Microsoft SharePoint 2010

Building Solutions for SharePoint 2010

Sahil Malik

Apress®

Microsoft SharePoint 2010: Building Solutions for Sharepoint 2010

Copyright © 2010 by Sahil Malik

ISBN-13 (pbk): 978-1-4302-2865-3

ISBN-13 (electronic): 978-1-4302-978-1-4302-2866-0

Printed and bound in the United States of America (POD)

President and Publisher: Paul Manning
Lead Editor: Jonathan Hassell
Technical Reviewer: Rob Garrett
Editorial Board: Clay Andres, Steve Anglin, Mark Beckner, Ewan Buckingham, Gary Cornell, Jonathan Gennick, Jonathan Hassell, Michelle Lowman, Matthew Moodie, Duncan Parkes, Jeffrey Pepper, Frank Pohlmann, Douglas Pundick, Ben Renow-Clarke, Dominic Shakeshaft, Matt Wade, Tom Welsh
Coordinating Editor: Debra Kelly, Tracy Brown
Copy Editors: Katie Stence, Nancy Sixsmith
Compositor: Lynn L'Heureux
Indexer: BIM Indexing & Proofreading Services
Artist: April Milne
Cover Designer: Anna Ishchenko

Distributed to the book trade worldwide by Springer-Verlag New York, Inc., 233 Spring Street, 6th Floor, New York, NY 10013. Phone 1-800-SPRINGER, fax 201-348-4505, e-mail orders-ny@springer-sbm.com, or visit www.springeronline.com.

For information on translations, please e-mail rights@apress.com, or visit www.apress.com.

Apress and friends of ED books may be purchased in bulk for academic, corporate, or promotional use. eBook versions and licenses are also available for most titles. For more information, reference our Special Bulk Sales–eBook Licensing web page at www.apress.com/info/bulksales.

The source code for this book is available to readers at www.apress.com.

I would like to dedicate this book to Tanya, Anish, and Shawn.

Contents at a Glance

Contents

About the Author

Sahil Malik, the founder and principal of Winsmarts, has been a Microsoft MVP and INETA Speaker for the past many years, author of numerous books and articles, consultant, and a trainer who delivers training and talks at conferences internationally.

About the Technical Reviewer

Rob Garrett has worked with SharePoint since the early beta version of MOSS 2007 and has leveraged his talents for SharePoint architecture and design with Portal Solutions—a SharePoint consultant company in Rockville, MD. Rob has extensive background in .NET technologies and has developed software for Microsoft Frameworks since the early days of C++ and MFC. In pursuit of his career dreams, Rob left his birthplace in England for a journey to the United States on Thanksgiving Day 1999. Upon arrival, he enjoyed his first American meal from a gas station.

Acknowledgments

No man is an island, and I am not a book writing machine. Thus my acknowledgements here are not just about this book, but about everything that made this book possible.

First, I would like to thank my family for providing me with a good upbringing to be strong, dedicated, respectful, and humble. I would then like to thank all my friends for their support and all the good times we've had together. I would like to thank all my co-workers, bosses, and subordinates for their support and encouragement in writing this book. Finally, I would like to thank my technical peers, who I have or have not directly ever worked with. This includes members of the MVP community, various Microsoft employees, and non-MVPs who are involved in the community.

I'd like to thank my special friend. Your biggest help to me was lifting my spirits when I was down. I'd like to thank the technical reviewer, Robert Garrett, for his thorough review, dedication, and skills he offerred to the book.

I'd like to thank the entire team at Apress, particularily my Lead Editor Jonathan for his trust and support. Also, Debra and Tracy for being stressed about the book when I was not (which we know never happened! HA!), and the cover editors for their attention to detail.

I'd like to thank my clients for all the experience they offerred me along with their trust and support. As it turns out, my clients are also my long-term best friends. There are so many of them to list here and I didn't take your permission before writing your names, so I am mentioning all your initials: FW, JF, JF, YT, ST, HM, FL, KS, GH, SG, and SK.

Finally, I'd like to thank all the students I have trained for asking me difficult questions, and keeping me on my toes. I am continually amazed at how smart some of you are, and I have learned a lot from you.

This book did require a lot of focus and attention, almost like a machine. It would not have been possible if it wasn't for the support of everyone around me.

Thank you!

CHAPTER 1

■ ■ ■

The First Chapter. Please read!

Your biggest investment in this book is not the money you spent on it, but the time you are going to spend reading it. Time is short, so I'll get straight to the point! Technology is exploding, there is so much to be learned that it is impossible for a single person to know it all, even within SharePoint. Yet, to functionally work in or lead a SharePoint project, you will need to know various facets of it. In a typical SharePoint project, like most other projects, you will find well defined roles, such as a developer, the IT Pro, designer, and the architect. Rather than focusing on an individual such role, in this book I will try to cover as much as necessary that I wish every SharePoint team member knew. As a result, I will probably not respect the boundaries between the architect, developer, IT Pro and designer, and instead focus on what you, as a productive SharePoint techie needs to know.

Technology is exploding faster than we can learn, so let me share the good news first. To read and understand this book, you need to know ASP.NET 2.0, and I will cover everything else necessary. The bad news next, there is plenty else to learn.

How to Read this Book

The first question I asked myself when I was writing this book was who am I writing this book for? The answer was that I'm writing this book for mainly two audiences:

- The first audience is an ASP.NET developer who is completely unfamiliar with SharePoint. He finds himself either interested in SharePoint or in the middle of a SharePoint project. To you my dear ASP.NET developer I must say, a SharePoint project is slightly different from a regular .NET project. First of all you will have to further your knowledge into the IT pro side of things. Secondly, you will have to realize that a typical SharePoint project is not 100% code. Finally, SharePoint being an implementation of .NET, will always be slightly behind the usual .NET world. You should definitely read this book cover to cover.

- The second audience I have focused on is the individual who is familiar with SharePoint 2007.Especially for you, at the start of every chapter I have mentioned if you can skip any particular given chapter. Thus you, the SharePoint 2007 developer, can skim through this chapter, or skim through the next chapter. Just make sure you have a development machine, with an active directory on it, called "sp2010.winsmarts.internal". Deal? Of course if you were to follow the instructions included in this chapter to setup your development environment, the examples in this book will work better for you.

SharePoint Environments

One of the most interesting things I have noticed in any SharePointproject, is that soon as SharePoint is introduced into an organization, the number of servers in that organization start multiplying like bunnies. As most IT projects, a SharePoint project will need a development environment, an integration environment, a QA environment, and a production environment. Depending upon certain specific needs, you may also need additional environments such as an environment to develop content for Internet facing sites. I am by no means a Microsoft licensing expert (do they even exist?), but at least your development environments do not need anything more than your MSDN subscription. You still have the necessary cost involved for hardware. It is important to realize that most of these environments are not 100% utilized all the time. Therefore, it makes sense to virtualize many of these environments. However, the minimum set of environments you will need in any SharePoint project are Development, Integration, QA and production. Let me describe each one of these one by one.

The SharePoint 2010 Development Environment

Developing for SharePoint requires a developer to have 100% administrator rights on the machine. You can still develop using least privilege, but frequently for certain configuration you will need to jump into administrative level privileges. This machine that the developer has 100% administrator rights on, can run Windows Vista or better, or preferably a server operating systems such as Windows 2008 or better. Starting with SharePoint 2010, you have to go with 64 bit operating systems and SQL server. On the same machine you will also need to install Visual Studio 2010, all other associated development tools, IIS, SQL server, active directory and SharePoint. Depending upon the specific project you're on, you may want to install either SharePoint foundation or SharePoint server.

That would be the ideal configuration. That would also be a configuration that I would try and insist upon in any project. However some boundaries are flexible. For instance, you could technically use a shared active directory, and a shared instance of SQL server.Sharing m eans contention, contention means loss of productivity. Therefore, so that it doesn't cost anything extra (thanks to your MSDN license), I prefer to give every developer their very own fully self contained development environment.

Certainly, some boundaries are absolutely not flexible. For instance, you cannot expect to develop for SharePoint without having a local instance of SharePoint server installed. Remote debugging doesn't work on a good day, forget having five developers attaching to one instance of IIS using their visual studio instances over a LAN.

I will describe your ideal SharePoint development machine shortly. For now I will mention, that if possible try to go with Windows server 2008 over Windows Vista or Windows 7. There are certain isolated instances which require an active directory, and thus require Windows server 2008.Also certain features such as HTTP Activation on IIS are not enabled by default on Windows 7/Vista, and therefore will cause unnecessary surprises for you. Not to mention, your production environment has to be Windows Server 2008, so why create an unnecessary difference between your development environment and production environment if you can avoid it.

The other thing I would like to mention, is that it is extremely productive to virtualize your SharePoint installation. This is for many reasons that follow:

- Developing for SharePoint will usually require a lot of configurations, things that typically are very admin/it-pro- related. These configurations are usually difficult to backup. If you were to use virtualization however, you could save such configurations, or multiple such configurations, by simply storing snapshots of your virtual machines.

- Developing for SharePoint will frequently require you to fork certain configurations and tweak them slightly. As you will see shortly, preparing a fresh development machine can be quite a task. If you do virtualize, storing snapshots allows you to store the state of the machine as you are building it, and thus is a huge time saver when creating new configurations of your development environment to support different needs.

- As a consultant, I, and I strongly suspect you will too, end up supporting multiple projects. Sometimes you will travel. Virtualization allows me to develop on a full workstation when I can, and on a laptop when I have to.

- If you do virtualize, introducing a new developer to your team with a consistent environment simply means giving the new developer an image of your virtual machine. Virtualization abstracts physical hardware, so as new developers or newer workstations are added to your project, your development continues seamlessly without a week spent in setting up the new team member's development environment.

- Virtualization will allow you to run multiple machines on the same hardware. Usually you won't have to run multiple machines for most development tasks, but for certain borderline tasks, or for certain testing related tasks you will end up running multiple machines at the same time.

- Virtualization means, your host machine stays clean and spiffy. So when Microsoft releases the new fancy operating system, or your IT administrator pushes down patches without informing you first, your development, if virtualized, is immune to such changes.

Consequently, as you can see, virtualization offers significant advantages. In fairness, virtualization has a huge disadvantage as well. It needs a really powerful host operating system. Assuming this book has a shelf life of two to four years, I will share my machine specifications as I am typing this book today. Chances are, in two to four years, you will be surprised how antiquated my hardware is.

I have two main machines.

My desktop has 8GB of RAM, and is a Quad Core Q9550 processor with RAID 0, 10,000 RPM disks. In my experience, the most critical piece of hardware here that made the most difference to my virtualization performance were the fast disks.

My laptop on the other hand has 16GB of RAM, a 256GB SSD, and runs the Core-i7 processor. Again, the most critical peicepiece here was the fast disk. I choose to invest more in my laptop, because I travel a lot. Your needs may be different.

In addition, to virtualize you will need virtualization software. Since you will need to virtualize a 64 bit operating system, your choices are limited to software such as the following:

- *VirtualBox from Sun*: This product as of writing this book is relatively less mature,,but it's free.

- Windows Server Hy*per-V*: This product is an offering from Microsoft. The same company that makes SharePoint. What I like about Hyper-V is that it is a very thin operating system that can virtualize quite well. Another thing I like about Hyper-V is that since Microsoft makes it, chances are they will bet on this horse when it comes to releasing sample VHDs going forward. What I don't like about Hyper-V is that it is indeed a server operating system, and my main host operating system is also my entertainment machine as well as my business machine running things such as email. While I could tweak Hyper-V to suit those needs, it still doesn't do things such as power management and sleep modes well, which are critical on long flights where you are reading documents to save battery, and the dominatrix, I mean, flight attendant comes and demands that you shut down the laptop and comply immediately! If you don't comply you're a terrorist. I don't want to be a terrorist, so I don't use Hyper-V on my laptop.

- *VMWare Workstation 7.0 or better*: This product allows you to virtualize an operating system with up to 4 processors and 32GB of RAM allocated to the virtual machine. More than plenty for the virtual machine. What I like the most about this option is that it has rich capabilities such as snapshots, networking support, etc., and that it doesn't require me to run a server operating system on the host. What I dislike the most about this option is that it costs money. However, given all pros and cons, I use VMware workstation over other choices for most of my needs. I could also use VMware server based products such as ESX, but they bring the disadvantages of Hyper-V, i.e., owning your entire machine, and giving you an abstracted layer of hardware in your virtual machines, thus turning your machine into a completely non-fun work only environment.

- Finally, you can boot a .VHD file directly if your host is running Windows 7 or better. What I like about this option is that it runs on bare metal, so the performance is quite good. Also, it's free with Windows 7. What I dislike about this option is that it owns your machine and nothing else runs on it while you run the Virtual machine. Finally, snapshots aren't exactly convenient when you are shuttling 40GB Virtual images on a 256GB SSD.

SharePoint Integration Environment

Every developer gets their very own SharePoint development machine. That allows them to attach to IIS and debug and diagnose their code as much as they want. It is from that machine that they are also connected to source control. However, there are certain issues with SharePoint that do not manifest themselves unless you test them on the load balanced environment. Thus, the SharePoint integration environment, is where multiple developers would put together their code as .wsps (windows solution packages), and pass their functionality in a load balanced environment, where the URL of the SharePoint site does not match the machine names. Windows solution packages are the standard way of deploying any new functionality on a SharePoint farm. Any custom code deployed to SharePoint must always be deployed using WSPs. WSPs in reality are nothing but simple cab files with a manifest.xml inside them telling SharePoint what they are all about.

This load balanced environment is typically what the architect or team lead has full administrative rights to, and the architect can delegate rights to other members on the team. It is on this environment where it is OK to diagnose and debug issues and make minor fixes by hand to verify and squash bugs. It is important to virtualize this environment, so you can restore it to a current production level release with a few point and clicks. Also, it is in this environment where you would force version control.

It is when you replicate desired functionality without any manual fixes done by hand, that you should turn over the installed .wsp packages to the QA manager so the QA manager can deploy them in the SharePoint QA environment.

SharePoint QA Environment

The SharePoint QA environment is another load balanced environment which mimics the production environment as closely as possible. The only difference between the production environment and the QA environment should be high availability. The QA environment is not something that developers are given access to—this includes the architect. But take that with a grain of salt, every SharePoint environment including the production environment, will require you to give some user level access to everyone. Therefore, perhaps a more accurate way of saying this would be, you should not give any additional level access to developers in the QA environment than what they would have in the production environment.

Code should be deployed to the QA environment using .wsps, and build scripts and instructions. The person deploying this code is not expected to know SharePoint in-depth. If the code deployment fails, or bugs are discovered during testing, no handcrafted manual fixes should be done in this environment to make the code work.

For that reason this environment should also be virtualized, so its state can be restored to the current production level release after a failed QA cycle.

Code that successfully deploys and tests in this environment can then if be handed over to the production environment.

SharePoint Production Environment

Finally, you have the production environment. The exact configuration of the production environment depends upon the nature of the project and the details of the organization. The IT administrators have full rights to this environment. The QA manager and the architect do not. In SharePoint 2010, however, there is a concept of managed services and appointing administrators for those managed services. Frequently depending upon the policies of an organization, the IT administrators will appoint administrators for certain managed services, thereby giving them limited access to central administration. There is no reason to panic, by appointing an administrator for a certain service, that newly appointed administrator will get access to central administration, but will be able to make changes only in their own section.

Your SharePoint Development Machine

I just described what every developer will need for their own development machine. This is the SharePoint development environment which is preferably virtualized. Now let me describe in detail, how exactly I'd like to configure my own development environment. Many of these steps are "preferences" rather than "necessities", but I am mentioning everything I do to my development machine to make me more productive.

Now, I know there are 35 steps below, but please don't skip them. It will take you a few hours to configure the ideal SharePoint development machine, but believe me it is well worth it. Let's get started with building your ideal SharePoint development machine.

1. Review the operating system and sql server requirements at `http://blogs.msdn.com/SharePoint/archive/2009/05/07/announcing-SharePoint-server-2010-preliminary-system-requirements.aspx`. Ensure that you are using the right operating system, etc.

2. Start by creating a windows 2008 server virtualized machine, allocate at least 40 GB to the disk. If using VMware Workstation, choose to create fixed disks with all space pre-allocated for performance reasons. You could also go with Windows 7, but for the purposes of this book, and my general preference, go with Windows Server 2008.

3. Make some changes to the Windows 2008 server machine, so it behaves more like a desktop operating system. I like to use a tool called the Windows 2008 Workstation Converter to make these changes. The Windows 2008 Workstation converter can be downloaded from `http://www.win2008workstation.com/win2008/windows-server-2008-workstation-converter`.The specific changes I like to make are as follows:

    a. Remove the shutdown tracker.
    b. Give the machine a decent name, I choose "sp2010", and will be referring to this name throughout the book.

     c.   Remove and disable screen saver.
     d.   Install desktop experience.
     e.   Enable graphic acceleration and sound.
     f.   Enable RDP.
     g.   Disable Internet Explorer Enhanced Configuration.
     h.   Install other browsers if you choose to.
     i.   Full update and patch the machine using Windows Update.

4.   The next step is to set up active directory on this machine. In order to do so, login as administrator and start the server manager and choose to add a role. The specific role you're adding is Active Directory Domain services is shown in Figure 1-1.

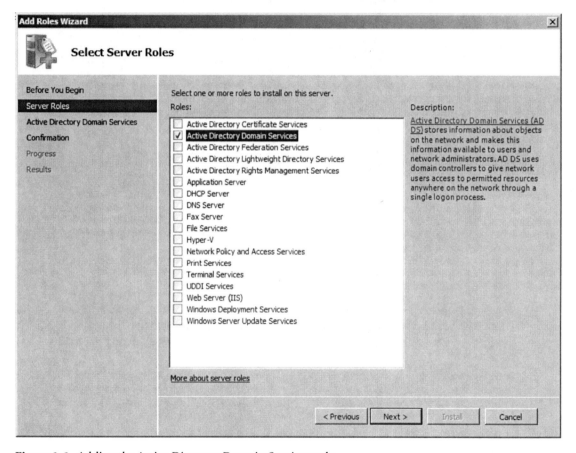

Figure 1-1. *Adding the Active Directory Domain Services role*

5.   Go through the preceding wizard, and on the last page run dcpromo.exe when prompted to do so.dcpromo.exe will prompt you to configure your domain. Choose to create a new domain in a new forest as shown bin Figure 1-2.

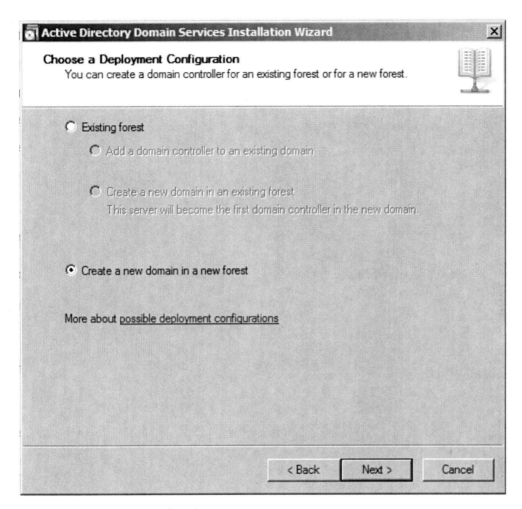

Figure 1-2. *Creating a new domain*

6. Provide a FQDN of: "winsmarts.internal", forest functional level of Windows 2003, and Domain Functional Level of Windows 2003.

7. In additional domain controller options also choose to add a dns server (see Figure 1-3).

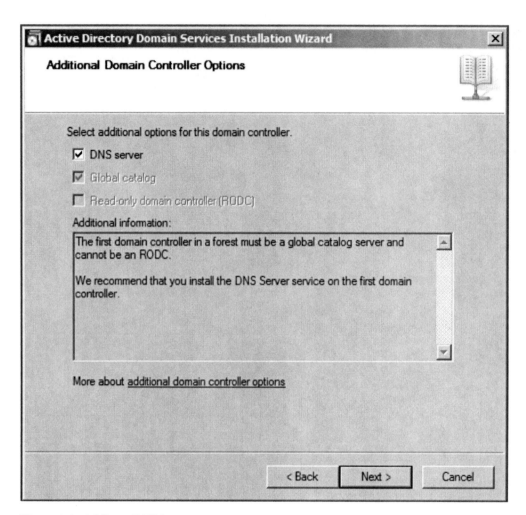

Figure 1-3. *Adding a DNS Server*

8. Windows 2008 will probably issue a warning at this point that you do not have a static IP configured for your server. This warning makes sense in production environments, but this is going to be your development machine, and you want a dynamic IP. So when prompted with a warning shown in Figure 1-4, choose yes.

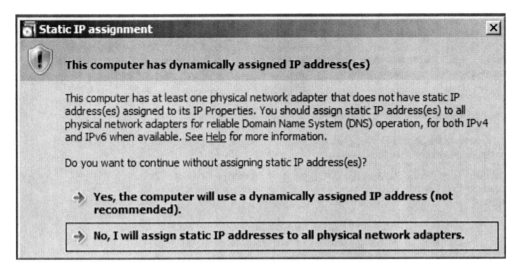

Figure 1-4. *IP Assignment, you need to choose yes*

9. At this point Windows 2008 will try to scare you with another warning as shown in Figure 1-5, just choose yes and continue.

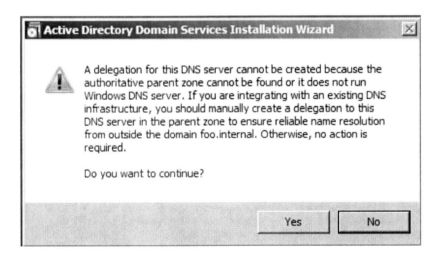

Figure 1-5. *DNS warning, choose yes*

10. Finally, it will ask you for a location for database folder, log files folder and sysvol folder. Accept the default provided locations and continue. You will also be prompted to provide a password. I always specify "p@ssword1" for my development machines, and I've found it very useful to have a dummy, everyone knows, sort of password only for development environments. But remember, production passwords are like underwear. They are good when fresh, long, and never shared!

11. If you care, my unattended dcpromo configuration file is shown in Listing 1-1.

12. Next, you will see the dialog box shown in Figure 1-6.

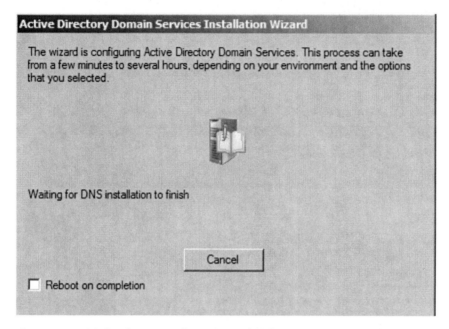

Figure 1-6. *Wait for the AD configuration to finish*

13. When the previous dialog box finishes your active directory is all set, so go ahead and restart your computer.

14. When your computer restarts, go back to server manager and choose to add the application server role. Adding the application server role will prompt you to add certain other required features, go ahead and accept the defaults. Remember that if you're doing this on Windows 7, be aware that the defaults do not include necessary features such as HTTP activation. When finished with this installation, reboot your machine.

15. Next install Visual Studio 2010.

16. Then make some optional minor tweaks to your operating system, such as start windows explorer, and make status bar visible. Go to tools ~TRA folder options ~TRA Make thumbnails visible and show file extensions.

17. Then install the 32 bit office client. You could choose to install the 64 bit office client version, and that may be a essential, if your project relies heavily on powerpivot. Installing a 64 bit office client version will put an additional limitation on you, however. The limitation is that your SharePoint Designer 2010 version will also need to be 64 bit. This is not such a problem, except that SharePoint Designer 2010 will not work with SharePoint 2007 sites. Therefore, if you need to install SharePoint Designer 2007 to manage SharePoint 2007 sites, you will need to go with side-by-side SharePoint Designer 2007 and SharePoint Designer 2010 installs. The problem is that there is no 64 bit version of SharePoint Designer 2007. If you choose to go with 64 bit office 2010, you are unable to use SharePoint Designer 2007 from the same machine. Of course, if you would have virtualized your development environments, then this would not be such an issue. Other than the specific need of Powerpivot, I have a slight preference for 32 bit over 64 bit. The preferences driven by the fact that 64 bit programs cause more memory fragmentation and, therefore, they need more memory allocated to the virtual machine for the same level of performance. Also, Powerpivot does work in 32 bit Excel, it just works a whole lot better with very large amounts of data in 64 bit Excel. Barring some borderline conditions, I prefer to install 32 bit office client.

18. Also install SharePoint Designer 2010, preferably 32 bit for reasons mentioned in the previous step.

19. Next, you need to install SQL server. Specifically, you need to install the developer edition of SQL Server from your MSDN downloads. SharePoint 2010 requires 64 bit versions of SQL Server that should be SQL Server 2005 SP3 or better. I would recommend going with at least SQL Server 2008 SP1. You will need to install cumulative updates to your SQL Server installation.

   a. Installation of SQL server will require you to configure your firewall in a certain way, and also download and install the Microsoft certificate revocation list from `http://crl.microsoft.com/pki/crl/products/MicrosoftRootAuthority.crl`. These instructions are documented well in SQL server install. In the pre-requisites check, you will probably get a warning that you are installing SQL server on the domain controller. You can safely ignore this warning for development environments.

   b. If this is your development machine, choose to install SQL Server 2008 development version, and choose to install the database engine, analysis services, and reporting services. The features selected are shown in Figure 1-7.

   c. Also, choose to start the SQL Server agent, SQL Server database engine, SQL Server analysis services, and SQL Server Reporting services.

   d. In database configuration, choose to enabled mixed mode authentication, and add the currently logged in user, "administrator" as a SQL server administrator.

   e. In analysis services configuration and reporting services configuration, add the current user, "administrator" as the administrator.

   f. Go ahead and install SQL Server 2008.

   g. Then install SQL Server 2008 service pack one.

   h. Install the necessary SQL Server cumulative updates.

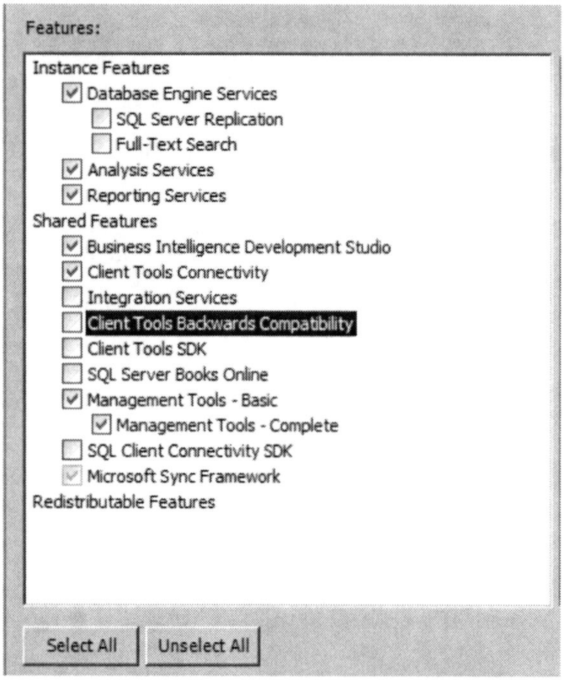

Figure 1-7. *The selected options for installing SQL Server*

20. Finally, run the SharePoint server installation. First, install software prerequisites. If any of these prerequisites fail, you need to examine the logs and make sure that your prerequisites install properly. One of the most common reasons of failing is if a previous version of a component (such as powershell) is already installed. You may need to manually uninstall that component and rerun the prerequisites wizard again. Ensure that you can run the prerequisites wizard successfully.

21. Finally, choose to install SharePoint server. After the installation finishes, on the last screen you're prompted to run the SharePoint products and technologies configuration wizard as shown in Figure 1-8.

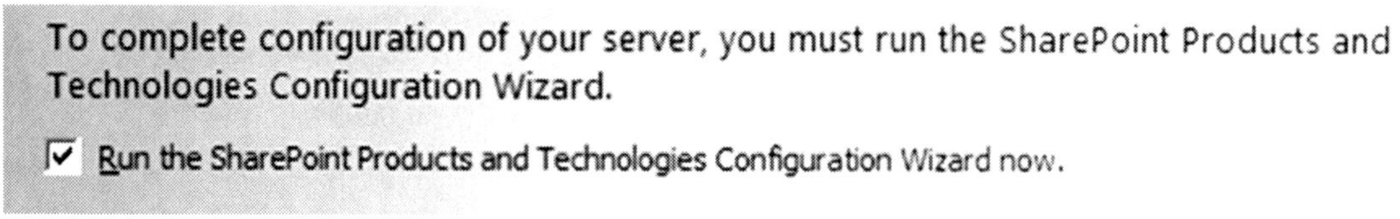

Figure 1-8. *Run the configuration wizard*

Choose to check the check box and hit the close button which will run the SharePoint products and technologies configuration wizard.

22. In the configuration wizard,

  a. Choose to create a new server farm

  b. You need to specify a new service account. To get started one service account is fine, but as you start using your SharePoint installation further, you will want to create more service accounts at a later date. But to get started you need at least one service account. Use the following steps to create a service account called sp_admin.

    i. Create a new account in your active directory called sp_admin, and give this account DBCreator and DBSecurity roles in the local SQL Server database.
    ii. In your active directory users and computers applet, right-click on your domain and choose to delegate control
    iii. Next, choose "Create Custom Task to Delegate" and choose to delegate control of "This folder, existing objects in this folder".
    iv. Then choose to pick replicating directory permissions as shown in Figure 1-9.
    v. Your service account is all set.

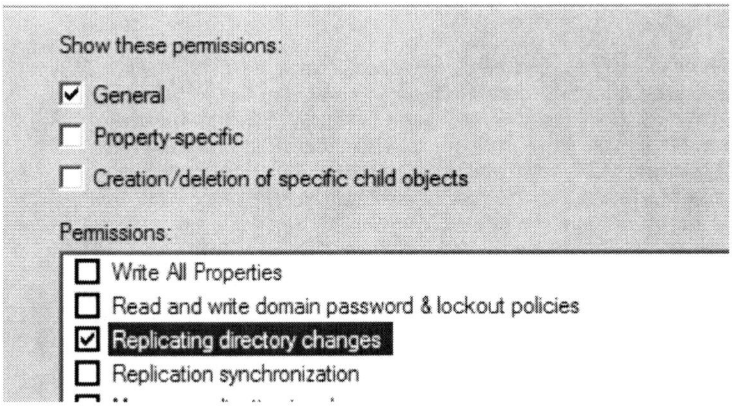

Figure 1-9. *Replicating directory changes*

  c. Back in the SharePoint configuration wizard, specify the winsmarts.internal\sp_admin user as the config account, and specify sp2010 as the database server.

  d. Enter a passphrase that you will remember. On development environments I usually go with p@ssword1.

  e. Specify port 40000 for central administration. If you prefer a different number that's fine, but in the various screenshots in my book when you see a web site running at port 40000 that will be the central administration site.

  f. Pick kerberos authentication. Picking Kerberos authentication will require you to perform certain additional steps on your machine. These steps are mentioned later in the chapter under "Enabling Kerberos".

  g. Then wait for 10 steps of the configuration wizard to finish.

23. Once the configuration wizard has finished, launch central administration. This will be the site at `http://sp2010:40000`.

24. As soon as you land into central administration, you are prompted to configure your SharePoint farm. You are given two choices; either you can let SharePoint do it for you, or you could fine tweak such configuration yourself. For a typical development machine, and to ensure all the examples of this book will work, and if you're a beginner with SharePoint, just let SharePoint automatically configure your installation as shown in Figure 1-10.

How do you want to configure your SharePoint farm?

This wizard will help with the initial configuration of your SharePoint farm. You can select the services to use in this farm and create your first site.

You can launch this wizard again from the Configuration Wizards page in the Central Administration site.

Yes, walk me through the configuration of my farm using this wizard.   [Start the Wizard]

No, I will configure everything myself.   [Cancel]

Figure 1-10. *Farm configuration wizard*

Once you're an expert at SharePoint 2010, you will probably find configuring the farm yourself by hand.

25. In the next screen, choose an existing managed account namely "sp_admin" to configure all the managed services. In SharePoint 2007, you used to have a concept called a shared service provider. The shared service provider has now been broken out into managed services. Each managed service, can now have multiple instances, can be shared across farms, and can have individual administrators appointed to them. This screen will automatically configure all managed services for you. Ensure that everything except the lotus connector is checked. I haven't covered a lotus connector in this book, but if your project involves the lotus connector, you probably want to leave that checked.

26. After all the managed services are configured for you, SharePoint will prompt you to create a site collection at `http://sp2010`. Create a site collection using the blank site definition. Technically, you could have chosen any other site definition, but start with a minimum out of the box site definition, so I can demonstrate all the pieces involved in building any particular solution.

27. Next, create favorites in your browser for `http://sp2010` and `http://sp2010:40000`

28. I also like to make the following changes to environment variables:

    a. Create a new environment variable called "14" with value C:\Program Files\Common Files\Microsoft Shared\Web Server Extensions\14.

    b. Add C:\Program Files\Common Files\Microsoft Shared\Web Server Extensions\14\BIN to path.

    b. Setup a menu on the toolbar to C:\Program Files\Common Files\Microsoft Shared\Web Server Extensions\14 for easy access to 14. 14 is a special directory, also referred to as SharePoint root. Some people also call it the 14 hive, because in SharePoint 2007 it used to have the 12 hive.

29. Finally, install office web apps, which will require you to run the SharePoint products and technologies configuration wizard and the farm wizard in central administration one more time. This is because the office web apps require you to configure certain new managed services.

30. Install Visio, preferably 32 bit.

31. Run the following command to enabled a developer dashboard on demand

    stsadm -o setproperty -pn developer-dashboard -pvOnDemand

32. Run the powershell script shown in Listing 1-2 to enable sandbox solutions on the domain controller.

33. Activate windows and office client.

34. Configure visual studio to work with your source control repository.

35. Take a snapshot of your virtualmachine, zip it and store it somewhere safe.This is what you want to hand over to every developer in your team.

Listing 1-1. *Unattended DCPromo Configuration File Contents*

```
; DCPROMO unattend file (automatically generated by dcpromo)
; Usage:
; dcpromo.exe /unattend:C:\Users\Administrator\Desktop\settings.txt
;
[DCInstall]
; New forest promotion
ReplicaOrNewDomain=Domain
NewDomain=Forest
NewDomainDNSName=foo.internal
ForestLevel=2
DomainNetbiosName=FOO
DomainLevel=2
InstallDNS=Yes
ConfirmGc=Yes
CreateDNSDelegation=No
DatabasePath="C:\Windows\NTDS"
LogPath="C:\Windows\NTDS"
SYSVOLPath="C:\Windows\SYSVOL"
; Set SafeModeAdminPassword to the correct value prior to using the unattend file
SafeModeAdminPassword=
; Run-time flags (optional)
; RebootOnCompletion=Yes
```

Listing 1-2. *Enabling Sandbox Solutions on a Domain Controller*

```
$acl = Get-Acl HKLM:\System\CurrentControlSet\Control\ComputerName
$person = [System.Security.Principal.NTAccount]"Users"
$access = [System.Security.AccessControl.RegistryRights]::FullControl
$inheritance = [System.Security.AccessControl.InheritanceFlags]"ContainerInherit,
ObjectInherit"
$propagation = [System.Security.AccessControl.PropagationFlags]::None
```

```
$type = [System.Security.AccessControl.AccessControlType]::Allow
$rule = New-Object System.Security.AccessControl.RegistryAccessRule($person,
$access, $inheritance, $propagation, $type)
$acl.AddAccessRule($rule)
Set-Acl HKLM:\System\CurrentControlSet\Control\ComputerName $acl
```

Congratulations your development machine is all set!

On production environments and in very special situations, even on a development environment, you will need to setup Kerberos as well. But for a single machine development environment only scenario, this step is optional. You can find more information about configuring Kerberos on a SharePoint 2010 environment at `http://technet.microsoft.com/en-us/library/ee806870(office.14).aspx`.

Summary

This chapter gave you a basic introduction of what to expect in a SharePoint project. It mainly focused on walking you through the steps of giving you your sandbox environment where you can play with and learn SharePoint. Once you have your SharePoint environment setup, the next step is to learn the basics of SharePoint. This is what I'll cover in the next chapter. If you are familiar with SharePoint 2007 feel free to rapid skim through Chapter 2 and then jump to Chapter 3.

CHAPTER 2

■ ■ ■

SharePoint Basics

Reading Key: If you're familiar with SharePoint 2007, in this chapter you might find the various UI improvements, the new central administration layout, and web.config changes in SharePoint 2010 interesting. I suggest that you skim the chapter even if you are familiar with SharePoint 2007.

In the previous chapter, you configured your basic SharePoint development machine. Before you move any further, ensure that you take a snapshot of that machine so you can get back to that position at any point in this book. In this chapter I will walk you through the basics of SharePoint. When I say basics, I mean user level features that end users will use through the browser. I will also talk a little bit about what you the developer needs to know about the bare minimum administration necessary at least on your development machine. Also this will make you sound a little bit smarter when talking to your infrastructure guys managing the production SharePoint environment.

What Did Installing SharePoint Do to My Machine?

In the last chapter you started with a bare bones Windows Server 2008 machine, and then you installed a whole bunch of things on that machine to turn it into your SharePoint development environment. Ignoring the client applications such as the Office client SharePoint designer and Visual Studio 2010, the question is what exactly did installing SharePoint server on your development machine do to your machine? Well it did four things:

First, it deployed certain DLLs in the GAC, which makes the SharePoint framework available to any running program on the operating system. In most scenarios, the running program will be various web sites that are configured to run SharePoint.

The second thing was to create a special folder called as the SharePoint root. This folder is located at c:\program files\common files\microsoft shared\web server extensions\14. I assure you that you will have this long path memorized (or laser-etched into your memory) by the time you start calling yourself a SharePoint developer. It is in this folder that a number of files necessary for the operation of SharePoint go.

The third thing that installing SharePoint on your server did was to configure numerous IIS web sites. These numerous IIS web sites are nothing special they are ASP.NET 2.0 web sites, with configuration files that turn them into SharePoint 2010 sites that use .NET 3.5. At the bare minimum, you would have a central administration web site, which is a SharePoint site used to manage the entire farm. And on top you will have some additional web applications configured to support web services or other SharePoint applications. By default you will find all SharePoint web applications created at C:\inetpub\wwwroot\wss\VirtualDirectories. If you run IIS Manager on your SharePoint development environment, you should see at least two but maybe three SharePoint web applications provisioned.

- The first web application is the central administration web application.

- The second web application is the SharePoint web services application being hosted at C:\Program Files\Common Files\Microsoft Shared\Web Server Extensions\14\WebServices\Root.

- And the third web application is a web application for your port 80, assuming that you created it per the instructions in the previous chapter.

For a moment, open any SharePoint site's web.config file (for instance, visit C:\inetpub\wwwroot\wss\VirtualDirectories). In any of those directories, open (but do not edit) the web.config file. In this web.config, you will see a custom section group called SharePoint with many extensions to the web.config schema done by the SharePoint team to store SharePoint-specific configuration information. There is also a Microsoft.SharePoint.Client section, which is new in SharePoint 2010, and is present for the client object model. I will talk more about the client object model in Chapter 5.

Finally, you have the standard .NET sections, such as System.Web, System.WebServer, System.ServiceModel; and then you have a huge runtime section. (There are some other important sections in the web.config that you should also look at.) Let's examine some of the major configuration details in some of these sections one by one:

- The runtime section specifies a lot of assemblyBinding elements. The purpose of these elements is to redirect calls of older versions of SharePoint DLLs to newer versions of DLLs transparently without the calling programs ever knowing about it. Thus if you had a DLL that was compiled to target SharePoint version 12 (SharePoint 2007), that would automatically be routed to SharePoint 14 (SharePoint 2010).

- The System.Web element is perhaps the most interesting. In this element you will find custom trust levels created called to the WSS_medium and the WSS_minimal. These are code access security policies that tie down your SharePoint installation and make it more secure. In addition you will see standard ASP.NET concepts powering SharePoint, such as sitemap providers and WebParts. If you're familiar with SharePoint 2007, one notable exception you will see here is that the httpModules element is empty.

- The System.WebServer element is something new with IIS 7. In this element because SharePoint 2010 works in the integrated pipeline mode, you will see the various httpModules configured. As you may note, an httpModule is a piece of code that executes with every incoming request. The modules section from a SharePoint web.config is shown in Listing 2-1. SharePoint chooses to eliminate a number of out of the box HTTP modules. Notably it removes the anonymous identification, file authorization, ASP.NET profiles, webDav module, and ASP.NET session module. Thus when you're writing functionality for SharePoint, you must remember that these facilities from ASP.NET are not applicable to a typical SharePoint site. Instead SharePoint provides its own implementations for each one of these facilities. What does this mean to you? This means that if your fellow team member wishes to rely on ASP.NET session state to build some SharePoint functionality, you need to sit down have a talk with them and discourage them from doing so! In other words, the emphasis in SharePoint is to write stateless code. Also you would note that SharePoint inserts the SPRequestModule in the HTTP pipeline. It is this SPRequestModule that turns an ASP.NET application into a SharePoint web application. In Chapter 4, I will dive into the details of the SPRequestModule and explain how that works with the VirtualPathProvider to provide the SharePoint file structure.

- The system.serviceModel element is what deals with WCF configuration. The details of the system.serviceModel can be seen in Listing 2-2. Before I explain what this particular element does, look under the system.web element one more time and look for an element that says <identity impersonate=true/>. What that element ensures is that all code running on the server will attempt to run as the identity of the user logged into the browser. In other words, the user's identity is impersonated on the server. This is what allows SharePoint to present a security trimmed UI and view of data when queried through the object model. Also starting with SharePoint 2010, SharePoint can now, out of the box, act as a WCF host. With SharePoint 2007, you needed to patch SharePoint to make it work as a WCF host (see http://spwcfsupport.codeplex.com for more details). The WCF, however, is much bigger in scope than just ASP.NET. Thus by default any web request that comes into the server is first handled by WCF and then handled by ASP.NET. As a result, WCF by default does not work in ASP.NET compatibility mode. This means httpcontext.current is null, SPContext.Current is null, and <identity impersonate=true/> and all other such ASP.NET elements are ignored. In order to make WCF work with ASP.NET, you need to explicitly allow the ASP.NET compatibility mode to be enabled. The code shown in Listing 2-2 ensures that behavior. There are some additional configurations required to the service itself, which I will talk about in more detail in Chapter 5. If you're interested in reading more about this topic, you may also read my article at http://blah.winsmarts.com/ 2008-9-Getting_SPContextCurrent_in_a_SharePoint_2007_WCF_Service.aspx.

Listing 2-1. *SharePoint HTTP Modules*

```
<modules runAllManagedModulesForAllRequests="true">
 <remove name="AnonymousIdentification" />
 <remove name="FileAuthorization" />
 <remove name="Profile" />
 <remove name="WebDAVModule" />
 <remove name="Session" />
 <add name="SPRequestModule" preCondition="integratedMode" type=".." />
 <add name="ScriptModule" preCondition="integratedMode" type=".." />
 <add name="SharePoint14Module" preCondition="integratedMode" />
 <add name="StateServiceModule" type=".." />
 <add name="PublishingHttpModule" type=".." />
</modules>
```

Listing 2-2. *SharePoint System.ServiceModel Element*

```
<system.serviceModel>
 <serviceHostingEnvironment aspNetCompatibilityEnabled="true" />
</system.serviceModel>
```

While we are talking about the SharePoint web.config file, I want to share a little trick with you. When you're writing code for SharePoint, and your custom code runs into an error, by default SharePoint will log that error and it will present the user with a generic error through the browser. In order to view the actual error message through the browser, you will need to make three changes to your web.config:

1. Change the SharePoint\SafeMode\@CallStack attribute to true.

2. Change System.Web\CustomErrors\@Mode attribute to Off.

3. Change System.Web\Compilation\Debug mode to true.

Making these changes will allow you to both attach to W3WP.exe and run your code in debug mode, and to view actual error messages through the browser. Note that you should not make these changes in production environments. Finally even this is not an exact science! Whenever I run into an error in SharePoint programming, I usually look at the following four places in sequence:

1. The browser window, assuming I have made the above-mentioned web.config changes.

2. The ULS logs available at 14\Logs. You may need to tweak the logging level in central administration to view your actual error message. Also, you should try out this fantastic tool at http://code.msdn.microsoft.com/ulsviewer.

3. The event log, especially for WCF-related errors.

4. The IIS log and tracing facilities.

If all these steps fail, I use the techniques described in this article http://www.code-magazine.com/Article.aspx?quickid=0907041. If even that fails, I call in sick and let my co-workers deal with it. Luckily that hasn't happened yet.

In addition to logging, SharePoint now comes with a database called WSS_Logging. This database contains a tonne of usage and log data, and Microsoft now actually invites you to read this database, and run reports against it.

The final thing that installing and configuring SharePoint did was to provision many databases in the appointed SQL Server. At the bare minimum, every SharePoint web application has one or more content databases. Also, in the entire farm, you will have a config database. In addition, various services such as managed metadata service, BCS service, secure store service, and so on will provision their own databases per their needs.

Central Administration

Central administration is a SharePoint site used to manage all other SharePoint sites. Because your SharePoint development machine is a single server SharePoint environment, you have a single instance of central administration provision. In production, however, you should choose to provision central administration on more than one web front end. This is best practice because if you lose central administration, you lose the entire farm. Well not entirely, but it will still make your life a lot harder if you lost the only single central administration site you had. On the other hand, if you lost the configuration database, you will probably have to rebuild your farm. So in backing up your SharePoint installations, you should worry about backing up code, having a good versioning strategy, and backing up all the content contained in various databases.

When you visit central administration in SharePoint 2010, you are greeted with the page shown in Figure 2-1.

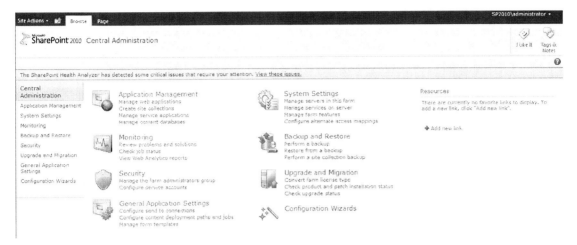

Figure 2-1. *Central Administration in SharePoint 2010*

As you can see, the page is split into various sections:

- The Application Management section allows you to configure and create various web applications and site collections across your farm. As I will describe shortly, SharePoint stores and manages all its data and functionality across various web applications and site collections. I talk more about this in the great SharePoint hierarchy section of this chapter. In this section you choose to configure the various web applications and site collections all across your SharePoint farm. In addition, you can also configure the various service applications and the various and involved content databases. This section can be shown in Figure 2-2.

Figure 2-2. *The Application Management section in central administration*

- Of special interest here is the Service Applications section. In SharePoint 2007 you used to have a concept called a shared service provider, which was a single web application in which you would configure various batch-oriented, heavy-duty tasks that would run in the background. It suffered with a limitation of not being able to appoint administrators on a per-service-level scenario, and one web application could be managed by only a single shared service provider at a given time. Also such services could not be shared across farms, and the SSP was a concept available only in SharePoint server. The managed services concept of SharePoint 2010 breaks out those various services into their own individually manageable entities. This rearchitected managed services model has the following important ramifications:

  - You can now appoint administrators on a per-service basis. You can do so by selecting a given service, and clicking the Administrators button on the ribbon. These users are then given access to central administration. However, they can only manage the designated service.

  - Services can now be offered to sites on an a-la-carte basis, rather than an all-you-can-eat buffet style. For example, if a web site does not need Excel Services, it does not get Excel Services. The administrator can pick and choose which services are made available to which web sites.

  - The third scenario is perhaps the most exciting. Farms can share services. In fact, now you can have an entire farm that can scale out, whose job is nothing but to provide services to other farms. This opens up immense scalability options and also a great deal of flexibility in the overall architecture considering things such as security, availability, and so on. Now, the cynical among you might wonder what SQL Server permissions you will need to give in this cross-farm implementation. The answer is none. Managed Farm Services communicate through each other via proxies, thus obviating the need for direct SQL permissions to the parent farm's configuration or service databases. One other point to consider is that not every service is shareable. You can also alter your custom services and, depending upon the nature of the service, if it makes sense to share it you have the ability to share it.

- The System Settings page allows you to configure various farm-wide settings. Various farm-level settings allow you to configure the services running on the servers, global e-mail level settings, and custom code that affects the entire farm. In addition, you can configure alternate access mappings. Alternate access mappings are extremely important in production SharePoint environments because the URL used by users to access your SharePoint site is probably different from the machine names that are running SharePoint itself. Sometimes the same content can be exposed on more than one web application. Using alternate access mappings, you would tell SharePoint what the actual URL on rich content is being rendered. This allows the various components of SharePoint such as Excel web access WebParts and many other such components to generate the right code pointing to the correct URLs. This section can be seen in Figure 2-3.

Figure 2-3. *System Settings under Central Administration in SharePoint 2010*

- The Monitoring section allows you to use the Health Analyzer, various timer jobs, and reporting functionality within SharePoint. That bar you see at the top of the central administration page is a rule in the Health Analyzer, telling me that my drives are running short on space. You can add to these rules and you can configure existing rules. This section can be seen in Figure 2-4.

Figure 2-4. *The Monitoring section in Central Administration in SharePoint 2010*

- The Backup and Restore section allows you to do some rudimentary backups from the user interface. These backups are not to be replaced with enterprise class automated backups. To view the proper process and various options available to you in backing up your SharePoint installation, please see this article http://blah.winsmarts.com/2007-10-Backup_and_Restore_Strategies_in_MOSS_2007.aspx. Even though the article was written for SharePoint 2007, the basic concepts are applicable to SharePoint 2010. One big enhancement in SharePoint 2010 over 2007 is the ability to do granular backups. This allows you to recover data from unattached content databases. SharePoint 2007 required you to have a backup and restore farm (see Figure 2-5).

Figure 2-5. *Backup and Restore section under central administration in SharePoint 2010*

- The Security section allows you to manage farm administrator users, service accounts, antivirus settings, and information policy–related settings, and so on. Farm administrators are those couple of users that have the eventual responsibility for maintaining your entire SharePoint farm. Usually they are from the infrastructure department in your organization and they should be no more than two of them. This section can be seen in Figure 2-6.

Users
Manage the farm administrators group | Approve or reject distribution groups | Specify web application user policy

General Security
Configure managed accounts | Configure service accounts | Configure password change settings
Specify authentication providers | Manage trust | Manage antivirus settings | Define blocked file types
Manage web part security | Configure self-service site creation

Information policy
Configure information rights management | Configure Information Management Policy

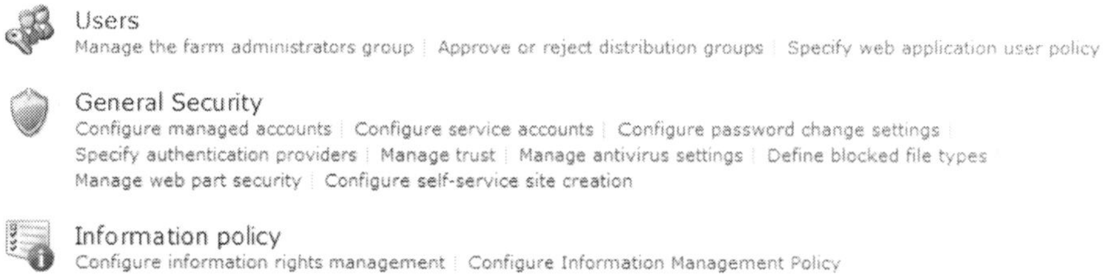

Figure 2-6. *The Security section under central administration in SharePoint 2010*

- The Upgrade and Migration section allows you to upgrade to different SKUs of your SharePoint license. For instance you can start with SharePoint foundation, and then move on to SharePoint standard or SharePoint enterprise at a later date. Also you can perform upgrades on individual databases. This section can be seen in Figure 2-7.

Upgrade and Patch Management
Convert farm license type | Enable Enterprise Features | Enable Features on Existing Sites |
Check product and patch installation status | Review database status | Check upgrade status

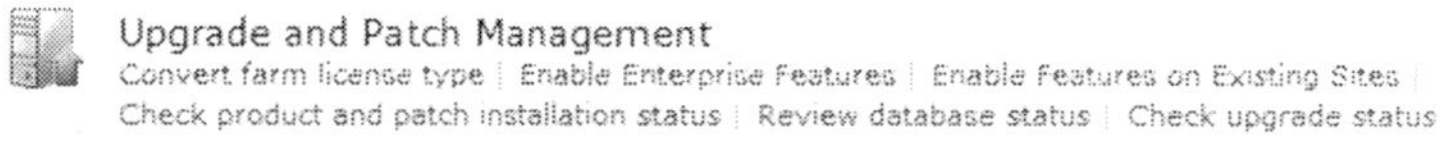

Figure 2-7. *The Upgrade and Migration section under central administration in SharePoint 2010*

- The General Application settings area is an area for everything else. By default, you have the ability to do the following:

  - Define external service connections and thereby customizing the send to locations in the ECB (Edit Control Block) menu on any item in a document library. The ECB menu is the menu that pops up on any list item and shows you options such as View/Edit. Or you can customize document conversions, which allows you to convert between different formats of documents such as .docx to HTML.

  - Manage various Infopath form services settings, such as uploading and making available various form templates, data connection files for external data sources, and other such settings.

  - A section for site directory to help you manage the various sites and site collections all across your farm.

- Global SharePoint designer–related settings, allowing you to restrict the usage of SharePoint designer on various site collections. SharePoint designer is a thick client application that is intended to be used with SharePoint site collections. While it is extremely powerful, in the wrong hands it can act as a sharp two-edged sword. Using this link you have the ability to restrict the usage of SharePoint designer on your farm. Note that you can further restrict the usage of SharePoint designer from SiteCollection[1] settings as well.

- Global search-related settings. Note the search itself is a managed service application, so there is a further level of configuration possible beyond what this page allows you to do.

- And finally content deployment related settings, which is primarily used where SharePoint is used as a web content management platform, but can be used in other scenarios as well. The purpose of content deployment is to produce and maintain content on one farm and be able to deploy that content on to another farm once that content is ready to be deployed. The settings related to that can be configured from this section.

This section can be seen in Figure 2-8.

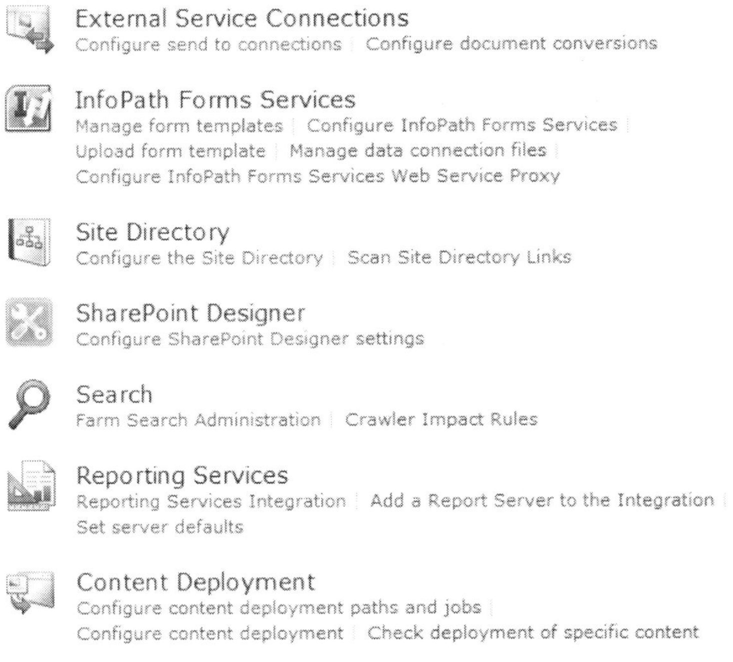

External Service Connections
Configure send to connections | Configure document conversions

InfoPath Forms Services
Manage form templates | Configure InfoPath Forms Services |
Upload form template | Manage data connection files |
Configure InfoPath Forms Services Web Service Proxy

Site Directory
Configure the Site Directory | Scan Site Directory Links

SharePoint Designer
Configure SharePoint Designer settings

Search
Farm Search Administration | Crawler Impact Rules

Reporting Services
Reporting Services Integration | Add a Report Server to the Integration |
Set server defaults

Content Deployment
Configure content deployment paths and jobs |
Configure content deployment | Check deployment of specific content

Figure 2-8. *The General Application Settings section under Central Administration in SharePoint 2010*

---

[1] What is a site collection? The challenge with teaching any topic is what comes first, the chicken or the egg? Keep reading this book; I promise that you will understand what a site collection is shortly.

The Great SharePoint Hierarchy

At the very top of the great SharePoint hierarchy is the farm. When I say the SharePoint *farm*, I am talking about everything—including all the servers, all the applications, and everything concerned with one installation of SharePoint. On your development virtual machine that you built in the last chapter, you have a single machine farm.

After the farm you have SharePoint *web applications*; there can be numerous web applications in a single SharePoint farm. One of those web applications is special the central administration but there can be others as well. These various SharePoint web applications are nothing but ASP.NET web applications with a custom web.config file that turns them into SharePoint web applications.

It is after this web application that things become a little bit interesting. Think of SharePoint web applications as any other ASP.NET web application. What does any ASP.NET web application in the world have? It has some code, typically ASPX files backed by some DLLs, and it has one or more databases. A SharePoint web application is very similar. There is code available as DLLs, various config files, various virtual directories, and one or more databases called *content databases*. It is in these content databases that the actual SharePoint content resides. So whenever you upload a document into a document library, usually that document goes into a content database. There's one slightly gray area called a site page, which is an .aspx page that lives in the content databases. I will talk more about site pages later on in this book.

Inside a SharePoint web application you have one or more content databases attached to the web application. The various content databases available in any particular web application are managed from the central administration\application management section.

Inside each one of these content databases can be one or more *site collections*, which are areas in which SharePoint logically likes to store its data. A content database is where SharePoint physically stores its data. And site collections live inside of a content database. A site collection is also the smallest entity you can put inside a content database; in other words, you cannot have a single site collection span across multiple content databases. This is a technique many of us use to provide different level of SLAs to different level of users in the same farm. We simply segregate the more important site collections into their own content databases living on their own servers.

You can create new site collections in any web application from the central administration\application management section by clicking the Create Site Collections link. When creating a new site collection, SharePoint central administration will ask you a few questions:

- It will ask you for a title and description of your new site collection.

- It will ask you under which web application you're creating the site collection. It doesn't ask you which content database this Site Collection will go into if you had multiple content databases in a site collection. Thus there is a concept of a default content database which is the last content database you added into the web application. If you wish to create a site collection in a specific content database you can do so using PowerShell or the object model.

- It will ask you what site definition you base the site collection on. Depending upon the site definition you pick, you will get certain out of the box features and functionality in your newly created site definition. You can further customize the created site collection using either custom code or SharePoint designer.

- It will ask you for a primary and secondary site collection administrator. A site collection administrator is a special user in a site collection who has the ability to give any permission he wants to. Note that a site collection administrator is not a special permission; it is merely a special flag on a particular user. I will talk more about SharePoint security in Chapter 12. Once the site collection is created, you can add more than two site collection administrators or appoint a SharePoint group as site collection administrators.

- Finally you have the ability to define and assign quota templates at the site collection level. Quota templates allow you to define settings such as user solution management, size allocation, and so on.

- This page will ask you on what URL you are creating the site collection on. This can be seen in Figure 2-9.

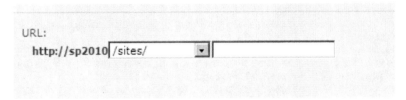

Figure 2-9. *Specifying the site URL*

As you can see there's a portion of the URL that you cannot edit the URL of the web application. Then there is a portion at the end in which you can type whatever you want. And then there is a portion that is driven using drop-downs, which is controlled by a concept called managed paths in a web application. In central administration under application management, click manage web applications, and select your port 80 web application. From the ribbon, click the Managed Paths button and you should see a dialog box as shown in Figure 2-10.

Define Managed Paths

Included Paths

This list specifies which paths within the URL namespace are managed by Microsoft SharePoint Foundation.

✗ Delete selected paths

	Path	Type
☐	(root)	Explicit inclusion
☐	sites	Wildcard inclusion
☐	my	Explicit inclusion
☐	my/personal	Wildcard inclusion

Add a New Path

Specify the path within the URL namespace to include. You can include an exact path, or all paths subordinate to the specified path.

Use the **Check URL** link to ensure that the path you include is not already in use for existing sites or folders, which will open a new browser window with that URL.

Path:

Check URL

Note: To indicate the root path for this web application, type a slash (/).

Type:

Wildcard inclusion ▾

Add Path

OK

Figure 2-10. *Specifying managed paths for a web application*

There are some managed paths defined, some with explicit inclusion type and some with wildcard inclusion type. When I define a managed path with explicit inclusion, I'm telling SharePoint that there will be one but only one site collection at that defined location. For instance, out of the box there will be a site collection that you can create at the root level in a web application. That is commonly also referred to as the root level web application. When I say that I'm creating a managed path using wildcard inclusion, I'm telling SharePoint that I can have as many site collections as I please at the URL in the format of http://webapplication/wildcardmanagedpath/*. Managed paths is a technique that we use very frequently for defining the logical layout of any SharePoint installation. Even though the site collections appear as a single site hierarchy, behind the scenes we can split the content among multiple site collections and content databases.

Under a site collection you can have various sites. In fact, you cannot have a site collection without any site in it. When you create a site collection from central administration, by default it will put in a top-level site in the site collection. For instance if I create a site collection at http://sp2010/sites/myfunsitecollection, I create a container for site collections at http://sp2010/sites/myfunsitecollection. In that container, I can then put a single top-level site at http://sp2010/sites/myfunsitecollection. Now I can visit this URL, http://sp2010/sites/myfunsitecollection, and from within this site I can create further child-level sites.

One important thing to realize is that a site collection is a boundary of various sorts. Most importantly, it is a boundary for security. Let's say that you have two site collections in a web application, one is at http://sp2010, and the other is at http://sp2010/sites/myfunsitecollection. Then adding a user at http://sp2010 has no bearing or effect on the site collection at http://sp2010/sites/myfunsitecollection. In fact, for all intents and purposes, the site collection at http://sp2010/sites/myfunsitecollection has no knowledge, interrelation, affection, feelings, or anything else for the site collection at http://sp2010. They are in the same web application by chance and they can be moved into another web application without affecting each other. Practically speaking, though, in order to scale out your SharePoint installation you will probably end up creating many site collections in a web application, and using some custom code you will probably also want to tie them together with each other, functionally speaking.

Finally inside the site collection and individual sites is where you create lists and document libraries where the actual content goes. So next let's look at the process of creating a list and define some basic security settings on a SharePoint list.

Creating and Using SharePoint Lists

The basic element in which data is stored inside of SharePoint is a SharePoint *list* (I also include a *document library*, which is a special kind of a SharePoint list whose primary storage element is a document).

In addition to allowing you to store a document in an item, a list also gives you a number of additional facilities on top. It lets you define the specific metadata you wish to capture with each added document or item, define views on the collected data, define security on the overall list on an individual list item, and do many other things that you will discover in this book.

But to get started, let's see the basic usage of a SharePoint list!

1. I assume that you have created a site collection on port 80. If you haven't done so, please visit central administration\application management\create site collections and create a site collection using the blank site definition, marking you the administrator as the site collection owner.

2. In your active directory, provision two new users called Joe and Jane.

3. Back in your site collection click the "site actions\site settings" link, and look for people and groups on the "site settings" page.

4. Under the "people and groups" section, add both Joe and Jane in the Members group, or with Contribute rights. This will allow both Joe and Jane to participate in content editing within the site collection.

5. Next, click "site actions\more options", and choose to create a new list called Discussions based on the Discussion Board list definition. This will give the newly created list discussion board like behavior and features.

6. With the list created, now logged in as administrator, add a new list item by clicking the Add New Discussion link, or visiting the list at `http://sp2010/list/discussions`, and going to the List Tools\Items tab in the ribbon, and clicking New Item. Fill in the new discussion thread details as shown in Figure 2-11.

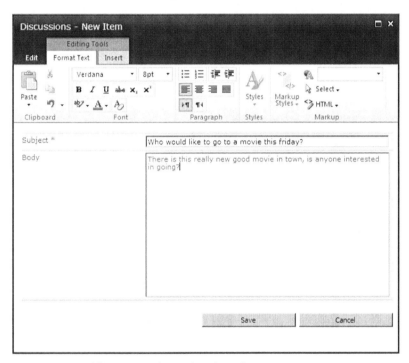

Figure 2-11. *Adding a new discussion thread*

7. Next, while still logged on as administrator, go to the home page of the site at `http://sp2010` and choose "site actions\edit page". You should see WebPart zones become available, as shown in Figure 2-12.

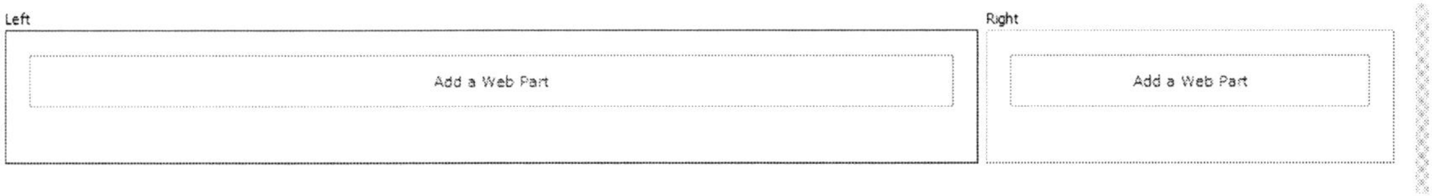

Left   Right

Add a Web Part   Add a Web Part

Figure 2-12. *WebPart zones on a SharePoint page*

8.   Click the left WebPart zone, and from Lists and Libraries, choose to add the Discussions list. Then under the page tab of the ribbon, click the Stop Editing button. Your SharePoint site should look Figure 2-13.

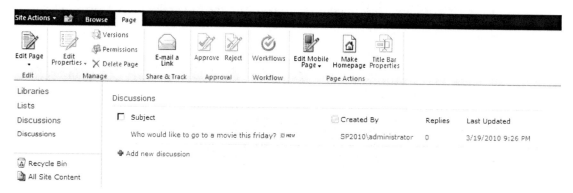

Figure 2-13. *The discussion forum on the site's home page*

9.   Now, click the Winsmarts\Administrator link on the upper right of your page, choose to Sign in as different user, and log in as Joe. Joe can now not only view the discussion item but also reply to it. Add a reply as Joe, as shown in Figure 2-14.

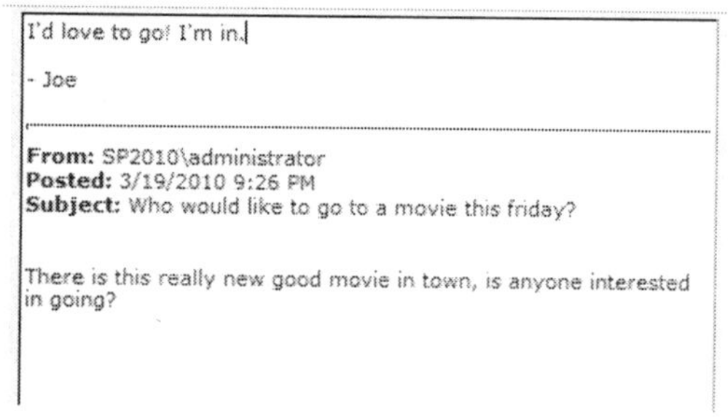

```
I'd love to go! I'm in.

- Joe
_____
From: SP2010\administrator
Posted: 3/19/2010 9:26 PM
Subject: Who would like to go to a movie this friday?

There is this really new good movie in town, is anyone interested
in going?
```

Figure 2-14. *Replying to an existing discussion*

10. Log in to the site as Jane and add Jane's reply as well, as shown in Figure 2-15.

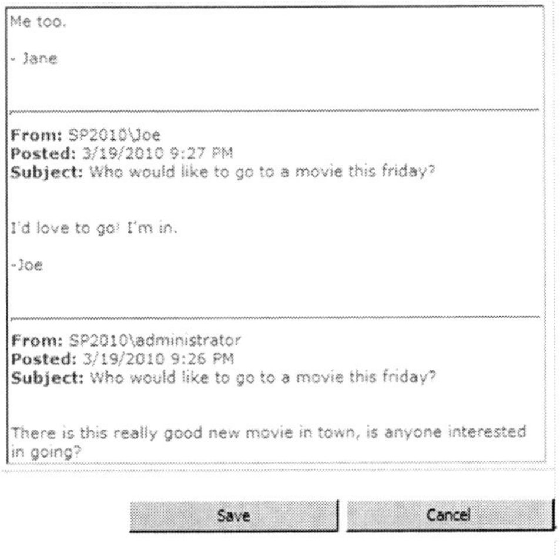

Me too.
- Jane
From: SP2010\Joe
Posted: 3/19/2010 9:27 PM
Subject: Who would like to go to a movie this friday?
I'd love to go! I'm in.
-Joe
From: SP2010\administrator
Posted: 3/19/2010 9:26 PM
Subject: Who would like to go to a movie this friday?
There is this really good new movie in town, is anyone interested in going?
Save
Cancel

Figure 2-15. *Jane's reply to the discussion*

11. Now, suppose that the last time we took Jane with us, she was a real pain. Not fun at all. Didn't even pay for her ticket and dinner. So you, as the administrator, want to have a private discussion with Joe, and not let Jane see that discussion. What should you do? You can log in as administrator.

12. When logged in as administrator, from the ECB Menu, choose to Manage Permissions on the specific discussion in progress (see Figure 2-16).

Discussions
Subject
Creat
Who would like to go to a movie this friday? NEW
SP20
Add new discussion
View Item
Edit Item
Manage Permissions
Delete Item

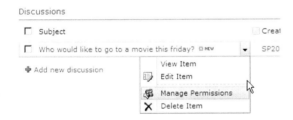

Figure 2-16. *Managing permissions on a discussion thread*

13. Note that neither Joe nor Jane had rights to configure permissions, but the administrator does! I'll cover further security related details in Chapter 12, but in short, Joe and Jane have Contribute rights, and the administrator has Full Control, which includes managing permissions (Contribute doesn't). On certain kinds of objects, called as SecurableObjects, you can choose to either inherit permissions from the parent or stop inheriting and define unique permissions. And that is exactly what you're going to do!

14. Clicking the Manage Permissions ECB menu item, will land you on the page shown in Figure 2-17.

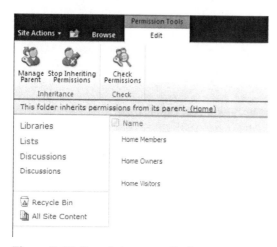

Figure 2-17. *Permissions on a list item*

15. Home Owners have Full Control rights, whereas Visitors have read only, and Members have Contribute rights. Remember you added Joe and Jane as Home Members? Well, they have Contribute rights. Click the Stop Inheriting Permissions button in the ribbon. See the warning that you are creating unique permissions, hit OK, choose to remove Home Members, add only Joe as Contribute (do not add Jane in any permission right on this list item). Thus you can either add permissions to a user or to a group.

16. Back as administrator, reply to Joe's reply on his own thread as shown in Figure 2-18.

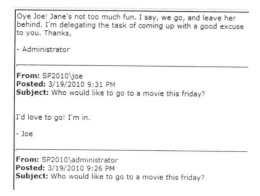

Figure 2-18. *The administrator's reply to Joe*

17. Now, log in to the site as Joe, and you should see Joe's view as shown in Figure 2-19.

Discussions

	Subject		Created By	Replies	Last Updated
□	Who would like to go to a movie this friday? ⌗NEW		SP2010\administrator	3	3/19/2010 9:39 PM

✦ Add new discussion

Figure 2-19. *Joe's view of the discussion board*

18. Finally, log in as Jane, and you should see Jane's view (see Figure 2-20).

Discussions

	Subject		Created By	Replies	Last Updated
□	Subject	□	Created By	Replies	Last Updated

There are no items to show in this view of the "Discussions" discussion board. To add a new item, click "New".

✦ Add new discussion

Figure 2-20. *Jane's view of the discussion board*

As you can see, Jane can no longer participate in the discussion. In fact, because we didn't even give her Read rights, she can't even view our discussion. Obviously, you and Joe will go and enjoy the movie and leave Jane behind! Serves her right!

So what exactly did you see in this simple example? You saw the basic use of SharePoint using a discussion list. At this point I invite you to play a little bit more around the site, create a few other kinds of lists, and see what else SharePoint is capable of out of the box. Specifically, when you create various lists, try creating columns in lists. You can now specify some simple validation rules on the columns right through the browser. Also, on lookup columns you can enforce cascade actions on related lists. These are new in SharePoint 2010.

If you have worked with SharePoint 2007 before, by now you would've also noticed some major UI differences between SharePoint 2007 in SharePoint 2010. Specifically the SharePoint user interface now is full of modal popover dialog boxes that keep the user in context of the list that he's working on. Also the user interface is now full of Ajax-related richness, thereby providing a less confusing and more useful user interface. Also the ribbon has now been extended from Office thick client applications all the way into SharePoint. Yes you will see that certain list definitions such as the image library still do not use the ribbon. There is no good reason for that except that Microsoft needed to ship this product on time. Both that dialog box and the ribbon UI are concepts that are extended to you as a developer. Using custom code you have the ability to define new ribbon buttons and new dialog boxes at various places inside SharePoint.

Summary

This was a short and sweet chapter that served as a basic introduction to SharePoint 2010 and its usage. Note that so far we haven't dealt even a little bit into the developing side of SharePoint. You learned about the basic administration a developer needs to know, how SharePoint organizes its data, and how you would go about using a standard SharePoint site and a standard SharePoint list.

Needless to say there's plenty more to learn. Starting in the next chapter I will start talking about the process of authoring custom code deployed to SharePoint installations as features and solutions. Hang tight! Things are about to become a whole lot more fun.

CHAPTER 3

The SharePoint 2010 Feature Solution Framework

Reading Key: If you are familiar with SharePoint 2007, you will find this chapter interesting.

So far within the first chapter of this book you installed and configured SharePoint. Since you are a techie and not a manager, you also dove into what SharePoint 2010 installation did to your machine behind the scenes. Subsequently, in the second chapter, you saw the wealth of features SharePoint 2010 provides out of the box.

Out of the box features are great. You don't have to write them, you don't have to maintain them, but you can claim full credit for them. On the other hand, say you had an out of the box feature called "Hammer". But the client asks for a "Plier". Well, here's a hammer—see how it goes! Sometimes, you need to both tweak out of the box features, and sometimes you need to write completely new features into SharePoint to meet your customers' needs.

In SharePoint, there are three ways to deliver functionality to the end user.

- Using out of the box features typically tweaked right through the browser.

- Using a thick client tool such as Excel, InfoPath, Access, and probably the most important of all, SharePoint Designer.

- Finally, if you really need to roll up your sleeves and seriously customize SharePoint in ways that both the previous options are unsuitable for, you would pop open Visual Studio 2010 or better and deliver such functionality.

I should also mention that most real projects will involve all three of the preceding. Also, sometimes you may start a customization in a tool such as SharePoint designer, and then take it to Visual Studio for further serious customization. Therefore, when working with Visual Studio 2010 to deliver new functionality into SharePoint, you would need to become familiar with the object model, better known as the SharePoint API. Now, the simplest way of getting familiar with the object model is by writing a simple Console Application. While you shouldn't deploy new functionality to production using Console Applications, it is worthwhile to learn how to write a console application for SharePoint 2010 since frequently you will write such applications as "use and throw" code to test concepts or learn the object model.

Writing Your First SharePoint Console App

Writing a SharePoint console app is quite simple.

1. On your SharePoint development machine, create a new Console Application in Visual Studio 2010. As shown in Figure 3-1, make sure your target framework is .NET 3.5. This is because SharePoint 2010 is built on .NET 3.5 SP1.

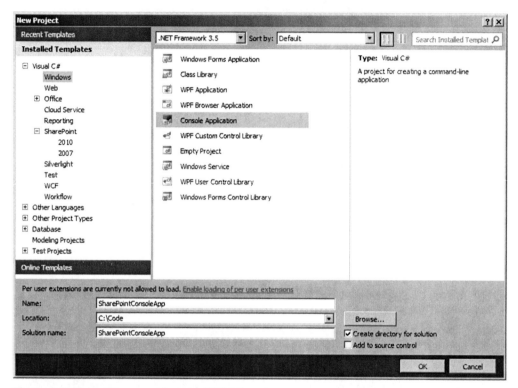

Figure 3-1. *Target Framework set to .NET 3.5*

2. Add a reference to Microsoft.SharePoint.dll. You will find this reference under the .NET tab of the Add References Dialog within Visual Studio. Look for Microsoft.SharePoint.

3. Right-click your project and choose properties. Under the Build section, change the platform of your console application to AnyCPU or x64. The default in Visual Studio 2010 is x86, because it is envisioned that for a very long time to come x86 apps will be the default application of choice unless an application needs to deal with massive amounts of data. x64 apps require too much segment calculation for them to be efficient in most scenarios. On the other hand, AnyCPU apps have an initial starting overhead, but once they are started, they run quite well. (I prefer to go with AnyCPU in most instances.)

4. Finally, write some code in your static void main, as shown in the following:

```
using (SPSite site = new SPSite("http://sp2010"))
{
    Console.WriteLine(site.RootWeb.Title);
}
```

Remember to add a using statement for Microsoft.SharePoint.

That's basically it. Hit F5 to run your application and now you should be able to view the title of the Site at http://sp2010. There is plenty else to learn in the SharePoint object model. Luckily, most of it is named well so it is easy to figure out what most of it does. You will see many classes, but for now please go ahead and familiarize yourself with the following basic classes in the SharePoint object model:

- SPFarm
- SPWebApplication
- SPSite
- SPWeb
- SPList
- SPListItem
- SPDocumentLibrary

There are many more objects to be familiar with and throughout this book as well as while working with SharePoint you will learn them as you go.

As I said earlier, you will never deploy new functionality to production using console applications. Also, when you write new functionality for SharePoint 2010, the only good and maintainable way to deploy such functionality is as a SharePoint solution. A solution is simply a .cab file, renamed to a .wsp file. If you were to simply rename a .wsp file to a .cab file and open it, you will most definitely see a manifest.xml file in there. The manifest.xml file is what SharePoint would use to understand what the solution contains.

What can any solution contain? A solution can contain plain artifacts being deployed to the file system, content database, or any new executable artifacts such as web pages, server controls, or WebParts. So, what does it take to write a simple feature or solution that deploys a new WebPart? Before I describe how to write a WebPart, first let's define WebParts.

What are WebParts?

Pardon me for being obvious, but in the interest of being complete, I have to describe what a WebPart is before using a WebPart in the demonstration feature and solution. I will cover writing WebParts in detail in Chapter 4, however. But if you are familiar with what a WebPart is, please feel free to skip to the end of this section and continue reading the section "Writing Your First Feature and Solution."

A WebPart is the Microsoft equivalent of a portlet or a widget. Imagine a webpage on which the administrator could drop a widget, *customize* it right through the browser, and provide some functionality to the users of the site. Not only that, imagine that if every end user could further tweak such widgets on the web page, or maybe even drop more widgets to fully *personalize* their experience on the site. Also, sometimes these widgets need to present their own complex UI to provide such customizability or personalization, and perhaps in certain scenarios, these widgets may also need to talk with each other.

Well, assuming that you're working with SharePoint, those "widgets" that you're dropping on the web page are called WebParts. Those complex UIs that these widgets, or WebParts, present to edit themselves are called WebPart Editors. Finally, the ability of WebParts to talk to each other is referred to as WebPart connections.

■**Note** Did you notice I said the administrator customized and the end user personalized the WebPart? WebParts is a big topic in itself and I'll dive into it in Chapter 4.

Let's try out a simple WebPart to solidify your understanding here.

Trying Out a Simple WebPart

In this exercise, you will create edit a SharePoint web page and add and customize a simple WebPart.

1. If you don't already have a web application on port 80, go ahead and create one.

2. Create a fresh site collection using the Blank site definition at the port 80 web site.

3. Visit the port 80 web site in the browser.

4. Click the Site Actions button on the top left of the page, and choose Edit Page. You should see two WebPart zones appear, as shown in Figure 3-2.

Figure 3-2. *The page in edit mode with two WebPart zones*

5. Those rectangles you see are WebPartzones. Now click one of them. You will notice that a new menu item appears on the ribbon called Page Tools/Insert, as shown in Figure 3-3.

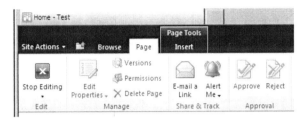

Figure 3-3. *The ribbon with the insert ribbon tab*

6. Click Insert and choose "WebPart" in the ribbon.

7. In the navigation area for available WebParts below the ribbon, choose the Content Editor WebPart and click the Add button, as shown in Figure 3-4.

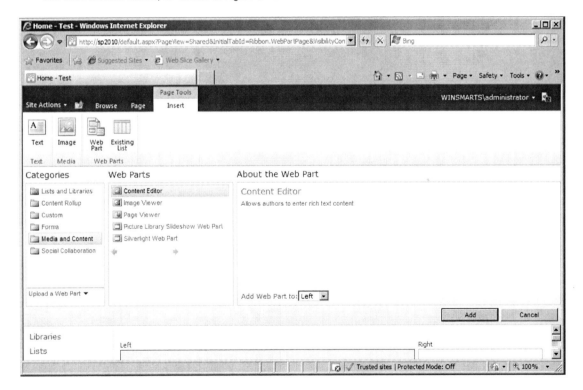

Figure 3-4. *Browsing for your WebPart*

8.   You will note that the content editor WebPart is now added to the left WebPart zone. In the WebPart, you will see a link that says "Click here to add new content". Go ahead and click that and type in some text.

9.   Next, in the ribbon under the Page tab, click Stop editing. Your final page should look like the one shown in Figure 3-5.

Figure 3-5. *Your WebPart in action*

Congratulations, you just worked with a WebPart! Go ahead and play with some other WebParts available to you in SharePoint.

Writing Your First Feature and Solution

Assuming that you're a developer, the previous exercise on dropping and creating a WebPart was just too easy for you. Let's sharpen your claws and write your first solution and feature in Visual Studio 2010.

Like any other project, you first create the project. Next, you add functionality into your project and then you deploy and debug. Finally, you may have to worry about things such as versioning, upgrades, and so forth.

Create the Project

On your SharePoint development machine, start Visual Studio 2010. Then, click File ➤ New Project, and look for the SharePoint 2010 group on the left, as shown in Figure 3-6.

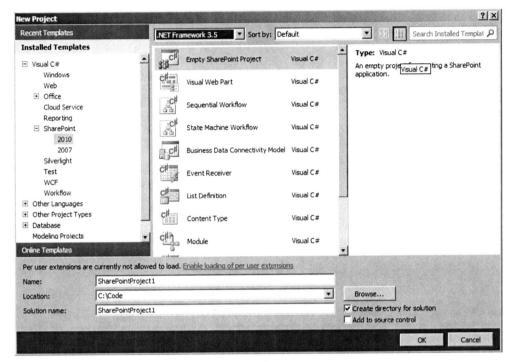

Figure 3-6. *The various SharePoint project templates*

There are so many different kinds of SharePoint 2010 projects you can create. Usually, I like to create a project that mimics a business need such as Invoice authorization or time sheet. I don't like to create solutions that have technical meanings such as "The TimeSheet List Definition" or "The Timesheet WebPart". One .wsp can contain many SharePoint artifacts. It makes sense that you should hand over a timesheetfunctionality.wsp rather than five or ten .wsps that deploy parts of timesheet functionality. In that vein, I find myself creating the Empty SharePoint Project the most, so create a new "Empty SharePoint Project", and call it "HelloWorld".

As soon as you try and create your new HelloWorld project, Visual Studio will present you with the dialogbox shown in the Figure 3-7.

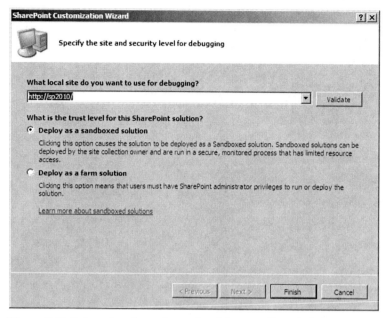

Figure 3-7. *Debugging site and trust level for your SharePoint project*

There are two questions being asked here. The first is, which local site do you want to use for debugging? This is the same machine that you are running SharePoint on. Some may wonder why Visual Studio has to ask such a silly question, because after all this is always your local machine. The reality is, sometimes you may have alternate URLs setup even for your local site, and that may be important in certain development tasks. Secondly, the site collection you intend to debug your code on may not be a root level site collection. Finally, if you have multiple web applications, this tells Visual Studio which w3wp.exe process to attach to for debugging. So you see, it's not such a silly question after all.

Providing the URL tells Visual Studio which web application you will debug your code on, and which w3wp.exe process visual studio should attach itself to during debugging, so you as a developer can now create a breakpoint, hit F5, and your breakpoint just hits. Something your fellow .NET developer brethren have been doing since 2000 is now finally available out of the box to SharePoint developers.

That was my marketing side talking. Although in simplistic scenarios F5 debugging will work, in many situations you will still find yourself attaching to processes. For example, sometimes your code may not run inside w3wp.exe. It may run under a separate EXE called SPUserCodeService.exe. That would be a sandboxed solution which I will cover in more detail later in this chapter, but for now, that is the second question Visual Studio wishes you to answer. Therefore, the second question is whether you intend to create a sandboxed solution or a farm solution?

A farm solution is what used to be a solution in SharePoint 2007. Basically, it had unfettered rights to your SharePoint farm, so it could do anything. Sounds like a good proposition, but this created an immense headache for the two poor farm administrators in your organization who were then expected to somehow review every line of code being deployed to the server. A task they intend to get around to doing right after they solve world peace and hunger. Frankly, it is unreasonable to expect two overtaxed IT Pro people to review every single developer's code. Plus since some developers can be really crafty, custom code, while being necessary, is the number one reason for support issues on SharePoint in general.

Tip I use the term IT Pro administrators and infrastructure ogres interchangeably.

In response, Microsoft came out with the concept of sandboxed solutions, sometimes also referred to as user solutions or user code. Put simply, a sandboxed solution is what runs inside a secure sandbox. It runs inside a separate process from W3WP.exe, and it is protected by a CAS policy, so you no longer have to craft custom CAS policies. Also, in addition to being more secure, it is also more easily monitored.

Being more restricted, secure, and being more easily monitored, sandboxed solutions can now be deployed with more confidence. Thus, they are now deployable and can be activated right through the site collection. The Farm Administrator doesn't even need to be bothered, because he is monitoring the solution anyway.

I will talk more about sandboxed solutions later in this chapter, but for now let me just say two things:

- Secure by default, you should create sandboxed solutions when you can. Creating a farm solution unnecessarily is bad practice. Perhaps a better way of saying this is, create farm solutions only when you cannot create a sandboxed solution.

- You can choose to change your mind later, i.e., change a sandboxed solution to a farm solution or vice versa if you need to.

There is much more to learn about sandboxed solutions, but for now the choice is quite obvious here. Go with a sandboxed solution and hit "OK". This will create a new HelloWorld project for you.

Now that the HelloWorld project is created, let's examine the structure of the project that is created for you. You can see this structure in Figure 3-8.

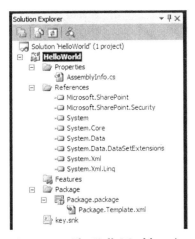

Figure 3-8. *The HelloWorld project structure*

There are some standard Visual Studio-like nodes here, and a few interesting things that are typical to a SharePoint project.

The Properties and References area are much like any other Visual Studio project, so I won't bother explaining those too much. However, you should poke around and see what's inside them. Also, there is a strongly named key called key.snk. Sometimes, especially when working with farm solutions, your code will go into the GAC. Therefore, it must be strongly named. You should replace that key.snk with a standard yourcompany.snk in real world projects, but for use and throw code, key.snk is just fine.

Other than standard .NET-like nodes, there are two nodes specific to SharePoint development. These are Features and Package.

The Feature is a container of various defined extensions for SharePoint. It's a set of XML files which are deployed to web front ends that can be bundled in site definitions or individually turned on in SharePoint sites. Put simply, a feature is something you activate on either the farm, web application, site collection, or a site. By activating a feature on any of these four scopes, you add new things into SharePoint that are logically bundled together by you. What can those things be? Things such as new WebParts, list definitions and instances, event receivers, or content types. You will discover many of these various extensions for SharePoint, which. I will show many of throughout this book. Therefore, no need to memorize the list just yet.

Package is where you specify what gets packaged into the final .wsp your Visual Studio solution will produce. This may contain features and other assets that are not directly a part of your features. By double-clicking the package node, you can view the package designer which lets you decide what gets deployed as a part of your .wsp.

Add Functionality to Your Project

Assuming that you've created an Empty SharePoint solution project to be deployed as a sandboxed solution, now let's begin adding some functionality. The simplest possible thing to write would be a simple WebPart that displays "Hello World!"

Doing so is quite simple. Just right-click the project and choose "Add New Item" (or hit CTRL_SHIFT_A like us cool kids). You will then be presented with various SharePoint Items (SPI) you can add into a SharePoint project, as shown in the Figure 3-9.

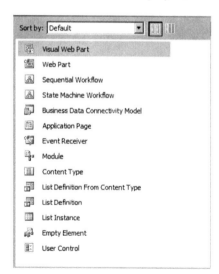

Figure 3-9. *The various SPIs you can add into your project*

Next, add a new WebPart and call it the "HelloWorldWebPart".

Before you start typing in code, quickly glance over to the solution explorer. Adding the WebPart related files also added a new feature for you. This is shown in Figure 3-10.

Figure 3-10. *The solution explorer with your WebPart included*

Obviously, I don't like the default "Feature1" names, but I'll leave it up to you to fix them. When you are poking around fixing the names of your feature also quickly examine the various properties for the feature. You can access the properties of the Feature1 node by double-clicking the "Feature1" node. This will both show properties and the feature designer dialog in the main client area.

The feature designer is where you can choose what portions of the solution get packaged in which feature. For instance, if your solution being deployed was "Consultant management", and it had two features "Timesheets" and "Invoice", the whole functionality could be deployed as a single solution and two features. You get to pick and choose what gets deployed, packaged, and how. And you do so by playing around with the feature designer and the package designer. Now would be an excellent time for you to poke around the feature designer and package designer on your own before moving on.

Back in the WebPart, you see there are three files.

Elements.xml

Elements.xml defines the WebPart to SharePoint. If you open it, you will see code that looks like Listing 3-1.

Listing 3-1. *Elements.xml for Your HelloWorld WebPart*

```xml
<?xml version="1.0" encoding="utf-8"?>
<Elements xmlns="http://schemas.microsoft.com/sharepoint/" >
  <Module Name="HelloWorldWebPart" List="113" Url="_catalogs/wp">
    <File Path="HelloWorldWebPart\HelloWorldWebPart.WebPart" Url="HelloWorldWebPart.WebPart"
Type="GhostableInLibrary">
      <Property Name="Group" Value="Custom" />
    </File>
  </Module>
</Elements>
```

There is a wealth of information embedded in the previous elements.xml. There is a Module node which you would typically use to deploy any file into the content database. It talks of a List with ID 113. List ID 113 is the template ID of the document library found at _catalogs/wp. That is where all .WebPart files go, which describe to SharePoint what WebParts are available for use in the current site collection. Note that this is just a document library, so item level permissions on the .WebPart files can be used to allow or disallow certain WebPart availability to certain users.

Besides the Module tag and the templateID, you will see various other things such as a file tag that signifies each individual file being copied into the content database. There is also a Path and URL attribute, which specifies the copied "from" location and copied "to" location. The idea is that the Visual Studio tools should make it unnecessary for you to know these details. My personal view is that every good SharePoint developer should know these details, because at some point the tools either won't work well enough, or trust me, on production environments you won't find the tools.

Also, you see Type = GhostableInLibrary. This is necessary when you are copying files into a document library.

Then there are various Property elements. These property elements set various properties to the added ListItem in the document library. These column values help you do things such as categorize your WebPart appropriately or give it a nice looking icon.

Remembering Template IDs

Perhaps you're wondering if you are supposed to remember the ID "113"? The answer is yes, but don't worry, as a SharePoint developer you will end up remembering many such IDs anyway. In case you forget the Template ID of any standard SharePoint document library, let me tell you a little trick to discover such IDs.

In the Server explorer of Visual Studio, add a SharePoint connection to your local SharePoint farm, in this case http://sp2010. This will give you the entire structure of your SharePoint farm right through visual studio. Too bad it's read only, but it is still helpful. You can, however, extend the SharePoint explorer to add your own nodes if you choose to.

When inside SharePoint explorer, find the Web Part Gallery under Lists and Libraries. With the WebPart Gallery selected, look at the properties for it in Visual Studio, and copy then paste the GUID that is right by the ID property. Remember, you are looking for the TemplateID, which is a number. The ID is a unique identifier for any SharePoint object. The ID for the WebPart Gallery on my machine is 9e7d064f-d9c8-42f0-8a4f-b02c9f4c259f, but yours is probably different.

Next, visit the following URL in your browser (remember to put the correct ID per your machine):

```
http://sp2010/_vti_bin/owssvr.dll?Cmd=ExportList&List=9e7d064f-d9c8-42f0-8a4f-b02c9f4c259f
```

That should spew out a lot of XML on the browser. The TemplateID is ready for you to consume under the List node as the ServerTemplate attribute. This can be seen in Figure 3-11.

Figure 3-11. *Finding template IDs for lists*

HelloWorldWebPart.WebPart

The HelloWorldWebPart.WebPart file is an XML file that provides an initial configuration to the WebPart. For instance, if you were creating a WebPart to display an RSS feed that had an RSSURL as a public property, you could specify an initial RSSURL property to point to a blog of your choice when the WebPart is first dropped on the page and is yet unconfigured.

The .WebPart file also has sufficient information to tell SharePoint where to find the class library for the WebPart. In doing so, if you open the .WebPart file, you will also see strings such as SharePoint that are automatically replaced to actual names.

You should open up the .WebPart file and examine the contents at this time.

HelloWorldWebPart.cs

Finally, there is the .cs file where your actual WebPart logic goes. This is a glorified server control. It inherits from the System.Web.UI.WebControls.WebParts.WebPart, which is a class that was introduced in .NET framework 2.0. There is also another .WebPart base class in the Microsoft.SharePoint namespace, but that is there only for backward compatibility reasons with WSS 2.0. If you're writing a WebPart today, you shouldn't inherit from that class.

■**Note** Since you are writing a WebPart as a sandbox solution, when you're online next, do check out the restrictions on a WebPart in a sandbox solution at http://blah.winsmarts.com/2009-12-You_can_deploy_WebParts_as_Sandboxed_solutions__but.aspx.

Let's make a minor modification to the code. In the RenderContents method, go ahead and add the following line of code:

```
writer.WriteLine("Hello World!");
```

That's basically it. Your WebPart is done. Save and hit CTRL_SHIFT_B to make sure that it builds. Assuming that you were able to build this WebPart, and thus your solution, let's move on to deploying and debugging.

Deploying and Debugging

Before you do this, I'd like you to enable the output window. This can be done by going to the View ➤ Output window menu or using the CTRL_W, O key combination. This is where you see deployment results.

Next comes perhaps the easiest part. Just hit F9 on the line of code you added and then hit F5 to deploy and debug.

A number of interesting things happen now. First, the output window quickly scrolls and shows an output, as shown in Listing 3-2.

Listing 3-2. *Output Window Details During Deployment*

```
------ Build started: Project: HelloWorld, Configuration: Debug Any CPU ------
  HelloWorld -> C:\Code\HelloWorld\HelloWorld\bin\Debug\HelloWorld.dll
  Successfully created package at: C:\Code\HelloWorld\HelloWorld\bin\Debug\HelloWorld.wsp
------ Deploy started: Project: HelloWorld, Configuration: Debug Any CPU ------
Active Deployment Configuration: Default
Run Pre-Deployment Command:
  Skipping deployment step because a pre-deployment command is not specified.
Recycle IIS Application Pool:
  Skipping application pool recycle because a sandboxed solution is being deployed.
Retract Solution:
  Deactivating feature 'HelloWorld_Feature1' ...
  Retracting solution 'HelloWorld.wsp'...
  Deleting solution 'HelloWorld.wsp'...
Add Solution:
  Found 1 deployment conflict(s).  Resolving conflicts ...
  Deleted file 'http://sp2010/_catalogs/wp/HelloWorldWebPart.WebPart' from server.
  Adding solution 'HelloWorld.wsp'...
  Deploying solution 'HelloWorld.wsp'...
Activate Features:
  Activating feature 'Feature1' ...
Run Post-Deployment Command:
  Skipping deployment step because a post-deployment command is not specified.
```

You might get an error at this time, telling you that "Cannot start service SPUserCodeV4". If that happens, go to Central Administration\System Settings\Manage Services on Server, and choose to start the "Microsoft SharePoint Foundation Sandboxed Code Service". This service allows you to run Sandbox Solutions, which I will describe later in this chapter.

Next, a dialog box pops up prompting you to attach to the appropriate process, as shown in Figure 3-12.

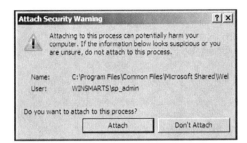

Figure 3-12. *Attaching to the right process in Visual Studio*

Click attach. The browser will then open and show the SharePoint site you had intended to use for debugging. Let's go ahead and add the WebPart to any of the two WebPart zones on the page. You would note that as soon as the WebPart is rendered, your breakpoint in your code gets hit.

Congratulations, you've just built, deployed, and debugged your first WebPart.

Go celebrate, but come right back because there is plenty more to learn. As you may have guessed, there is more to the picture than this.

First of all, you can right-click the project and choose menu items such as "Deploy" and "Package". Sometimes you want to redeploy without doing a rebuild, perhaps to run through something called as Feature Receivers, which are custom code blocks that run at certain conveniently placed events during the feature lifetime.

On the other hand, package just builds, packages the .wsp, but does not deploy. This is quite useful in scenarios such as automating using MSBUILD, where you want to hand over a .wsp to another environment such as the QA or Production environment. Another example where I see myself packing and not deploying directly is when I want to hand over code to the infrastructure ogre to deploy to production. Yet another example is where I want to test out feature upgrade code, as you will see later in this chapter.

Therefore, go ahead and right-click the project and choose Properties to view the project properties. Then view the SharePoint tab. You should see an area that allows you to specify pre-deployment commands and post-deployment commands. These are quite useful when you wish to perform steps before and after deployment steps. You will frequently need to perform such steps. You can also add to these steps using custom code. To be honest, I find writing custom batch files or powershell scripts executed as a post-build deployment step a whole lot more convenient and maintainable. An example of such a situation is when you have a silverlight .xap file that is built as a separate project and needs to be packaged up in your SharePoint project as a module. This is done much easier using a post-build command. I will demonstrate this in Chapter 5.

Also, you will see Deployment configurations. There are two deployment configurations that you cannot edit: Default and No Activation. The names make it quite obvious what they do, but the following explains them in detail.

- Default runs the pre-deployment command line, packages the WSP file, recycles the application pool, retracts the previous version of the solution, adds the solution, activates all features, and runs the post-deployment command line.

- No Activation on the other hand runs the pre-deployment command line, packages the WSP file, recycles the application pool, retracts the previous version of the solution, adds the solution, and runs the post-deployment command line. It is obvious this configuration does not call the activate all features step.

You can also create newer deployment configurations per your needs as your project demands, and trust me you will need it frequently as you start writing more and more interesting SharePoint projects.

There is one more thing I'd like to point out before moving on to other real-world scenarios such as versioning and upgrade. That is what happens during debugging or otherwise, if you keep redeploying this project over and over again, which is typical behavior during iterative building. There are exceptions to this rule, but as a very rough rule of thumb you can think that most items that go in the content database are not overwritten or deleted for you when the feature reinstalls or is retracted. Most items that go on the file system are overwritten or deleted during deploys and retracts. Remember I said there are exceptions to this very rough rule of thumb, so always verify the actual behavior when you are coding.

During iterative development, however, you will see yourself hit F5 constantly as you develop your functionality. The .WebPart class by default will not be overwritten. However, during iterative deployment you would want the .WebPart file to be overwritten. Luckily, SharePoint 2010 development tools in Visual Studio 2010 have this problem sorted out for you.

With the solution already deployed, and the WebPart already in use, right-click the project, choose Deploy one more time, and observe the output window closely. You should see output that looks like the following code:

```
Found 1 deployment conflict(s).  Resolving conflicts ...
Deleted file 'http://sp2010/_catalogs/wp/HelloWorldWebPart.WebPart' from server.
Adding solution 'HelloWorld.wsp'...
Deploying solution 'HelloWorld.wsp'...
```

Let me explain what is going in here. There is a HelloWorldWebPart.WebPart file at _catalogs/wp, which ended up there as a result of the first deployment of the WebPart. If you look at the properties of HelloWorldWebPart in Visual Studio, there is a property called "Deployment Conflict Resolution". The values are None because the previous WebPart file is left as is, untouched, much like SharePoint 2007 solutions did and much like deploying from command line would do. The value of "Automatic" will make a best guess scenario, which in this case will replace the old .WebPart file with the new .WebPart file. This is exactly what happened here; the deployment process automatically resolved the conflict for you. The value of "Prompt" will ask you before overwriting your file.

Thus, the scenario of deploying the same WebPart over and over with the same version number at least is handled quite well. However, what if you wanted a real versioning and upgrade strategy?

Versioning and Upgrade

Wouldn't it be nice if you could just write code and leave the maintenance to the next guy? For some crazy reason, I always end up being that next guy, so I have to share my pain and tell you about the new and much improved Versioning and Upgrade story in SharePoint 2010.

In SharePoint 3.0, there was really no good way to upgrade features. You did have a "version" attribute in the feature node of the feature.xml file, but it didn't do anything. It was simply ignored. In SharePoint 2010, however, the version attribute takes good meaning. When a feature is activated at a specified scope, a feature instance is created that is associated with the current version of that feature. If a new and higher version of the feature is deployed, SharePoint 2010 detects that the associated feature instance needs an upgrade.

There is an upgrade infrastructure present in SharePoint that calls the QueryFeatures methods, the SPWebService, SPWebApplication, SPContentDatabase, and SPSite classes. This method tells which features need to be upgraded during deployment. There are many suitable overloads available for this method.

- *SPWebService*: Find server farm, web application, site collection, and web site-scoped feature instances, or activated Features, in the farm that conform to filtering criteria.

- *SPWebApplication*: Find activated Features at site collection scope that conform to the specified filtering criteria. Querying is done across all content databases in the Web application object and the returned collection is ordered by content database.

- *SPContentDatabase*: Find Features in the content database that are scoped for site collection and web sites that conform to the specified filtering criteria. The collection that is returned is ordered with respect to web site hierarchy. For example, parent web site Features are represented before child web site Features and the hierarchy is traversed from the top down.

- *SPSite*: Find Features scoped to the web site within the site collection that conform to the specified filtering criteria. The returned collection is ordered with respect to web site hierarchy. Parent web site Features are represented before child web site Features, and the hierarchy is traversed from the top down.

Once SharePoint knows which features need an upgrade, it will then call the Upgrade method on the SPFeature object. Calling that tells the feature to run its upgrade process.

The upgrade process can be defined in custom code or as declarative code. The feature.xml now has a new section that can be used to tell SharePoint the specific upgrade actions that need to take place during the upgrade process. The custom upgrade code can be attached to the appropriate events in the feature receiver. I know I haven't yet talked about feature receivers. I will soon though, but for now it is enough to understand that feature receivers are classes that give you a hook into various events on a feature and allow you to write custom code. One such hook is the "FeatureUpgrading" event. This is called right before the upgrade on the feature occurs.

The declarative way of describing feature upgrade actions is the <UpgradeActions> section at the beginning or end of the feature.xml file.

It is also important to understand the sequence in which features are upgraded. The features are upgraded in a top-down model: farm first, web application, site collection, and then individual sites. Within an individual site collection, the sites at the top are upgraded first. Also, features are upgraded in order of activation dependencies. It is important to note that features are upgraded in an optimistic manner. If one upgrade breaks, the upgrade process will continue.

With this in mind, let's look at a simple basic feature upgrade scenario.

Here you will be adding a new list instance into your existing WebPart feature. Also, since you are adding a new SPI into the feature, you will upgrade the feature version from 0.0.0.0 to 1.0.0.0. This will then demonstrate that only the upgrade action, i.e., only the list instance creation, gets called.

Let's make that happen!

First, right-click your project and add a new SharePoint Item (SPI). Add a new list instance, base it on the "Custom List" template, and call it "ANewList". You can see the filled out details in Figure 3-13.

By default, the List Instance is added to your feature definition, which makes total sense. If someone deployed version 1.0.0.0 (and not version 0.0.0.0) to a SharePoint site collection, you'd want both the WebPart and the list instance to be deployed as a part of the same feature.

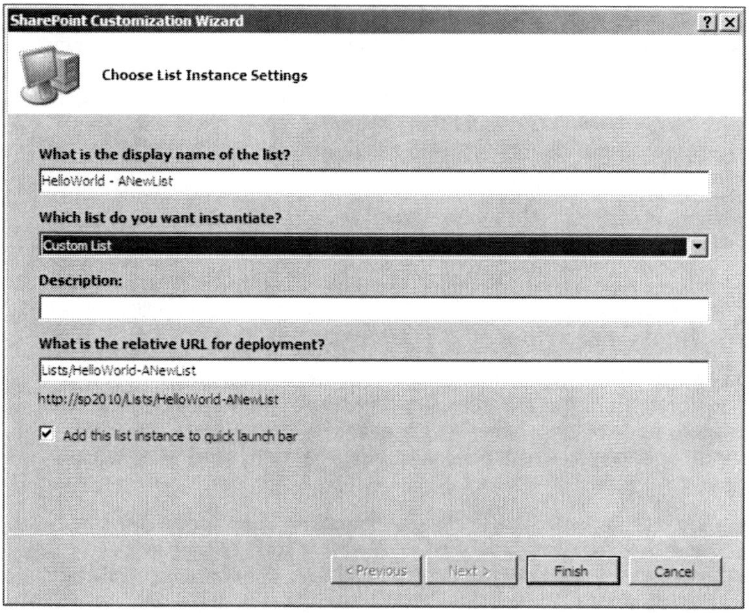

Figure 3-13. *Adding a list instance*

However, let's talk about the upgrade scenario. You already have feature version 0.0.0.0 activated on the site collection. However, let's tell SharePoint that when this feature upgrades from version 0.0.0.0 to 1.0.0.0, to go ahead and provision the list instance, but do not redeploy the WebPart.

In order to do so, double-click the Feature1.feature node to open the feature designer in Visual Studio. At the bottom, you should see two tabs, Design and Manifest. Click Manifest and you should see a non-editable area which shows you how feature.xml looks as of now. This can be seen in Figure 3-14.

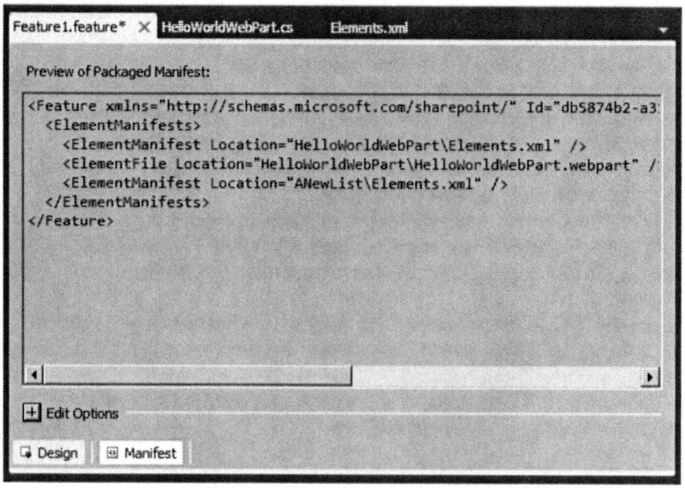

Figure 3-14. *The feature.xml, in a non-editable form*

This is non-editable, because Microsoft Visual studio wrote this for you and doesn't want you to mess with it. However, instead of editing it, you can add to it by clicking on the "Edit options" button at the bottom. Here you can add more stuff to the feature.xml file directly in that multiline textbox, or as I prefer to do it, click the Open in XML Editor link, so you can edit with Schema and intellisense enabled.

For the hawk-eyed amongst you, you might have noticed that the preceding steps to open in XML editor really opened the Feature1.Template.xml file from your project structure. You could have double-clicked that directly, but this scenic tour allowed me to show you a full feature.xml file, along with your changes included. Feel free to take that shortcut next time.

With the feature1.template.xml file open, go ahead edit it to look like Listing 3-3.

Listing 3-3. *Edited Feature1.template.xml with Custom Upgrade Actions*

```
<?xml version="1.0" encoding="utf-8" ?>
<Feature xmlns="http://schemas.microsoft.com/sharepoint/">
  <UpgradeActions>
    <VersionRange BeginVersion="0.0.0.0" EndVersion="1.0.0.0">
      <ApplyElementManifests>
        <ElementManifest Location="ANewList\Elements.xml" />
      </ApplyElementManifests>
    </VersionRange>
  </UpgradeActions>
</Feature>
```

Save the code and revert back to the feature designer. What do you see? The feature.xml has now included your changes in an additive manner.

You need to do one more thing. Double-click the Feature1.Feature node and in its properties in Visual Studio give it a version # of 1.0.0.0. Also, verify that the Feature.xml, i.e., the manifest of your feature, shows a Version of 1.0.0.0 under the feature element in the version attribute.

Good job! Your code changes are done. Now go ahead and build it, and then right-click package your solution (Not DEPLOY!). This will create a .wsp for you. Next, go to your bin/debug folder and rename the HelloWorld.wsp to HelloWorld_1_0_0_0.wsp to reflect the new version number. I didn't want you to do a deploy directly through Visual Studio to demonstrate the upgrade process. If you upload a new solution in a site collection with a solution ID the same as an existing solution, SharePoint interprets that as an upgrade scenario and will prompt you to upgrade your code.

Next, go to your site collection through the browser and click Site Actions ➤ Site Settings, and then click the Solutions Gallery. Go ahead and upload the HelloWorld_1_0_0_0.wsp into your solution gallery.

As soon as the file is uploaded, you will see a dialog box, as shown in Figure 3-15 (with a different solution ID of course).

Brilliant! SharePoint detected that an existing feature needs an upgrade, so hit the "Upgrade" button. After upgrading, you will see:

- The previous version is now deactivated.

- The new version is activated.

- The new HelloWorld-ANewList list is created for you.

- The .WebPart file has been left untouched.

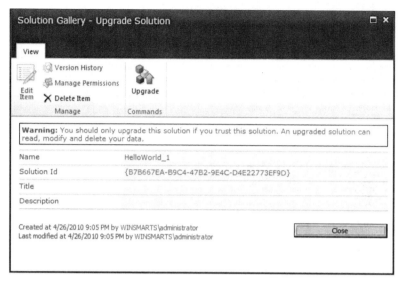

Figure 3-15. *SharePoint prompting you to upgrade a solution*

Interestingly, you can pick any solution file with a matching solution ID in the solution gallery and hit the upgrade button. What happens behind the scenes is that the framework will call QueryFeatures and then find all features that need upgrades. Next it will call the Upgrade method on each of those features. After repeatedly trying to upgrade simply upgrades to the latest possible version, it then stops upgrading (because subsequent calls to QueryFeatures will return no new features to be upgraded). However, this behavior is slightly broken in sandbox solutions, or let's be politically correct, and say that the behavior in sandbox solutions is slightly different than farm solutions. In Sandbox solutions, the upgrade detection works on SolutionID. However, solution's manifest.xml doesn't have any version attribute on it, so the onus of clicking "Upgrade" on the right version is on the end user. Also, the user has to go through the process of renaming the .wsp packages with the right version numbers as I demonstrated to keep things well organized. In contrast, farm solutions do work well based on feature.xml version numbers.

You just saw an example of doing a simple upgrade on a feature using the ApplyElementManifests element. There are a few other options available to you.

- *AddContentTypeField*: This allows you to add a new field to an existing content type. What is really neat about this upgrade is that it has an attribute called "PushDown". Specifiying PushDown = true pushes down the changes to child content types and lists that content type. This used to be a major sore spot in SharePoint 2007.

- *MapFile*: If there is a file that was deployed to a content database, but has not yet been customized via SharePoint designer or any other means, this element will let you rename such files in a feature. In addition to just renaming, you can also move files relative to the Features directory.

- *CustomUpgradeAction*: All the preceding upgrade mechanisms are great, but you know you will need to write code at some point. CustomUpgradeAction allows you to execute custom code when a Feature instance is being upgraded. When an action is specified in an upgrade action sequence, SharePoint 2010 calls the SPFeatureReceiver.FeatureUpgrading method synchronously with other upgrade actions in order of declaration.

This brings us to the rather interesting topic of Feature Receivers.

Feature Receivers

As I mentioned earlier, a Feature Receiver is a class you can add to your feature definition that give you hooks into various methods which execute during different times of the lifetime of the feature. This class inherits from the SPFeatureReceiver base class. One of those events is the FeatureUpgrading event.

In order to add a feature receiver, right-click your feature and choose "Add Event Receiver". You will note that you are provided five possible event handlers that you can hook into to execute your custom code. Starting SharePoint 2010, you override only the methods the events for which you wish to tap into. These methods are the following:

- *FeatureActivated and FeatureDeactivating*: Both are respectively called after the feature is activated and before the feature has been deactivated.

- *FeatureInstalled and FeatureUninstalling*: Called after the feature has been installed and before the feature is being uninstalled.

- *FeatureUpgrading*: Called right before the upgrade on the feature has taken place.

Next, update the version number of the feature to 2.0.0.0 and add a feature receiver. The feature receiver will do the following two things:

- Implement a FeatureActivated event to change the title of the site.

- Implement a FeatureUpgrading event to add a new list item into the list created by version 1.0.0.0 or earlier.

My FeatureActivated and FeatureUpgrading event handlers look similar to what is shown in Listing 3-4.

Listing 3-4. *FeatureActivated and FeatureUpgrading Events*

```
public override void FeatureActivated(SPFeatureReceiverProperties properties)
{
    properties.UserCodeSite.RootWeb.Title = "Changed Title!";
    properties.UserCodeSite.RootWeb.Update();
}

public override void FeatureUpgrading(SPFeatureReceiverProperties properties,
    string upgradeActionName,
    System.Collections.Generic.IDictionary<string, string> parameters)
{
    SPSite site = properties.UserCodeSite;
    if (site != null)
```

```
        {
            SPList customList = site.RootWeb.Lists["HelloWorld - ANewList"];
            SPListItem item = customList.Items.Add();
            item["Title"] = parameters["Title"];
            item.Update();
            customList.Update();
        }
    }
}
```

Finally, edit your Feature1.Template.Xml to what is shown in Listing 3-5.

Listing 3-5. *Feature1.Template.Xml with CustomUpgradeAction Included*

```xml
<?xml version="1.0" encoding="utf-8" ?>
<Feature xmlns="http://schemas.microsoft.com/sharepoint/">
  <UpgradeActions
         ReceiverAssembly="..removed for brevity.."
         ReceiverClass="..removed for brevity..">
    <VersionRange BeginVersion="0.0.0.0" EndVersion="1.0.0.0">
      <ApplyElementManifests>
        <ElementManifest Location="ANewList\Elements.xml" />
      </ApplyElementManifests>
    </VersionRange>
    <VersionRange BeginVersion="1.0.0.0" EndVersion="2.0.0.0">
      <CustomUpgradeAction Name="Version1To2">
        <Parameters>
          <Parameter Name="Title">From the Upgrade Process</Parameter>
        </Parameters>
      </CustomUpgradeAction>
    </VersionRange>
  </UpgradeActions>
</Feature>
```

As before, package the feature, but don't deploy it. Since you are working with a sandbox solution, you will have to rename the .wsp and upload and upgrade manually. Hitting F5 to deploy it will also work, but you'll miss out on two things:

- The fun of deploying it yourself and also the ability to break up the various parts of the execution/action and examine them as you upgrade and deploy.

- Understanding the end user experience, because they won't deploy using F5 and Visual Studio. As mentioned, you're working with sandbox solutions, so you have to take the end user route of rename/upload/upgrade to truly test this.

With either version 0.0.0.0 or version 1.0.0.0 deployed and activated, visit the site collection solution gallery again and upload your new .wsp, which contains Version 2.0. Note that you will have to choose a different name for the new .wsp, because you don't want to overwrite the existing activated solution.

Now, as soon as you upload the new .wsp, you are prompted to Upgrade, as shown in Figure 3-16.

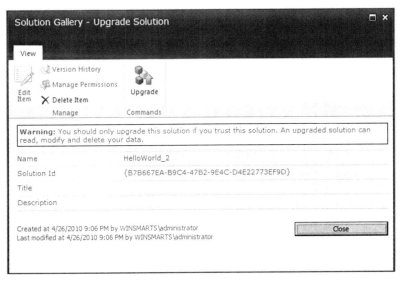

Figure 3-16. *Being prompted to upgrade to version 2*

Don't hit upgrade just yet! Well, if you hit upgrade now, the code will still work, but I want to take this golden opportunity to show you how to debug user solutions and upgrade features.

The problem is, simply hitting F5 through Visual Studio in its default deployment configurations will retract and delete the older solution, and then add and deploy the newer solution. Therefore, you aren't really doing an upgrade, you're doing a redeploy!

In an upgrade process, you would upgrade existing instances of the solution/feature without having to deactivate the features or delete the older solution itself. This is typical real-world flow that was so difficult to implement in SharePoint 2007.

In order to debug the upgrade process of a sandbox solution, also known as user code, you need to attach your visual studio to the SPUCWorkerProcess.exe process. This is the process that actually runs your user code/sandbox solution code. I will talk more about user code and sandboxed solutions later in this chapter. If you were upgrading a farm solution, you would instead attach to the relevant w3wp.exe process.

Now, set a breakpoint in both FeatureActivated and FeatureUpgrading methods and hit the upgrade button. What do you see?

You see that the FeatureUpgrading method is called, and it successfully picks the values from the feature.xml values you had specified. This is great because now you have a place where you can execute code as the feature is transitioning from one version to another. However, you will also see that the FeatureActivated method doesn't get called. This is to be expected because you are only upgrading the feature from version 1 to version 2. The feature is already activated. You aren't deactivating and then reactivating the feature, as you had to do in SharePoint 2007. If you did deactivate and reactivate then perhaps the FeatureActivated event handler should get called.

With the debugger still attached, deactivate your version 2.0 feature and then reactivate it. What do you see this time? You see that the FeatureActivated event gets called and the FeatureUpgrading event does not get called. This is truly a wonderful way for you to write much more maintainable code. You can now deploy newer versions of your code, and at every such version (or for multiple versions) have as many upgrade code blocks.

When your code goes from version 1 to version 2 the upgrade mechanism kicks in. However, when the code goes directly from version 0 to version 2, then the Activated mechanism kicks in. Think of this in terms of disaster recovery. You now no longer have to maintain separate versions of your code base: one for upgrades and one for disasters. For the SharePoint 2007 brethren, please ask yourself did you really maintain two version paths? I'm guessing most of you didn't. Where would you look if your server blew up on Version 99 one day? Personally speaking, I'd look at monster.com for a new job.

Writing Sandboxed Solutions

All this time you've been writing, debugging, maintaining, and version controlling a sandboxed solution, but I haven't yet gotten a good chance to explain what a sandboxed solution really is. This is the problem with any new and interesting topic to learn: It looks like a big hamburger. You know it's tasty, but no matter where and how you start, you will find yourself scraping cheese off the paper with a fork at the end. It's time to scrape some of that yummy half-burned cheese.

Let me begin by saying this, sandboxed solutions are awesome!

The Basics

A sandboxed solution is a new concept introduced in SharePoint 2010. As mentioned earlier, a solution is how you deploy new custom code to your SharePoint server. Custom code is that essential evil that is impossible to deliver real-world projects without, but also cause the most headaches and effort.

A sandboxed solution is custom code that runs in a safe sandbox. It runs under some standard nonnegotiable restrictions, so it can only do certain things and is prevented from doing certain other things. Mostly, those other things that it's prevented from doing are the ones that cause the most headaches.

In addition to being restricted, a sandboxed solution can be monitored by two levels of administrators. The site collection administrator can monitor them through Site Actions ➤ Site Settings ➤ Solution Gallery and the farm administrator can monitor them through central administration on a per site collection basis.

In addition, the farm administrator to monitoring these sandboxed solutions can also set limits on the resource allocation to sandboxed solutions on a per site collection basis using the standard quota mechanism. There are fourteen different metrics that contribute to such resource allocation, and it is done using a points-based system. The farm administrator allocates a certain number of points to a site collection. If any sandboxed solution causes the number of points to jump over the total allocated points, all sandboxed solutions in that site collection are halted until a timer job that runs every 24 hours resets the site collection. Also, while you are under the allocated number of points, try doing something naughty like format my c: drive. You will see that the execution is blocked, a certain number of configurable points are charged, and the solution can attempt to do something naughty again (only to be blocked again and charged more points). On each of these metrics, you have the ability to set an absolute limit of resource points before the execution is halted, or an incremental number of points that are charged, without blocking resource allocation. This is useful since sometimes you want to halt execution and increment resource usage points. Sometimes you just want to count resource usage points, but not yet halt.

I like to think this level of monitoring very much like a family cell phone plan. Dad, mom, sister, and son have a pool of 2000 minutes to share. If the son somehow starts calling his Russian internet girlfriend a little too much and goes over the minute quota, everyone's cell phones quit working. Now dad has to call the phone company and request the entire family plan to be allowed to run, and the offending solution (the son's cell phone) can now be blocked execution. Similarly, the farm administrator also has a concept called "Blocking sandboxed solutions". Certain sandboxed solutions that are known to be troublesome can be blocked by the farm administrator.

Finally, if you have code that is more restricted, better monitored, and less damaging to your server environment in general, you can be more confident when you deploy it. Therefore, the biggest advantage of sandboxed solutions is that they can be deployed by the site collection administrator of a site collection. They are deployed directly into the solution gallery in a site collection, as you have been doing throughout this chapter. Also, if a sandboxed solution does not deploy any assemblies, it can even be deployed by individuals with full control to a site collection. This greatly alleviates the headache of the farm administrator.

A brief overview of sandboxed solutions: They are restrictive and thus secure, better monitored, better administered, and easier to deploy. Before diving into the individual details of a sandboxed solution, let's meet the elder brother of sandboxed solutions first, which is writing a farm solution.

Writing a Farm Solution

To understand a sandboxed solution, it is important to understand farm solutions—its elder, more capable, yet more issue-bound brother. Put simply, farm solutions came first. They were what solutions used to be in SharePoint 2007. These were .wsp files, which were .cab files renamed to .wsp that had unfettered access to your server farm. When deployed, they could run any kind of code and they could make any kinds of changes to the servers themselves. You had to restrict them using CAS policies on their DLLs, something many never cared to do. This caused support issues, and the infrastructure ogres to get mad and break servers, rip cables and hair, tear their clothes, and howl at late hours in the office when everyone had left work and they were still stuck there!

Now you can see why sandboxed solutions were necessary. I must say, however, that even in SharePoint 2010, you cannot treat farm solutions as an obsolete/deprecated mechanism of delivering functionality. Sometimes you have no choice but to deliver a farm solution. In fact, in most projects, I try and segregate my functionality into as few as possible farm solutions that provide my sandboxed solutions with trusted elder brothers (farm solutions) on the server side with a secure way of restricted functionality via a proxy or other such means. This way, at the beginning of a project, I can approach the Infrastructure Ogre in my organization to deploy a farm solution with a higher level of confidence, because he knows it is necessary but there aren't many more farm solutions coming.

Once you have a farm solution deployed that sandboxed solutions can talk with, the rest of my functionality is delivered mostly as sandboxed solutions.

Let's write one such functionality.

You can write many different kinds of farm solutions. One of the things sandboxed solutions cannot do is make changes to the file system during deployment. Therefore, you are going to write a simple solution that deploys an Image to the _layouts/images folder in the SharePoint root. You will try and deploy and activate it as a sandboxed solution, which will fail as you will see shortly. After, you will change it to a farm solution, which will allow it to succeed. Here you go!

1. Start with a clean and fresh site collection and http://sp2010. Create a sandbox solution project. For this example, use "FarmSolution". Perhaps that's confusing because you are naming a sandbox solution as a farm solution, but you will change it to a farm solution shortly.

2. Add a very simple WebPart to it that writes out "Hello World".

3. Right-click the project and add a SharePoint mapped folder. Choose to add the Images Folder, as shown in Figure 3-17.

4. The idea now is that anything you put in the images folder will get deployed in the [SharePoint Root]_layouts\images folder. Also, you will see that SharePoint tools for Visual Studio automatically creates a folder called "FarmSolution" under the Images directory to keep your images from interfering with other images. Go ahead and drop a sample image in the FarmSolution directory. This example drops in the logo for this company, so the filename is wslogo.gif.

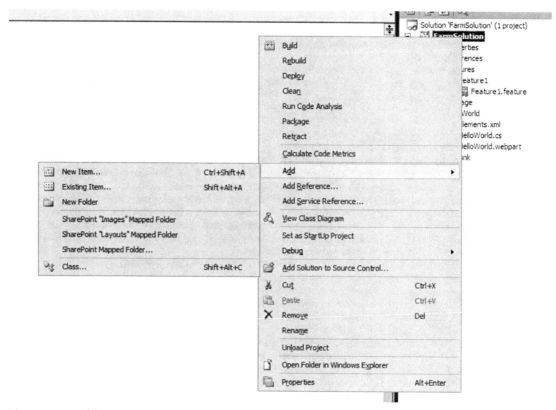

Figure 3-17. *Adding a mapped folder in your solution*

5. To make the example a bit more interesting, the Feature1 feature, let's give feature a thumbnail image. Go to the properties of the feature, and change its "Image URL" property to /farmsolution/wslogo.gif (or whatever image you uploaded in step 4).

6. Right-click and deploy the solution. Remember you're still trying to deploy this as a sandbox solution. You will see that the deployment will fail and you should see messages such as "The deployment type "TemplateFile" of file "wslogo.gif" in Project Item "Images" is not compatible with a Package in a Sandboxed Solution." and "The Project Item "Images" cannot be deployed through a Package in a Sandboxed Solution."

That proves my point! You were not able to deploy an image as a part of a sandbox solution. In fact, anything that deploys to the file system will not work as a sandbox solution.

7. Now let's change it over to a farm solution. This is rather easy to do. Click the solution, and in the properties window, change SandBox value from true to false, as shown in Figure 3-18.

Figure 3-18. *Changing the SandBox Solution property from True to False*

Note that by changing this value from False to True, the assemblyinfo.cs edits itself and removes the AllowPartiallyTrustedCallers attribute.

8. If you hit F5 and start to debug, Visual Studio will package and deploy the WSP as a farm solution. But, we're developers. Forget Visual Studio, let's see what's happening behind the scenes. Simply right-click the project and choose Package instead of Deploy.

9. Open a command line window in Administrator mode (right-click command prompt and choose Run as Administrator). Change directory to where your farmsolution.wsp file is. Issue the following command on command line:
   ```
   stsadm -o addsolution -filename farmsolution.wsp
   ```

10. After command line says Operation Completed successfully, open the browser, and visit central administration and then the system settings section. Under System Settings, look for Manage Farm Solutions. You will see that farmsolution.wsp has been added to the farm.

11. You can deploy the solution to the various web applications from the browser or you can issue the following stsadm command:
    ```
    stsadm -o deploysolution -name farmsolution.wsp -allowGacDeployment -immediate
    -url http://sp2010
    ```

12. If you're doing everything properly, you should see a message on command line saying "Timer job successfully created". Here SharePoint queued the deployment job and is now waiting for the job to be picked up by the SharePoint timer service.

13. After a little bit, the solution will get deployed. Here comes the interesting part: verify that now you have a folder at [SharePoint Root]\14\Template\Features\FarmSolution_Feature1. A sandbox solution would not have created such a folder. Then, verify you have a folder at [SharePoint Root]\Images\FarmSolution. A sandbox solution cannot create such a folder.

14. Next, visit the site collection at http://sp2010 then visit site settings, and look for a link called Site collection features under the Site Collection Administration section. You should see the feature you just wrote with a neat little logo, as shown in Figure 3-19.

Figure 3-19. *Farm Solution with a custom logo*

15. You can activate the feature and use it just like a sandbox solution feature would let you. However, the big difference here is that a farm solution places no restrictions on you whatsoever. While they are powerful, and even essential, they should be used sparingly. You know, with great power comes great headache and current squared resistance. Be careful!

Now that you've written a farm solution, let's go back to sandbox solutions. I described in brief what sandbox solutions are, and why they are cool. To name a few more positive aspects:

- They are restricted to what they can do.

- They are much more manageable.

- They are much more monitorable.

- They are easier to deploy.

- They are possible to validate.

- They can be extended using full trust proxies.

Let's dive into each one of these topics one by one!

Sandbox Solution Restrictions

It is clear that sandbox solutions run under certain restrictions. You saw one of those restrictions, i.e., not being able to make changes to the file system, even during deployment. However, it is important to understand the architecture of how sandbox solutions work before I can talk about the specific restrictions.

The word "sandbox" in computers is generally used to refer to a safe area where you can play, without damaging the outside hosting environment. The sandbox in SharePoint is implemented as a separate process where your sandbox solution code will run. In fact, there are three processes.

Sandboxed Code Service

SPUCHostService.exe, also known as the Sandboxed Code Service, runs on each server on the farm that you are going to allow to work in the sandbox. Therefore, the infrastructure ogres can choose to run this service on all or only a certain subset of the servers in the farm. This is an important consideration, because this constitutes an important part around the administration of sandbox solution infrastructure, namely the load balancing aspects. There are two approaches to load balancing sandbox solutions on your SharePoint Farm.

You could turn on the Sandboxed Code Service on every front end in the farm. In that scenario, the solution would run on the web front end on which the request was made. The code is executed on the WFE. This is very low administration overhead, but has lower scalability.

Alternatively, you can choose to spin up the sandboxed code service on only certain web front ends and use only certain web front ends to run sandbox solutions. This allows you to offload the execution load on different servers.

In order to choose one or the other mechanism, the infrastructure administrator needs to perform two steps in central administration.

1. Start the sandboxed code service on the relevant web front ends. This can be done by accessing Central Administration\System Settings\Manage Services on Server. The Microsoft SharePoint Foundation Sandboxed Code service can be seen started in Figure 3-20. If you built your development machine based on the steps identified in Chapter 1, this service should already be running on your machine.

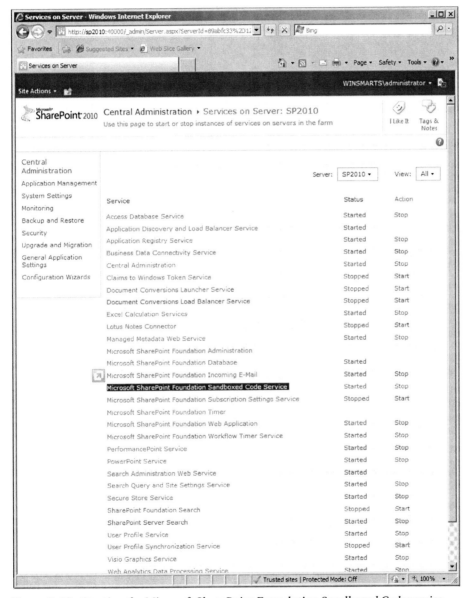

Figure 3-20. *Starting the Microsoft SharePoint Foundation Sandboxed Code service*

2. Go to Central Administration\System Settings\Manage User Solutions and specify the desired load balancing behavior, as indicated in Figure 3-21.

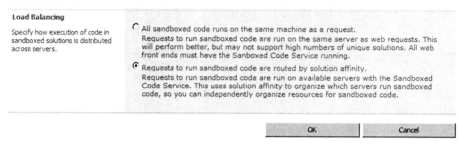

Figure 3-21. *Sandbox solutions load balancing behavior*

The Sandbox Worker Process

The sandbox worker process is where your actual code runs. This is in contrast to having the code run inside of w3wp.exe. This is why you don't have to restart the application pool every time your redeploy a sandbox solution. If you wish to debug a sandbox solution, and for any reason F5 debugging is not working, you will need to attach your visual studio debugger to the SPUCWorkerprocess.exe process. It is important to note, however, that the sandbox solution management infrastructure of SharePoint 2010 can choose to destroy the SPUCWorkerProcess.exe anytime your code tries doing something naughty, such as an infinite resource crunching loop. During debugging, don't be too surprised if SharePoint kills your process without asking first.

Sandbox Worker Process Proxy

Finally, there is the sandbox worker process proxy, or the SPUCWorkerProcessProxy.exe, which is built on the new services infrastructure in SharePoint.

Inside the SPUCWorkerProcess.exe sandbox, you have the ability to run only a subset of the Microsoft.SharePoint namespace. What does that subset include? In sandbox solutions, you are free to use the following:

- Microsoft.SharePoint: *Except* SPSite constructor, SPSecurity, SPWorkItem and SPWorkItemCollection, SPAlertCollection.Add, SPAlertTemplateCollection.Add, SPUserSolution and SPUserSolutionCollection, and SPTransformUtilities

- Microsoft.SharePoint.Navigation

- Microsoft.SharePoint.Utilities: *Except* SPUtility.SendEmail and SPUtility.GetNTFullNameandEmailFromLogin

- Microsoft.SharePoint.Workflow

- Microsoft.SharePoint.WebPartPages: *Except* SPWebPartManager, SPWebPartConnection, WebPartZone, WebPartPage, ToolPane, and ToolPart

As long as you can fit your solution within the previous constraints, you can deliver very compelling functionality. It is important to note, however, that when you create a new Visual Studio SharePoint project, and choose to make the solution a sandbox solution, Visual Studio will trim its intellisense to reflect the restricted API. However, if you choose to hand type in one of the preceding restricted APIs and compile and deploy your project, it will still compile and deploy. It just won't execute. This is because your sandbox solution code is validated against the restricted API as indicated, but it is compiled against the full API.

Here is a little trick: If you want to make sure that you aren't using any of the restricted APIs *before* you deploy your solution, manually reference your project against [SharePoint Root]\UserCode\assemblies\Microsoft.SharePoint.dll. If your code compiles, then you're pretty safe. Of course, never deploy code with the user code Microsoft.SharePoint dll references, instead reference the Microsoft.SharePoint.dll in the [SharePoint Root]\ISAPI folder.

While you are in the [SharePoint Root]\UserCode folder, you will also note a web.config there. If you open that web.config, you will see a trust level entry as shown in the following:

```
<trustLevel name="WSS_Sandbox" policyFile="..\config\wss_usercode.config" />
```

As you can see, the sandboxed solutions are also restricted by an out of the box CAS policy. Therefore, the sandbox is non-negotiable. You shouldn't edit this file to define the boundaries of your own sandbox, you should stick with the boundaries that Microsoft defined for you. Specifically, the CAS policy for sandbox solutions grants you the following policy permissions:

- SharePointPermission.ObjectModel
- SecurityPermission.Execution
- AspNetHostingPermission.Level = Minimal

There are two other important points to note in this out of the box CAS Policy:

- While your code is restricted to the CAS policy permissions previously defined, it allows the SharePoint framework code full trust.

- If your custom code needs to break out of this sandbox's boundaries, you can always write a full trust proxy, as I will describe shortly.

Sandbox Solution Monitoring, Management, and Deployment

Sandbox solutions are inherently secure because they are restricted on what they can and cannot do. This means you can be confident that they won't format your c:\ drive, and that's a good thing. But, what if someone put the following code block in their sandbox solution?

```
while (true) { i++;}
```

The previous will chew up CPU resources of your high end server processors. However, it's not a security violation is it? Neither is it part of the restricted API.

Therefore, it is important that sandbox solutions also be monitored. Monitored and punished if they do something naughty.

Monitoring goes a step beyond punishment. A good traffic system is not what is designed around ambulances but around each intersection. A good traffic system is designed around placing good traffic lights so those ambulances are not necessary.

Therefore, step number one around monitoring is allowing the site collection administrator, or the application owners, to get some visibility into how good or bad their sandbox solutions are behaving. If you visit the solution gallery in your site collection, at the top of your solution gallery, you will see how much resource quota has been allocated to you, how much of it you have been using lately, and how much of it you have used today. This can be seen in Figure 3-22.

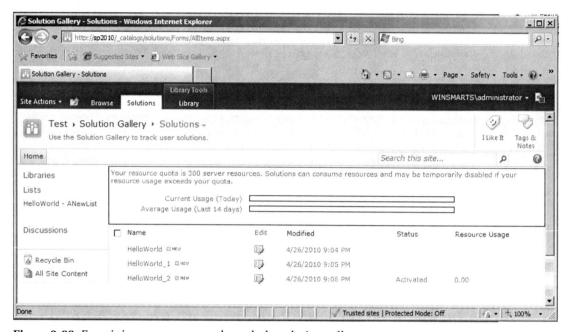

Figure 3-22. *Examining resource usage through the solution gallery*

This is great, but if you are a site collection owner, there are some obvious questions.

- Who decided that my site collection should get 300 server resources or resource points?

- Is 300 points a lot? What does it mean? What constitutes a resource point? Can you ask for more points?

- Perhaps you see that the solutions will be temporarily disabled if you exceed the allocated quota. Will you get a warning if you exceed a certain amount of resource usage, so you can plan before you are completely shut down?

- What exactly does temporary disabled mean? How long is temporary?

The answers to all the previous questions are quite simple. The farm administrator decided that your site collection should have 300 resource points. If you go to central administration and visit Application Management\Configure quotas and locks, you will see there is a section called User Solutions Resource Quota. This can be seen Figure 3-23.

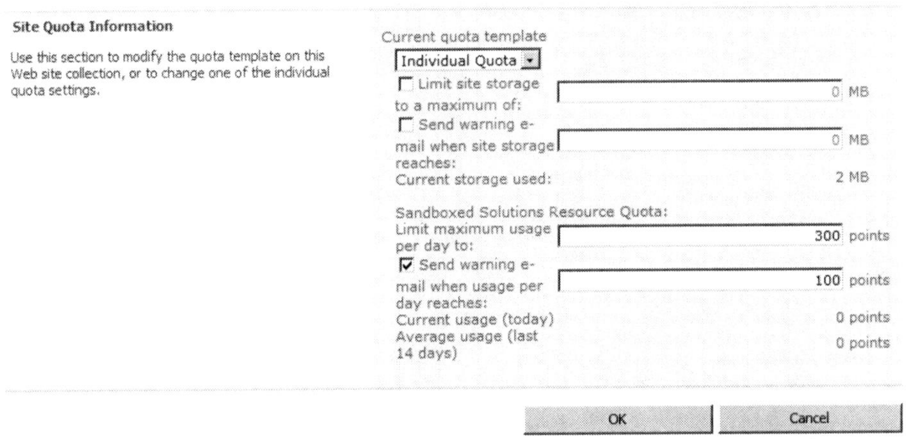

Figure 3-23. *Specifying sandbox solution limits in the Site Quota Information*

That also answers the second question about sending a warning e-mail when you use a certain number of points in a day. Also, this indirectly answers the fourth question about, "How long is temporary?" Temporary is approximately a day.

Essentially, your entire site collection has been allocated a certain number of points to be shared across all sandbox solutions. If one of those solutions ends up using all of those points, all of those sandbox solutions are shut down for about a day.

What exactly does using 300 points mean? How did someone come up with this number of 300?

Earlier, I was talking about the various restrictions placed on your sandbox solutions, namely CAS policies and a restricted subset of the API. Also, I referred to the fact that excessive CPU usage is perhaps a metric that you should monitor. All these metrics that should be monitored are given some weight, and they collectively contribute to the 300 resource point limit.

Specifically, there are 14 metrics that are monitored by SharePoint. To view the metrics, open powershell and execute the following command:

```
[Microsoft.SharePoint.Administration.SPUserCodeService]::Local.ResourceMeasures
```

■**Tip** If your SharePoint powershell commands are not running, you may need to load the SharePoint powershell snap in first. You can do so by executing this command on powershell:

```
Add-PSSnapin Microsoft.SharePoint.Powershell
```

You will see all the various resource monitoring metrics print out. Also, there is an interesting property on each one of them, namely ResourcesPerPoint. Specifically, the metrics (also known as ResourceMeasure) and ResourcesPerPoint you will see are as follows:

- `AbnormalProcessTerminationCount: 1`
- `CPUExecutionTime: 3600`
- `CriticalExceptionCount: 3600`
- `InvocationCount: 100`
- `PercentProcessorTime: 85`
- `ProcessCPUCycles: 100000000000`
- `ProcessHandleCount:10000`
- `ProcessIOBytes: 10000000`
- `ProcessThreadCount: 10000`
- `ProcessVirtualBytes: 100000000`
- `SharePointDatabaseQueryCount: 20`
- `SharePointDatabaseQueryTime: 120`
- `UnhandledExceptionCount: 50`
- `UnresponsiveprocessCount: 2`

In other words, if you have a single AbnormalProcessTermination, you consume one resource point and so on. These resource points are customizable using the SharePoint object model. My suggestion would be to try out what you have out of the box, and then see if you need further tweaking.

The ResourcesPerPoint contributes to the additive resource points calculation. However, if there was a solution that did something really naughty, like tried to format your C:\, should you wait to keep letting it try until it hits an additive count? Obviously not! You need to have the capability of shutting a bad solution immediately. There is another property on the ResourceMeasure called AbsoluteLimit. The solution is terminated immediately, even if the daily usage limit hasn't been reached yet. As an example, AbnormalProcessTerminationCount's AbsoluteLimit is set to 1. So, a solution that causes an AbnormalProcessTermination is immediately shut down. The additive count is bumped up, so the solution can try again, but it will be immediately shut down again. If the solution keeps causing problems, chances are the farm administrator will notice it.

If there is such an awful solution that causes nothing but headaches, the farm administrator can go into Central Administration\System Settings\Manage User Solutions and add a solution to the Blocked Solutions list. This can be seen in Figure 3-24.

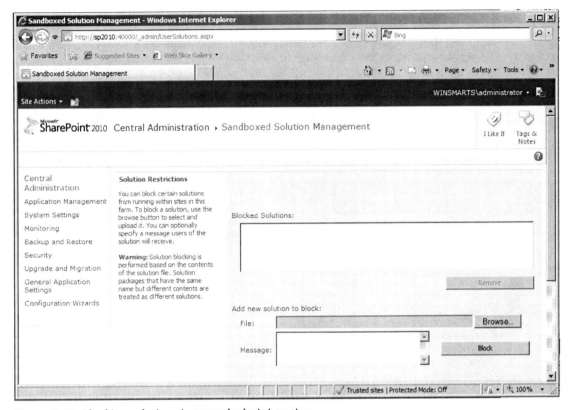

Figure 3-24. Blocking solutions in central administration

Now the infrastructure ogre farm administrator can force the developer to fix the code before it will run again. How nice!

All of this seems a bit after the fact, but the approach here seems to make sure you have enough ambulances, once an accident occurs. If a solution has gone awry, you can throttle it. But, can you do anything when the solution is uploaded into the site collection? Perhaps validate it?

Sandbox Solution Validations

Farm administrators can be proactive in deploying solution validators to their farm. These validators are run when a solution is uploaded to a solution gallery. If a solution fails validation, the user is shown a suitable message and their solution cannot be activated.

If a validator is added after solutions have been activated, the validator will be called the next time the solution is executed. If a validator is updated, the solutions are validated again the next time they are executed.

Writing a solution validator is as simple as inheriting from the SPSolutionValidator class.

Once such a class is written, you need to add the solution validator to the SPUserCodeService SolutionValidators collection. This requires writing a Farm level feature or a powershell script.

You can also iterate through existing validators in the farm by executing the following powershell command:

```
[Microsoft.SharePoint.Administration.SPUserCodeService]::Local.solutionvalidators
```

Let's look at a simple solution validator. I am going to keep this simple. This solution validator will invalidate every uploaded solution. You can write real validation logic at the indicated portions in the provided code.

Start by creating a farm solution called SolutionValidator and add a class to it called WinsmartsSolutionValidator. Add a new class and put the code, as shown in Listing 3-6.

Listing 3-6. *Code for WinsmartsSolutionValidator*

```
[Guid("3014EB40-A067-4A21-BB83-B787229A7FC1")]
class WinsmartsSolutionValidator : SPSolutionValidator
{
    private const string validatorName = "Winsmarts Solution Validator";

    public WinsmartsSolutionValidator() { }

    public WinsmartsSolutionValidator(SPUserCodeService userCodeService)
        : base(validatorName, userCodeService)
    {
        this.Signature = 1111;
    }

    public override void ValidateSolution(SPSolutionValidationProperties properties)
    {
        base.ValidateSolution(properties);

        // Write some validation logic here.
        properties.Valid = false;

        properties.ValidationErrorMessage = "The uploaded solution is invalid";
        properties.ValidationErrorUrl = "/_layouts/SolutionValidator/WinsmartsErrorPage.aspx";
    }

    public override void ValidateAssembly(SPSolutionValidationProperties properties,
SPSolutionFile assembly)
  {
    base.ValidateAssembly(properties, assembly);
    properties.Valid = true;
  }
}
```

As you can see, there is a public default constructor, which is necessary for serializing and deserializing the feature during deployment. Then there is a specific overload of the constructor in which you set the signature to a number. If you wish to update the validator, it is this signature that you'll need to change. There are two overrides, one to validate the solution and another to validate the assembly. Under ValidateSolution, you also have access to all the files inside the solution. The idea here is that you would write some validation logic on the solution. If you set properties.Valid = false, the solution won't get activated. Note that you are also setting a ValidationErrorUrl here. Go ahead and add a layouts page in your solution at the specified URL. You will need to add a mapped _layouts folder as described earlier in this chapter (see Figure 3-17). This page can be made as smart as you wish, but this simply shows a message saying "Your Solution Validation Failed". You can see the customizations in Listing 3-7.

Listing 3-7. *Application Page Used to Display the Validation Error*

```
<asp:Content ID="Main" ContentPlaceHolderID="PlaceHolderMain" runat="server">
Your solution failed validation.
</asp:Content>

<asp:Content ID="PageTitle" ContentPlaceHolderID="PlaceHolderPageTitle" runat="server">
Winsmarts Error Page
</asp:Content>
```

That's basically it! Now go ahead and add a feature scoped at site collection or higher, along with a feature event receiver. The code for the feature event receiver adds the solution validator in the FeatureActivated event and removes the solution validator in the FeatureDeactivating event. This is shown in Listing 3-8.

Listing 3-8. *Feature Event Receiver Used to Register and Unregister the Solution Validator*

```
public override void FeatureActivated(SPFeatureReceiverProperties properties)
{
    SPUserCodeService.Local.SolutionValidators.Add(
        new WinsmartsSolutionValidator(SPUserCodeService.Local));
}

public override void FeatureDeactivating(SPFeatureReceiverProperties properties)
{
    SPUserCodeService.Local.SolutionValidators.Remove(
        new Guid("3014EB40-A067-4A21-BB83-B787229A7FC1"));
}
```

The GUID you see in the FeatureDeactivating event is the same GUID you used to decorate your SPSolutionValidator class with.

Your project is done! The final project structure should look like the one shown in Figure 3-25.

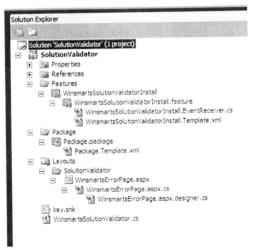

Figure 3-25. *Solution Validator, the final project structure*

At this point, press F5 to run and debug your farm solution. You may be prompted to edit your web.config to allow debugging, as shown in Figure 3-26.

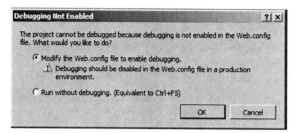

Figure 3-26. *Enable Debugging on your web site*

Next, go to your site collection and upload any sandbox solution .wsp. Since you are invalidating every single .wsp, you will be able to upload the solution. As you try and activate your solution, you will be greeted by the error dialog box shown in Figure 3-27. Note that this is the same application page you deployed along with your SolutionValidator solution.

Figure 3-27. *Your solution has failed validation. Hooray!*

This gives you all the necessary flexibility in tying down sandbox solutions. You can now be confident that sandbox solutions will work inside their respective boundaries. Boundaries? How do you deliver any functionality in these boundaries? What if sometimes you need to break these boundaries that your solution requires? You would do so by creating sandbox solution full trust proxies.

Sandbox Solution Full Trust Proxies

How can you expect to deliver a real solution by placing yourself under boundaries? The thing is, sandbox solutions are great, because they restrict the average Joe developer, and they allow the farm administrator to manage and monitor. Sometimes you need to negotiate the boundaries of what a sandbox solution can do. For example, let's say you are presented with a crazy requirement that through a sandbox solution you need to create a file on the disk of the web server. To make things even more interesting, the sandbox solution packages a WebPart, which presents the user with a simple textbox. The file contents will be whatever the user typed into that text box, through a web- based solution, in a sandboxed solution. Yes, it's a crazy requirement, but I am using this only as an extreme example to demonstrate my point.

■**Note** Even though for sake of completion I am describing sandbox solutions full trust proxies, the reality is this is not my personal preferred approach to break out of sandboxes. In Chapter 5, I describe how to write a WCF service, which for many reasons I feel is a much more elegant and maintainable way of delivering functionality consumable for sandbox solutions.

The solution to this problem is to write a full trust proxy.

The obvious question you may have here is, if you can get around the whole notion of sandbox solutions using full trust proxies then why even bother with sandbox solutions? What is that boundary good for, if it can be broken!?

The idea here is to break your architecture down into two major pieces:

- The first piece that you will deliver completely using sandbox solutions.

- The second piece is the API you will build using full trust proxies that the sandbox solutions can leverage.

The big idea here is that the architect creates an acceptable API that is available for all sandbox solutions to use. Therefore, as the architect, you still maintain significant control on what portions of the API are open for access. The process of opening this API using a full trust proxy is in fact rather simple to write. It basically involves five simple steps.

1. Decide on what operation you wish to perform in the full trust proxy and implement it as a class that inherits from Microsoft.SharePoint.Usercode.SPProxyOperation.

2. Choose what arguments need to be passed to the SPProxyOperation that you just created. This is a serializable class you implement that inherits from Microsoft.SharePoint.Usercode.SPProxyOperationArgs.

3. Compile the previous classes in a DLL, strong name the DLL, and then put it in the GAC.

4. The preceding steps would create a full trust proxy, which you will then need to register for use with SharePoint.

5. Finally, you consume the proxy in a sandbox solution using the SPUtility.ExecuteRegisteredProxyOperation method.

I told you it is rather simple. Basically, you create the operation, create the arguments, register the proxy with SharePoint, and use it merrily.

Let's solidify this understanding with real code. You are going to write a simple sandbox solution that displays the user a simple UI, as shown in Figure 3-28.

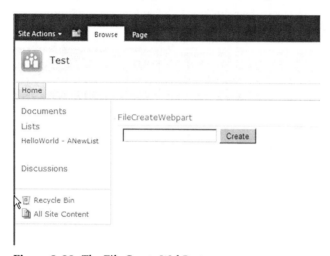

Figure 3-28. *The File Create WebPart*

The idea here is that the user will type in some text and hit the Create button. Whatever text was entered in the textbox, will be written to a file called C:\inetpub\wwwroot\wss\VirtualDirectories\80\SampleFile.txt.

1. Start by creating an empty SharePoint project. Create a folder within the SharePoint project and call the folder ProxyCode.

2. Inside ProxyCode, add a class called FileCreateOperation. The code for FileCreateOperation can be seen in **Listing 3-9.** Note to override the Execute Method. Execute returns an object. As long as the return type is serializable, you can return whatever you wish to the calling code (in this case a sandbox solution WebPart, which you will write shortly).

Listing 3-9. *FileCreateOperation with the Execute Method Overridden*

```
public class FileCreateOperation : SPProxyOperation
{
    public override object Execute(SPProxyOperationArgs args)
    {
        if (args != null)
        {
            FileArgs fileArgs = args as FileArgs;
            FileStream fStream =
                new FileStream(@"C:\inetpub\wwwroot\wss\VirtualDirectories\80\SampleFile.txt",
                    FileMode.CreateNew);
            fStream.Write(
                System.Text.ASCIIEncoding.ASCII.GetBytes(fileArgs.FileContents), 0,
                fileArgs.FileContents.Length);
            fStream.Flush();
            fStream.Close() ;
            return fileArgs.FileContents;
        }
        else return null;
    }
}
```

3. Similarly, add another class under ProxyCode called FileArgs. This will serve as the input arguments sent to the proxy. The code for FileArgs can be seen in Listing 3-10. As you can see, the FileArgs class is decorated with the Serializable attribute.

Listing 3-10. *FileArgs, the Input Arguments to the Proxy*

```
[Serializable]
public class FileArgs : SPProxyOperationArgs
{
    public string FileContents { get; set; }

    public FileArgs(string fileContents)
    {
        this.FileContents = fileContents;
    }
}
```

4. Usually, you would create the proxy as a separate DLL, but for this example keep things simple by adding a WebPart to the project. Therefore, add a new FileCreateWebPart to your project.

5. The code for the FileCreateWebPart can be seen in Listing 3-11. As is evident from the code, you are using the SPUtility.ExecuteRegisteredProxyOperation method to call code in the full trust proxy. Thus a registered proxy (which you will register next), is available for any sandbox to use. It is not split per site collection.

Listing 3-11. *The FileCreateWebPart*

```
public class FileCreateWebPart : WebPart
{
    private TextBox fileContents = new TextBox();
    private Button createFileButton = new Button() { Text="Create" };
    private Label results = new Label();

    public FileCreateWebPart()
    {

createFileButton.Click += (object sender, EventArgs e) =>
        {
            results.Text =
                SPUtility.ExecuteRegisteredProxyOperation(
                "SandBoxWebPartWithProxy, Version=1.0.0.0, Culture=neutral,
PublicKeyToken=64b818b3ff69ccfa",
                "SandBoxWebPartWithProxy.ProxyCode.FileCreateOperation",
                new ProxyCode.FileArgs(fileContents.Text)).ToString();
        };
    }

    protected override void CreateChildControls()
    {
        Table layoutTable = new Table();
        layoutTable.Rows.Add(new TableRow());
        layoutTable.Rows[0].Cells.Add(new TableCell());
        layoutTable.Rows[0].Cells.Add(new TableCell());
        layoutTable.Rows.Add(new TableRow());
        layoutTable.Rows[1].Cells.Add(new TableCell() { ColumnSpan = 2 });

        layoutTable.Rows[0].Cells[0].Controls.Add(fileContents);
        layoutTable.Rows[0].Cells[1].Controls.Add(createFileButton);
        layoutTable.Rows[1].Cells[0].Controls.Add(results);

        this.Controls.Add(layoutTable);

        base.CreateChildControls();
    }

    protected override void RenderContents(HtmlTextWriter writer)
    {
        base.RenderContents(writer);
    }
}
```

6. Finally, build this project, put the DLL in GAC, and use the simplistic powershell script show in Listing 3-12 to register your newly created full trust proxy with SharePoint.

Listing 3-12. *Registering the Full Trust Proxy with SharePoint*

```
Param($assemblyName, $typeName)
$userCodeService = [Microsoft.SharePoint.Administration.SPUserCodeService]::Local
$proxyOperationType = new-object -typename Microsoft.SharePoint.UserCode.SPProxyOperationType
-argumentlist $assemblyName, $typeName
$userCodeService.ProxyOperationTypes.Add($proxyOperationType)
$userCodeService.Update()
```

7. Go ahead and run the previous powershell script using a command as shown in the following:

```
.\RegisterProxy.ps1 -assemblyName "SandBoxWebPartWithProxy, Version=1.0.0.0,
Culture=neutral, PublicKeyToken=64b818b3ff69ccfa" -typeName
"SandBoxWebPartWithProxy.ProxyCode.FileCreateOperation"
```

Keep in mind your proxy runs in the SPUserCodeService.exe, so every time you make changes to your project and redeploy the DLL to GAC, you will need to restart the SPUserCodeV4 service. You can stop the service by using net stop SPUserCodeV4 and start it again by using net start SPUserCodeV4.

Note In the previous example and various other places in SharePoint, you will need to point it to the correct assembly with the correct PublicKeyToken per your development environment. Please see http:// blah.winsmarts.com/2009-12-SharePoint_Productivity_Tip_of_the_day.aspx for an easy way to generate assembly signatures of your visual studio projects

---

With your WebPart compiled and deployed, add it to a WebPart zone. Type in some text, and click the Create button. You should see a sample file get created at the path you specified. If you need help debugging, remember that the WebPart itself runs under SPUserWorkerProcess.exe, but the full trust proxy runs under SPUserCode.exe. Therefore, remember to attach it the right process.

Summary

This chapter is important. I cannot emphasize this point more. You really need to read this chapter five times and suck it all in. In every single SharePoint project you do, you will end up using most of these concepts. Writing features and solutions, maintaining them properly, establishing a versioning and upgrade story, and drawing lines between sandbox solutions, farm solutions, and proxies are decisions you will have to make in almost every SharePoint project you will undertake. So, don't skim this chapter. Read it well before moving on.

■ ■ ■

WebParts and SharePoint Pages

Reading Key: If you are familiar with SharePoint 2007, you may find the topics of SharePoint Designer, editing an XSLTListViewWebPart, and the new tooling along with Visual WebParts interesting. The rest of the chapter, you can skim over.

In Chapters 1 and 2 of this book, you learned some SharePoint basics. In Chapter 3, you learned what every SharePoint developer needs to know—writing features and solutions.

As I mentioned in Chapter 3, features and solutions are what you would use to package almost any new functionality into SharePoint. Every SharePoint developer must know how to write features and solutions. This is especially important when you are moving code between different environments such as moving functionality from QA to Production. In the rest of the book, you will continue to learn how to write and package different SharePoint elements as features of solutions. Starting with this chapter, I will start talking about WebParts and SharePoint Pages. In the next chapter, I will talk about a rather exciting new introduction from Microsoft, called the Client Object Model. In addition, you will also read about the ADO.NET(WCF) Data Services as it applies to SharePoint 2010. Also, I will demonstrate some interesting and practical techniques that you can use when developing applications for SharePoint 2010, such as custom WCF services and WebParts that can communicate without causing postbacks.

Before I dive deep into each one of these topics let me first cover the very basic introduction of the topics covered in this chapter.

What Are WebParts?

Modern web sites have different elements on their web pages. Each one of these elements provides unique functionality to end users. Sometimes these elements can be configurable or sometimes these events can talk to each other. These elements occupy rectangular areas on a web page. Different technologies use different words for these elements. Some technologies call them portlets. Some technologies call them widgets. SharePoint chooses to call them WebParts.

WebParts is an integral portion of ASP.NET 2.0. They were first introduced with SharePoint 2003 before ASP.NET 2.0. ASP.NET 2.0 adopted them, and SharePoint 2007 WebParts were largely built upon the ASP.NET 2.0 WebPart framework. In the previous chapter, I had an overview of what a basic WebPart is and how you would use and configure a basic WebPart. If you are unfamiliar with WebParts, I would strongly recommend reading that section before reading this chapter. In the previous chapter, you also wrote a simple HelloWorld WebPart. In this chapter, you will further your knowledge and look at all aspects of writing more involved and complicated WebParts.

What Are SharePoint Pages?

SharePoint pages are simply ASPX's that you would use to browse through your SharePoint web site. Some of these pages come from the file system and are called application pages, whereas some other pages come from the database and are called site pages. There are unique differences between the usage and deployment of application pages and site pages. Also, some of these pages can be used to host WebParts. Sometimes they are called as WebPartPages, but WebPartPages are usually site pages. Technically speaking, you can have an application page host WebParts as well, but as you will learn by convention application pages seem to have a different purpose in SharePoint than site pages.

By the end of this chapter, you should have a clear understanding of how to write and use an application page and a site page. You will be able to make this important architectural decision based on what you learn in this chapter.

Using SharePoint Designer with WebParts

As I mentioned Chapter 3, there are three ways to deliver functionality in SharePoint.

- Through the browser

- Through SharePoint Designer

- Through Visual Studio

Each one of these options is successively more complicated and more compelling in its effort and results. In the previous chapter, you customized the content editor WebPart through the browser. Subsequently, in this chapter, you will start by looking at customizing a rather important out of the box WebPart using SharePoint Designer.

The specific WebPart you will be working with is the XSLT List View WebPart, referred to in code as the *XsltListViewWebPart*. There used to be a rather important WebPart in SharePoint 3.0 called the *DataViewWebPart*. The XsltListViewWebPart is a better and improved replacement for the DataViewWebPart. The DataViewWebPart is still available, but the XsltListViewWebPart is much easier and better to use, and I hope you will agree with me by the end of a real-world example.

To begin, I created a simple list based on the Custom List template. Then I added a column and called it "Population". This column will hold numeric data, so I made it a "Number" kind of a column. Then, I went to http://www.census.gov/ipc/www/idb/ranks.php and got myself some sample data. You can tell that I am trying to come up with some data for a real-world example. If you prefer to be adventurous and create your very own sample data, be my guest!

Once my list is populated with some sample data, I will next start using the XsltListViewWebPart to customize the presentation of data in my List.

To recap, my source data is a Custom List with a column called "Population". I put in some sample data to show populations of the top 50 most populous countries in the world.

First, start SharePoint Designer 2010. SharePoint Designer 2010 is a tool that ships with Office 2010. It is intended for use by developers and moderately sophisticated business users. The equivalent tool in SharePoint 2007 was SharePoint Designer 2007. SharePoint Designer 2010 can be used only with SharePoint 2010 sites; it cannot be used with SharePoint 2007 sites. Therefore, if you have SharePoint 2007 sites to manage as well, you can install SharePoint Designer 2007 and SharePoint Designer 2010 side by side on the same machine. However, it is important to note that if you need to install SharePoint Designer 2007 and SharePoint Designer 2010 on the same machine both of them will need to be 32 bit only. You cannot have 64 bit office 2010 and SharePoint Designer 2007 on the same machine. Personally speaking, I virtualize my work, so this is never an issue for me anyway.

■**Note** You cannot have 64 bit Office 2010, 64 bit SharePoint Designer 2010, and SharePoint Designer 2007 on the same machine. You can have them side by side in 32 bit versions.

Assuming that you have SharePoint Designer 2010 open and running on your machine now, click the open site button in SharePoint Designer, as shown in Figure 4-1.

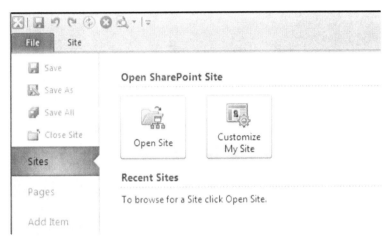

Figure 4-1. *Opening a site in SharePoint Designer*

When prompted to enter a site name enter, http://sp2010. If you have worked with SharePoint Designer 2007 before, you would note that SharePoint Designer 2010 presents a completely different task oriented UI. What you should intend to do next is to edit the site home page and use the XsltListViewWebPart to display the information from the countries list in a user-friendly form.

In SharePoint Designer 2010 with your site open in the customization section, click the edit sites home page link, as shown in Figure 4-2.

Figure 4-2. *Editing the site home page*

Clicking on the edit site home page link opens the home page of the site in edit mode. Next, click the left WebPartZone and then click the Insert tab on the ribbon in SharePoint Designer. Under the insert, look for the data view button. Click the data view button and choose the countries list under lists, as shown in Figure 4-3.

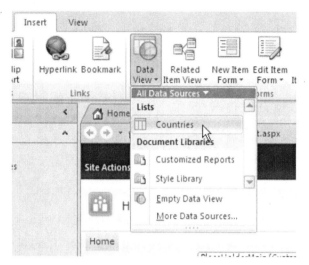

Figure 4-3. *Inserting the countries list*

This would insert the country's list using the XsltListViewWebPart, as shown in Figure 4-4.

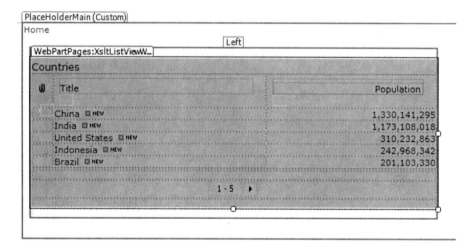

Figure 4-4. *The XsltListViewWebPart displaying the countries list*

If you saved the homepage in SharePoint Designer, refresh the page in your browser and you should see the countries list data surface on the home page of the site.

But let's make it a little bit more interesting. Go ahead and click any of the numeric population cells you see on the right. With your cursor in the numeric population cell, look for the options tab under list view tools in the SharePoint Designer ribbon. Click the conditional formatting button and then choose format column, as shown in Figure 4-5.

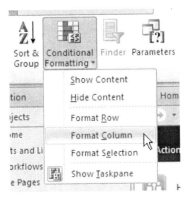

Figure 4-5. *Choosing to format a column in SharePoint Designer*

You will next be prompted with two dialog boxes: the first asks you for a condition for the column and the second asks you for a visual formatting style. Using these two dialog boxes, choose to format countries with population greater than 80,000,000 with a background color of pink. Next, save the page and using your browser visit http://sp2010. Note that the country's list information is showing on the homepage. Go ahead and sort the title column in ascending order. Now note that the formatting information you specified is carried through even when the sort order is changed. This can be seen in Figure 4-6.

As you can see, the XsltListViewWebPart gives you immense flexibility in formatting how your list looks in the browser. Before jumping into the next section, I'd like you to try two other things.

First, I'd like you to see some other WebParts you can insert using SharePoint Designer on a web page and how you can customize them. Go ahead and play with SharePoint Designer 2010 a little.

The second thing, and perhaps the more interesting, I'd like you to try is to visit the countries list in the browser one more time, and click the list tab in the ribbon. Look for the Modify View dropdown and choose Modify in SharePoint Designer, as shown in Figure 4-7.

Countries

☐	🔗	Title↑	Population
		Afghanistan ☼NEW	29,121,286
		Algeria ☼NEW	34,586,184
		Argentina ☼NEW	41,343,201
		Bangladesh ☼NEW	158,065,841
		Brazil ☼NEW	201,103,330
		Burma ☼NEW	53,414,374
		Canada ☼NEW	33,759,742
		China ☼NEW	1,330,141,295
		Colombia ☼NEW	44,205,293
		Congo (Kinshasa) ☼NEW	70,916,439
		Egypt ☼NEW	80,471,869
		Ethiopia ☼NEW	88,013,491
		France ☼NEW	64,768,389
		Germany ☼NEW	82,282,988
		Ghana ☼NEW	24,339,838
		India ☼NEW	1,173,108,018
		Indonesia ☼NEW	242,968,342
		Iran ☼NEW	67,037,517
		Iraq ☼NEW	29,671,605
		Italy ☼NEW	58,090,681
		Japan ☼NEW	126,804,433
		Kenya ☼NEW	40,046,566
		Korea, South ☼NEW	48,636,068
		Malaysia ☼NEW	26,160,256
		Mexico ☼NEW	112,468,855
		Morocco ☼NEW	31,627,428
		Nepal ☼NEW	28,951,852
		Nigeria ☼NEW	152,217,341
		Pakistan ☼NEW	177,276,594
		Peru ☼NEW	29,907,003

1 - 30   ▶

✚ Add new item

Figure 4-6. *The countries list with conditional formatting applied*

Figure 4-7. *Modifying the view of a list*

As you can see, the view pages in SharePoint 2010 are also customized using the XsltListViewWebPart. This is a major improvement over SharePoint 2007's CAML-based views.

Writing Visual WebParts

Next, you are going to start writing WebParts using Visual Studio 2010. These WebParts are deployed using WSP's or solution packages. The first kind of WebPart you will write is a Visual WebPart. The word visual simply refers to the fact that you get visual editing experience when developing this WebPart in Visual Studio. This is possible because a Visual WebPart is based on an ASCX, also known as a user control. This WebPart being an ASCX also presents a significant limitation. The deployment of this WebPart requires an ASCX file to be copied on the file system. Since the deployment requires you to make changes to the file system, a Visual WebPart always has to be deployed as a farm solution. If you read Chapter 3 intently, this goes against my advice of delivering as much of your solution as possible using sandbox solutions instead. There are some hacky ways to deploy the ASCX to the content database, but that isn't quite how the Visual WebPart SharePoint Item works in Visual Studio 2010.

■**Note** The other kind of WebPart, simply known as "WebPart" can also present visual elements on a SharePoint page. Visual WebPart simply refers to the Visual Editing Experience during Development. Visual WebPart is based on a User Control; the other WebPart is a server control.

However, the visual editing experience during development is quite useful as well. Let's go ahead and master this technology of developing a Visual WebPart.

Start by creating a new solution in Visual Studio 2010 and base it on the Visual WebPart project type. Note that SharePoint asks you which web site you intend to debug this solution on, but it does not allow you to create it as a sandbox solution. Once your solution is created, Visual Studio will open the ASCX file that will contain the UI for your Visual WebPart. You can go ahead and give your feature a proper name, by renaming your files to something meaningful. However, the examples stick with the default names for brevity.

Once the ASCX opens, you can use various controls that ship with SharePoint and ASP.NET to build a UI for your Visual WebPart. You may also write code-behind to enhance the logic of your Visual WebPart. This can be done by right-clicking the Visual WebPart ASCX and choosing view code.

However, this example uses only declarative code in the ASCX to demonstrate a way of showing the countries list using both SharePoint and ASP.NET controls. To achieve this, go ahead and add the code shown in Listing 4-1 in your ASCX.

Listing 4-1. *Visual WebPart Code*

```
<h1>My Visual WebPart</h1>
<br />

<SharePoint:SPDataSource runat="server" ID="countriesList" DataSourceMode="List"
SelectCommand="<Query><OrderBy><FieldRef Name='Title' Ascending='true'/></OrderBy></Query>">
  <SelectParameters>
    <asp:Parameter Name="ListName" DefaultValue="Countries" />
  </SelectParameters>
</SharePoint:SPDataSource>

<asp:GridView ID="GridView1" runat="server" DataSourceID="countriesList"
```

```
  EnableModelValidation="True" AutoGenerateColumns="False"
  AllowPaging="True">
  <Columns>
    <asp:BoundField DataField="Title" HeaderText="Country Name"/>
    <asp:BoundField DataField="Population" HeaderText="Country Population" />
  </Columns>
</asp:GridView>
```

Note that the code used for this ASCX uses both SharePoint controls and ASP.NET controls running in tandem.

Go ahead and build then deploy your solution. Note that this is a farm solution so it will do an IISReset. Drop the WebPart on the homepage of your site collection, and you should see the WebPart in action, as shown in Figure 4-8.

VisualWebPart1

My Visual WebPart

Country Name	Country Population
Afghanistan	29121286
Algeria	34586184
Argentina	41343201
Bangladesh	158065841
Brazil	201103330
Burma	53414374
Canada	33759742
China	1330141295
Colombia	44205293
Congo (Kinshasa)	70916439

1 2 3 4 5

Figure 4-8. *Your Visual WebPart in action*

SharePoint Pages

As I mentioned earlier, there are two kinds of pages that are available in SharePoint. The first are application pages that are read from the disk while the second are site pages that are read from the content database. Whenever SharePoint gets an HTTP request, it uses an ASP.NET concept called as the VirtualPathProvider to fetch the actual contents of the page. The VirtualPathProvider class in ASP.NET provides a set of methods that enable a web application to retrieve resources from a virtual file system. SharePoint has one such class located at Microsoft.SharePoint.ApplicationRuntime.SPVirtualPathProvider.

Let me take you into a quick dive into the innards of SharePoint. In order to do so, download a free tool called reflector from http://reflector.red-gate.com. In this deep dive, you will be decompiling important pieces of SharePoint. Please note that it is OK to do so for learning purposes only.

Once you have downloaded and installed reflector on your SharePoint machine, drag and drop all the Microsoft.SharePoint.* dlls from the 14\ISAPI folder into reflector. This will allow you to examine the internal class structures of the SharePoint 2010 framework. I should mention that the code you are about to look at is Microsoft code and Microsoft can choose to change it at any point without consulting us first.

With the Microsoft SharePoint classes loaded, look for the Microsoft.SharePoint.ApplicationRunTime.SPRequestModule class. This is an extremely important class in the Microsoft SharePoint framework. This class is an HttpModule. In fact, it is the first HttpModule that runs in the SharePoint pipeline. You can verify this by opening the web.config of any SharePoint web site and looking for a section, as shown in Listing 4-2.

Listing 4-2. *HttpModules in a SharePoint web.config*

```
<modules runAllManagedModulesForAllRequests="true">
 <remove name="AnonymousIdentification" />
 <remove name="FileAuthorization" />
 <remove name="Profile" />
 <remove name="WebDAVModule" />
 <remove name="Session" />
 <add name="SPRequestModule" preCondition="integratedMode"
type="Microsoft.SharePoint.ApplicationRuntime.SPRequestModule, Microsoft.SharePoint,
Version=14.0.0.0, Culture=neutral, PublicKeyToken=71e9bce111e9429c" />
 <add name="ScriptModule" preCondition="integratedMode"
type="System.Web.Handlers.ScriptModule, System.Web.Extensions, Version=3.5.0.0,
Culture=neutral, PublicKeyToken=31bf3856ad364e35" />
 <add name="SharePoint14Module" preCondition="integratedMode" />
 <add name="StateServiceModule" type="Microsoft.Office.Server.Administration.StateModule,
Microsoft.Office.Server, Version=14.0.0.0, Culture=neutral, PublicKeyToken=71e9bce111e9429c"
/>
 <add name="PublishingHttpModule" type="Microsoft.SharePoint.Publishing.PublishingHttpModule,
Microsoft.SharePoint.Publishing, Version=14.0.0.0, Culture=neutral,
PublicKeyToken=71e9bce111e9429c" />
</modules>
```

Put simply, possibly to the risk of inaccuracy, the SPRequestModule class is what turns an ASP.NET site into a SharePoint site.

Back in reflector, look for the Init method of the SPRequestModule. Somewhere in the Init method, you will see a code block as shown in the following:

```
SPVirtualPathProvider provider2 = new SPVirtualPathProvider();
HostingEnvironment.RegisterVirtualPathProvider(provider2);
_virtualPathProviderInitialized = true;
```

The SPVirtualPathProvider class shown previously is what SharePoint uses to provide a virtual file system to SharePoint. The SPVirtualPathProvider inherits from the VirtualPathProvider abstract base class and provides implementations for the necessary methods such as GetFile and GetDirectory. For the sake of space, let me get to the point, but you can poke more around the framework using Reflector if you so wish. The GetFile method creates an instance of SPVirtualFile, which depending upon the request type would return either a Microsoft.SharePoint.ApplicationRuntime.SPDatabaseFile or a Microsoft.SharePoint.ApplicationRuntime.SPLocalFile. Most of these classes are internal and sealed, but they are great tools for learning how the product actually works.

As you can see, one of those files comes from the database (site pages), and another comes from the file system (application pages).

The behavior of application pages and site pages are quite different from each other. Let's write a small Visual Studio Solution that deploys an application page and a site page, and then examine the differences between the two.

Deploying Pages: A Quick Example

Open Visual Studio 2010 and create a new empty SharePoint project called SomePages. You will have to create this as a farm solution because application pages live on the file system and sandbox solutions cannot edit the file system.

Application pages live in a standard SharePoint folder called the layouts folder. To add the layouts folder in your project, right-click the project and choose add\SharePoint "layouts" mapped folder. This action will add a layouts "SomePages" folder into your solution structure. This is a good practice because the file system is potentially shared across many solutions. Putting your application pages in your own folder ensures that you don't accidentally overwrite somebody else's pages.

Next, right-click the SomePages folder and choose to add a new item. When prompted, go ahead and add the new application page called MyApplicationPage.aspx. In a similar manner, add the new element called Elements.xml and add a new module called SitePageModule. In the SitePageModule, rename the sample.txt file to SitePage.aspx.

Finally, add a new feature called SomePages. Your project structure should look like the one shown in Figure 4-9.

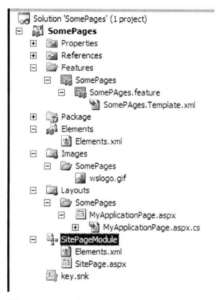

Figure 4-9. *The SomePages project structure*

The package is going to deploy an application page and the SomePages feature. The SomePages feature when activated creates a new custom action to access the application page under the site actions menu, and it creates a new site page in the content database.

Open the MyApplicationPage.aspx file, and change the PlaceHolderMain ContentPlaceHolder content to the following:

```
<h1> Current Trust Level is:
  <asp:Label ID="currentTrustLevel" runat="server" Text="Label"></asp:Label>
</h1>
```

Edit the code-behind of MyApplicationPage.aspx to what is shown in Listing 4-3.

Listing 4-3. *Code-Behind for MyApplicationPage.aspx*

```
protected void Page_Load(object sender, EventArgs e)
{
  currentTrustLevel.Text = GetCurrentTrustLevel().ToString();
}

private AspNetHostingPermissionLevel GetCurrentTrustLevel()
{
  AspNetHostingPermissionLevel[] permissionLevels = new AspNetHostingPermissionLevel[]
  {
    AspNetHostingPermissionLevel.Unrestricted,
    AspNetHostingPermissionLevel.High,
    AspNetHostingPermissionLevel.Medium,
    AspNetHostingPermissionLevel.Low,
    AspNetHostingPermissionLevel.Minimal
  };

  foreach (AspNetHostingPermissionLevel trustLevel in permissionLevels)
  {
    try
    {
      new AspNetHostingPermission(trustLevel).Demand();
    }
    catch (System.Security.SecurityException)
    {
      continue;
    }

    return trustLevel;
  }

  return AspNetHostingPermissionLevel.None;
}
```

As you can see, the preceding code tries to get the current AspNetHostingPermissionLevel and displays it on the page. Deploying the application page makes it accessible for use to all SharePoint web applications. After such a page is deployed, typing the URL directly in the browser will open the page. However, you still need to make it easier for the user to access it using a convenient link. One possible way to add such a link is to add a custom action in SharePoint. There are many places within SharePoint where a custom action can be added. One such place is the site actions menu. In order to add a custom action under the site actions menu, edit your elements.xml to what is shown in Listing 4-4.

Listing 4-4. *Elements.Xml Used to Add the Custom Action*

```
<?xml version="1.0" encoding="utf-8" ?>
<Elements xmlns="http://schemas.microsoft.com/SharePoint/">
 <CustomAction
            Id="MyApplicationPage"
            GroupId="SiteActions"
            Location="Microsoft.SharePoint.StandardMenu"
            Sequence="2001"
```

```
                 ImageUrl="_layouts/images/somepages/wslogo.gif"
                 Title="My ApplicationPage"
                 Description="This page will tell you what security level it is operating
under.">
  <UrlAction Url="~site/_layouts/SomePages/MyApplicationPage.aspx"/>
 </CustomAction>
</Elements>
```

That finishes your application page so now you need to start working on the SitePage.
Under the SitePageModule folder, edit the SitePage.aspx file to include the following code:

```
<%@ Page Language="C#" MasterPageFile="~masterurl/default.master" %>
<asp:Content ID="Main" ContentPlaceHolderID="PlaceHolderMain" runat="server">
<h1>
  Current Date and Time is: <% Response.Write(DateTime.Now); %>
</h1>
</asp:Content>
```

In the elements.xml in the SitePageModule folder, add the following code block:

```
<?xml version="1.0" encoding="utf-8"?>
<Elements xmlns="http://schemas.microsoft.com/SharePoint/">
 <Module Name="SitePageModule">
  <File Path="SitePageModule\SitePage.aspx" Url="SitePageModule/SitePage.aspx">
   <NavBarPage ID="1002" Name="SitePage" Position="1002"/>
  </File>
 </Module>
</Elements>
```

As you saw in Chapter 3, the module tag allows you to deploy artifacts into the content database. In
this case, you are deploying the SitePage.aspx file into the SitePageModule folder in the content
database. In addition, you are also creating a menu on the navigation bar for easy access to the site page.

Next, go ahead and build then deploy the solution. After deploying, visit http://sp2010 in your web
browser and go to site actions\site settings. Click the Manage site features link under the site actions
section. You should see the SomePages feature activated, as shown in Figure 4-10.

Figure 4-10. *The Some Pages feature activated*

Also, since the feature is now active, pay close attention to the navigation bar of the web site. You
should see a link to the SitePage menu as well. This can be seen in Figure 4-11.

Figure 4-11. *Navigation link for SitePage*

In SharePoint Designer if you were to open your site and click all files link on the left, you should see the SitePageModule folder in the content database. This can be seen in Figure 4-12.

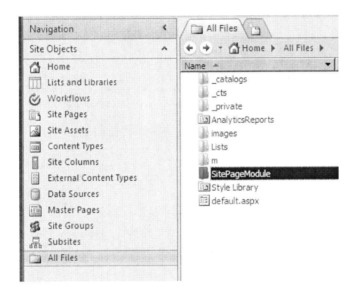

Figure 4-12. *The SitePageModule folder in the content database*

Inside that folder, you should see your SitePage.ASPX file deployed. Back in your browser, go ahead and click the SitePage link on the NAV bar an attempt to access the SitePage. You should see the page run, as shown in Figure 4-13.

Figure 4-13. *The SitePage running in SharePoint*

Next, make the following changes to the SharePoint web.config:

1.   Change the SharePoint\SafeMode\@CallStack attribute to true.

2.   Change System.Web\CustomErrors\@Mode attribute to On.

3.   Change System.Web\Compilation\Debug mode to true.

The above changes will allow you to view any errors in their full detail through the browser.

With the above changes made, edit your site page in either visual studio or SharePoint designer, and embed some server side code using the <script runat="server"> tag, and you will notice that SharePoint informs you that server side script/code blocks are prohibited from running in SitePages by default.

You get this error because by default code blocks are not allowed in site pages. To allow code blocks in site pages, you have to allow for exceptions, using PageParserPaths element in the web.config of SharePoint.

Specifically, you would have to add the following code block under the SharePoint element in the web.config of your SharePoint web site.

```
<PageParserPaths>
  <PageParserPath VirtualPath="/SitePageModule/*" CompilationMode="Always"
  AllowServerSideScript="true" IncludeSubFolders="true"/>
</PageParserPaths>
```

However, using PageParserPaths is not a good practice. This is because now anyone with access to the content database via SharePoint Designer or otherwise will have the ability to upload and run any arbitrary code on the server. The second disadvantage of this approach is the necessity to edit the web.config to make your code run.

Next, let's look at the application page in action. With your feature now activated, you should see a link to your application page under the site actions menu, as shown in Figure 4-14.

Figure 4-14. *The Custom Action your feature added*

Accessing the application page would successfully run it in SharePoint. Note the URL of the application page is the following: `http://sp2010/_layouts/SomePages/MyApplicationPage.aspx`.

Next, try visiting the same application page in central administration by changing the URL to: `http://sp2010:40000/_layouts/SomePages/MyApplicationPage.aspx`.

■**Note** 40000 is the port for Central Administration on my machine.

Also, create a subsite called "SubSite" under your port 80 root level site collection, and visit the same application page at the URL: `http://sp2010/subsite/_layouts/SomePages/MyApplicationPage.aspx`.

Notice that the same application page is available at every single location within SharePoint. I didn't even have to activate the feature, because the physical file for the above URL is being shared under each of these locations. In fact, it is being served by the same physical file, so by editing that one file you change it everywhere within SharePoint. This behavior is different from site pages because editing a site page only changes it at the specified location. Also, running the page should present you the current trust level, as shown in Figure 4-15.

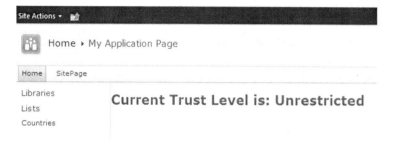

Figure 4-15. *Current running trust level for the page*

Also, note that the application page runs under the ASP.NET trust level of unrestricted. Therefore, if you're deploying custom application pages you should always think of securing them as well. In order to secure an application page, you have two choices. Either you can require the user to be a site collection administrator or you can specify an explicit permissions string necessary to access the application page. Permissions strings and SharePoint security in general is something I will cover in a later chapter of this book.

In order to secure your application page and restrict its usage to only the site collection administrator, you need to make the following code changes.

1. To secure the page itself, add the following code in the code behind of MyApplicationPage.aspx:

    ```
    protected override bool RequireSiteAdministrator
    {
      get
      {
        return true;
      }
    }
    ```

2. In the elements.xml used to create the CustomAction, add the following attribute under the CustomAction element:

    ```
    RequireSiteAdministrator="true"
    ```

Now redeploying and reactivating your feature will give you an access denied if you try accessing the application page as a user who is not a site collection administrator. If, instead, you wanted to restrict using a permission string, you would have to overwrite the RightsRequired property in the code behind, and specify the rights attribute in the custom action element.

One other thing I'd like you to try before leaving this exercise is to deactivate the feature and retract a solution from Central Administration. Note that deactivating the feature successfully removes the custom action under site actions. Also, retracting the solution removes the application page from the file system. Interestingly, the site page in the content database and the relevant navigation bar link are not removed when the feature is deactivated or the solution is retracted. Therefore, to clean up the site page artifacts, you would have to write a custom feature receiver and override the feature deactivating event.

This technique was demonstrated in Chapter 3. Remember when I had mentioned, as a very rough rule of thumb, stuff that goes in the content database is left up to you to clean and stuff that goes on the file system is generally cleaned up for you?

The following list summarizes the major differences between an application page and a site page:

- An application page is deployed to the file system and a SitePage is deployed to the content database.

- An application page requires a farm solution and a SitePage can be deployed using a sandbox solution.

- An application page is shared all across the web front end, but a SitePage is unique to its location.

- A SitePage can be easily customized through SharePoint Designer, but an application page usually requires Visual Studio.

- Custom application pages should be secured and PageParserPaths for site pages should be avoided.

- Feature Receivers are necessary to clean up after a site page feature is deactivated. Application page artifacts are removed from the file system when the solution is retracted.

The obvious question here is what is an application page or site page good for? In which situation would you pick which? Application pages generally are great for administrative-like functions. For example, all the layouts pages (those that appear at _layouts URLs) are application pages that Microsoft wrote. You should never edit out of the box Microsoft pages or any other out of the box files for that matter. But if you wish to deploy custom application pages, your own folder in the layouts directory is the right place to deploy your custom application pages.

On the other hand, site pages are great for presenting content and functionality to the end user. They also easily adapt the look and feel using the default.master of your SharePoint web site. WebPart pages are special example of SitePages. These are simply SitePages with WebPartZones in them. The WebPart manager itself lives on the master page. Therefore, putting WebPartZones on a site page, allows you to create a page in which during feature activation, or at a later date you can put WebParts.

In the next section, I will cover writing the details of a WebPart and also deploy that WebPart using a site page that has WebPartZones.

Writing a WebPart

Earlier in this chapter, you've already written a Visual WebPart. Visual WebParts are great because they give you a visual editing experience during development time. Their biggest disadvantage, however, is that they need to make changes to the file system and thus have to be deployed as a farm solution.

As I mentioned in Chapter 3, you should prefer to deliver your functionality as much as possible using sandbox solutions instead. Therefore, I suspect that you would be writing more and more normal WebParts rather than Visual WebParts.

A normal WebPart is a server control, whereas a Visual WebPart is based on a UserControl.

As mentioned earlier, WebParts are widgets that you can drop on a page, and they present a unique functionality to the end user. Sometimes these WebParts are also editable. The administrator can customize them for everyone or an individual user can personalize them for their own needs. Also, sometimes, these WebParts can talk to each other.

I'm going to build a crawl, walk, run approach example for you.

1. You will begin by writing a WebPart that renders an RSS feed for you. You will also deploy this WebPart using a site page that has WebPartZones. (I will also demonstrate an easy way to get a runtime configuration experience by allowing the end user to specify the RSS feed URL.) Let's call this the RSSFeed WebPart.

2. Next, you will write a second WebPart, which will allow you to host a number of RSS URLs. (In order to host a number of RSS URLs, I will demonstrate writing a custom editor for this WebPart. Let's call this the OPML WebPart.)

3. Finally, you will connect the OPML WebPart with the RSSFeed WebPart. This will allow the OPML WebPart to communicate the RSS URL of the selected RSS Feed, so it can be rendered in the RSSFeed WebPart.

Writing the RSSFeed WebPart

Start by creating a new empty SharePoint project in Visual Studio 2010 called "FeedReader". I intend to put the RSS WebPart and the OPML WebPart in this project. Specifically, the RSS WebPart is going to make a call to an external web service. While I could (and probably should) have written a full trust proxy, to keep things to the point, I will simply write this as a farm solution instead.

Next, right-click the features node and choose add feature, then go ahead and rename the added Feature1 to something more meaningful such as RSSWebParts. While you're at it, also give the feature a decent title, description, and ImageURL. Finally, in the feature properties, make sure that the feature is scoped to Site Collection. You can access the feature properties by double-clicking the feature itself and changing the scope, as shown in Figure 4-16.

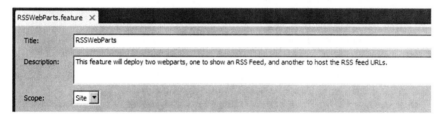

Figure 4-16. *The RSSWebParts feature properties*

Next, right-click the project and add the new SharePoint item, then choose to add a new WebPart called RSS WebPart, as shown in Figure 4-17.

Adding the RSSWebPart will also add the associated Feature1 feature for you in the solution. Since you intend to package the RSSWebPart you just added in the RSSWebParts feature you just created a moment ago, delete the Feature1 feature. You can do so by right-clicking the Feature1 node and then choosing delete.

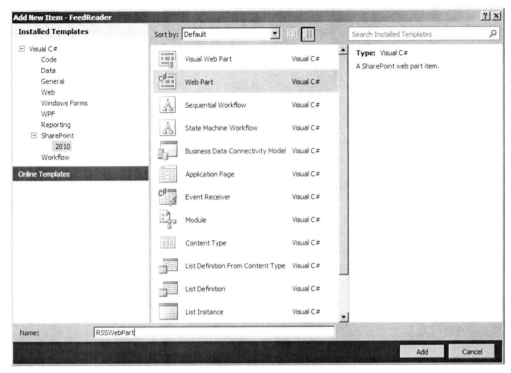

Figure 4-17. *Adding a new WebPart*

Next, you need to package the RSSWebPart WebPart in the RSSWebParts feature. To do this, double-click the RSSWebParts feature to open the feature designer. You should see the RSSWebPart WebPart in the items in the solution pane on the left side. Select it and move it to the items in the feature pane using the buttons provided. This can be seen in Figure 4-18.

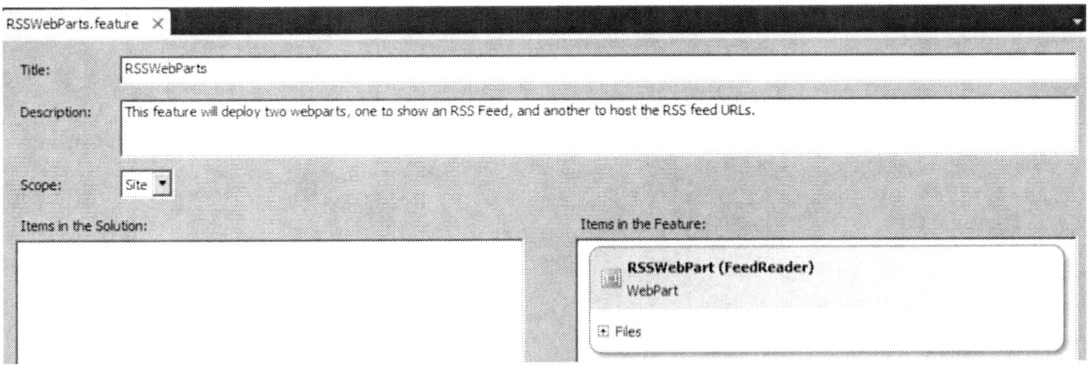

Figure 4-18. *The RSSWebPart webpart is now a part of the RSSWebParts feature.*

Next, you need to add some logic to the RSSWebPart WebPart. Edit the RSSWebPart.cs class to include the code, as shown in Listing 4-5.

Listing 4-5. *Code for RSSWebPart.cs*

```
using System;
using System.ComponentModel;
using System.Runtime.InteropServices;
using System.Web.UI;
using System.Web.UI.WebControls;
using System.Web.UI.WebControls.WebParts;
using Microsoft.SharePoint;
using Microsoft.SharePoint.WebControls;
using FeedReader.BO;

namespace FeedReader.RSSWebPart
{
  [ToolboxItemAttribute(false)]
  public class RSSWebPart : WebPart
  {
    [WebBrowsable(true)]
    [Personalizable(PersonalizationScope.Shared)]
    public string RSSUrl { get; set; }

    protected override void RenderContents(HtmlTextWriter writer)
    {
      RSSFeed feed = new RSSFeed(RSSUrl);
      HyperLink newLink = new HyperLink();
      foreach (RSSItem singleRssItem in feed)
      {
        newLink.Text = singleRssItem.Title;
        newLink.NavigateUrl = singleRssItem.Href;
        newLink.Target = "rssSite";
        newLink.RenderControl(writer);
        writer.WriteBreak();
      }
      base.RenderContents(writer);
    }
  }
}
```

As you can see in Listing 4-5, I'm using custom business objects called RSSFeed and are RSSItem. The code for RSSFeed and RSSItem are shown in Listings 4-6 and 4-7.

Listing 4-6. *Code for RSSFeed*

```
internal class RSSFeed : List<RSSItem>
{
  internal RSSFeed(string RssURL)
  {
    try
    {
      XmlDocument rssDoc = new XmlDocument();
      XmlTextReader xRead = new XmlTextReader(RssURL);
      rssDoc.Load(xRead);

      XmlNodeList xNodes = rssDoc.SelectNodes("./rss/channel/item");

      foreach (XmlNode xNode in xNodes)
      {
        this.Add(new RSSItem(xNode)) ;
      }
    }
    catch (Exception)
    {
      this.Add(new RSSItem());
    }
  }
}
```

Listing 4-7. *Code for RSSItem*

```
internal class RSSItem
{
  public string Title { get; internal set; }
  public string Href { get; internal set; }

  internal RSSItem()
  {
    Title = "Feed not available at this time" ;
    Href = "~" ;
  }

  internal RSSItem(XmlNode xNode)
  {
    Title = xNode.SelectSingleNode("./title").InnerText;
    Href = xNode.SelectSingleNode("./link").InnerText;
  }
}
```

The list of WebParts available in a site collection is generally controlled by the WebPart gallery. The WebPart gallery is a document library at the top-level site in a site collection. You will look at this document library shortly. For your WebPart to be available in the site collection you need to deploy a file with the extension .WebPart into the WebPart gallery. A sample RSSWebPart.WebPart file has already been created for you in the project. Go ahead and edit the RSSWebPart.WebPart file to look like what is shown in Listing 4-8.

Listing 4-8. *The RSSWebPart.WebPart File*

```xml
<?xml version="1.0" encoding="utf-8"?>
<webParts>
 <webPart xmlns="http://schemas.microsoft.com/WebPart/v3">
  <metaData>
   <type name="FeedReader.RSSWebPart.RSSWebPart, $SharePoint.Project.AssemblyFullName$" />
   <importErrorMessage>$Resources:core,ImportErrorMessage;</importErrorMessage>
  </metaData>
  <data>
   <properties>
    <property name="Title" type="string">RSSWebPart</property>
    <property name="Description" type="string">This WebPart displays an RSS Feed rendered in
the browser.</property>
    <property name="CatalogIconImageUrl"
type="string">/_layouts/images/FeedReader/wslogo.gif</property>
    <property name="TitleIconImageUrl"
type="string">/_layouts/images/FeedReader/wslogo.gif</property>
    <property name="RSSUrl" type="string">http://feeds.feedburner.com/winsmarts</property>
   </properties>
  </data>
 </webPart>
</webParts>
```

As a side note, I am also deploying an image with my solution. This technique was demonstrated in the FarmSolution example of Chapter 3.

You would notice some interesting properties being set in the RSSWebPart.WebPart file. All of these properties surface at different places within SharePoint helping to categorize your WebPart and also provide helpful information to the user about the usage of the WebPart. They can also be used to preconfigure the WebPart with some initial values as necessary. When you see this WebPart running in action come back to Listing 4-8 and compare what you see on the screen with what you specified in the RSSWebPart.WebPart file.

Before you build and deploy this solution, let's revisit Listing 4-5 one more time. Specifically, observe the code shown in the following lines:

```
[WebBrowsable(true)]
[Personalizable(PersonalizationScope.Shared)]
public string RSSUrl { get; set; }
```

The [WebBrowsable(true)] attribute tells ASP.NET that this WebPart property is editable from the UI. SharePoint at runtime will provide you with a simple text box to edit the string value. If the property type was an enum, it would instead provide you with a dropdown. The Personalizable attribute specifies the scope of personalization available on the property.

However, PersonalizationScope.User means that individual users can personalize this property to their own needs. In other words, a change that you make using personalization is available only to you and not to the other users on the web site. This process is referred to as personalization of the WebPart and is generally accessed by choosing the "personalize this page" menu item, as shown in Figure 4-19.

Figure 4-19. *Personalize a page*

PersonalizationScope.Shared means that any changes done to the property are shared amongst all users using the web site. This is also referred to as customization and is generally accessed by putting the page in edit mode using the ribbon in SharePoint. Since the RSSUrl Property is marked as PersonalizationScope.Shared only, that property is not available for Personalization but it is available for customization.

Go ahead and deploy your WebPart and let's see it working in action. This can be done by right-clicking your project and choosing deploy. Launch your browser and visit your SharePoint site. Go to site actions\site settings and under the site collection administration section click site collection features. You should see your RSSWebParts feature activated, as shown in Figure 4-20.

Figure 4-20. *The RSSWebParts feature is activated.*

Now go back to the home page of the site collection and put the page in edit mode. Click the left WebPartZone and choose the insert tab from the ribbon. Click the WebPart button and under the custom category on the left look for the RSSWebPart. This can be seen in Figure 4-21.

Figure 4-21. *Adding the RSSWebPart to a WebPartZone*

At this time, I would like you to quickly glance over Listing 4-8 and compare what you see on the screen with what you specified in **Listing 4-8.** *Go ahead and add the RSSWebPart to the left WebPartZone. You should see the WebPart running, as shown in Figure 4-22.*

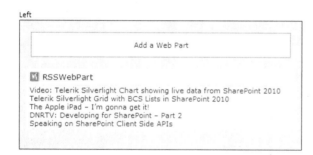

Figure 4-22. *The RSSWebPart running in SharePoint*

Again, quickly glance over Listing 4-8, and you will note that by default this WebPart is pointing to the RSSFeed of my blog. Also, as you can see, I've been blogging about SharePoint 2010 quite a lot. Let's go ahead and repoint this WebPart to CNN.com. Choose to edit the WebPart, as shown in Figure 4-23.

Figure 4-23. *Editing the WebPart*

When the editor zone pops open on the right-hand side under the miscellaneous section, point the RSSUrl property to `http://rss.cnn.com/rss/cnn_topstories.rss` instead. This is as shown in the Figure 4-24.

Figure 4-24. *Specifying an alternate RSS Feed*

Next, hit OK and stop editing the page. You can stop editing the page by clicking on the page tab in the ribbon and clicking on the stop editing button. Your final WebPart in action can be seen in Figure 4-25.

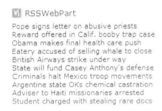

Figure 4-25. *The RSSWebPart pointed to CNN News*

Congratulations you've written and deployed the RSSWebPart successfully!

Configuring the WebPart During Deployment

In the previous example, you just wrote an RSSWebPart and deployed and used it successfully. Using it and configuring it, however, was done by the end user through the browser. Sometimes during deployment, you may also want to add a custom SitePage with WebPartZones on it, configure the WebPart automatically during deployment, and drop it in one of the WebPartZones of the SitePage. I'm going to extend this example next by adding a SitePage that has WebPartZones in it. I will configure this WebPart to the CNN RSS feed instead of my blog, and drop this configured WebPart into one of the WebPartZones on the custom SitePage.

Back in the solution in Visual Studio 2010, add the new SharePoint item, and choose to add a new module called WebPartPage. Rename the sample.txt file to WebPartPage.aspx. Note that the associated element.xml also fixes itself when you renamed the sample.txt. Also, ensure that the RSSWebParts feature includes the WebPartPage module that you just added. Open the WebPartPage.ASPX file, and change it to include the code shown in Listing 4-9.

Listing 4-9. *WebPartPage.aspx Code Containing WebPartZones*

```
<%@ Page language="C#" MasterPageFile="~masterurl/default.master"
meta:WebPartpageexpansion="full" meta:progid="SharePoint.WebPartPage.Document"
Inherits="Microsoft.SharePoint.WebPartPages.WebPartPage,
Microsoft.SharePoint,Version=14.0.0.0,Culture=neutral,PublicKeyToken=71e9bce111e9429c" %>
<%@ Register Tagprefix="WebPartPages" Namespace="Microsoft.SharePoint.WebPartPages"
Assembly="Microsoft.SharePoint, Version=14.0.0.0, Culture=neutral,
PublicKeyToken=71e9bce111e9429c" %>
<asp:Content ContentPlaceHolderId="PlaceHolderMain" runat="server">
        <table cellpadding="4" cellspacing="0" border="0" width="100%">
                <tr>
                <td height="100%" width="50%">
                <WebPartPages:WebPartZone runat="server" ID="Left" Title="Left"/>
                </td>
                <td height="100%" width="50%">
                <WebPartPages:WebPartZone runat="server" ID="Right" Title="Right"/>
                </td>
                </tr>
        </table>
</asp:Content>
```

At this time, if you were to package and deploy the solution, you would get a site page with WebPart zones at http://sp2010/WebPartPages/WebPartPage.aspx. But don't deploy yet! Before you deploy, using a feature receiver, you will preconfigure this WebPartPage to contain an instance of the RSSWebPart displaying top stories from CNN.

To do this, add a feature event receiver to the RSSWebParts feature and add the code shown in Listing 4-10 to the feature event receiver.

Listing 4-10. *Code for the Feature Event Receiver*

```
[Guid("34ed6466-8f0e-4330-b910-5a7c8a7d0feb")]
public class RSSWebPartsEventReceiver : SPFeatureReceiver
{
  public override void FeatureActivated(SPFeatureReceiverProperties properties)
  {
    SPFile file = (properties.Feature.Parent as
SPSite).RootWeb.GetFile("/WebPartPage/WebPartPage.aspx");
    SPLimitedWebPartManager lwpm = file.GetLimitedWebPartManager(PersonalizationScope.Shared);
    lwpm.AddWebPart(
      new RSSWebPart.RSSWebPart()
      {
        Title = "CNN News",
        RSSUrl = "http://rss.cnn.com/rss/cnn_topstories.rss "
      },
      "Left",
      1);
  }
```

```
public override void FeatureDeactivating(SPFeatureReceiverProperties properties)
{
    SPFolder folder = (properties.Feature.Parent as SPSite).RootWeb.GetFolder("/WebPartPage");
    folder.Delete();
}
}
```

Now, go ahead and package and deploy the solution one more time. After deployment is completed visit http://sp2010/WebPartPage/WebPartPage.aspx. You should see a CNN News WebPart running, as shown in Figure 4-26.

Figure 4-26. *A preconfigured webpart deployed*

Overall, you were able to configure and deploy a WebPart and add it to a WebPartZone, using a feature receiver.

Writing the OPML WebPart and a WebPart Editor

You just wrote the RSSWebPart. The RSS WebPart required some runtime configuration, specifically you needed to specify an RSS URL to the RSSWebPart. The WebBrowsable(true) attribute provided you a convenient way to allow SharePoint to give you an Editing UI for that property.

Next, you are going to write the OPML WebPart. The OPML WebPart will host a number of RSS URLs and will present the user with the RSS URLs laid out with radio buttons next to them. The idea is that the user can select any of the RSS URLs. In the next section, I will connect the two WebParts so the selected RSSURL in the OPML editor is rendered as an RSS feed in the RSSWebPart.

While it was convenient to edit one single RSS feed URL using a simple text box, editing the OPML WebPart's numerous RSS Feeds perhaps requires a different UI. To keep things simple instead of creating a single line text box, I will instead create a multiline text box allowing the user to enter multiple RSS URLs as comma separated values. This multiline text box would be the custom editor for the OPML WebPart.

In this section, you look at the process of writing yet another WebPart and connecting it to its custom editor. Let's get started.

Back in your Visual Studio project, add another WebPart and call it the OPMLWebPart. In the OPMLWebPart.cs file, write the code shown in Listing 4-11.

Listing 4-11. *The OPMLWebPart Code without the Editor*

```
[ToolboxItemAttribute(false)]
public class OPMLWebPart : WebPart
{
    private RadioButtonList rbl;

    [Personalizable(PersonalizationScope.Shared)]
    public List<String> FeedURLS { get; set; }

    public OPMLWebPart()
    {
      FeedURLS = new List<string>();
    }

    protected override void CreateChildControls()
    {
      rbl = new RadioButtonList() { AutoPostBack=true };

      foreach (string rssFeed in FeedURLS)
      {
        rbl.Items.Add(new ListItem(rssFeed));
      }

      this.Controls.Add(rbl);
    }
}
```

If you look at the code in Listing 4-11, note that you've created a simple WebPart with the public property called FeedURLs. What you haven't done though is provide the ability for the user to edit the value of FeedURLs. The WebBrowsable(true) attribute is not going to work here for two reasons.

First, the single line text box is not a good UI to enter multiple RSS Feed URLs, and secondly, List<String> is a complex object. It is not a simple string, or an enum, so the framework won't be able to intelligently serialize or deserialize it. In order to edit the FeedURLs, you have to write a custom editor.

Writing a Custom Editor

Writing a custom editor for a WebPart is rather simple and involves two steps. First, your WebPart has to implement the IWebEditable interface, and second you have to implement a class that inherits from the EditorPart abstract base class. This inherited class will be the WebPart editor.

Go ahead and implement the IWebEditable the interface in the OPMLWebPart. Implementing the IWebEditable interface would require you to make the change shown in Listing 4-12 to your OPMLWebPart.

Listing 4-12. *IWebEditable Implementation*

```
#region IWebEditable Members


EditorPartCollection IWebEditable.CreateEditorParts()
{
  List<EditorPart> editors = new List<EditorPart>();
  editors.Add(new OPMLEditor());
  return new EditorPartCollection(editors);
}

object IWebEditable.WebBrowsableObject
{
  get { return this; }
}


#endregion
```

As you can see from Listing 4-12, the CreateEditorParts method returns you an EditorPartCollection. Therefore, numerous editors can work on one single WebPart at the same time. This makes sense considering that there may be numerous properties on the WebPart and each of them may acquire a different editor. The second property simply returns an object, which is an instance of what is being edited. In this case, the WebPart is being edited so you simply return this.

In the CreateEditorParts method, note that you are adding an instance of a new class called as the OPMLEditor. This is the actual editor which inherits from the EditorPart abstract base class. Therefore, add a new class in your project and call it OPMLEditor.cs. The code for OPMLeditor.cs can be seen in Listing 4-13.

Listing 4-13. *OPMLEditor Class*

```
public class OPMLEditor : EditorPart
{
  private TextBox opmlCSV;

  public OPMLEditor()
  {
    this.ID = "MyEditorPart";
  }

  protected override void CreateChildControls()
  {
    opmlCSV = new TextBox()
    {
      TextMode = TextBoxMode.MultiLine,
      Width = new Unit("300px"),
      Height = new Unit("100px")
    };
    Controls.Add(opmlCSV);
  }
```

```
public override bool ApplyChanges()
  {
    EnsureChildControls();
    OPMLWebPart part = WebPartToEdit as OPMLWebPart;
    if (part != null)
    {
      List<String> feeds = new List<String>();
      string[] rssfeeds = opmlCSV.Text.Split(',');
      foreach (string rssfeed in rssfeeds)
      {
        feeds.Add(rssfeed.Trim());
      }
      part.FeedURLS = feeds;
    }
    else
    {
      return false;
    }
    return true;
  }

  public override void SyncChanges()
  {
    EnsureChildControls();
    OPMLWebPart part = WebPartToEdit as OPMLWebPart;
    if (part != null)
    {
      StringBuilder sb = new StringBuilder();
      foreach (String rssFeed in part.FeedURLS)
      {
        sb.Append(rssFeed);
        sb.Append(",");
      }
      if (part.FeedURLS.Count != 0)
        sb.Remove(sb.Length - 1, 1);

      opmlCSV.Text = sb.ToString();
    }
  }
}
```

As you can see, the EditorPart abstract base class requires you to implement two methods.

The ApplyChanges method takes the data entered on the EditorPart and applies it to the WebPart. The SyncChanges method goes in the reverse direction. When the WebPart is put in edit mode, the SyncChanges method reads the data from the WebPart, and applies it to the editing user interface. The editing user interface can be seen in the CreateChildControls method of the OPML editor.

At this point, you can also edit the feature receiver to add an instance of the OPMLWebPart to the WebPartPage.aspx that you had created earlier. Since the steps for that are pretty much the same as what I've already shown for RSSWebPart, I'm going to skip describing them. If you prefer, you can also configure the WebPart at runtime right through the browser.

With the code finished, go ahead and build then deploy the project. Visit the site in your browser and drop an instance of the OPMLWebPart in a WebPartZone. Edit the WebPart and you should you be able to see a multiline text box that would allow you to enter multiple RSS Feed URLs as comma seperated values. This can be seen in the Figure 4-27.

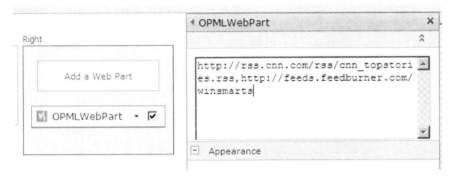

Figure 4-27. *Editing the OPMLWebPart using a custom editor*

So far so good since the page is coming along well. You now have two WebParts, one that shows the RSS feed and another that lets you host a number of RSS feed URLs and allows you to pick one of them. Wouldn't it be nice if you picked the RSS feed URL from the OPML WebPart and that feed was rendered in the RSSWebPart on the right?

What you will do next is to make the necessary code changes so these two WebParts can talk with each other.

WebPart Communication

Sometimes different WebParts on the same page have a need to talk to each other. Events in one WebPart need to reflect changes in another WebPart. Enabling this process is commonly referred to as WebPart communication.

WebPart communication requires you to do the following four things:

- Decide on what needs to be communicated. This becomes your communication contract, usually implemented as an interface.

- Create a provider WebPart that returns an instance of the interface that represents the contract.

- Create one or more consumer WebParts that will get an instance of the interface and suitably act upon it.

- Connect those consumers and the provider.

So, let's begin. In the RSS WebParts, what you intend to communicate is an RSS URL. Therefore, your communication contract looks like the following code:

```
public interface IRSSFeedContract
{
    String RSSUrl { get; set; }
}
```

Go ahead and add the preceding code as an interface in your project.

Next, you need to decide on who the provider is. In this case since the RSSWebPart holds an instance to the RSS URL in question, that seems to be the suitable candidate to be a provider. In RSSWebPart.cs, make the public class RSSWebPart implement the IRSSFeedContract interface. This will require you to make some changes to the RSSWebPart class. The final code for the RSSWebPart class can be seen in Listing 4-14.

Listing 4-14. *RSSWebPart Class with the Communication Code*

```
[ToolboxItemAttribute(false)]
public class RSSWebPart : WebPart, IRSSFeedContract
{
  [WebBrowsable(true)]
  [Personalizable(PersonalizationScope.Shared)]
  public string RSSUrl { get; set; }

  protected override void RenderContents(HtmlTextWriter writer)
  {
    RSSFeed feed = new RSSFeed(RSSUrl);
    HyperLink newLink = new HyperLink();
    foreach (RSSItem singleRssItem in feed)
    {
      newLink.Text = singleRssItem.Title;
      newLink.NavigateUrl = singleRssItem.Href;
      newLink.Target = "rssSite";
      newLink.RenderControl(writer);
      writer.WriteBreak();
    }
    base.RenderContents(writer);
  }

  [ConnectionProvider("Rss service Provider")]
  public IRSSFeedContract GetRssCommunicationPoint()
  {
    return this as IRSSFeedContract;
  }
}
```

If you note closely, the RSSUrl Property of the RSSWebPart acts as the implementation for the IRSSFeedContract. Also, you will notice a method decorated with the ConnectionProvider attribute. This method is called by the SharePoint framework when it needs to get a reference to the provider. This reference to the provider in turn is provided to all the consumers on the page. Since RSSWebPart implements IRSSFeedContract, you simply return this.

Next, let's make changes to the consumer. The consumer in this case is the OPMLWebPart. Go ahead and add the code is shown in Listing 4-15 to the OPMLWebPart.

Listing 4-15. *OPMLWebPart's Consumer Code*

```
private IRSSFeedContract theProvider;


[ConnectionConsumer("Rss service Consumer")]
public void InitializeProvider(IRSSFeedContract provider)
{
  theProvider = provider;
}

protected override void OnPreRender(EventArgs e)
{
  base.OnPreRender(e);

  if (theProvider != null)
  {
    theProvider.RSSUrl = rbl.SelectedValue;
  }
}
```

As you can see from Listing 4-15, the InitializeProvider method is called by the framework after it has a reference to the provider (which it got by calling the GetRssCommunicationPoint method in Listing 4-14). The instance of IRSSFeedContract is passed as a parameter to InitializeProvider. By using this parameter in the OnPreRender method, your WebPart now has the opportunity of setting the appropriate value of the RSSUrl. Setting a value on RSSUrl thereby renders the proper RSS Feed in the provider.

Go ahead and build then deploy the WebPart. In your browser, go to any suitable page with two WebPartZones in it. Drop an instance of the OPMLWebPart and the RSSWebPart in each of the zones. Then like before, edit the OPMLWebPart and provide a few RSS Feed URLs. Next connect the two WebParts, as shown in Figure 4-28.

Figure 4-28. *Connecting WebParts through the browser.*

You should see this running in action. You will note that choosing an alternate feed from the OPMLWebPart changes the RSSFeed displayed in the RSSWebPart. The WebParts are now talking with each other.

Some Closing Thoughts about WebParts

Closing thoughts? What a misnomer you've barely started with this book! Well, think of this as an intermission. WebParts is an inherent topic of SharePoint. You cannot call yourself a SharePoint developer without the ability to write WebParts. At the same time, WebParts is not the only thing you can write for SharePoint. A mark of a beginner SharePoint developer is that he likes to solve every problem he sees as a SharePoint WebPart. Followed by perhaps a semi-beginner SharePoint developer who likes to write workflows for everything he sees.

The reality is WebParts is just one of the arrows in your quiver. SharePoint 2010 is a huge topic. I would never be able to fit everything I wanted to talk about in a single book if I covered everything in super extreme detail. However, there are some important salient points about WebParts that I should point out before moving on to other interesting topics.

- WebParts is an ASP.NET 2.0 concept. WebParts were first introduced in SharePoint 2003 before ASP.NET 2.0. For backwards compatibility reasons, you will find a WebPart abstract base class in the Microsoft.SharePoint namespace and another WebPart abstract base class in the System.Web namespace. When writing WebParts today you should not inherit from the Microsoft.SharePoint base class, instead you should inherit from the WebPart abstract base class in the system.web namespace.

- WebPart communication causes post backs. There is a way to allow WebParts to communicate purely on the client side as well. WebParts can be deployed using sandbox solutions as well. However, WebParts deployed as sandbox solutions have a number of limitations that are identified in this article http://blah.winsmarts. com/2009-12-You_can_deploy_WebParts_as_Sandboxed_solutions__but.aspx.

- You can write Visual WebParts or normal WebParts, but personally I find myself writing normal WebParts a lot more than Visual WebParts.

If you've been reading this chapter for a couple of hours, you should give yourself a small coffee break and come back to read the next chapter.

In Chapter 5, I will talk about a rather interesting new development in SharePoint 2010 called the client object model. Also, I will talk about similar and relevant technologies such as ADO.NET REST or WCF Data services and writing custom WCF Services. I will then mix and match my examples with WebParts and Pages to show you how all these work together!

■ ■ ■

Client Object Model, ADO.NET Services, and Custom Services

Reading Key: If you are familiar with SharePoint 2007, you will probably find this entire chapter interesting and important.

By now, you should be familiar with the basic concepts of SharePoint. You should also understand writing features and solutions, and packaging WebParts and pages as features and solutions.

Writing WebParts and pages is critical for any SharePoint developer. However, most of that code runs on the server. This is very much like the world we used to live in during ASP.NET 2.0 times, when any rich functionality you wanted to provide to the end user required you to cause a postback.

The reality today is a little bit different. Web applications are extremely rich and sophisticated, and almost feel like desktop applications. This is made possible with client-side technologies such as Silverlight and Ajax, which provide a rich running framework right inside the browser, which is then able to talk to the server side on demand. In order to satisfy this growing need in a market, Microsoft introduced a few new and interesting additions in SharePoint 2010, which will be discussed in this chapter. In discussing these three technologies (the client object model, ADO.NET data services, and custom services), I will leverage upon what you already learned in this book. Because by now you should know how to write WebParts, I will write WebParts that will leverage the client object model, ADO.NET services, and custom WCF services.

Let's begin with a brief introduction of these three technologies.

The Client Object Model

SharePoint comes with a rich object model, but it is entirely server-based. However, most clients access SharePoint from a web browser. Modern web applications are increasingly sophisticated these days. They use technologies such as Ajax and Silverlight to create more and more compelling applications that feel like desktop applications instead of web applications. While feeling like desktop applications, they run under the security and deployment ease of a web application.

Because the SharePoint object model is entirely server-based, it can be cumbersome to bring all that rich functionality into the web browser. The client object model solves that problem.

Put simply, the client object model brings a major portion of that rich server-side functionality as a client-side API, which can be used in a NET client such as a WPF application, in a Silverlight application, or in a simple client such as ECMAScript.

This opens up numerous possibilities for you as the application architect. Just think of what you can do with the combination of ECMAScript with ASP.NET, Ajax and jQuery, and Silverlight if they have *secure* and *efficient* access to SharePoint object model.

ADO.NET Data Services and the REST API

ADO.NET Data Services are a set of patterns and libraries that allow you to create access and update data using web-based semantics. In other words, you can use standard HTTP verbs such as GET, PUT, POST, DELETE, and MERGE to interact with your data. They are also commonly referred to as semantics of Representational State Transfer (REST). If you are interested in reading more about REST, you should read this article: http://en.wikipedia.org/wiki/REST.

What confuses me most about REST is that it is such a simple technology, yet big thick books have been written about it. The way I understand REST is that other web-based API calls such as SOAP and web services had gotten way too complex. So people came out with a new mechanism to interact with their data over HTTP using very simple semantics. They could issue commands to both change or query data using a simple HTTP URL. Data would be formatted as JSON or ATOM feeds, and could be consumed in any kind of application.

Later in this chapter when I discuss ADO.NET Data Services as applied to SharePoint 2010 in detail, you will see specific examples that will make this concept clear. But for now it is important to understand that using REST-based APIs is yet another way that you can interact with SharePoint 2010 data from the client side.

■**Note** People have begun calling ADO.NET Data Services WCF Data Services or even oData. I wish they'd quit changing their mind on technology names. But it's the same technology, and a monkey by any other name is still a monkey.

Even though ADO.NET Data Services was pioneered by the data access team at Microsoft (hence the name "ADO.NET"), it is now fully applicable to SharePoint 2010 as well. In ADO.NET, generally the ADO.NET Data Services work against any Entity Data Model (EDM). In SharePoint, such an EDM is driven by the structure of the schema of the lists in your SharePoint site. You can simply visit a service at http://sp2010/_vti_bin/ListData.svc, which exposes ADO.NET data services for SharePoint 2010 that are ready to be consumed in all sorts of clients.

Custom WCF Services

Now here's the best part. The client object model and ADO.NET Data Services both build upon Windows Communication Foundation (WCF). WCF is an inherent block of .NET that was introduced with .NET 3.0. It is that part of .NET that allows you to build connected systems (any sort of possible communication that would occur between any two entities within a program). This could be interprocess communication, communication between different services on the same machine, communication across the network, or even communication that occurs over a queuing mechanism such as MSMQ. WCF truly is a very flexible technology.

You could have used WCF in SharePoint 2007, but in SharePoint 2010, WCF is an inherent part. It is thus not a surprise that technologies such as the client object model and ADO.NET Data Services are both built upon WCF. At numerous other places inside of SharePoint you will find usage of WCF as well.

In this chapter, I will focus on the practical usage of custom WCF services inside of SharePoint. If you are unfamiliar with WCF I would first recommend taking a mini-crash course in WCF by reading the following articles:

- "What is WCF?" http://blah.winsmarts.com/2008-4-What_is_WCF.aspx

- "Writing the WCF Hello World App." http://blah.winsmarts.com/2008-4-Writing_the_WCF_Hello_World_App.aspx

- "Writing your first WCF Client." http://blah.winsmarts.com/2008-4-Writing_your_first_WCF_client.aspx

- "Host a WCF Service in IIS7." http://blah.winsmarts.com/2008-4-Host_a_WCF_Service_in_IIS_7_-and-amp;_Windows_2008_-_The_right_way.aspx

WCF is a very important .NET technology, and every .NET developer must learn it. It is highly applicable in SharePoint, and there will be many other technologies from Microsoft that will leverage WCF.

With a basic introduction of all three topics that covered in this chapter, let's start diving into details about each one.

The Client Object Model

There are numerous ways to get data out of SharePoint. One of those ways is WCF services (including the old time ASMXs). However, out of the box WCF services provide you with a limited API. You can author your own WCF services, but a rather interesting out of the box WCF service in SharePoint 2010, is available at /_vti_bin/client.svc. This client.svc service is your entry point to the client object model.

But what is the client object model? SharePoint comes with a rich API with various objects such as SPSite, SPWeb, SPList, and so on. All these objects have proven very effective in interacting with SharePoint sites and data. However, modern day applications use plenty of client-side technologies such as Ajax and Silverlight. Also there is an emergence of distributed applications in which the application consuming SharePoint data may not be running on the SharePoint server. The client object model provides you with a client-side API that mimics a large portion of the server-side API. This client-side API can be called from regular .NET applications, Silverlight applications, or Ajax applications using JavaScript. The best way to understand the client-side object model is to look at examples of each of these. However before we dive into specific examples, it is important to understand some basics first.

I should point out that even though I'm describing the client object model using WebParts as examples, the client object model is something that is not limited to just WebParts. You can use this in any part of SharePoint or even outside of SharePoint in regular .NET applications!

Client Object Model Design

The client object model has been designed with two things in mind

- It is as similar as possible to the server-side model. This eliminates a serious learning curve.

- It is designed in to give you, the developer, full control on when the round trips to the server are made, and what data is loaded when those round trips are made.

When I say that the client object model has been designed to be as similar as possible, Table 5-1 makes that absolutely clear.

Server	.NET Managed and Silverlight	ECMAScript
Microsoft.SharePoint.SPContext	Microsoft.SharePoint.Client.ClientContext	SP.ClientContext
Microsoft.SharePoint.SPSite	Microsoft.SharePoint.Client.Site	SP.Site
Microsoft.SharePoint.SPWeb	Microsoft.SharePoint.Client.Web	SP.Web
Microsoft.SharePoint.SPList	Microsoft.SharePoint.Client.List	SP.List
Microsoft.SharePoint.SPListItem	Microsoft.SharePoint.Client.ListItem	SP.ListItem

Table 5-1. *SharePoint 2010 Client Object Model Design*

If you are familiar with the server object model, you should have no problem picking up the client object model. Besides the similarities, there are some notable differences as well. For instance, the client object model does not provide any objects scoped higher than SPSite. Also the various administration-related objects are missing in the client object model. Also, the querying semantics in the client object model are somewhat different because when working with the client object model, you are always dealing with a distributed application. The objects shown in Table 5-1 are also referred to as ClientObjects because all of them inherit from a ClientObject base class. There are also base classes in the framework to represent collections of such ClientObjects. There is however a whole other category of objects in the client object model called infrastructural objects.

Infrastructural Objects

The SharePoint 2010 client object model uses several objects to transfer data between the server and client. When I say transfer data between the server and client, I do not mean an object that represents the site or web. Instead I am referring to objects that will help you fill and interact with other objects that represent the site or web. The objects that represent site or web are called ClientObjects. Infrastructural objects let you fill and persist ClientObjects.

Perhaps the most important infrastructural object is the ClientContext object. The process of working with the server from the client starts with the ClientContext object. It is best to understand the usage of ClientContext with a very simple example. I'm going to write a simple console application that retrieves the title of the site using the client object model.

Start by opening Visual Studio 2010, and create a simple console application targeting .NET framework 3.5. Call it **COMHelloWorld**. Next go ahead and add references to the Microsoft.SharePoint.Client.dll and Microsoft.SharePoint.Client.Runtime.dll. You can find these assemblies in the 14\ISAPI folder. Next, edit your console application to include the code shown in Listing 5-1.

Listing 5-1. *HelloWorld Client Object Model Code*

```
static void Main(string[] args)
{
  string siteUrl = "http://sp2010";
  using (ClientContext myContext = new ClientContext(siteUrl))
  {
    myContext.Load(myContext.Site);
    myContext.ExecuteQuery();
    Console.WriteLine(myContext.Site.Url);
  }
}
```

Now if you run your console application, you will note that your console application can successfully read the title of your site. But this code looks slightly different from the regular server-side code. For starters, there is a ClientContext object, which seems to act as the central policeman in the client object model. The process of obtaining and working with sites and data in the client object model begins by retrieving a ClientContext object.

The second interesting thing is a ClientContext.Load method. In your console application, if you were to comment out the Load and ExecuteQuery statements, and then try and access site.Url, you would get a PropertyOrFieldNotInitializedException.

The Load method allows you to specify to the ClientContext what you're interested in retrieving. But it isn't until you execute the ExecuteQuery method that the object is actually retrieved. Another method similar to Load is the LoadQuery method.

Note The ExecuteQuery method loads your requested object. Load and LoadQuery help you specify what you wish to load in ExecuteQuery.

Now, comment out the Console.WriteLine statement and replace it with the code shown following:

```
foreach (List list in myContext.Web.Lists)
{
  Console.WriteLine(list.Title);
}
```

If you were to run the preceding code, you would get CollectionNotInitializedException. However if you were to edit your Load statement to look like the following, your code would then run just fine:

```
myContext.Load(myContext.Web,
web => web.Lists.Include(list => list.Title).Where(field => field.Hidden == false));
```

Thus the ExecuteQuery method only loads what you specify to be loaded in the Load method (or the LoadQuery method, as you will see shortly). In the previous line of code, you are only loading titles of lists that are visible.

The above code will work, but the syntax is not a pleasure to read. There is yet another way for you to specify what you wish to have loaded from SharePoint: the LoadQuery method. Go ahead and modify your console application code to look like Listing 5-2. Note that the code in Listing 5-2 still needs to be between the using statements you see in Listing 5-1.

Listing 5-2. *Client Object Model Using the LoadQuery Method*

```
var query = from list in myContext.Web.Lists
      where list.Hidden != false
      select list;

var lists = myContext.LoadQuery(query);
myContext.ExecuteQuery();

foreach (var list in lists)
{
  Console.WriteLine(list.Title);
}
```

As you can see, the code shown in Listing 5-2 is much easier to read. Also the object loaded is an object in itself; it is not a property of ClientContext. You still need to call ClientContext.ExecuteQuery in order to load such an object.

■**Tip** You can use the Load or LoadQuery methods to specify what you wish to have loaded, and how.

If you were to run the code shown in Listing 5-2, you would still see that many properties are not evaluated. In debug mode, trying to access those properties will give you a PropertyOrFieldNotInitializedException or a CollectionNotInitializedException.

Other than the Load and LoadQuery methods, yet another way of loading data using the client object model is by using *object prototypes*, which allow you to specify the data to be retrieved for an object even if the object hasn't been retrieved yet. This is extremely useful when you're trying to save on the number of roundtrips executed to the server. This same scenario, can also be achieved by using the LoadQuery method.

As an example, suppose that you want to retrieve all views of a list, but you don't have a viable list object yet. Usually you would first have to get a list object and then execute a second round trip to get its views! Wouldn't it be nice to get all this information in a single roundtrip? Prototypes solve that problem. Observe the code shown in **Listing 5-3.** This code fetches the various lists and views in the lists. Using the Retrieve method, you specify the specific object you wish to have retrieved, but in a single ExecuteQuery (round trip to the server), you are able to fill the information necessary.

Listing 5-3. *Prototype-based Code to Fetch Lists and List Views in One Round Trip*

```
ClientOobjectPrototype<List> listProtoype =
  myContext.Web.Lists.RetrieveItems();
ClientObjectCollectionPrototype<View> viewProtoType =
  listProtoype.RetrieveCollectionObject<View>(ListObjectPropertyNames.Views);
```

```
viewProtoType.RetrieveItems().Retrieve();
listProtoype.Retrieve();

myContext.ExecuteQuery();

foreach (var list in myContext.Web.Lists)
{
  Console.WriteLine("The views in list: " + list.Title);
  foreach (View view in list.Views)
  {
    Console.WriteLine(view.Title);
  }
}
```

If you were to select the ClientObjectPrototype object in Visual Studio and press F12 to examine the metadata for this object, you would see something like this:

```
[EditorBrowsable(EditorBrowsableState.Never)]
public ClientObjectPrototype<T> RetrieveItems();
```

By doing so, Microsoft is intentionally hiding these objects from you and is discouraging their use. The .Retrieve and .RetrieveItems methods are not intended to be used by developers. Instead, developers should use LINQ-based semantics, which are the .Load and .LoadQuery methods.

Besides just fetching data from SharePoint, note that the client object model will also let you update data back to the SharePoint server. Updating data raises a whole new set of challenges, however. One such relevant concept is a concept of object identity.

Object Identity

When you work with simple objects in .NET code, you access them through variables. When two variables hold a reference to the same object, editing the data from one variable would immediately reflect the changes in the other variable.

Objects that are inherently tied to a central data store such as SharePoint, or even a database server, cannot work under this behavior. This is because their identity is constrained by their unique identifiers in the central store (in this case, SharePoint), and the main issue is that objects when being modified as variables are now disconnected from the actual store they live in; they are now being modified on the client.

Thus, the data that would then be queried out of the same items in the SharePoint server will probably not correspond to the same object instances your client object model represents.

This discrepancy is resolved by having the ClientContext manage object identities. Whenever an object is retrieved from SharePoint, its identity is remembered by its unique identifier. Whenever the same object is retrieved again, the original object instance is handed back to the application running the client object model. This way, the ClientContext translates SharePoint's concept of identities (unique identifier or GUID) into .NET language's concepts (object instances). This way, the application consuming the object model sees the object only in the state it was first retrieved. If newer data is encountered, it is discarded.

New data is discarded? That cannot possibly be good, right? Well, no; it really isn't as bad as it sounds. If you were writing an application, you would expect the data in your objects to remain the same until you persist the changes back to the SharePoint server. If in the meantime some other user has modified the same data you were working with, the client object model will give you a concurrency exception. But the whole idea here is that your business logic gets the same data it expects to get your business logic will not get confused by data magically changing under the carpet because of other user's actions until you try and issue an update, at which point optimistic concurrency checks are performed.

This process of ensuring the identity of retrieved objects across multiple retrieves between updates is referred to as the concept of object identity.

Updating Data Using the Client Object Model

Updating data from the client object model is rather simple. The following code snippet updates the title of the site:

```
myContext.Load(myContext.Web);
myContext.ExecuteQuery();
myContext.Web.Title = "New title";
myContext.Web.Update();
myContext.ExecuteQuery();
```

Adding a new list or a new list item requires you to create a ClientObjectCreationInformation object or a class that inherits from that. The word "ClientObject" is important in the client object model because ClientObject is an abstract base class from which most client objects, such as SPList and SPWeb in the Microsoft.SharePoint.Client namespace, inherit from. Thus ClientObjectCollection is the abstract base class for most client object collection–like objects. And ClientObjectCreationInformation is the abstract base class for classes such as ListCreationInformation.

The code shown in Listing 5-4 adds a new list into your site.

Listing 5-4. *Adding a New List into SharePoint Using the Client Object Model*

```
// Add a new list into the SharePoint site.
List newlyAddedList = myContext.Web.Lists.Add(
  new ListCreationInformation()
  {
    Title = "A New List",
    Description = "Some Description",
    TemplateType = (int) ListTemplateType.Announcements
  }
  );
newlyAddedList.Update();
myContext.ExecuteQuery();
```

This covers the basic theory of the client object model. All the code snippets you saw were in pure .NET-managed code. But perhaps the best feature of the client object model is that it is also accessible from Silverlight and JavaScript.

Next, let us solidify our understanding of the client object model by building an interesting application that uses both Silverlight and JavaScript. What I intend to build here is a Silverlight WebPart that shows calendar information from a list based on the calendar list template in SharePoint. I will use the client object model to display the information in a visually appealing way. To make the WebPart visually appealing and also to demonstrate the integration with third-party products, I will integrate the client object model with popular third-party products such as telerik's Silverlight suite. This suite is freely downloadable for trial purposes, but you are more than welcome to use the same concepts for any Silverlight front end. For your convenience I have included a non-telerik version of the described code sample in the associated code download as well.

I will also write another WebPart that uses JavaScript as its main execution engine. Using JavaScript I will also consume the client object model. Specifically, given the ID of the list item I will use the ClientObject model from JavaScript to load the details of that list item.

Finally I will make these two WebParts, the Silverlight WebPart and the JavaScript WebPart, talk to each other using WebPart connections. What will be different this time around, however, is that the two WebParts when communicating with each other will communicate purely on the client side. They will not cause postbacks. In short, I intend to do the following:

1. Write the Silverlight WebPart that consumes the client object model and integrates it with a third-party product.

2. Write a JavaScript WebPart that consumes the client object model.

3. Establish communication between the Silverlight WebPart and JavaScript WebPart without postbacks.

Before we get started, I'd like to point out two additional things. First, that by now you understand WebPart basics and I will be going over the steps and little bit faster than before. If you do not understand WebPart basics by now I recommend reading chapter 4 first. And second that the client object model concepts as shown here, are applicable to more than just WebParts. WebParts are simply my test pony here.

So let's get started. If you want to watch the below as a Video, you can do so at http://tv.telerik.com/Silverlight/video/telerik-Silverlight-controls-and-SharePoint

Writing the Silverlight WebPart

As usual, start Visual Studio 2010. Create a new project, but this time create a Silverlight application project and call it **SLScheduler**. As soon as you create the SLScheduler project, Visual Studio will ask you how you intend to debug your Silverlight application. In certain situations, I have found it useful to have a separate ASP.NET web application project. So usually I go ahead and generate the SLScheduler.Web web application project.

In the same solution, go ahead and add an empty SharePoint project and call it **Scheduler**. I would love to be able to say that this should be a sandbox solution, but unfortunately it cannot be because the WebParts you will write intend to communicate with each other. This communication is done through WebPart connections, and WebPart connections internally use reflection, so they are not allowed in sandbox solutions. So choose this to be a farm solution. I will demonstrate WebParts talking with each other using a custom postback-free mechanism later in this chapter.

The Silverlight XAP file will be generated out of the SLScheduler project. The Scheduler SharePoint project will deploy the XAP file into SharePoint as a module. Add a SilverlightXAP module into your Scheduler SharePoint project. In order to automatically copy the XAP file from the SLScheduler project into the SharePoint Scheduler project, right-click Properties on the SLScheduler project, and under Build Events in the Post-Build Event command line, add the following command:

```
copy $(TargetDir)\SLScheduler.XAP $(SolutionDir)\Scheduler\SilverlightXAP
```

The above command will ensure that the XAP file is copied into your Scheduler SharePoint project. It is still not however included in the final packaged solution. For it to be included in the final package solution, build the SLScheduler project once, so the XAP file is copied over to the SilverlightXAP folder. Then click the Show All Files button in the Visual Studio Solution Explorer toolbar, so you can see the SLScheduler.XAP file (see Figure 5-1).

Figure 5-1. *The Show All Files button*

With the SLScheduler.xap file visible, right-click the SLscheduler.xap file and choose to include it in your project. While you're at it, go ahead and delete the sample.txt file as well. Finally, ensure that the elements.xml file looks like Listing 5-5. Note that you don't have to make this change; Visual Studio should have edited the elements.xml for you soon as you included the SLSCheduler.XAP file in your project.

Listing 5-5. *The Elements.XML File to Deploy the Module*

```xml
<?xml version="1.0" encoding="utf-8"?>
<Elements xmlns="http://schemas.microsoft.com/SharePoint/">
 <Module Name="SilverlightXAP">
  <File Path="SilverlightXAP\SLScheduler.xap" Url="SilverlightXAP/SLScheduler.xap" />
 </Module>
</Elements>
```

Now in the same SharePoint project, add a feature called Scheduler. Using the feature designer, include the module shown previously as a part of the feature. Make sure that the feature is scoped to site collection or higher because you are next going to add a WebPart into the same project, and WebParts cannot be added to features whose scope is lower than a site collection. The responsibility of this WebPart would be to download and run the SLScheduler.XAP file within SharePoint. There is an out-of-the-box Silverlight WebPart as well. While you could use that for simplistic cases, in this particular scenario, I intend to add postbacks free WebPart communication, which is why I am choosing to create my own WebPart.

So go ahead and add a new WebPart called ScheduleOverview. Also include the ScheduleOverview WebPart to be deployed by the Scheduler feature.

■**Note** I know I am skipping hand-holding point and click steps here. But if you have been reading this book from Chapter 1 diligently, you shouldn't have a problem following these steps.

Your project structure is now set up.

In short, you created a solution with a Silverlight project and a SharePoint project. The SharePoint project includes a Scheduler feature. The Scheduler feature includes a ScheduleOverview WebPart and a SilverlightXAP module. The Silverlight project copies the XAP file into the proper module location in the SharePoint project.

Your project structure should now look like Figure 5-2.

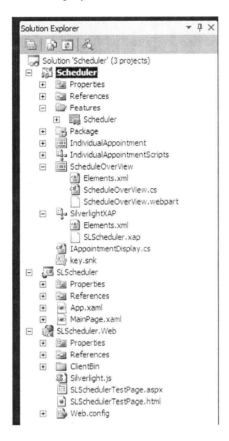

Figure 5-2. *The Scheduler Project Structure*

With the basic structure of your project set up, it is time to write some code. There are two places where you will need to write code. The first is the WebPart itself. The WebPart is rather simple and simply downloads and displays the XAP file from a well known URL. The code can be seen in Listing 5-6.

Listing 5-6. *Code for the ScheduleOverView WebPart*

```
public class ScheduleOverView : WebPart
{
  protected override void RenderContents(HtmlTextWriter writer)
  {
    StringBuilder sb = new StringBuilder();
    sb.AppendLine("<object style=\"display:block\" data=\"data:application/x-Silverlight-2,\"
type=\"application/x-Silverlight-2\" width=\"600px\" height=\"500px\">");
    sb.AppendLine("<param name=\"source\" value=\"/SilverlightXAP/SLScheduler.xap\" />");
    sb.AppendLine("<param name=\"onError\" value=\"onSilverlightError\" />");
```

```
    sb.AppendLine("<param name=\"initParams\" value=\"MS.SP.url=" + SPContext.Current.Site.Url
+ "\" />");
    sb.AppendLine("</object>");
    writer.Write(sb.ToString());
    base.RenderContents(writer);
  }
}
```

As you can see, this code is rather simple; it just renders out an object tag into the HTML. Silverlight in a browser is just an object tag that loads the necessary ActiveX control to run the Silverlight application. Most parameters are quite straightforward, but of special mention is the initParams parameter for the Silverlight object. Specifically, we are using a special variable name called MS.SP.url to pass in the URL for the current running site. This is necessary for the client object model to get a handle to ClientContext.current. This is something that you didn't have to do in the previous .NET examples of the client object model because all those .NET examples were running as a separate exe outside of SharePoint. In this case, however, your Silverlight application is running within the context of SharePoint, so you shouldn't create a client context if you don't need to. Instead, you should try and hook into the ClientContext.Current.

Next, let's start writing the Silverlight application itself. The Silverlight application is going to read appointments out of an appointments list based on the calendar template. It will read this data using the client object model. It will then present the data in a visually appealing manner. I'm using the telerik RADScheduler component, but you can choose to render the content in any manner you wish. The final result is still a XAP file, which is easy to deploy and run.

In order to use the client object model from the Silverlight application, add references to the following two DLLs in your Silverlight project:

- Microsoft.SharePoint.Client.Silverlight.dll

- Microsoft.SharePoint.Client.Silverlight.Runtime.dll

These DLLs can be found in the 14\TEMPLATE\LAYOUTS\ClientBin folder.

In order to use Telerik's controls, you will need to download and install the Silverlight suite from its website at http://www.telerik.com. You would then need to add references to the Telerik.Windows.Controls and Telerik.Windows.Controls.Scheduler dlls.

With the references in place, let's start writing the code for the Silverlight application. The XAML code can be seen in Listing 5-7. As you can see, I've declared an instance of RadScheduler, which I am using in a read-only form.

Listing 5-7. *MainPage.XAML Code*

```
<UserControl
  xmlns:my="clr-
namespace:Telerik.Windows.Controls;assembly=Telerik.Windows.Controls.Scheduler"
  x:Class="SLScheduler.MainPage"
  xmlns="http://schemas.microsoft.com/winfx/2006/xaml/presentation"
  xmlns:x="http://schemas.microsoft.com/winfx/2006/xaml"
  xmlns:d="http://schemas.microsoft.com/expression/blend/2008"
  xmlns:mc="http://schemas.openxmlformats.org/markup-compatibility/2006"
  mc:Ignorable="d"
  d:DesignHeight="600" d:DesignWidth="500">

  <Grid x:Name="LayoutRoot" Background="White">
    <my:RadScheduler Name="schedule" ViewMode="Day" IsReadOnly="True">
      <my:RadScheduler.DayViewDefinition>
        <my:DayViewDefinition
```

```
        DayStartTime="07:00:00" DayEndTime="19:00:00"
        TimeSlotLength="0:30:0"/>
      </my:RadScheduler.DayViewDefinition>
    </my:RadScheduler>
  </Grid>
</UserControl>
```

Now before we can start writing the code for code-behind, let's create some sample data first. The sample data is simply going to be a SharePoint list based on the calendar template. I'm going to call this list **Appointments** and add a few sample appointments in there. My list looks like Figure 5-3.

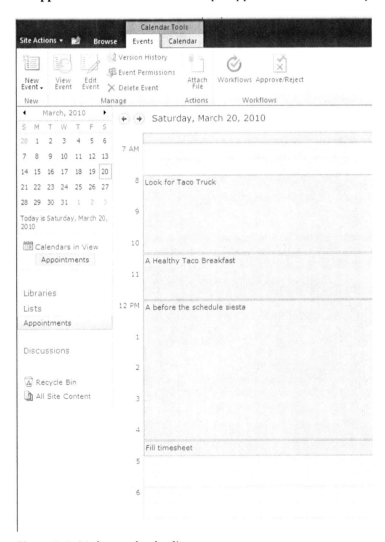

Figure 5-3. *My busy calendar list*

Next let's start writing the code for the code-behind. The code for the code behind can be seen in Listing 5-8.

Listing 5-8. *MainPage.XAML.cs Code*

```
public partial class MainPage : UserControl
{
  private IEnumerable<ListItem> appointments = null;

  public MainPage()
  {
    InitializeComponent();
    this.Loaded += new RoutedEventHandler(MainPage_Loaded);
  }

  void MainPage_Loaded(object sender, RoutedEventArgs e)
  {
    ClientContext context = ClientContext.Current;
    CamlQuery camlQuery = new CamlQuery()
    {
      ViewXml = "<Query><OrderBy><FieldRef Name='EventDate'/></OrderBy></Query>"
    };
    var query = from item in context.Web.Lists.GetByTitle("Appointments").GetItems(camlQuery)
          select item;
    appointments = context.LoadQuery(query);
    context.ExecuteQueryAsync(succeededCallBack, failedCallback);
  }

  void succeededCallBack(object sender, ClientRequestSucceededEventArgs e)
  {
    this.Dispatcher.BeginInvoke(() =>
        {
          foreach (var appointment in appointments)
              {
            schedule.Appointments.Add(new Appointment()
              {
                Subject = appointment.FieldValues["Title"].ToString(),
                Start =
Convert.ToDateTime(appointment.FieldValues["EventDate"]).ToLocalTime(),
                End = Convert.ToDateTime(appointment.FieldValues["EndDate"]).ToLocalTime(),
                Body = appointment.FieldValues["Description"].ToString()
              }
            );
              }
        }
      );
  }

  void failedCallback(object sender, ClientRequestFailedEventArgs e)
  {
    MessageBox.Show(e.ErrorDetails.ToString(), "Error", MessageBoxButton.OK);
  }
}
```

As you can see from Listing 5-8, in the MainPage_Loaded method, I'm getting a handle to ClientContext.Current. Then using the ClientContext and the LoadQuery method, I'm executing a query asynchronously to fetch the items out of the appointments list sorted by EventDate. In Silverlight and JavaScript, I have to call ExecuteQuery methods asynchronously. Then in the succeededCallBack, I'm creating an instance of the object that I can add to the RadScheduler instance declared earlier in my XAML in Listing 5-8. In the failedCallback, I'm simply showing a message box with the error message.

Now go ahead and build and deploy your project, and drop an instance of the SchedulerWebPart on the home page of your site. You should see the WebPart running in action as shown in Figure 5-4.

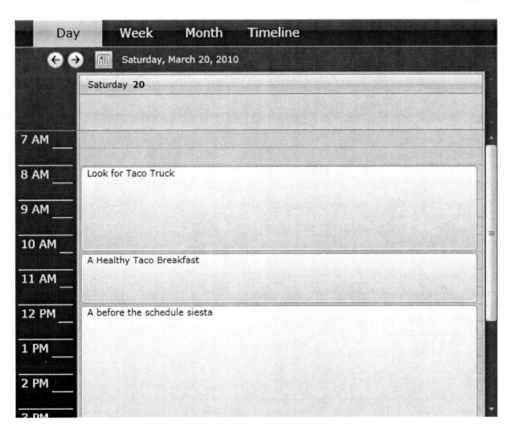

Figure 5-4. *My busy calendar as shown in a Silverlight WebPart*

Thus by using Silverlight and the Client object model, I'm able to read the various list items and display them in a visually appealing manner.

Next, I'm going to demonstrate the loading of a single appointment or a single list item, given the ID of that list item. I will do so using JavaScript consuming the client object model.

And then eventually I will connect these two WebParts in a postback-free manner, so a selected appointment from the Silverlight WebPart can show its details in the JavaScript WebPart.

Writing the JavaScript WebPart

In this WebPart, I intend to start with a given ID for a list item and using the client object model I will fetch the details of that item and display them to the end user. You could have written this JavaScript in the Content Editor WebPart, but to keep consistency with my project, I will write this as my own WebPart. Also in the next section I will connect this JavaScript WebPart to the previous Silverlight WebPart and establish WebPart communication that works without postbacks.

So let's begin writing the JavaScript WebPart. In your same Scheduler SharePoint project that you have been working with, add a new WebPart called **IndividualAppointment**. Go ahead and modify the code of the WebPart as shown in Listing 5-9.

Listing 5-9. *IndividualAppointment WebPart*

```
public class IndividualAppointment : WebPart
{
  protected override void CreateChildControls()
  {
    this.Controls.Add(
      new ScriptLink()
      {
        ID = "SPScriptLink",
        Localizable = false,
        LoadAfterUI = true,
        Name = "sp.js"
      }
      );
    this.Page.ClientScript.RegisterClientScriptInclude(
      "IndividualAppointmentScript",
      ResolveClientUrl("/IndividualAppointmentScripts/appointment.js"));

    base.CreateChildControls();
  }

  protected override void RenderContents(HtmlTextWriter writer)
  {
    writer.WriteLine("<div id=\"appointmentDetails\"/>");
    base.RenderContents(writer);
  }
}
```

As you can see from Listing 5-9, in the CreateChildControls method I'm adding an instance to ScriptLink. This adds the necessary framework files required to use the client object model in JavaScript. Next I read a custom script called /IndividualAppointmentScripts/appointment.js. Obviously, this is a script that I need to write and deploy along with my WebPart. This will be deployed as a module. This script will fetch the details of a particular item, and write the contents in the <div> being written in the RenderContents method.

So go ahead and add a new module into your project and call it **IndividualAppointmentScripts**. In this directory, add an appointment.js file and delete the sample.txt file. In the appointment.js file, go ahead and write the code as shown in Listing 5-10.

Listing 5-10. *Code for Appointment.js*

```
var idToFetch = 1;
var appointments;
function FetchAppointment() {
  var context = SP.ClientContext.get_current();
  var site = context.get_web();
  var list = context.get_web().get_lists().getByTitle("Appointments");
  var camlQuery = new SP.CamlQuery();
  camlQuery.set_viewXml("<View><Query><Where><Eq><FieldRef Name='ID'/><Value
Type='Number'>1</Value></Eq></Where></Query></View>")
  appointments = list.getItems(camlQuery);
  context.load(appointments);
  context.executeQueryAsync(onSucceeded, onFailed);
}

function onSucceeded(sender, args) {
  var listItemEnumerator = appointments.getEnumerator();
  while (listItemEnumerator.moveNext()) {
    var listItem = listItemEnumerator.get_current();
    $get("appointmentDetails").innerHTML = "<b>" + listItem.get_item('Title') + "</b><br/>" +
listItem.get_item('Description');
  }
}

function onFailed(sender, args) {
  alert('request failed' + args.get_message() + '\n' + args.get_stackTrace());
}


_spBodyOnLoadFunctionNames.push("FetchAppointment");
```

As you can see from Listing 5-10, I have a couple of global variables. One is the ID of the appointment I intend to fetch. I'm including this ID in a CAML query, which is then executed on the server using the client object model. This ID is currently hardcoded to "1", but I will change that later in the chapter. For now, to get our functionality running, let's go with the hardcoding. Then there is the appointments global variable, which will contain the fetched appointments from the server. Because our CAML query matches on ID, you will have only one appointment matched at any given point.

Also you will note at the end of the script that is an interesting command, as follows:

```
_spBodyOnLoadFunctionNames.push("FetchAppointment");
```

This command is a part of the standard SharePoint JavaScript infrastructure. This results in the FetchAppointment method being called after the entire page is done loading.

When the FetchAppointment method is called, you get an instance to the current ClientContext using the client object model. Once you have a handle to the ClientContext, the code is quite similar to the Silverlight equivalent. The notable differences are that instead of using the LoadQuery method, I'm using the Load method. Also, I'm using SET and GET methods to set the various properties as necessary. But similar to Silverlight, I call the ExecuteQuery method and pass in the callback methods of onSucceeded and onFailed.

In the onFailed method, I'm simply showing a message box to the end user, informing him of the error. But in the onSucceeded method handler, I'm getting a handle to the listItemEnumerator using the appointments global variable that I created earlier. Using this enumerator, I get a handle to the selected list item and then I can format some HTML and put it in div, which I created in my code-behind.

That's basically it. Go ahead compile and deploy your WebPart and drop it on the home page of your SharePoint web site. You should see the WebPart running as shown in Figure 5-5.

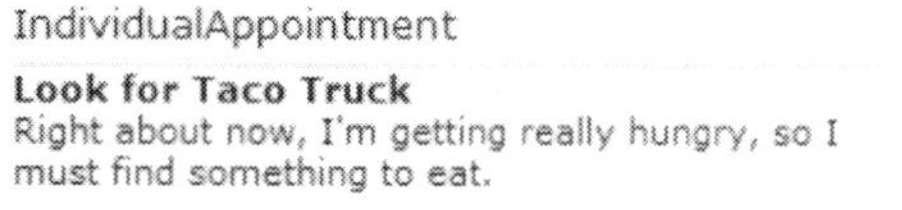

IndividualAppointment

Look for Taco Truck
Right about now, I'm getting really hungry, so I
must find something to eat.

Figure 5-5. *Details of a single appointment in Javascript client object model*

As you can see, your JavaScript code can successfully call the client object model from the client side and can fetch the details of the list item with ID = 1 because the ID=1 has been hardcoded in the JavaScript, which is great.

Now you have two WebParts: the Silverlight WebPart that shows you all the list items and the JavaScript WebPart that shows you a single list item. Now wouldn't it be nice if selecting a particular list item in the Silverlight WebPart updates the details on the JavaScript WebPart?

This sounds like a job for WebPart communication, something you've already seen. So obviously I can extend these WebParts to communicate the ID of the selected appointment among each other. Also, I can probably figure out the JavaScript ID variable var idToFetch, to be driven by a property in the code-behind. But wouldn't it be nice if selecting appointments from the Silverlight WebPart automatically updates the JavaScript WebPart without causing postbacks? In other words, the communication between WebParts would work without using postbacks. Let's implement that next.

WebPart Communication Without Postbacks

WebPart communication is a standard portion of ASP.NET 2.0. Out of the box, WebPart communication will require postbacks. Now I'm not going to edit the source code of .NET and enable the establishment of such communication without postbacks. I intend to leverage upon the existing WebPart communication infrastructure and allow the establishment of communication between WebParts using the standard WebPart communication mechanisms. Thus the initial establishment of such communication will still require a postback, but the actual communication itself will be done using Ajax.

We have a Silverlight WebPart ready that shows me a list of appointments and a JavaScript WebPart that, given an ID, is able to fetch the appointment detail from SharePoint. Once these two WebParts are connected with each other, the user should be able to select an appointment from the Silverlight WebPart and view the details in the JavaScript WebPart–without postbacks.

Thus it is clear that the process of selecting an appointment and communicating it with the JavaScript WebPart has to be done on the client side using JavaScript only. So if somehow Silverlight could call a JavaScript method to set the value of the idToFetch in Listing 5-10 and then call the FetchAppointment method in Listing 5-10, this client-side communication would work.

Silverlight can call JavaScript methods using the HTML Bridge, so that is not a problem. The problem however is that Silverlight doesn't know which JavaScript method to call. This is because there could be multiple consumers of one provider WebPart, and as a result, there could be multiple FetchAppointment methods on the same HTML page.

Did you note? I said *multiple FetchAppointment methods*. That is not going to work because JavaScript expects unique method names. If you're using the JavaScript client object model inside a WebPart, you will have to write some code to generate unique method and variable names. I haven't done that in my previous example (to keep things to the point), but I will demonstrate that going forward while establishing this client-side WebPart communication.

Tip As a rule of thumb, if you're using the JavaScript client object model inside a WebPart, you have to write some code to generate unique method and variable names. Another option is to send in an ID as a parameter.

So when Silverlight calls a JavaScript method, it needs to know the unique ID of the consumer WebPart. This will allow Silverlight to affect the correct WebPart on the page. Thus, as a part of establishing WebPart communication, I will need to communicate the ID of the WebPart. So let's start writing our WebPart communication code.

From the previous chapter, WebPart communication requires you to do three things:

- Define a communication contract.

- Implement the provider.

- Implement the consumer.

The communication contract in this case looks like this:

```
public interface IAppointmentDisplay
{
  void AddListener(string clientID);
}
```

The next step is to implement the provider. The provider in this case will be the Silverlight WebPart that shows an overview of the schedule. Open the ScheduleOverview.cs class in your project and edit it as shown in Listing 5-11 to turn it into a provider of IAppointment display.

Listing 5-11. *ScheduleOverview.cs as a Provider*

```
public class ScheduleOverView : WebPart, IAppointmentDisplay
{
  private string displayClientID = String.Empty;

  protected override void RenderContents(HtmlTextWriter writer)
  {
    StringBuilder sb = new StringBuilder();
    sb.AppendLine("<object style=\"display:block\" data=\"data:application/x-Silverlight-2,\"
type=\"application/x-Silverlight-2\" width=\"600px\" height=\"500px\">");
    sb.AppendLine("<param name=\"source\" value=\"/SilverlightXAP/SLScheduler.xap\" />");
    sb.AppendLine("<param name=\"onError\" value=\"onSilverlightError\" />");
    sb.AppendLine("<param name=\"initParams\" value=\"MS.SP.url=" + SPContext.Current.Site.Url
+ "\" />");
    sb.AppendLine("</object>");

    writer.Write(sb.ToString());
    base.RenderContents(writer);
  }

  public void AddListener(string clientID)
  {
    displayClientID = clientID;
  }
```

```
[ConnectionProvider("Appointment Display Provider")]
public IAppointmentDisplay GetAppointmentDisplayCommunicationPoint()
{
  return this as IAppointmentDisplay;
}
}
```

As you can see from the provider code, I'm getting the clientID of the consumer WebPart and storing it as a private member variable. Later on, I will edit the code further to pass this clientID to a client-side JavaScript method so that method knows which FetchAppointment method to call. Another thing you will note is that there could be multiple consumers and a single provider. Thus technically you would have to maintain an array of clientIDs of all connected consumer WebParts. I'm going to keep things simple and to the point, and demonstrate my concept using only a single clientID. You can extend the provided code to add support for multiple consumer WebParts an exercise for you.

Next let's go ahead and implement the consumer WebPart. The consumer WebPart in this scenario will be the JavaScript WebPart that shows an individual appointment. Open the IndividualAppointment.cs file and add the code shown in Listing 5-12 in the IndividualAppointment class.

Listing 5-12. *Consumer Code for the IndividualAppointment class*

```
private IAppointmentDisplay theProvider;
private string pseudoRandomID = RandomString(4, true);

[ConnectionConsumer("Appointment Display Consumer")]
public void InitializeProvider(IAppointmentDisplay provider)
{
  theProvider = provider;
}

protected override void OnPreRender(EventArgs e)
{
  base.OnPreRender(e);
  if (theProvider != null)
  {
    theProvider.AddListener(pseudoRandomID);
  }
}

private static string RandomString(int size, bool lowerCase)
{
  StringBuilder builder = new StringBuilder();
  Random random = new Random();
  char ch;
  for (int i = 0; i < size; i++)
  {
    ch = Convert.ToChar(Convert.ToInt32(Math.Floor(26 * random.NextDouble() + 65)));
    builder.Append(ch);
  }
  if (lowerCase)
    return builder.ToString().ToLower();
  return builder.ToString();
}
```

Similar to normal consumer WebPart communication code, I'm getting an instance to the provider and storing it as a private member variable. In the OnPreRender method, if the provider is not null (i.e., the provider has been connected to this consumer), I'm calling its AddListener method and passing in a pseudoRandomID. The pseudoRandomID is a four-character, randomly generated string. Remember that I will need to pass this clientID to client-side JavaScript, so I didn't want to send a long GUID or some other ugly number like that.

Now with this much code, your WebParts are connectable. In other words, you now have the ability to pass in the clientID from a consumer (JavaScript individual appointment WebPart) to the provider (Silverlight schedule overview WebPart).

Now the Silverlight WebPart has enough information to call the proper FetchAppointment JavaScript method on the client side. However, instead of calling the FetchAppointment JavaScript method directly, I will instead create an entry point method in my IndividualAppointment WebPart. This will greatly simplify my Silverlight JavaScript method. In order to achieve this, edit the RenderContents method of the IndividualAppointment WebPart to what is shown in Listing 5-13.

Listing 5-13. *RenderContents Method of the IndividualAppointment WebPart*

```
protected override void RenderContents(HtmlTextWriter writer)
{
  writer.WriteLine("<div id=\"appointmentDetails\"/>");

  StringBuilder sb = new StringBuilder();
  sb.AppendLine("<script language=\"JavaScript\">");
  sb.Append(
    @"
    function [clientID]DisplayData(appointmentID)
    {
      idToFetch = appointmentID ;
      FetchAppointment() ;
    }
    "
  );
  sb.AppendLine("</script>");
  writer.Write(sb.ToString().Replace("[clientID]", pseudoRandomID));
  base.RenderContents(writer);
}
```

I'm injecting a JavaScript method into the rendered client-side code. The function name of this method is dynamically generated based on the pseudoRandomID that you calculated earlier. This same pseudoRandomID was also passed on to the provider WebPart. This way if there are multiple consumers, the provider will be able to call the right method of the right consumer. Technically you will have to make all other such methods and global variables unique as well. Again, so I can explain my code clearly, I am going to skip on those redundant details and will leave them as an exercise for you.

Now that you have an entry point declared in your IndividualAppointment WebPart, I need to call this entry point from the Silverlight WebPart. The Silverlight XAP file itself can call a JavaScript method using the HTML Bridge, but first we need to inject that JavaScript into the rendered client side code. Thus in the ScheduleOverview.cs file, edit the RenderContents method as shown in Listing 5-14.

Listing 5-14. *RenderContents Method of the ScheduleOverview WebPart*

```
private string clientScript =
  @"function sendmessage(selectedID)
  {
    var methodName = '[clientID]' + 'DisplayData';
    eval(methodName + '(' + selectedID + ')');
  }";

protected override void RenderContents(HtmlTextWriter writer)
{
  StringBuilder sb = new StringBuilder();
  sb.AppendLine("<object style=\"display:block\" data=\"data:application/x-Silverlight-2,\"
type=\"application/x-Silverlight-2\" width=\"600px\" height=\"500px\">");
  sb.AppendLine("<param name=\"source\" value=\"/SilverlightXAP/SLScheduler.xap\" />");
  sb.AppendLine("<param name=\"onError\" value=\"onSilverlightError\" />");
  sb.AppendLine("<param name=\"initParams\" value=\"MS.SP.url=" + SPContext.Current.Site.Url +
"\" />");
  sb.AppendLine("</object>");

  // Add JavaScript;
  if (displayClientID.Length != 0)
  {
    sb.AppendLine("<script language=\"JavaScript\">");
    sb.Append(clientScript.Replace("[clientID]", displayClientID)) ;
    sb.AppendLine("</script>");
  }

  writer.Write(sb.ToString());
  base.RenderContents(writer);
}
```

I'm declaring a clientScript private variable that holds the code for the JavaScript method. What is interesting is that I do not know the method name until the consumer is connected to this provider. Thus once I have a consumer, (when the displayClientID is no longer null), I inject this JavaScript method in the rendered HTML with the appropriate clientID replaced. Then I use some JavaScript magic to call the appropriate method using that eval method.

This will now allow my Silverlight WebPart to call the JavaScript WebPart on the client side. All I need to do next is to make changes to my XAP file, so this sendmessage JavaScript method that I added in Listing 5-14 is actually called.

The changes to the XAP file are twofold. First we need to make some change to the UI itself, allowing the selection of an appointment and passing it to another WebPart. Note that passing it another WebPart simply means calling the sendmessage JavaScript method. The changes to the XAML portion of the Silverlight XAP are shown in Listing 5-15.

Listing 5-15. *MainPage.xaml for the ScheduleOverview WebPart*

```
<Grid x:Name="LayoutRoot" Background="White">
  <Grid.RowDefinitions>
    <RowDefinition Height="20"/>
    <RowDefinition Height="*"/>
  </Grid.RowDefinitions>
  <Button x:Name="showDetails" Grid.Row="0" Click="showDetails_Click" Content="Show Details
>>"/>
  <my:RadScheduler Name="schedule" ViewMode="Day" IsReadOnly="True" Grid.Row="1">
    <my:RadScheduler.DayViewDefinition>
      <my:DayViewDefinition
        DayStartTime="07:00:00" DayEndTime="19:00:00"
        TimeSlotLength="0:30:0"/>
    </my:RadScheduler.DayViewDefinition>
  </my:RadScheduler>
</Grid>
```

I've added a button to the UI. Clicking that button calls the showDetails_click method, which simply calls the sendmessage JavaScript method (see Listing 5-16).

Listing 5-16. *showDetails_Click method*

```
private void showDetails_Click(object sender, RoutedEventArgs e)
{
  if (schedule.SelectedAppointment == null)
  {
    MessageBox.Show("You need to select an appointment below first!");
  }
  else
  {
    HtmlPage.Window.Invoke(
      "sendmessage",
      "'" + (schedule.SelectedAppointment as Appointment).UniqueId + "'");
  }
}
```

That's it. Now rebuild your solution and deploy to SharePoint again. On a web page of your choice, drop an instance of the Silverlight WebPart and another instance of the JavaScript WebPart. Go ahead and establish communication between them, which leverages the WebPart framework and will cause a postback. Then select an appointment from the Silverlight WebPart and click the showDetails button. The details are now shown in the JavaScript WebPart without postbacks! This can be seen in Figure 5-6.

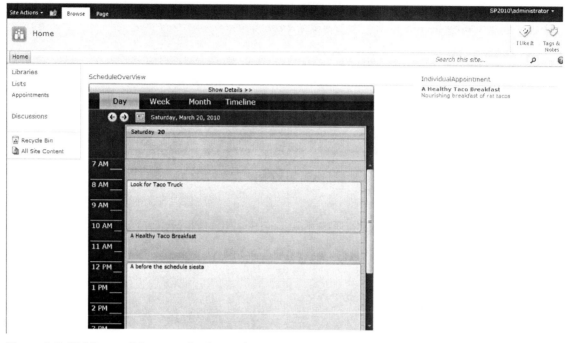

Figure 5-6. *WebParts talking to each other without postbacks*

Just to drive home the point of how compelling this really is, remember that this client side, without postback communication that is occurring, has access to the SharePoint API using the client object model.

ADO.NET Data Services and REST

ADO.NET Data Services is yet another way for you to access your SharePoint data at client side. Under this technology you would use patterns and libraries that make data accessible over simple HTTP-based technologies. This means that you can access the data over simple HTTP-based URIs and use of standard HTTP verbs such as GET, PUT, POST, and DELETE. Data is fetched in JSON or ATOM formats, so it is portable across all platforms. Before I dive into real working examples using ADO.NET Data Services and REST, let's examine some basics about REST and ADO.NET Data services first.

ADO.NET Data Services and REST Basics

In order to begin playing with ADO.NET Data Services in SharePoint 2010, let's begin by setting up some sample data in a sample site. You can either create this data manually or use the RawData.wsp solution package provided to create the data for you. Just upload the RawData.wsp package to the Solution Gallery, activate, and create a subsite based on the newly created site definition.

Start with a blank SharePoint site and create three lists, all of them based on the "Custom List" template.

- Artists with just one column: Title

- Albums: add a look up column pointing to Artists.Title

- Songs: add two lookup columns, pointing to Artists.Title and Album.Title

What I just did is define my EDM (Entity Data Model). Go ahead and fill the lists with some data. I have included RawData.wsp as an export of my own site at this point with the associated code download. If you wish, you can create a new site based on the blank site definition, upload RawData.wsp as a user solution, and activate it to get a site definition with the same data that I am working with.

With some data loaded, I can now start executing some simple REST-based queries right through my web browser. So open Internet Explorer and disable the feed reading view so you can view the actual XML being sent back to you by the server. In Internet Explorer 8, you can do this by going to Tools\Internet options\Content and click Settings under the Feeds and Web Slices section . In the dialog box that pops up, uncheck the check box next to Turn on feed reading view.

Great! Now visit `http://sp2010/_vti_bin/ListData.svc`. You should see some XML come back from the server, as shown in Figure 5-7.

```
<?xml version="1.0" encoding="utf-8" standalone="yes" ?>
- <service xml:base="http://sp2010/_vti_bin/ListData.svc/"
    xmlns:atom="http://www.w3.org/2005/Atom" xmlns:app="http://www.w3.org/2007/app"
    xmlns="http://www.w3.org/2007/app">
  - <workspace>
      <atom:title>Default</atom:title>
    - <collection href="Albums">
        <atom:title>Albums</atom:title>
      </collection>
    - <collection href="Artists">
        <atom:title>Artists</atom:title>
      </collection>
      <collection href="Attachments">
```

Figure 5-7. *XML coming back from the server*

The ListData.svc should work for you if you built your machine per the instructions in Chapter 1. In the scenario that it doesn't work telling you that the system could not load "System.Data. Services.Providers.IDataServiceUpdateProvider", please see `http://blah.winsmarts.com/ 2010-4-WCF-ADONET_Data_Services_-_Could_not_load_type_'SystemDataServicesProviders IDataServiceUpdateProvider'.aspx`.

If you observe closely, this is nothing but an ATOM feed. It is telling you all the lists that are available in this site. Next visit this URL: `http://sp2010/_vti_bin/ListData.svc/$metadata`.

This URL sends you a little bit more XML back, basically giving you the detailed structure of all the entities available in the site. Think of this as WSDL for REST.

Now let's start querying individual lists. Visit this URL: `http://sp2010/_vti_bin/ListData.svc/Artists`. This should send back, again as an ATOM feed, all the artists in the Artists list. But what if I intended to filter based on a particular artist? Could I pass the primary key for the artist and load only a single entity instance?

Try visiting `http://sp2010/_vti_bin/ListData.svc/$metadata` one more time, and examine the metadata for the "ArtistsItem" EntityType closely. You should see a section as shown in Figure 5-8.

```
- <EntityType Name="ArtistsItem">
  - <Key>
      <PropertyRef Name="ID" />
    </Key>
```

Figure 5-8. *AristsItem EntityType definition*

What this is telling you is that the ArtistsItem has a key property, the equivalent of a primary key called ID. Thus it is valid to pass in a URL such as http://sp2010/_vti_bin/ListData.svc/Artists(2) to fetch all the details for Artist with ID = 2. Go ahead, try it!

So now you can not only fetch a list of all artists, but you can also filter on the primary key. Because the result is just an ATOM feed it is very easy to consume it in very thin clients such as JavaScript. Later on, I will also demonstrate getting results as JSON, which is even easier for JavaScript to consume.

Now, could you do more interesting things, perhaps sort by a column? You can do so by visiting a URL such as http://sp2010/_vti_bin/ListData.svc/Artists?$orderby=Title.

Could you do paging? You can fetch the top few items by visiting a URL such as http://sp2010/_vti_bin/ListData.svc/Songs?$top=3. And then you can in effect do paging by skipping the first few rows by passing in a URL such as http://sp2010/_vti_bin/ListData.svc/Songs?$skip=3&top=3. You can also choose to add orderby and visit a URL such as http://sp2010/_vti_bin/ListData.svc/Songs?$skip=3&top=3&orderby=Title. In fact, you can continue to stack as many of these actions as you want. You can see how powerful this can get.

How about relationships between multiple entities? You can do that, too. If I want to fetch a particular album and its artist information in a single HTTP query, I could visit a URL such as http://sp2010/_vti_bin/ListData.svc/Albums(1)?$expand=Artist. This allows me to go from child to parent. What if I want to go from parent to child? I can use the $filter action to achieve that. For instance, if I want to fetch all songs by Madonna, I could use a query such as this:

http://sp2010/_vti_bin/ListData.svc/Songs?$filter=Artist/Title eq 'Madonna'.

Of course, I can use the $filter action to do simple filtering within a single list, such as this:

http://sp2010/_vti_bin/ListData.svc/Songs?$filter=Title eq 'Careless Whisper'.

So far, all the data you're getting back is an ATOM feed. ATOM being xml can be extremely wordy. Frequently in Ajax base scenarios, we have preferred to use JSON over ATOM. This is because JSON is comparatively much more lightweight, and easily parsable in JavaScript. Lucky for us, the REST-based APIs can easily return any of the above results as either as ATOM or JSON, whichever you prefer. If you wish to receive the results as JSON, instead of ATOM, all you need to do is to modify the HTTP Header "Accept: application/json".

As far as I know, the only browser at the time of writing this book that allows you to modify HTTP headers on requests is Firefox with a custom add-on. You can choose to use that add-on if you wish, but I'm going to demonstrate viewing and debugging REST-based APIs using a tool that I find invaluable, which is the Fiddler tool (http://www.fiddlertool.com).

When you download and install Fiddler, it will register itself as a proxy in Internet Explorer settings. It will then be able to trace all the requests going between your browser to external sites. Fiddler can also allow you to handcraft a request, and view both the request and response all the way down to raw bytes.

However, the problem with using Fiddler with SharePoint is that most SharePoint sites a protected behind some kind of authentication. Fiddler cannot perform authentication for you, but it does let you modify requests on the fly. Some simple modifications can be done right through the UI, and some require a simple script or writing a Fiddler extension.

In order to view the JSON equivalent of any particular request, start Fiddler, start capturing traffic (File\Capture Traffic), and go to the Filters tab and check the check box "Use Filters". Also in the request headers section, choose to set the request header Accept to application/json. This is shown in Figure 5-9.

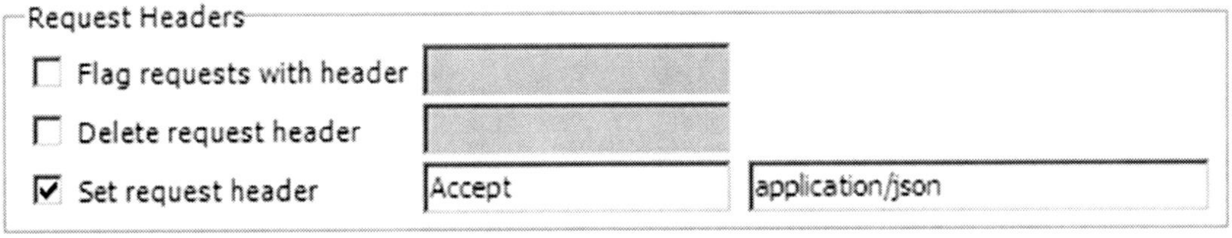

Figure 5-9. *Fiddler configuration to make JSON work*

Now back in Internet Explorer, visit http://sp2010/_vti_bin/ListData.svc/Songs?$skip=3&top=3 URL. You will probably see an error, as shown in Figure 5-10.

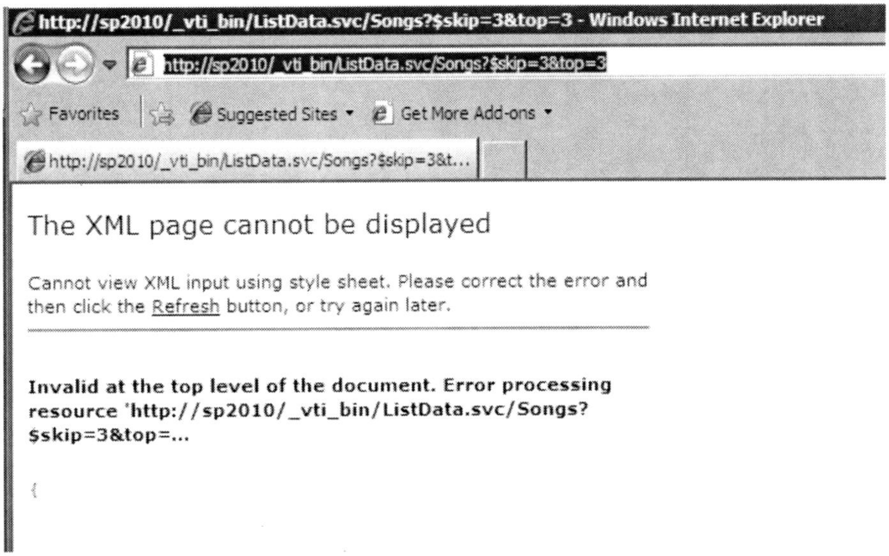

Figure 5-10. *JSON isn't shown nicely in the browser*

This is because Internet Explorer was expecting an XML return, but instead the server sent JSON. However back in Fiddler, double-click the HTTP 200 requests that were captured, and click the Raw tab in the response. You should see the return JSON as shown in Figure 5-11.

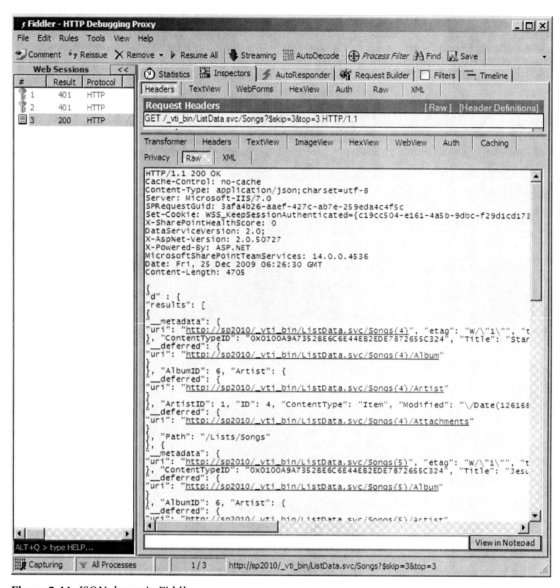

Figure 5-11. *JSON shown in Fiddler*

All the examples that you've seen so far in this section are the client telling the server that it wishes to query some information. Querying is incredibly flexible. As you just saw, you have the ability to query individual entities, lists of entities filtered by criterion, parent-child relationships, and child to parent expansions. Also the results are returned as either ATOM or JSON. I demonstrated the usage of ATOM results right through the browser, and using Fiddler to get the results formatted as JSON. You can do all this without having to write a single line of code. Once we are over the basics, I will also demonstrate writing real applications using the REST API.

So far, all the querying was done using a single HTTP verb called GET. You can however also update, delete and add new entities using the following HTTP verbs:

- GET: Query

- POST: Create

- PUT: Update

- DELETE: Delete

- MERGE: Used to merge a portion of data after a delete or insert, so you don't have to execute a full query all over again

While all of these commands will work, it is probably a lot easier to demonstrate to GET-based commands. This is because GET-based commands can be easily executed from the browser. Because Fiddler won't support NTLM or Kerberos or claims-based authentication, to really view the behind-the-scenes usage of verbs other than GET, you need to write a simple application using System.Net APIs. You can see an example of calling and parsing JSON from C# code at http://blah.winsmarts.com/2009-12-How_to_parse_JSON_from_C-.aspx.

In the real world, however, consuming such services doesn't require you to write such low-level code. Because this is a SharePoint book, let me just point out a link for further reading on examples of various operations that are possible with ADO.NET Data Services, and move on to more real-world scenarios that you will actually use. You can see such examples at http://msdn.microsoft.com/en-us/library/cc907912.aspx.

So far, all the examples demonstrated interacting with ADO.NET Data Services, through the browser and maybe hacking them a bit with Fiddler. In the real world, however, you will consume ADO.NET data services in standard .NET applications, Silverlight applications, and through JavaScript. Let's see an example of each one of these. In each one of the examples, I will continue to use the same sample data I had set up earlier.

Consuming ADO.NET Data Services in .NET Applications

When I say .NET applications, I mean applications that have access to the full .NET stack. This means console applications, windows applications, and WPF applications, but not Silverlight.

I'm going to demonstrate this by using a console application, so start Visual Studio and create a new console application using the .NET 3.5 framework and call it **RestConsoleApp**. In this console application, add a service reference to http://sp2010/_vti_bin/ListData.svc, call the generated service reference RESTReference. If you look closely in your project, it would generate a few files (see Figure 5-12).

Figure 5-12. *Your project after adding the RESTReference*

Of particular interest here is the service.edmx file. That describes your EDM. Once that EDM has been described, ADO.NET Data Services can work on the EDM without much consideration to where the actual data is coming from. The actual data could be coming from SharePoint, a database, or an in memory structure; the ADO.NET Data Services code approach will remain consistent. In the real world, however, you have to be somewhat careful and consider where the data is actually coming from. For instance, the SharePoint content database has been designed for appropriate functioning with minimal oversight; it has not been designed for extremely high levels of I/O. Thus when persisting changes using the SaveChanges method, if you use SaveChangesOptions.Batch on extremely large amounts of data, you may run the risk of locking your SharePoint content database. Considerations like these are important in the practical world.

Another thing you would note is that adding the service reference also generated a strongly typed DataContext for you. This DataContext reflects the structure of your entire site. This is similar to LINQ to SharePoint. If the structure of your site changes, this DataContext is no longer valid. Luckily, they are other approaches in REST-based APIs that allow you to write code that is slightly more resistant to schema changes. Those other approaches involve issuing HTTP requests yourself and parsing the return ATOM or JSON results manually. An example of that can be seen at http://blah.winsmarts.com/2009-12-How_to_parse_JSON_from_C-.aspx.

Back in our example, go ahead and create an instance of the DataContext:

```
RESTReference.TestDataContext ctx =
  new RESTReference.TestDataContext(
  new Uri("http://sp2010/_vti_bin/listdata.svc"))
  {
    Credentials = CredentialCache.DefaultCredentials
  };
```

The "Test" part of TestDataContext in the code snippet is reflecting the title of my site. The title of my site was Test; yours might be different, which also begs this question: is this approach of adding a reference tying your code too tightly to the site structure? Yes it certainly is, and you can use other approaches to work with REST, such as parsing the JSON or ATOM feeds directly, but adding a reference directly makes your code a lot more readable, perhaps at the expense of inflexible code.

Because this is a console application I'm passing in default NTLM credentials. With your DataContext ready to go, you can now start querying for songs using simple LINQ queries:

```
var songs = (from item in ctx.Songs
        where item.Artist.Title == "George Michael"
        select item) as DataServiceQuery<SongsItem>;

foreach (var song in songs)
{
  Console.WriteLine(song.Title);
}
```

When you run that query, also open the Fiddler tool on the side. You will see the results of the query, showing you the songs for George Michael (see Figure 5-13).

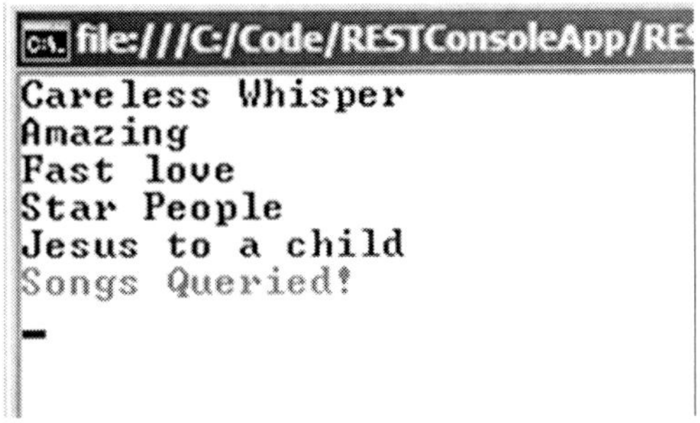

Figure 5-13. *Songs queried written out to the console*

In Fiddler, the request being made was as shown here:

```
GET /_vti_bin/listdata.svc/Songs()?$filter=Artist/Title%20eq%20'George%20Michael' HTTP/1.1
```

Feel free to examine and fiddle (ha!) a little bit more with headers that were sent to the server and the results sent back to the client.

Similar to querying, inserting new data is possible with code shown following:

```
    ctx.AddToArtists(
      new ArtistsItem()
      {
        Title = "Aerosmith"
      }
      );
    ctx.SaveChanges();
```

The result of inserting new data is captured in Fiddler and is shown in Listing 5-17.

Listing 5-17. *Request Used to Insert New Data in ADO.NET Data Services*

```
POST /_vti_bin/listdata.svc/Artists HTTP/1.1
User-Agent: Microsoft ADO.NET Data Services
Accept: application/ATOM+xml,application/xml
Accept-Charset: UTF-8
DataServiceVersion: 2.0
Content-Type: application/ATOM+xml
Authorization: NTLM
Host: sp2010
Content-Length: 1108
Expect: 100-continue

<?xml version="1.0" encoding="utf-8" standalone="yes"?>
<entry xmlns:d="http://schemas.microsoft.com/ado/2007/08/dataservices"
xmlns:m="http://schemas.microsoft.com/ado/2007/08/dataservices/metadata"
xmlns="http://www.w3.org/2005/ATOM">
 <category scheme="http://schemas.microsoft.com/ado/2007/08/dataservices/scheme"
term="Microsoft.SharePoint.DataService.ArtistsItem" />
 <title />
 <updated>2009-12-25T09:21:12.4876525Z</updated>
 <author>
  <name />
 </author>
 <id />
 <content type="application/xml">
  <m:properties>
   <d:ContentType m:null="true" />
   <d:ContentTypeID m:null="true" />
   <d:Created m:type="Edm.DateTime" m:null="true" />
   <d:CreatedByID m:type="Edm.Int32" m:null="true" />
   <d:ID m:type="Edm.Int32">0</d:ID>
   <d:Modified m:type="Edm.DateTime" m:null="true" />
   <d:ModifiedByID m:type="Edm.Int32" m:null="true" />
   <d:Owshiddenversion m:type="Edm.Int32" m:null="true" />
   <d:Path m:null="true" />
   <d:Title>Aerosmith</d:Title>
   <d:Version m:null="true" />
  </m:properties>
 </content>
</entry>
```

A post request was used to insert new data. If you were to format a POST request like this through JavaScript or System.NET, you would get the same results. Sure, the request is extremely wordy because we are using ATOM. When I describe the JavaScript equivalent shortly, I will use JSON, and you will then see how much more terse JSON syntax can be. At this time, verify in the Artists lists that indeed a new artist was added.

Finally you can delete an artist using this code:

```
var aeroSmithArtist = from artist in ctx.Artists
          where artist.Title == "Aerosmith"
          select artist;
```

```
ctx.DeleteObject(aeroSmithArtist.First());
ctx.SaveChanges();
```

As you can see, I'm first querying for the artist I intend to delete. And then I pass in that entity into the DeleteObject method. Deleting the artist causes a DELETE HTTP request, as shown in Listing 5-18.

Listing 5-18. *DELETE Http Request to Delete an Artist from SharePoint*

```
DELETE /_vti_bin/listdata.svc/Artists(5) HTTP/1.1
User-Agent: Microsoft ADO.NET Data Services
Accept: application/ATOM+xml,application/xml
Accept-Charset: UTF-8
DataServiceVersion: 2.0
Content-Type: application/ATOM+xml
If-Match: W/"1"
Host: sp2010
Content-Length: 0
```

As you can see from Listing 5-18, DELETE passes in the ID of the specific entity you intend to delete. The one other scenario that I haven't shown here is updating data inside a SharePoint list, which will cause a PUT query to be executed. I leave that as an exercise for you to try out.

Consuming ADO.NET Data Services in Silverlight

Earlier in this chapter, I described how you can write and deploy a Silverlight XAP file into SharePoint using a solution package. So I will skip mentioning the specific detailed steps here, but if the following instructions are difficult for you to follow, please go through the "Writing the Silverlight WebPart" section in this chapter first.

In order to test ADO.NET services in a Silverlight XAP, go ahead and create a Visual Studio 2010 Empty SharePoint Project called **SLRESTApp**. This project can be a sandbox solution because all it will do is deploy a XAP file to the content database. Even though the XAP file itself was deployed as a sandbox solution, the XAP however, can make WCF calls to the server to the same server. The XAP could also make calls to a different web server, as long as cross-domain policy allows it. To read more about cross-domain policy, and Network Security access restrictions in Silverlight, please see http://msdn.microsoft.com/en-us/library/cc645032(VS.95).aspx. Also, note that with Silverlight 4.0, you have the ability of creating trusted out of browser Silverlight applications, which can do even crazier things such as instantiate word objects on the client machine. Even they can be deployed as sandbox solutions. Remember, the purpose of sandbox solutions is to keep the server safe! Deploying trusted out-of-the-browser Silverlight applications is something sandbox solutions can easily do.

Also add the new Silverlight project called SLRest inside your solution. Because I will be deploying and debugging this inside of SharePoint, I didn't create a new web site for testing the Silverlight app. However (just like the previous chapter when I used build actions), I did copy over the XAP file into a module in the SLRESTApp. I named the Module SilverlightModule. Also ensure that the SLRest.xap file is included in the SLRESTApp project's SilverlightModule module. This will ensure that the SLRest.xap file gets deployed to the SharePoint content database.

My postbuild action command on the SLRest project is shown here:

```
copy $(TargetDir)\SLRest.XAP $(SolutionDir)\SLRESTApp\SilverlightModule
```

Finally rename the automatically added feature to **SLRest**. My final project structure looks like Figure 5-14.

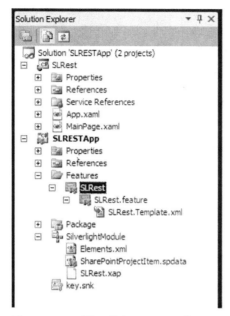

Figure 5-14. *Silverlight REST application project structure*

With your basic project structure set up, now we're ready to start writing Silverlight code that consumes ADO.NET Data Services. As in the console application earlier, add a service reference to http://sp2010/_vti_bin/listdata.svc. Name this reference **RESTReference**.

With the project structure fully set, we can finally begin writing some Silverlight code. Edit the grid in the MainPage.xaml as shown in Listing 5-19.

Listing 5-19. *MainPage.xaml for the SLRest App*

```
<Grid x:Name="LayoutRoot" Background="White">
  <Grid.ColumnDefinitions>
    <ColumnDefinition Width="*"/>
    <ColumnDefinition Width="80"/>
  </Grid.ColumnDefinitions>
  <ListBox Grid.Column="0" x:Name="songsList">
    <ListBox.ItemTemplate>
      <DataTemplate>
        <TextBlock Text="{Binding Path=Title}"/>
      </DataTemplate>
    </ListBox.ItemTemplate>
  </ListBox>
  <StackPanel Orientation="Vertical" VerticalAlignment="Center" Grid.Column="1" Margin="10 0
10 0">
    <Button x:Name="queryItems" Content="Query" Margin="0 10 0 10" Click="queryItems_Click"/>
    <Button x:Name="insertItem" Content="Insert" Margin="0 10 0 10" Click="insertItem_Click"/>
    <Button x:Name="deleteItem" Content="Delete" Margin="0 10 0 10" Click="deleteItem_Click"/>
  </StackPanel>
</Grid>
```

This will cause the user interface to look like Figure 5-15.

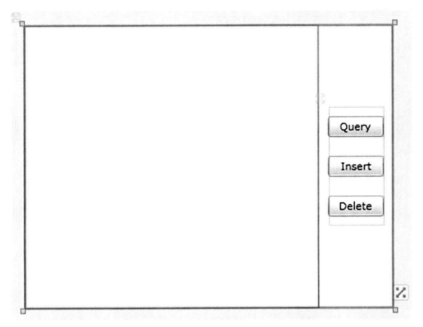

Figure 5-15. *Silverlight UI created and shown in design mode*

By clicking the query button, I will fill the list box with some data. So let's look at the method handler for the query portion first. This method handler can be seen in Listing 5-20. Also note that in Listing 5-20, the "Test" part of TestDataContext is the title of the site you are targeting; yours might be different.

Listing 5-20. *Silverlight Code Used to Query Data from ADO.NET Data Services*

```
private void queryItems_Click(object sender, RoutedEventArgs e)
{
  TestDataContext ctx = GetContext();

  var songsQuery = (from item in ctx.Songs
          where item.Artist.Title == "George Michael"
          select item) as DataServiceQuery<SongsItem>;

  songsQuery.BeginExecute(
    (IAsyncResult asyncResult) => Dispatcher.BeginInvoke(() =>
      {
        songsList.ItemsSource = songsQuery.EndExecute(asyncResult);
      }), songsQuery
    );
}
```

I'm creating a new TestDataContext. GetContext is a static method:

```
private static TestDataContext GetContext()
{
  TestDataContext ctx =
    new RESTReference.TestDataContext(
    new Uri("http://sp2010/_vti_bin/listdata.svc"));

  return ctx;
}
```

Then I write a simple LINQ query to query all artists with title = "George Michael". So far, it is absolutely the same as the .NET console application written earlier. But now is when things become different. In a Silverlight app, I need to execute the query asynchronously. Thus I execute that query asynchronously and I bind results to the list box. In order to get the actual results, I need to call the EndExecute method. You can see the data binding syntax in Listing 5-19. Go ahead and build and deploy the Silverlight application to SharePoint, and use the out-of-the-box Silverlight WebPart to host the XAP file. You should see the Silverlight application running in SharePoint as shown in Figure 5-16.

Figure 5-16. *Songs being queried and displayed in the Silverlight UI*

Next let's examine the code for inserting a new item. The code for inserting a new item can be seen in Listing 5-21.

Listing 5-21. *Code for Inserting a New Item Using ADO.NET Data Services*

```
private void insertItem_Click(object sender, RoutedEventArgs e)
{
  TestDataContext ctx = GetContext();
  ctx.AddToArtists(
    new ArtistsItem() { Title = "Aerosmith" }
    );
  ctx.BeginSaveChanges(
    (IAsyncResult asyncResult) => Dispatcher.BeginInvoke(() =>
      {
        MessageBox.Show("New Artist Saved");
      }), null
    );
}
```

Just as before, the code is exactly the same as the .NET console application. The only difference is that the code is being executed asynchronously because we are running in Silverlight. For brevity I'm skipping mentioning the details being captured in Fiddler. You should however have Fiddler running when you're done this example, and you should examine the data being sent and received from SharePoint.

Finally let's give a quick examination to the delete code. The code for deletion can be seen in Listing 5-22.

Listing 5-22. *Code to Delete an Artist Using ADO.NET Data Services*

```
private void deleteItem_Click(object sender, RoutedEventArgs e)
{
  TestDataContext ctx = GetContext();

  var aeroSmithArtistQuery = (from artist in ctx.Artists
              where artist.Title == "Aerosmith"
              select artist) as DataServiceQuery<ArtistsItem>;

  aeroSmithArtistQuery.BeginExecute(
      (IAsyncResult asyncResult) => Dispatcher.BeginInvoke(() =>
      {
        var aeroSmithArtist =
          aeroSmithArtistQuery.EndExecute(asyncResult);
        ctx.DeleteObject(aeroSmithArtist.First());
        ctx.BeginSaveChanges(
          (IAsyncResult asyncResult2) => Dispatcher.BeginInvoke(() =>
          {
            MessageBox.Show("Artist Deleted");
          }), null
          );
      }), aeroSmithArtistQuery
    );
}
```

As before, deletion will require you to fetch the entity you wish to delete first. Also you need to fetch this entity asynchronously. The process of fetching this entity is exactly the same as the process of querying that you've already seen. Once this entity has been fetched, you will need to call the

DeleteObject method, and execute another call to SharePoint and call the BeginSaveChanges method to persist the changes back into SharePoint.

Consuming ADO.NET Data Services in JavaScript

Perhaps the biggest advantage of the simplicity of the ADO.NET services REST-based API is the possibility to consume it in any platform. The formatted data is simply utf-8, so it can be consumed in Java (or JavaScript for that matter).

Let's look at a few examples of consuming the service in JavaScript. You will find all the associated code in the code download for this chapter, in the TestPage.aspx file. You can choose to drag and drop the TestPage.aspx using SharePoint designer into the content database, or you can choose to wrap it and deploy it as a solution.

Let's look at the example of querying data using JavaScript first. The necessary JavaScript required to fetch data over the REST-based API can be seen in Listing 5-23.

Listing 5-23. *Querying Data using JavaScript*

```
function load()
{
                var request = new Sys.Net.WebRequest();
                request.set_httpVerb("GET");
                request.set_url(
  "http://sp2010/_vti_bin/ListData.svc/Songs?$filter=Artist/Title eq 'George Michael'");
                request.get_headers()['Accept'] = 'application/json';
                request.add_completed(handleRequestComplete);
                request.invoke();
}

function handleRequestComplete(response, userContext)
{
                var songs = response.get_object().d;

                var outputHtml = "" ;
                for (var i = 0; i < songs.results.length ; i++)
                {
                                outputHtml = outputHtml + "<br/>" + songs.results[i].Title ;
                }

                $get("results").innerHTML = outputHtml;
}

Sys.Application.add_load(load);
```

I'm using the System.Net.WebRequest class to formulate my HTTP request. This is a simple GET request using the $filter action to find all songs by George Michael. After I invoke that request asynchronously, the results are handled in the handleRequestComplete method. Using the response.get_object method, I am able to get a handle to the actual object returned by SharePoint. Using Fiddler you can also verify that the return is in JSON. I can then easily parse the results and stick them in a DIV for the user to see. The results can be seen in Figure 5-17.

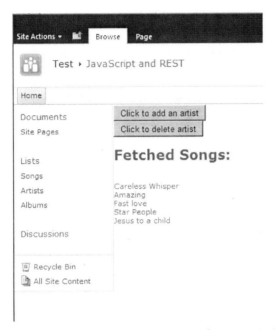

Figure 5-17. *Using the REST services from JavaScript*

Next is an example of inserting new entities into SharePoint lists using REST-based API and JavaScript. As is evident from Figure 5-17, pressing the "Click to add an artist" button will call a JavaScript method that will insert a new artist. This is where the simplicity of JSON over ATOM shines. The code required to insert a new artist into the list can be seen in Listing 5-24.

Listing 5-24. *Code Required to Insert a New Artist Using JSON*

```
function AddNewArtist()
{
            var request = new Sys.Net.WebRequest();
            request.set_httpVerb("POST");
            request.set_url("/_vti_bin/listdata.svc/Artists");
            request.get_headers()['Accept'] = 'application/json';
            request.get_headers()['Content-Type'] = 'application/json';
            request.set_body("{Title: \"Aerosmith\"}")
            request.add_completed(handleInsertCompleted);
            request.invoke();
}

function handleInsertCompleted(response, userContext)
{
            alert('New artist created') ;
}
```

I am sending a POST request, which is consistent with the desire to be able to insert a new artist. Also pay attention to the URL and calling, "/vti_bin/listdata.svc/Artists". I have set the format and content-type to application/json, which allows me to specify a rather terse and simple string identifying the data I wish to insert in the following line:

```
request.set_body("{Title: \"Aerosmith\"}")
```

Now pressing the Click to add an artist button will cause the Aerosmith artist to get inserted into the list. If you were to open Fiddler, you would also note that the response to your POST HTTP command is a JSON-formatted representation of the newly inserted entity. This can be seen in Listing 5-25.

Listing 5-25. *Response of the POST Command*

```
HTTP/1.1 201 Created
Cache-Control: no-cache
Content-Type: application/json;charset=utf-8
ETag: W/"1"
Location: http://sp2010/_vti_bin/listdata.svc/Artists(15)
Server: Microsoft-IIS/7.0
SPRequestGuid: bb765472-1671-4d60-bd7c-8ab7c96d30f0
Set-Cookie: WSS_KeepSessionAuthenticated={c19cc504-e161-4a5b-9dbc-f29d1cd1733d}; path=/
X-SharePointHealthScore: 0
DataServiceVersion: 1.0
X-AspNet-Version: 2.0.50727
X-Powered-By: ASP.NET
MicrosoftSharePointTeamServices: 14.0.0.4536
Date: Fri, 25 Dec 2009 13:05:32 GMT
Content-Length: 575

{
"d" : {
"__metadata": {
"uri": "http://sp2010/_vti_bin/listdata.svc/Artists(15)", "etag": "W/\"1\"", "type":
"Microsoft.SharePoint.DataService.ArtistsItem"
}, "ID": 15, "ContentTypeID": "0x010055431F18E21FD240854A20B8B30D9FA0", "ContentType": "Item",
"Title": "Aerosmith", "Modified": "\/Date(1261728332000)\/", "Created":
"\/Date(1261728332000)\/", "CreatedByID": 1, "ModifiedByID": 1, "Owshiddenversion": 1,
"Version": "1.0", "Attachments": {
"__deferred": {
"uri": "http://sp2010/_vti_bin/listdata.svc/Artists(15)/Attachments"
}
}, "Path": "/Lists/Artists"
}
}
```

Next let us look of an example of deleting an artist from the SharePoint list. Deletion requires you to query the entity you wish to delete first and then pass in the appropriate ID to be deleted. The code required to delete an artist from the SharePoint list can be seen in Listing 5-26.

Listing 5-26. *Code Required to Delete Using JavaScript and JSON*

```
function DeleteArtist()
{
                var request = new Sys.Net.WebRequest();
                request.set_httpVerb("GET");
                request.set_url("http://sp2010/_vti_bin/ListData.svc/Artists?$filter=Title eq
'Aerosmith'");
                request.get_headers()['Accept'] = 'application/json';
                request.add_completed(handleDeleteQueryCompleted);
                request.invoke();
}

function handleDeleteQueryCompleted(response, userContext)
{
                var artists = response.get_object().d;

                var aerosmithID = "" ;
                for (var i = 0; i < artists.results.length ; i++)
                {
                                aerosmithID = artists.results[i].ID ;
                }

                var request = new Sys.Net.WebRequest();
                request.set_httpVerb("DELETE");
                request.set_url("/_vti_bin/listdata.svc/Artists(" + aerosmithID + ")");
                request.get_headers()['Accept'] = 'application/json';
                request.get_headers()['Content-Type'] = 'application/json';
                request.add_completed(handleDeleteCompleted);
                request.invoke();
}

function handleDeleteCompleted(response, userContext)
{
                alert('Artist Deleted') ;
}
```

Again, there are two asynchronous calls here. The first call is to fetch data matching the Aerosmith artist. Like before, because I have access to the entire object in JavaScript, I can easily extract the ID of Aerosmith. Once I have that ID, I can execute another HTTP command asynchronously, except in this case my HTTP verb is DELETE, which causes the Aerosmith artist to be deleted from the SharePoint list. Also because we are working in JavaScript we do not have lambda expressions such as c#. So my code has been broken down into three separate functions. You can however use inline functions in Javascript and in effect achieve the same simplicity of code as lambda expressions.

Some Architectural Thoughts Before We Move On

I like the REST API. The simplicity of it simply amazes me. But what is evident is that in querying data from SharePoint you have numerous possibilities. You can use the server-side object model; you can use LINQ to SharePoint. Or if you intend to work on the client side, you can choose to use the client object model, or you can use the REST API. Neither of these approaches is perfect, so you will find yourself picking the right tool for the right job.

The server object model and a LINQ to SharePoint mechanisms are restricted to server-side operations only. Specifically, LINQ to SharePoint is somewhat inflexible because it restricts the further schema changes you can make on your SharePoint site. However, it is much more productive for the end developer as compared with working with the server-side API.

I would venture to guess that most of the code you will write going forward will require some sort of client-side interaction. Client-side interaction means you will most definitely find yourself using the client object model or the REST-based APIs. In working with the client object model, I find my code to be very maintainable. It does not suffer from schema changes on the web server, breaking my code too often. In REST-based APIs, however, if I choose to generate a reference, my generated reference is very closely tied to the schema of my SharePoint site. I do not like that. This is primarily because it results in fragile code that will break more often as the schema changes. The beauty of REST-based APIs is that you don't have to use the strongly typed data context. As you saw in the JavaScript example, nothing really stops you from sending your own hand-crafted HTTP WebRequests. And this is where the REST-based API is so amazing all the work is done simply over URL using simple HTTP requests. Which means your functionality can be consumed from any platform; it is platform-independent.

I was saving the best part for last: the client object model and the REST-based APIs are built on a singular .NET technology: WCF. The advantage of the client object model and REST-based APIs is that they are out of the box you didn't have to write them; Microsoft wrote them for you. But when Microsoft writes something for you; they create a one-size-fits-all approach. They don't author business objects that map the structure of your own business needs, so the data going over the wire does not have a hierarchical structure that maps your business needs, vocabulary, or even data validations. This reminds me very much of DataSets in ADO.NET 2.0. There used to be a big discussion around whether DataSets or business objects are better. The reality is that there are pros and cons of each. You can read my views on DataSets vs. Business Objects here: http://blah.winsmarts.com/2006/06/02/are-you-a-business-object-person-or-a-dataset-person.aspx.

The client object model and the out-of-the-box REST-based APIs are the equivalent of datasets in SharePoint. They are dumb, they do not have the structure of your business data, they do not reflect the right vocabulary, and they do not have custom validations. Their payload is what is commonly referred to as data transfer objects (DTOs). Also, you have a limitation on which clients or technologies can be used to consume these services! The entire server-side API is not open for use using the client object model and the REST-based APIs. The advantage of course is that you don't have to write the client object model - it is already written for you.

The beauty of SharePoint 2010, however, is that you can author your own custom WCF services. These custom WCF services can then choose to expose custom business objects, which buys you all the advantages of using custom business objects. Also you have the ability to switch bindings at will and support different technologies and WS-* standards on your services.

Think of the client object model and REST-based APIs, as a one-size-fits-all approach. And think of WCF as a custom-tailored suit. One is cheaper, but not as architecturally good. The other is more expensive, but also architecturally superior.

Now look at your wardrobe! How many custom-tailored suits do you have? If you are anything like me, I'm guessing you have more one size fits all T-shirts than you have custom-tailored suits.

For larger and more complex projects, you will find yourself writing more WCF services, but for a large percentage of projects, the out-of-the-box client object model and REST-based APIs are just fine.

Another instance when I personally find myself writing WCF services is when I need to break out of the limits of a sandbox solution. As I mentioned in chapter four, one of the possible ways of breaking out of the sandbox solution boundaries is to write a full trust proxy. The full trust proxy architecture however is very rigid, it requires you to shoe-horn everything you need into a few classes you have to inherit from. That makes it very inflexible. Also deployment requires you to touch the actual API. The full trust proxy has to be registered with SharePoint by calling an API method. Thus instead of using a full trust proxy, I find myself writing custom WCF services instead. This is simply because it is better architecture.

So let's next learn about writing custom WCF services in SharePoint 2010.

Writing Custom WCF Services

In this section, I will demonstrate writing a custom WCF service, deploying it in SharePoint as a solution and then using it in Silverlight and JavaScript front ends. The WCF service has access to the entire object model and it can expose custom business objects, thereby allowing scenarios such as WCF RIA services.

■**Tip** If you want to see an equivalent video version of this section, please see the video at http://blah.winsmarts. com/2010-3-Video__Telerik_Silverlight_Chart_showing_live_data_from_SharePoint_2010.aspx.

Start Visual Studio 2010 and create a new project based on the empty SharePoint project template. Call this project **CustomWCFService** and require it to be a farm solution. It has to be a farm solution because we will deploy an .svc, and its .config file to the file system. In the same solution, add a new project of template type WCF service library and call it **MyServiceLibrary**. By default, the WCF service library project type will add a Service1 service for you. Because we don't want the default service added, go ahead and delete the IService1.cs and Service1.cs files. Also open the app.config for your service library, and delete everything under the system.serviceModel element.

Next, right-click the MyServiceLibrary project and add a new WCF service called **ListService**. The intent of this service is to return the lists available in the SharePoint site. In this example, I will only show querying, but you have access to the entire object model, so you can easily extend it to update data as well.

The purpose of ListService is to return all the lists available within the site. Thus go ahead and modify the IListService.cs interface to as shown here:

```
[ServiceContract(Namespace="Winsmarts")]
public interface IListService
{
  [OperationContract]
  List<BO.List> GetLists();
}
```

As you can see, the methods that take part in the WCF operation are decorated with the [OperationContract] attribute. I'm returning a custom business object of type BO.List. The definition of BO.List is as follows:

```
[DataContract]
public class List
{
  [DataMember]
  public string Name { get; set; }
  [DataMember]
  public string Author { get; set; }
}
```

What I just did is declare the contract for the WCF service and declare the data contract of my custom business objects being sent across the wire. WCF works in an opt-out mechanism by default. Unless I decorate something with an attribute to explicitly opt in, be it a method or a property, WCF by default will choose to exclude it in the WCF contract. This minimizes the attack surface for security reasons. Also I'm returning a custom business object that has nothing to do with SharePoint yet.

It is in the actual implementation of the service that we actually talk with SharePoint. It is important to understand that you could choose to swap the implementation to a non-SharePoint implementation and develop the rest of the solution completely outside of SharePoint. You can see that technique demonstrated in this video: http://www.dnrtv.com/default.aspx?showNum=142.

However, in this scenario I will keep things to the point, so add a reference to Microsoft.SharePoint.dll in your service library project. Then modify the implementation of the service in the ListService.cs file to as shown in Listing 5-27.

Listing 5-27. *Implementation for the Service*

```
[AspNetCompatibilityRequirements(RequirementsMode=AspNetCompatibilityRequirementsMode
.Allowed)]
public class ListsService : IListsService
{
  public List<BO.List> GetLists()
  {
    List<BO.List> toReturn = new List<BO.List>();
    foreach (SPList list in SPContext.Current.Web.Lists)
        {
      toReturn.Add(
        new BO.List()
        { Name = list.Title, Author = list.Author.Name}
        );
        }
    return toReturn;
  }
}
```

The code for Listing 5-27 is quite simple. I'm simply querying for all the lists available in the site, and stuffing them into my custom business object and returning that to the caller. Of special mention here is the AspNetCompatibilityRequirements mode. Because the service will run in SharePoint 2010, by default it will run under the AspNetCompatibilityRequirements mode enabled. This makes sense because WCF is a lot bigger than just a web-based application, so for WCF to get a handle to SPContext.Current, it needs to run under the ASP.NET compatibility mode. Also what happens behind the scenes is that if you examine the web.config of any SharePoint site, it is configured to send the identity of the logged-in user to the server. It does so using the following web.config element:

```
<identity impersonate="true"/>
```

Thus when running under the ASP.NET compatibility mode, and with the end user's identity, the results that you query from SharePoint API are automatically security trimmed.

My ListsService is now written. I next need to deploy this into SharePoint using a solution package. In order to do so, I will strongly name the MyServiceLibrary.dll so it can be put in the GlobalAssemblyCache (GAC). Thus, go ahead and strongly name your MyServiceLibrary.dll by going to the project properties\signing tab.

Back in your SharePoint project, double-click the package node to open the package designer. Then at the bottom you will see the links for Design, Advanced, and Manifest, as shown in Figure 5-18.

Click the advanced button, click the Add button, and choose Add Assembly from Project Output to add the MyServiceLibrary.dll into the solution. This can be seen in Figure 5-19.

Figure 5-18. *The Design, Advanced, and Manifest buttons in a package*

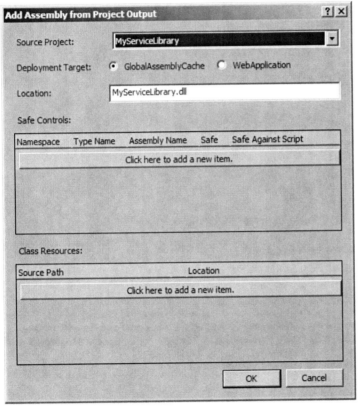

Figure 5-19. *Adding the WCF Assembly to deploy to the GAC with the solution*

At this point, your service library will get deployed into the GAC. You still need to create an endpoint within SharePoint to expose the services in the service library running inside SharePoint. To do so, right-click the CustomWCFService and add a SharePoint mapped folder. Choose to add the ISAPI mapped folder because this folder is mapped to the _vti_bin virtual directory on any SharePoint site. Adding the ISAPI mapped folder will also add a folder under ISAPI specifically for your project. This is good practice because your solution files will not accidentally overwrite some other solution files or other Microsoft files. Inside this folder, add two files called listservice.svc, and web.config. Your project structure at this time should look like Figure 5-20.

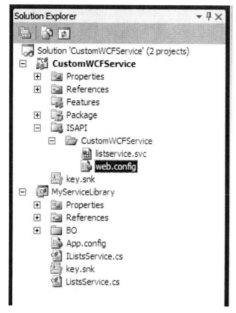

Figure 5-20. *Adding the listservice.svc and web.config at the right location*

Inside the ListService.svc file, enter the following code:

```
<%@ Assembly Name="MyServiceLibrary, Version=1.0.0.0, Culture=neutral,
PublicKeyToken=63237040b75dd29c"%>
<%@ ServiceHost Service="MyServiceLibrary.ListsService" %>
```

The ListService.svc file simply serves as an endpoint from which the service will be accessible. The name attribute in the assembly element is the assembly signature for the MyServiceLibrary.dll. Please see http://blah.winsmarts.com/2009-12-SharePoint_Productivity_Tip_of_the_day.aspx for a quick and easy way to get the assembly signatures for any assembly.

Inside the web.config file, enter the code shown in Listing 5-28.

Listing 5-28. *Contents of web.config for ListService*

```xml
<?xml version="1.0" encoding="utf-8" ?>
<configuration>
 <system.serviceModel>
  <serviceHostingEnvironment aspNetCompatibilityEnabled="true"/>
  <bindings>
   <basicHttpBinding>
    <binding name="customBasicHttpBinding">
     <security mode="TransportCredentialOnly">
      <transport clientCredentialType="Ntlm"/>
     </security>
    </binding>
   </basicHttpBinding>
  </bindings>
  <services>
   <service name="MyServiceLibrary.ListsService">
    <endpoint address="" binding="basicHttpBinding"
        contract="MyServiceLibrary.IListsService"
        bindingConfiguration="customBasicHttpBinding">
    </endpoint>
   </service>
  </services>
 </system.serviceModel>
</configuration>
```

The web.config file specified in Listing 5-28 contains the configuration information for the WCF service. Specifically, we're exposing the service over basicHttpBinding, and in order to call the service we are requiring that the NTLM credential be sent along with the request. Note that if you're using Kerberos, you will have to change the clientCredentialType to "Windows". Also we're allowing the service to run under the ASP.NET compatibility mode. Build and deploy the solution and then visit http://sp2010/_vti_bin/CustomWCFService/listservice.svc. You should see the service running, as shown in Figure 5-21.

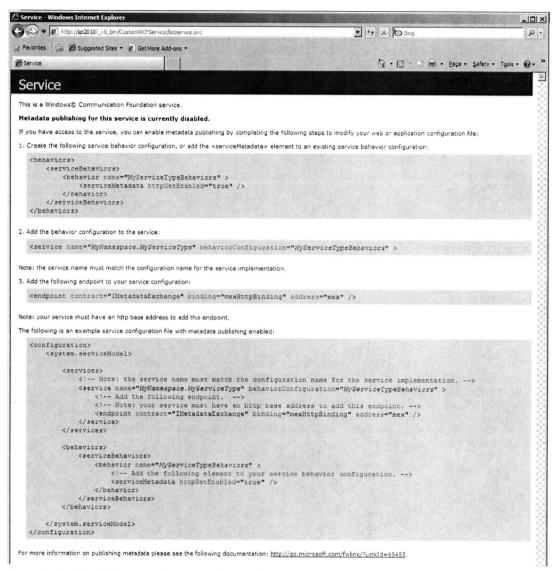

Figure 5-21. *The WCF service is now running in SharePoint*

Good! Your service is now running, and you're ready to consume it in various kinds of clients. These clients could be anything; all they require is a little bit of tweaking to your web.config file. I'm going to demonstrate the following clients:

- A simple .NET app

- A Silverlight app

- JavaScript and the ASP.NET Ajax framework

■**Tip** If you are inclined to do so, read a good book on WCF, and you will find that you can use this service in numerous other scenarios such as REST-based APIs, interprocess communication, MSMQ queues, or literally anything else.

Consuming the Service in a .NET Application

Start Visual Studio and create a new console application targeting the .NET 3.5 framework. Call it **TestWCFConsoleApp**. They are two main ways to consume a WCF service in a .NET app.

In the first approach, you add a service reference and generate a proxy. This requires the service to either support mexHttpBinding or publish previously generated metadata statically. But somehow the client application needs to access the metadata. Metadata in basicHttpBinding is simply the WSDL of the service. It is recommended that you publish previously generated metadata statically. In this approach, because the proxy is generated from the metadata, you do not need to send a DLL. This means that the consuming client can be something as different as Java and it can be on the other side of the globe on a machine over which you have no influence. But the downside of this approach is that all the validations that are embedded inside your business objects will not work on the client side.

In the second approach, the client has direct access to DLLs that hold your business objects. The disadvantage is that you have to ship the DLL in advance, but you are working with your own business objects, with your own custom validations.

If you are interested, you should also check out WCF RIA Services, in which a portion of the business objects is copied over to the front end such as Silverlight, thereby allowing you full access to business objects logic both in back ends and front ends.

Let's look at both these approaches one by one.

Approach #1: Adding a Service Reference

Because the service running inside of SharePoint does not expose the mex endpoint, you need an alternate location where the proxy can be generated. The easiest way to do this is to set the MyServiceLibrary as your startup project and add a service reference to the service running from the MyServiceLibrary. To achieve this, simply right-click the MyServicelibrary project and choose it to be the startup project. Press F5, and the service will be hosted in the system tray web server.

Examine the URL on which the service is running and add a service reference to that URL. In this case, the service was running at `http://localhost:8732/Design_Time_Addresses/MyServiceLibrary/ListsService`. Call the service reference generated proxy ServiceReference1. Adding a service reference through Visual Studio makes some inferences about the service and generates a client-side configuration file for you. Now you need to edit this file because we generated the proxy from a location different from the actual service address. Also, the proxy location was running the service under wsHttpBinding under anonymous security, whereas the real service is running inside SharePoint under

NTLM security. Thus, you need to edit the app.config file of the TestWCFConsoleApp as shown in Listing 5-29.

Listing 5-29. *The app.config File for the WCF Test Console App*

```xml
<?xml version="1.0" encoding="utf-8" ?>
<configuration>
 <system.serviceModel>
  <bindings>
   <basicHttpBinding>
    <binding name="authenticatedBasicHttpBinding">
     <security mode="TransportCredentialOnly">
      <transport clientCredentialType="Ntlm" proxyCredentialType="Ntlm"/>
      <message clientCredentialType="UserName"/>
     </security>
    </binding>
   </basicHttpBinding>
  </bindings>
  <client>
   <endpoint
    address="http://sp2010/_vti_bin/CustomWCFService/listservice.svc"
    binding="basicHttpBinding"
    bindingConfiguration="authenticatedBasicHttpBinding"
    contract="ServiceReference1.IListsService">
   </endpoint>
  </client>
 </system.serviceModel>
</configuration>
```

The edits to the app.config file simply specify that I will use basicHttpBinding and that I have to send the NTLM identity to a specific URL (SharePoint service) with my requests!

Your service reference is all set! You can now go ahead and write code as shown in Listing 5-30 in your static void main of your console application.

Listing 5-30. *Code to Call a WCF Service from a Console Application*

```csharp
ServiceReference1.ListsServiceClient client =
  new ServiceReference1.ListsServiceClient();

client.ClientCredentials.Windows.AllowedImpersonationLevel =
  TokenImpersonationLevel.Impersonation;

ServiceReference1.List[] lists = client.GetLists() ;

foreach (var list in lists)
{
            Console.WriteLine(list.Name);
}

client.Close();
```

Build and compile your application. You should see the results as shown in Figure 5-22.

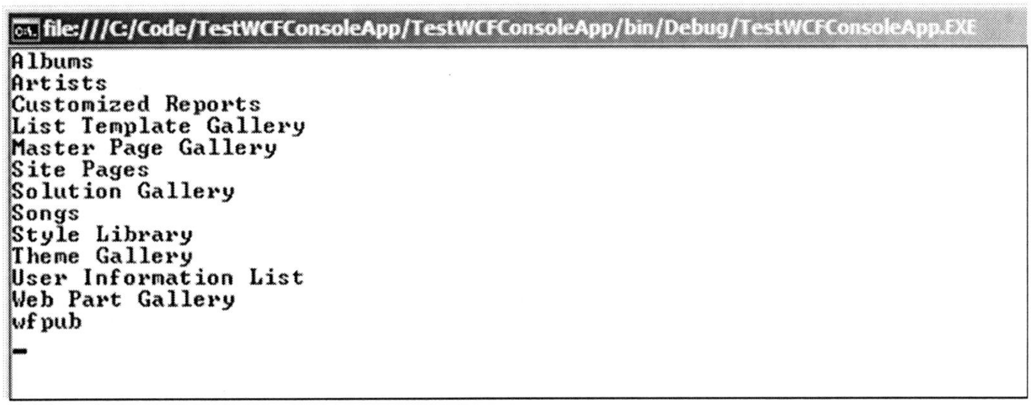

```
file:///C:/Code/TestWCFConsoleApp/TestWCFConsoleApp/bin/Debug/TestWCFConsoleApp.EXE
Albums
Artists
Customized Reports
List Template Gallery
Master Page Gallery
Site Pages
Solution Gallery
Songs
Style Library
Theme Gallery
User Information List
Web Part Gallery
wfpub
_
```

Figure 5-22. *Results queried from the WCF service*

Your console application, which might as well be a .NET 4.0 or even a Java app, can query the WCF service and show security trimmed SharePoint data.

Approach #2: Adding a DLL Reference

Create a new console application, again targeting the .NET 3.5 framework, and call it **TestWCFConsoleApp2**. In this application, add a reference to the MyServicelibrary project, which will give the console application visibility into the business objects and interfaces necessary to consume the WCF service. Also go ahead and add a reference to System.ServiceModel.

Then write code as shown in Listing 5-31 in your static void main.

Listing 5-31. *Calling a WCF Service from a Console Application Without a Reference*

```
BasicHttpBinding myBinding = new BasicHttpBinding();
myBinding.Security.Mode = BasicHttpSecurityMode.TransportCredentialOnly;
myBinding.Security.Transport.ClientCredentialType = HttpClientCredentialType.Ntlm;
myBinding.Security.Transport.ProxyCredentialType = HttpProxyCredentialType.Ntlm;
myBinding.Security.Message.ClientCredentialType = BasicHttpMessageCredentialType.UserName;

ChannelFactory<IListsService> channelFactory = new ChannelFactory<IListsService>(
  myBinding,
  new EndpointAddress("http://sp2010/_vti_bin/CustomWCFService/listservice.svc")
  );
channelFactory.Credentials.Windows.AllowedImpersonationLevel =
  System.Security.Principal.TokenImpersonationLevel.Impersonation;
```

```
IListsService listService = channelFactory.CreateChannel();

var lists = listService.GetLists();

foreach (var list in lists)
{
  Console.WriteLine(list.Name);
}
```

Execute this application and you should see the lists being written out on console just like before.

If you look at the code in Listing 5-30 and Listing 5-31 closely, you should notice some similarities. In both instances, we are getting an instance to basic HTTP binding and are configuring it to work under the NTLM authentication. We're setting the client impersonation level. The only difference is how we're getting a handle to a proxy. In one instance, the proxy is generated based on the published metadata. In the second instance, the proxy is generated using the channel factory and strongly typed to the actual business object.

Consuming the Service in a Silverlight application

In your CustomWCFService SharePoint project, add a Silverlight application called **SLLists**. When prompted to host the Silverlight application in a new web site, choose to not create that web site. As a mentioned earlier, WCF allows you to swap both the front end and back end as long as the contract remains the same. Thus sometimes it is helpful to add this external web application, not debug in SharePoint, and send dummy objects. These dummy objects can then be used for TDD purposes or to build UI inside Expression Blend or such! This technique is described in depth in a video you can find at http://www.dnrtv.com/default.aspx?showNum=142.

Back in your Silverlight application, choose to add a service reference. When prompted, click the Discover button to add the service reference being generated directly from MyServiceLibrary. You can also use a utility called SLSVCUtil.exe to generate proxies and add them manually to your Silverlight project. Just like the console application, in order to generate a ServiceReference in Silverlight, the service needs to publish metadata. Because the SharePoint service is not publishing metadata, we can choose to generate the service proxy from MyServiceLibrary instead. However before you can successfully generate such a ServiceReference in Silverlight, you need to edit the app.config file of your MyServicelibrary to use basicHttpBinding instead of wsHttpBinding. To do this, look for the following line of code in the App.config of MyServiceLibrary:

```
<endpoint address="" binding="wsHttpBinding" contract="MyServiceLibrary.IListsService">
```

Change it to this:

```
<endpoint address="" binding="basicHttpBinding" contract="MyServiceLibrary.IListsService">
```

You have to make this change because Silverlight can talk only to basicHttpBinding endpoints or REST-based APIs. Call the proxy **ServiceReference1**.

With the ServiceReference added, now you can start writing some Silverlight Code. Go ahead and edit the MainPage.xaml file to look like Listing 5-32.

Listing 5-32. *Code for MainPage.xaml*

```
<Grid x:Name="LayoutRoot" Background="White">
  <ListBox x:Name="lists">
    <ListBox.ItemTemplate>
      <DataTemplate>
        <StackPanel Orientation="Horizontal">
          <TextBlock Text="{Binding Path=Name}" Margin="10 0 10 0"/>
          <TextBlock Text="{Binding Path=Author}" Margin="10 0 10 0"/>
        </StackPanel>
      </DataTemplate>
    </ListBox.ItemTemplate>
  </ListBox>
</Grid>
```

I've declared a simple listbox, in which I intend to databind my custom business object. Back in MainPage.xaml.cs, add the code shown in Listing 5-33.

Listing 5-33. *Code for MainPage.xaml.cs*

```
public MainPage()
{
  InitializeComponent();
  this.Loaded += new RoutedEventHandler(MainPage_Loaded);
}

void MainPage_Loaded(object sender, RoutedEventArgs e)
{
  ServiceReference1.ListsServiceClient client = new ServiceReference1.ListsServiceClient(
    new BasicHttpBinding(),
    new EndpointAddress("http://sp2010/_vti_bin/CustomWCFService/listservice.svc"));

  client.GetListsCompleted += (sender1, e1) =>
    {
      lists.ItemsSource = e1.Result;
    };

  client.GetListsAsync();
}
```

The code is quite similar to what you have seen before. I'm making an asynchronous called to the WCF endpoint and data binding the results to the list box I had declared in Listing 5-32. You would also note that for simplicity I hardcoded the endpoint address. If you wanted to not hardcode the endpoint address you should follow the instructions shown at `http://blah.winsmarts.com/2009-5-Specifying_relative_URLs_to_Silverlight_WCF_EndPoints.aspx`.

Deploy the XAP output of SLlists as a module in the custom WCF service SharePoint project. Build and deploy the solution and use the out-of-the-box Silverlight viewer WebPart in SharePoint to view the Silverlight application running inside SharePoint. You should see the lists and the author of the lists retrieved, as shown in Figure 5-23.

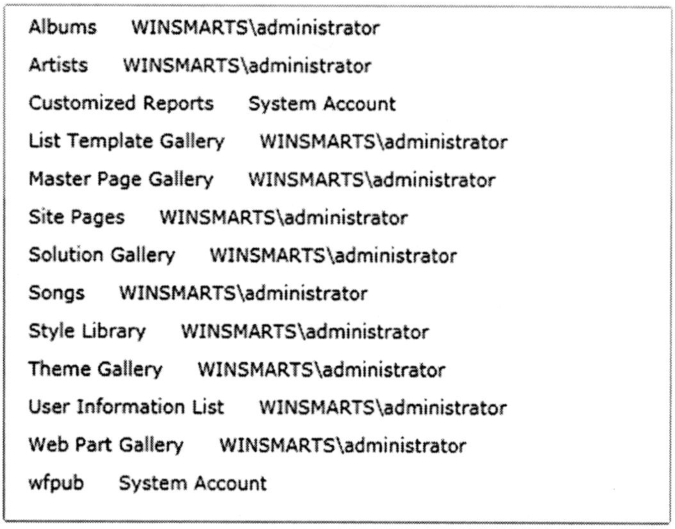

```
Albums      WINSMARTS\administrator

Artists     WINSMARTS\administrator

Customized Reports    System Account

List Template Gallery    WINSMARTS\administrator

Master Page Gallery    WINSMARTS\administrator

Site Pages    WINSMARTS\administrator

Solution Gallery    WINSMARTS\administrator

Songs    WINSMARTS\administrator

Style Library    WINSMARTS\administrator

Theme Gallery    WINSMARTS\administrator

User Information List    WINSMARTS\administrator

Web Part Gallery    WINSMARTS\administrator

wfpub    System Account
```

Figure 5-23. *WCF service results being shown in a Silverlight UI*

Consuming the Service in ASP.NET Ajax

ASP.NET Ajax cannot consume services that are exposed over basicHttpBinding. However, it can consume services that are exposed over webHttpBinding and use the enableWebScript behavior.

What this means to you is that with a little tweak in the web.config file of the service itself, you can easily consume this service in ASP.NET Ajax JavaScript–based code without any changes to the service. Now you can see where the client object model and ADO.NET Data Services get their good looks.

Go ahead and modify the web.config file under CustomWCFService\web.config, as shown in Listing 5-34.

Listing 5-34. *Modified web.confg to Add Support for a JavaScript Proxy*

```xml
<?xml version="1.0" encoding="utf-8" ?>
<configuration>
 <system.serviceModel>
  <serviceHostingEnvironment aspNetCompatibilityEnabled="true"/>
  <bindings>
   <basicHttpBinding>
    <binding name="customBasicHttpBinding">
     <security mode="TransportCredentialOnly">
      <transport clientCredentialType="Ntlm"/>
     </security>
    </binding>
   </basicHttpBinding>
```

```
      <webHttpBinding>
       <binding name="customWebHttpBinding">
        <security mode="TransportCredentialOnly">
         <transport clientCredentialType="Ntlm"/>
        </security>
       </binding>
      </webHttpBinding>
     </bindings>
     <behaviors>
      <endpointBehaviors>
       <behavior name="webScriptBehavior">
        <enableWebScript/>
       </behavior>
      </endpointBehaviors>
     </behaviors>
     <services>
      <service name="MyServiceLibrary.ListsService">
       <endpoint address="" binding="basicHttpBinding"
           contract="MyServiceLibrary.IListsService"
           bindingConfiguration="customBasicHttpBinding">
       </endpoint>
       <endpoint address="/javascript" binding="webHttpBinding"
           behaviorConfiguration="webScriptBehavior"
           contract="MyServiceLibrary.IListsService"
           bindingConfiguration="customWebHttpBinding">
       </endpoint>
      </service>
     </services>
    </system.serviceModel>
</configuration>
```

Listing 5-34 may seem large, but don't be overwhelmed; it is actually quite simple. Let's break it down. First you added a new endpoint:

```
<endpoint address="/javascript" binding="webHttpBinding"
    behaviorConfiguration="webScriptBehavior"
    contract="MyServiceLibrary.IListsService"
    bindingConfiguration="customWebHttpBinding">
</endpoint>
```

This endpoint uses webHttpBinding. It also uses the binding configuration of customWebHttpBinding, which is exactly the same as customBasicHttpBinding. It simply forces the browser to send the identity of the logged-in user to the server.

Also, it uses webScriptBehavior as its endpoint behavior. This behavior, as you can see from the web.config file, specifies the enableWebScript behavior.

Another thing to note is that the address of this service is different from the basicHttpBinding service. You cannot have two services with the same contracts at the same URL.

Now, in your browser, visit this site: http://sp2010/_vti_bin/CustomWCFService/ listservice.svc/javascript/jsDebug.

SharePoint will prompt you to download a file, as shown in Figure 5-24.

Figure 5-24. *A jsDebug file that the browser is prompting to download*

This file contains the automatically generated JavaScript proxy that can now be used with ASP.NET Ajax. With the JavaScript proxy now set up, you can write very simple object-oriented Javascript code to fetch results from the WCF service from JavaScript. The code can be seen in Listing 5-35.

Listing 5-35. *ASP.NET Ajax Javascript Code to Query the WCF Service*

```
<asp:ScriptManagerProxy ID="ScriptManagerProxy1" runat="server">
  <Services>
    <asp:ServiceReference Path="/_vti_bin/CustomWCFService/listservice.svc/javascript" />
  </Services>
</asp:ScriptManagerProxy>

<script type="text/javascript">
  function GetResults()
  {
                            var resultsDiv = $get("results");

    resultsDiv.innerHTML = "Fetching results .. ";

    var proxy = new Winsmarts.IListsService();
    proxy.GetLists(onSuccess, onFail) ;
  }
```

```
function onSuccess(listsResult)
{
  var result = "" ;
  for (var list in listsResult)
  {
    var listDetails = listsResult[list] ;
    result = result + listDetails.Name + " : " + listDetails.Author + "<br/>"
  }
  var resultsDiv = $get("results");
  resultsDiv.innerHTML = result ;
}

function onFail(err){
  var resultsDiv = $get("results");
  resultsDiv.innerHTML = err._message;
}

_spBodyOnLoadFunctionNames.push("GetResults");
</script>
<div id="results"/>
```

I'm using the ScriptManagerProxy to register a reference to my WCF service. This will automatically translate into /jsDebug or /js, depending on whether you're in debug mode. Once the service reference is set up, it is a matter of executing an asynchronous call to the GetLists method and then passing in the onSuccess and onFail event handlers. The event handlers can then take care of displaying the results or the error message appropriately. This can be seen in Figure 5-25.

The ASPX with the code is available in the associated code download as WCFTestPage.aspx.

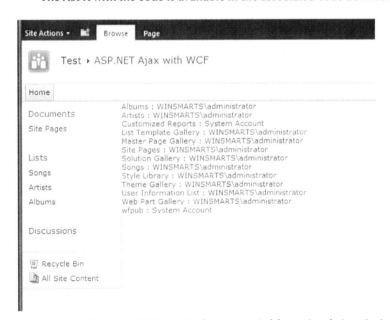

Figure 5-25. *The same WCF service being queried from simple JavaScript*

Summary

It would be a vast understatement to say that this chapter covered a lot of new ground. Computers are simply information management machines. So far in this book you should be familiar with the ability to query data and update data into SharePoint servers. You also looked at various facilities to query both on the server side and on the client side.

On the client side, I presented various options in this chapter: the client object model, ADO.NET Data Services, and custom WCF services.

You also created some interesting lists as we went along. Lists are how SharePoint stores information. These lists can be organized in numerous ways, and come with a number of associated concepts to learn, such as list definitions, content types, custom field types, and so on and so forth.

Now that you understand how to save data into and query data out of SharePoint, it is now time to focus your attention on organizing data into SharePoint.

We will start doing that in the next chapter.

CHAPTER 6

■ ■ ■

Managing SharePoint Data: Part 1

Let me guess, every software program that you've ever worked with stores data. SQL server stores data, excel stores data, even notepad saves data. What differentiates one program with another is in their ability to manage the data they store. Put very simplistically, SharePoint is nothing but a huge data management and storage engine. However, it is in the management aspects of its data storing where SharePoint truly shines. The SharePoint platform comes with many features that allow you to effectively manage and control the collection, lifecycle, and presentation of this information in your organization. It is all these functions combined together that allow SharePoint to act as a very effective content management system.

At a very fundamental level, SharePoint stores all of its data in lists. Lists are represented by the SPList object in the object model. Another class that inherits from SPList is the SPDocumentLibrary class. SPDocumentLibrary is a document library. Therefore, all document libraries are lists. In Chapter 2, you looked at the ability to create some basic lists and document libraries. Many of these lists were based on certain preset definitions. For example, there was the announcements list and there was the contacts list. There was the wiki page library and a simple document library. By creating any such list, you got certain facilities out of the box. These are the views that were created on the list, the columns that were created for you and perhaps a few other things. All of these constitute the list definition. Based on existing list definitions, you could create newer list instances. Once you create a list instance then in that list instance, or in short, list, you can add new items.

Once you create such a list various other questions arise. What rules can be associated with such a list? How can I use this data properly? What conditions or validations can I put in this list? How much data can I put in this list? You may be able to answer a few of these based on what you saw in Chapter 2. In this section of the book, I will delve into all of these details in much further detail.

Another concept that may not have been very apparent yet was the concept of content types. Content types are an invaluable tool that allows you to organize and manage information in SharePoint. Content types are an indispensable feature of SharePoint foundation, and by defining a content type you really are defining a number of things for your data. You are defining the structure, workflows, policies, etc., in a content type. Also, content types can inherit from one another. In defining the structure of a content type, you also define the various columns that can exist in the content type based on existing field definitions. A field definition controls various aspects of the kind of data you can put in a field and some rules around such data.

Starting with this chapter, I will begin to explore each one of these topics in greater depth. At the very least, I assume that you understand how to create a list from the SharePoint user interface, you are familiar with some of out of the box list definitions, and you have the ability to do developer-like tasks such as writing WebParts, features, solutions, and client-side APIs such as the client object model and so forth.

Given that you have the background knowledge, let's begin with content types.

Content Types

Content types are a fundamental concept of SharePoint foundation. Any data that you put inside SharePoint gets associated with some content type. Any content type gives you a number of reusable settings. The reusable settings consist of the structure of information, associated workflows, information management policies, field rendering templates, and in the case of documents—document information panels and document formats and templates.

As an example in your organization, you may produce proposals for clients or software defect bug reports. It is possible that both of these are Word documents, but their meanings are quite different. The workflows that they need to be routed through are quite different and the associated collected metadata on each of these can also be quite different. Therefore, it makes sense to differentiate between them as their own content types.

In fact, any content that you put inside of SharePoint automatically gets associated with some content type. At the very base, you have the "item content type," with just one possible column in it called Title. For every document that you upload into SharePoint, it gets associated with that document type content type. So any further content types you create you are basically inheriting from these base content types, or another content type that in turn inherits from these base content types. The document content type also inherits from the item content type, so the granddaddy of all content types is the item content type.

Let's examine this as a practical example. Let's say you're setting up the SharePoint site to collect information about zoo animals. You could just create a custom list and add the necessary columns in it to capture all the metadata necessary for a zoo animal. That would allow you to capture data as the default "item" content type, thus making your zoo animal of about the same category as school supplies. A better way of storing zoo animals would be to give zoo animals their own content type.

To create a content type for zoo animals, visit your SharePoint site at http://sp2010 and click site actions\site settings. Then, under the gallery section click the site content types link and you will see all the existing content types that are currently set up in your SharePoint site. As you can see, even out of the box Microsoft has made plenty of use of content types. Next, click the create button, as shown in Figure 6-1 to create a new content type.

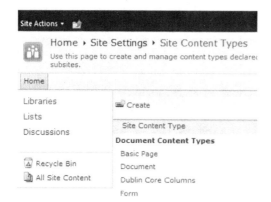

Figure 6-1. *The Site Content Types Page. The Create Content Type Button.*

Fill in the provided form, as shown in Figure 6-2.

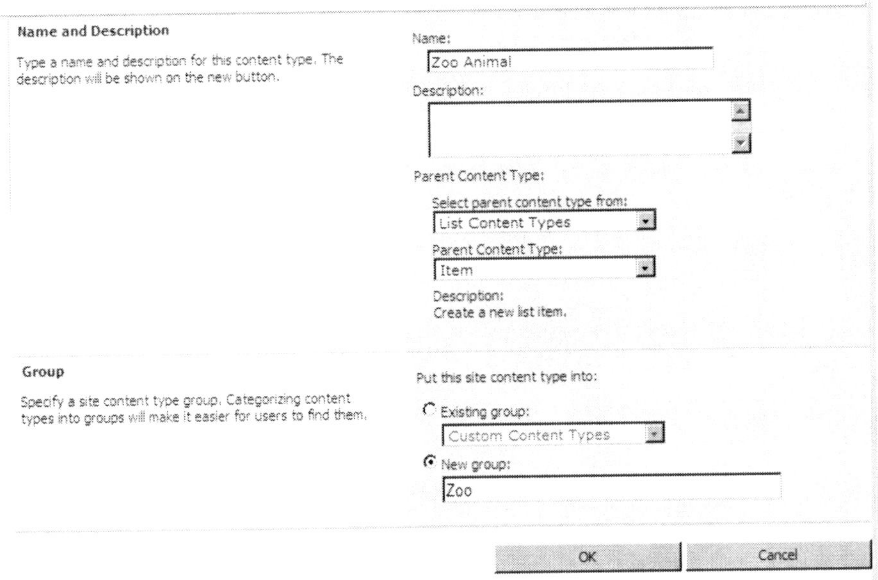

Figure 6-2. *New content type details*

As you can see, you've created a new zoo animal content type and are inheriting that content type from the base item content type. Also, you've put this content type in its own group called zoo. Click the OK button to create the new content type. SharePoint will now take you to a page that shows you the details of the newly created content type. The URL of this page will look a little bit like this: /_layouts/ManageContentType.aspx?ctype=0x010070A9BD7BBA699D48B92FE21F1632CC28.

This ctype querystring parameter is the content type ID of your newly created content type. Your ID might be different, but it would start with "0x01". This is because "0x01", is the content type ID for Zoo Animal's parent content type which is the item content type. Also, on the same page you will see a number of other things. You will see a settings section where you can specify additional settings available on the content type such as associated workflows. Under the columns section is where you can set up the structure of your content type, i.e., what columns are available in the content type. When setting up the structure for your content type, you can either choose to add from an existing site column or you can choose to create a new site column. Site columns are what define individual columns in a content type.

Open a new browser window and visit the site settings for your http://sp2010 site one more time. Under the Galleries section, you will see a link for site columns. Clicking on that link will show you all the site columns that have already been set up for you in the SharePoint site. One site column can be used across multiple content types. Perhaps you found out in an earlier zoo that if you mix Carnivores and Herbivores together, somehow you are only left with Carnivores? For the zoo animal content type, intend to differentiate between carnivores and herbivores. In the site columns gallery, click the create button to create a new site column. Go ahead and fill out the form, as shown in Figure 6-3.

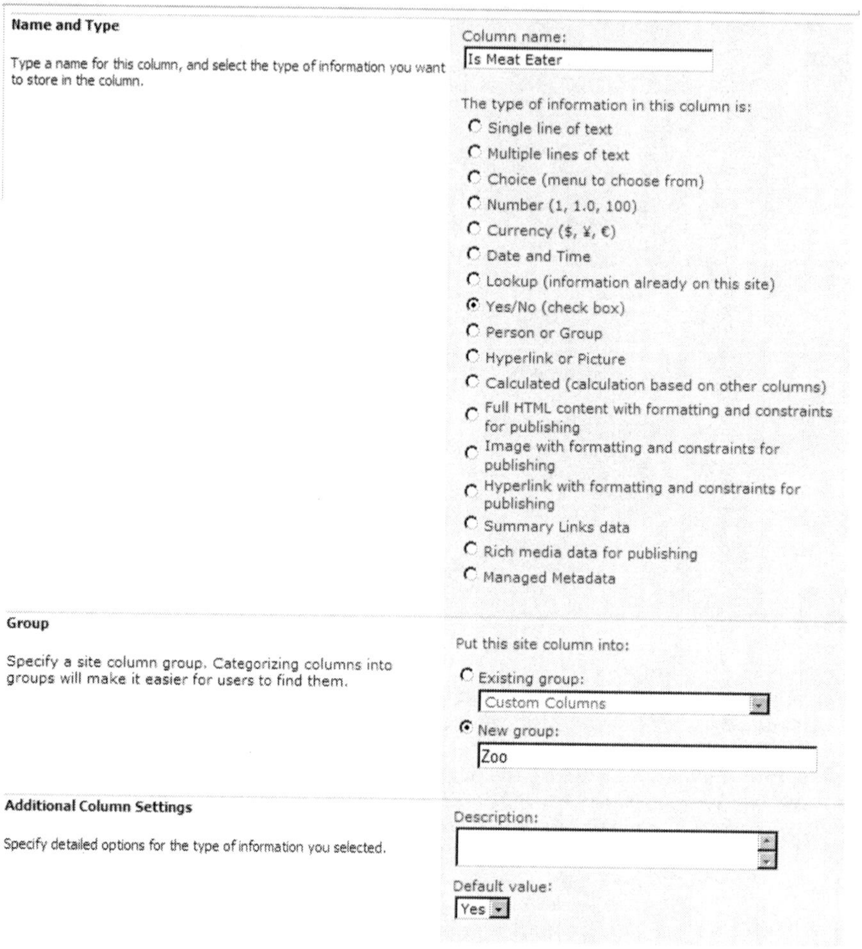

Name and Type

Type a name for this column, and select the type of information you want to store in the column.

Column name:

Is Meat Eater

The type of information in this column is:

○ Single line of text
○ Multiple lines of text
○ Choice (menu to choose from)
○ Number (1, 1.0, 100)
○ Currency ($, ¥, €)
○ Date and Time
○ Lookup (information already on this site)
◉ Yes/No (check box)
○ Person or Group
○ Hyperlink or Picture
○ Calculated (calculation based on other columns)
○ Full HTML content with formatting and constraints for publishing
○ Image with formatting and constraints for publishing
○ Hyperlink with formatting and constraints for publishing
○ Summary Links data
○ Rich media data for publishing
○ Managed Metadata

Group

Specify a site column group. Categorizing columns into groups will make it easier for users to find them.

Put this site column into:

○ Existing group:

Custom Columns

◉ New group:

Zoo

Additional Column Settings

Specify detailed options for the type of information you selected.

Description:

Default value:

Yes

Figure 6-3. *New site column details*

As you can see, you're creating a new site column called "Is Meat Eater". This will be a yes/no check box, with the default value of yes. Also, put this site column in its own group called "Zoo".

Note that you can base your new site column on a number of preexisting definitions such as single line of text, multiple lines of text, choice, and so forth. These preexisting definitions are referred to as field types. As you will see in the section "Custom Field Types," it is possible to write your own custom field types as well. Go ahead and play with the site columns a little bit and explore some of the additional field types available. I should point out that all your work so far is limited to the individual site collection you're working in, so if you completely mess up your site collection just delete the site collection and recreate it, and you'll start from zero again.

Once you have created that "is meat eater" site column, return to the browser instance where you are managing your "Zoo Animal" content type. If you have accidentally closed the previous browser window, you can find that content type again by visiting the site content types gallery under site settings and clicking on the zoo animal content type under the groups zoo at the bottom of the page.

Back in the zoo animal content type, under the Columns section, click that add from existing site columns link. In the form that shows up, look for the new "Is Meat Eater" site column you had set up previously and add it to your zoo animal content type.

Your content type is now set up. Next let's use it in a list. Create a new custom list called "SharePoint Zoo". The list definition for the custom list determines that there is only one content type associated with the newly created list instance. That single content type is the item content type. Using the ribbon under the list tab, visit the list settings link. On the list settings page, you will see various settings you can manage for the list. Click the advanced settings link under the general settings section. At the very top under advanced settings, you should see a section allowing or disallowing the management of content types in the list. This can be seen in Figure 6-4.

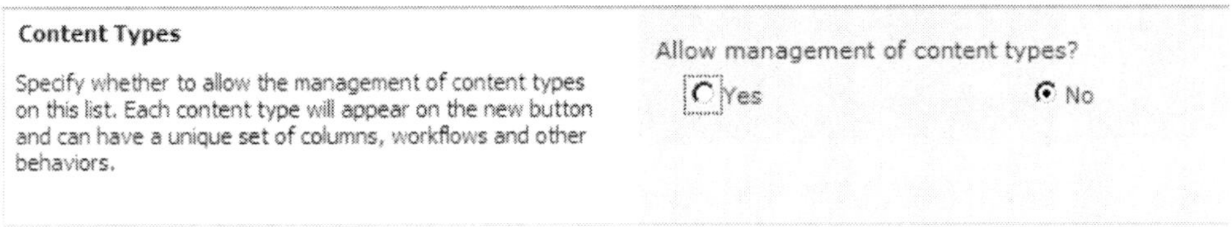

Content Types

Specify whether to allow the management of content types on this list. Each content type will appear on the new button and can have a unique set of columns, workflows and other behaviors.

Allow management of content types?

○ Yes   ◉ No

Figure 6-4. *Enabling management of content types*

By default, the custom list definition locks its list instances to the content types that are defined in the list definition. Since you need to associate the zoo animal content type with the SharePoint zoo list, choose to allow management content type by selecting the yes radio button, and then hit OK at the bottom of the page.

This will take you back to the list settings page except now a section for the management of content types will become available. This can be seen in Figure 6-5.

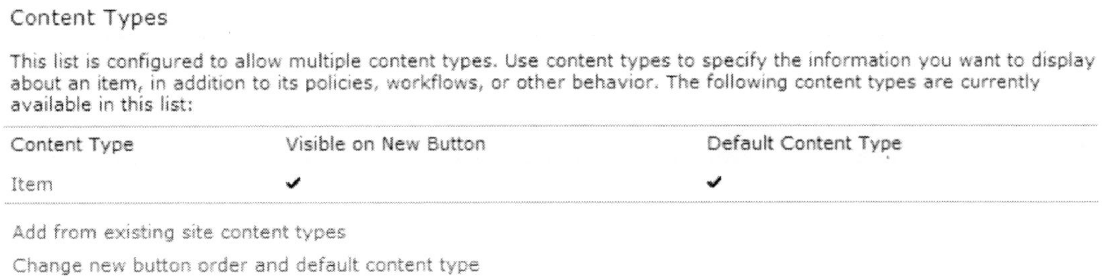

Content Types

This list is configured to allow multiple content types. Use content types to specify the information you want to display about an item, in addition to its policies, workflows, or other behavior. The following content types are currently available in this list:

Content Type	Visible on New Button	Default Content Type
Item	✔	✔

Add from existing site content types

Change new button order and default content type

Figure 6-5. *Management of content types*

Click the add from existing site content types link and add the zoo animal content type to this list. If you wish, you can associate more content types in the list, delete the existing item content type, or you can change the default content type as well. While still under lists settings, click the item content type link and choose to delete the item content type from the SharePoint zoo list.

■**Note** Did you just delete the item content type? Yes, you did. What happens to all the other content types that inherit from the item content type? What is important to realize here is that when you associate a content type with a list, a copy of that content type is created in the list. Therefore, if you delete a particular content type from the list settings page, you're only deleting the copy. You're not deleting it from the Content Types gallery from the site settings page. This also means that you can edit a content type by editing the copy of it that has been created in a list. Editing the copy will not affect the master content type in the content type gallery, and thus will not affect everything that inherits from the master. This is a technique that you will find yourself using frequently.

Now let's go back to the SharePoint zoo list and click the add new item link in the SharePoint zoo list. You should see a form, as shown in Figure 6-6.

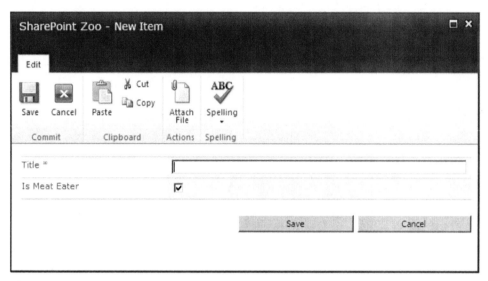

Figure 6-6. *Your content type in action*

As you can see, the definition of the content type now drives the forms of the list. Creating new items in this list will now also automatically associate them with the zoo animal content type. Now you could argue that you could have just created the "is meat eater" column in the list directly. What is the benefit of taking the content type route? There are many benefits. Because your data is now segregated from normal list items, it is more findable, you can execute custom search queries against the content type only, you can associate workflows, and many other such advantages. Let's see one of those in action.

Next, add a few animals in this list. Now let's say you had a business problem of aggregating all instances of the zoo animals from various lists in a singular view. How would you do that?

Because you segregated your data as its own content type it is now possible to do that. In order to do so, go into site actions\site settings and under site collection administration, click the site collections feature link. Then activate the SharePoint Server Publishing Infrastructure feature. This will make the content query WebPart available for use. Back on the homepage of the site, drop an instance of the content query WebPart. You will find this WebPart in the content rollup section. Now edit the content query WebPart, and configure it to show all items of the zoo animal content type from all lists that are based on the custom list definition. This can be seen in Figure 6-7.

Figure 6-7. *Query based on content type*

Your final configured WebPart can be seen in Figure 6-8.

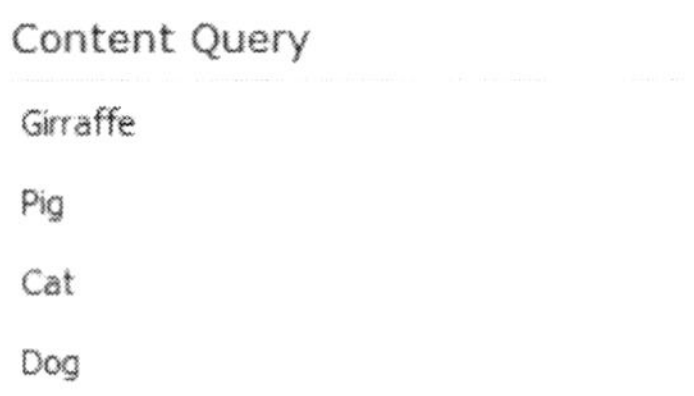

Content Query

Girraffe

Pig

Cat

Dog

Figure 6-8. *Results of content query*

The content query WebPart is an invaluable tool in your arsenal. Play with it a little bit more and see what else you can do.

You just created a new content type through the browser. You might have also noticed that, SharePoint generated a content type ID for you. What if you wanted to control this content type ID? This is important especially considering that you may have multiple environments in which you may want the content type ID to be consistent. Or you may want to content type ID to be consistent across site collections? What if you wanted your content type ID to use a site column that uses a custom field type? There are many other such scenarios that a developer will find useful in delivering a typical SharePoint project. Let's start by looking at how you would write your own custom field types.

Custom Field Types

When you add a new site column into the site columns gallery in a site collection, or you add a new column into a list, you base that column based on a bunch of preexisting field definitions. For example, you could choose to create the new column as a single line of text, multiple lines of text, be driven by Metadata, or even be driven by external data. When making that choice, SharePoint prompts you with a user interface with many radio buttons. This is shown in Figure 6-9.

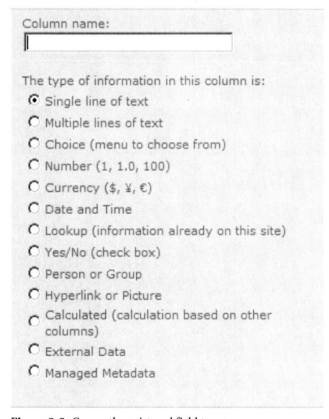

Figure 6-9. *Currently registered field types*

Those various choices in those radio buttons are referred to as field types. You can write your own field type which is referred to as a custom field type.

The custom field type I intend to write will present the end user with a google auto suggest like experience. The values will be driven from a list, and to keep things simple you're going to create a list based on the Custom List definition. The name of the list would be "Songs," and you will put some of my favorite songs in this list. When the user begins to type "Aer" in this textbox, the system will prompt the user with Aerosmith's "Dude looks like a lady" or "Crazy," and Jefferson Aeroplane's "Need somebody to love." Obviously, I have prepopulated these and other such songs in the "Song" list beforehand. Typing the first three characters in this textbox executes a CAML query on the "Songs" list, and these results are somehow shown as a list on the client side.

To achieve this, you will have to write a custom field type. In order to write this custom field type, you could take many approaches. You could use the ClientObject model and jQuery or you could write the JavaScript yourself. The approach taken in this book is that you will write a custom field type that builds upon the Ajax toolkit for .NET 3.5. Note that since the latest version of .NET is 4.0, the latest version of the Ajax tool kit available is targeted at .NET 4.0. That won't work with SharePoint 2010 until SharePoint 2010 works on .NET 4.0. You can, however, download the .NET 3.5 Ajax tool kit from the following URL: http://ajaxcontroltoolkit.codeplex.com/Release/ProjectReleases.aspx?ReleaseId=33804.

Start by creating a new empty SharePoint project in Visual Studio 2010, call it "SongTypeField". In this project, add a reference to the AjaxControlToolkit.dll that you just downloaded from codeplex. Writing a custom field type requires you to deploy a file at SharePointRoot\Template\XML. This file must have a filename that starts with fldTypes_*.xml. Whenever SharePoint starts, or whenever the IIS application pool starts or restarts, all these xml files in this directory are read, and they contain the field type definitions for all available fields in SharePoint. In your project, add a mapped folder for TEMPLATE\XML and inside that folder drop in a file called fldTypes_AutoComplete.xml. The contents of this file can be seen in Listing 6-1.

Listing 6-1. *Contents of fldTypes_AutoComplete.xml*

```xml
<?xml version="1.0" encoding="utf-8" ?>
<FieldTypes>
 <FieldType>
  <Field Name="TypeName">AutoCompleteField</Field>
  <Field Name="ParentType">Text</Field>
  <Field Name="TypeDisplayName">Auto Complete Song</Field>
  <Field Name="TypeShortDescription">Auto Complete Song</Field>
  <Field Name="UserCreatable">TRUE</Field>
  <Field Name="ShowInListCreate">TRUE</Field>
  <Field Name="ShowInSurveyCreate">TRUE</Field>
  <Field Name="ShowInDocumentLibraryCreate">TRUE</Field>
  <Field Name="ShowInColumnTemplateCreate">TRUE</Field>
  <Field Name="FieldTypeClass">
   SongTypeField.AutoCompleteField, SongTypeField, Version=1.0.0.0, Culture=neutral,
PublicKeyToken=c1944463f56d857a
  </Field>
 </FieldType>
</FieldTypes>
```

You can view the full possible schema for this file on MSDN. In Listing 6-1, I had to find some basic attributes of the new custom field type I intended to code. Whenever I am authoring a custom field type, I have to specify a FieldTypeClass. This attribute tells SharePoint with the actual implementation of my custom field type is. The implementation for AutoCompleteField can be seen in Listing 6-2.

Listing 6-2. *AutoCompleteField Implementation*

```
public class AutoCompleteField : SPFieldText
{
  public AutoCompleteField(
    SPFieldCollection fields, string fieldName) :
    base(fields, fieldName) { }
  public AutoCompleteField(
    SPFieldCollection fields,
    string typeName, string displayName) :
    base(fields, typeName, displayName) { }

  public override BaseFieldControl FieldRenderingControl
  {
    get
    {
      BaseFieldControl fieldControl = new AutoCompleteFieldControl();
      fieldControl.FieldName = InternalName;
      return fieldControl;
    }
  }
}
```

As you can see, I'm overriding the FieldRenderingControl property and I am returning an instance of the AutoCompleteFieldControl class. The AutoCompleteField control class is where the actual implementation of my field type goes. This can be a pure server control or it can be something that loads a user control. The AutoCompleteFieldControl class will directly or indirectly inherit from the BaseFieldControl base class.

In this particular implementation, since you intend to use the Ajax toolkit, it is a lot easier to write this code as a user control rather than a server control. Therefore, the implementation of the AutoCompleteFieldControl can be seen in Listing 6-3.

Listing 6-3. *Implementation for the AutoCompleteFieldControl*

```
public class AutoCompleteFieldControl : BaseFieldControl
{
  protected TextBox autoCompleteField;

  public override object Value
  {
    get
    {
      EnsureChildControls();
      return autoCompleteField.Text;
    }
    set
    {
      EnsureChildControls();
      autoCompleteField.Text = this.ItemFieldValue as String;
    }
  }
```

```
protected override void CreateChildControls()
{
  if (this.Field == null || this.ControlMode == SPControlMode.Display)
    return;
  base.CreateChildControls();

  autoCompleteField = TemplateContainer.FindControl("autoCompleteField") as TextBox;
}

protected override string DefaultTemplateName
{
  get
  {
    return "AutoCompleteFieldTemplate";
  }
}
}
```

In Listing 6-3, there are a number of interesting things. Let's start from the bottom. There is a property DefaultTemplateName. This should return the ID of the SharePoint:RenderingTemplate control that contains the actual implementation of the user interface of my custom feed control. This SharePoint:RenderingTemplate is in any of the ASCX files in the SharePointRoot\ControlTemplates virtual directory.

Therefore, add the ControlTemplates SharePoint mapped folder in your project and add an AutoCompleteField.ascx file in this folder. When adding this as ASCX, there are two important things to watch out for. First, that this ASCX cannot have a code behind, and second, this ASCX needs to live in the ControlTemplates directory not in a sub directory under ControlTemplates. This new ASCX and the code in Listing 6-3 together provide the actual implementation of the custom field type. The code for the ASCX can be seen in Listing 6-4.

Listing 6-4. *AutoCompleteField.ascx Implementation*

```
<SharePoint:RenderingTemplate ID="AutoCompleteFieldTemplate" runat="server">
  <Template>
    <asp:TextBox runat="server" ID="autoCompleteField" Width="100%" autocomplete="off" />
    <ajaxToolkit:AutoCompleteExtender
        runat="server"
        BehaviorID="AutoCompleteEx"
        ID="autoComplete1"
        TargetControlID="autoCompleteField"
        ServicePath="/_vti_bin/SongTypeField/AjaxToolkitMusic.svc"
        ServiceMethod="GetTopSongs"
        MinimumPrefixLength="1"
        CompletionInterval="1000"
        EnableCaching="true"
        CompletionSetCount="10"
        ShowOnlyCurrentWordInCompletionListItem="true"
        FirstRowSelected="true">
    </ajaxToolkit:AutoCompleteExtender>
  </Template>
</SharePoint:RenderingTemplate>
```

Do note that I omitted the assembly, register and import tags from Listing 6-4 for brevity. You can find those in the associated code download. Now to understand how the custom field definition works, compare Listing 6-4 and Listing 6-3 in tandem. Note that Listing 6-4 contains a textbox called autoCompleteField. You will find a protected textbox by the name of autoCompleteField in Listing 6-3 as well. Also, in the CreateChildControls method of the AutoCompleteFieldControl, you will see the value of this textbox being set as shown in the following:

```
autoCompleteField =
  TemplateContainer.FindControl("autoCompleteField") as TextBox;
```

Once this value has been set, in Listing 6-3 with in the AutoCompleteFieldControl, override the "Value" property to set and get the value of this autoCompleteField, which is also the value for this custom field type.

Now focus your attention on the rest of Listing 6-4. In Listing 6-4, you also see an entry for the AutoCompleteExtender. This is a standard control in the Ajax toolkit, which fetches various values as a string array from a WCF service, and shows them in a google suggest/autocomplete like behavior under the target textbox. As you can see from the various properties on the AutoCompleteExtender in Listing 6-4, you are querying a service located at /_vti_bin/SongTypeField/AjaxToolkitMusic.svc, and you are querying a method called GetTopSongs.

Therefore, you need to implement a WCF service in your project as well, which will be located at /_vti_bin/SongTypeField/AjaxToolkitMusic.svc and will have a method called GetTopSongs, which will return a string array. Add the new class in your project and call it AjaxToolkitSongQuery.cs. The code for the WCF service implemented in AjaxToolkitSongQuery.cs can be seen in Listing 6-5.

Listing 6-5. *AjaxToolkitSongQuery WCF Service*

```
[ServiceContract(Namespace = "winsmarts")]
[AspNetCompatibilityRequirements(RequirementsMode =
AspNetCompatibilityRequirementsMode.Allowed)]
public class AjaxToolkitSongQuery
{
  [OperationContract]
  public string[] GetTopSongs(string prefixText, int count)
  {
    List<string> songs = new List<string>();

    XmlDocument camlDocument = new XmlDocument();
    camlDocument.LoadXml(
      @"<Where>
        <Contains>
          <FieldRef Name='Title' />
          <Value Type='Text'>[prefixText]</Value>
        </Contains>
      </Where>".Replace("[prefixText]", prefixText));


    SPWeb web = SPContext.Current.Site.RootWeb;

    SPQuery query = new SPQuery();
    query.Query = camlDocument.InnerXml;

    SPListItemCollection items = web.Lists["Songs"].GetItems(query);
```

```
    IEnumerable<string> sortedItems =
      from item in items.OfType<SPListItem>()
      orderby item.Title
      select item.Title;

    songs.AddRange(sortedItems);
    return songs.ToArray();
  }
}
```

As you can see from Listing 6-5, the WCF Service expects to run under the asp.net compatibility mode. It exposes a method called GetTopSongs, which returns a string array of all matched top songs. Internally, it executes a simple CAML query to fetch the actual objects. It then uses a linq query to create a projection of the data that you are interested in and then it then returns that as a string array.

Since this class is a part of your SharePoint project, and thus a part of the associated DLL, it will get deployed to the GAC. Now all you need to create is an endpoint so this service is accessible.

Just as you did in the previous chapter, create an endpoint for the WCF Service by adding a SharePoint map folder at ISAPI, and under the ISAPI\SongTypeField folder add two files.

First, the endpoint, call it AjaxToolkitMusic.svc (note that this name matches what you specified in Listing 6-4). The contents for this file are as follows:

```
<%@ Assembly Name="SongTypeField, Version=1.0.0.0,
Culture=neutral,PublicKeyToken=c1944463f56d857a"%>
<%@ ServiceHost Service="SongTypeField.AjaxToolkitSongQuery" %>
```

Obviously, the public key token you generate might be different.

Secondly, the web.config file which provides all the configuration information for this endpoint can be seen in Listing 6-6.

Listing 6-6. *Configuration Information for the AjaxToolkitMusic.svc Service Endpoint*

```xml
<?xml version="1.0" encoding="utf-8" ?>
<configuration>
 <system.serviceModel>
  <serviceHostingEnvironment aspNetCompatibilityEnabled="true" />
  <bindings>
   <webHttpBinding>
    <binding name="customWebHttpBinding">
     <security mode="TransportCredentialOnly">
      <transport clientCredentialType="Ntlm"/>
     </security>
    </binding>
   </webHttpBinding>
  </bindings>
  <services>
   <service name="SongTypeField.AjaxToolkitSongQuery">
    <endpoint address=""
         behaviorConfiguration="SongQueryBehaviorAjaxToolkit"
         bindingConfiguration="customWebHttpBinding"
         binding="webHttpBinding"
         contract="SongTypeField.AjaxToolkitSongQuery"/>
   </service>
  </services>
```

```
  <behaviors>
   <endpointBehaviors>
    <behavior name="SongQueryBehaviorAjaxToolkit">
     <enableWebScript/>
    </behavior>
   </endpointBehaviors>
  </behaviors>
 </system.serviceModel>
</configuration>
```

As you can see from Listing 6-6, you're choosing to expose the service over webHttpBinding and are requiring the NTLM credential to be sent before the service can be run. Also, you have required aspNetCompatibilityEnabled to true.

There's one last thing that needs to be done. The Ajaxcontroltoolkit.dll that you add it towards the beginning of the project also needs to be deployed to the GAC. As demonstrated in the previous chapter, double-click the package designer, click the advanced tab, and choose to "Add an Existing assembly". Deploy the Ajaxcontroltoolkit.dll assembly in the bin\debug or bin\release folder.

Your final project structure should look like the one shown in Figure 6-10.

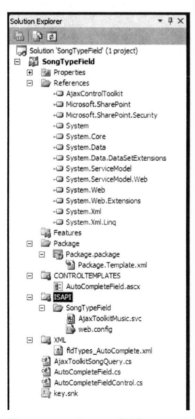

Figure 6-10. *Custom field type project structure*

Next, build and deploy your SharePoint project.

Create a list based on the custom list template and call it "Songs". This list contains only the title column, so enter a few of your favorite songs. The list looks like the one in Figure 6-11.

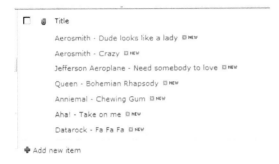

Figure 6-11. *The Songs list*

Next, create another list based on the custom list template and call it "My Favorite Songs". In this list, choose to add a new column. You should see your "Auto Complete Song" custom field type as one of the kinds of columns you can create. This can be seen in Figure 6-12.

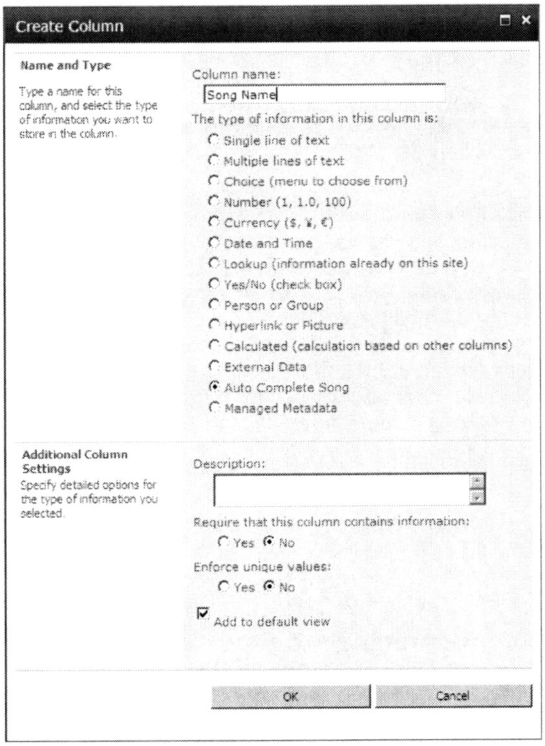

Figure 6-12. *Your custom field type is now available for use.*

After you have created the column, try creating a new list item in this "My favorite songs" list. You should see and autocomplete like user interface show up inside SharePoint, as shown in Figure 6-13.

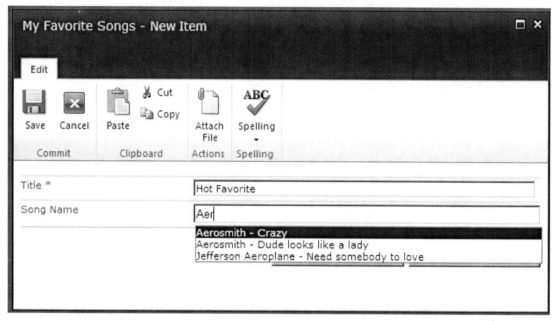

Figure 6-13. *Your custom field type in action*

The same user interface will also surface when you're trying to edit an item. Obviously a custom field type has many other possibilities. Now that you understand how to write a basic custom field type, you can refer to MSDN and learn how to add things such as custom validations. Also, do you think you can write the same custom field type using jQuery and the Client Object Model? Of course, you can! I'll give you a starter hint, the jQuery script registration and the ClientObject model ScriptLink control registration will go in the CreateChildControls method of the AutoCompleteFieldControl.

Also, check and see if you can use this custom field control in a site column. Can you use it in a site column? Can you use it in a content type? I think you'll find that the answers to these questions are yes. And while you can easily do this through the browser, it is useful to learn how you can do this as a .WSP as well.

Next, let's look at how you can create a site column and an associated content type using this field type that you just created through a Visual Studio project.

Creating Site Columns and Content Types in Code

Earlier in this chapter, you created a site column and content type through a browser. The question is, if you can do it through the browser why should you ever do it in code? The answer is they are many situations in which doing it through code is necessary. Frequently, many overloads of some methods in the SharePoint API expect the content type ID. While you could write 100% generic code to filter out the content type ID based on a content type name, that code is neither reliable nor a pleasure to write.

Frequently, you will need to keep content IDs across various environments (Development, QA, and Production) consistent.

Secondly, there may be a time where you have a single content ID across many site collections that has the same meaning. While in SharePoint 2010 you have the ability of synchronizing content types across cross site collections, the synchronization may take a while. Therefore, if you are running custom search scopes based on a content type name, or any cross site collection functionality that relies on the content type name, you probably also want to control the actual definition, ID, the value and structure of that content type across site collections.

It is in these scenarios that you will find yourself writing and deploying content types through code.

Also, as I mentioned earlier, content types live in content type gallery and are built using site columns.

Let's write up a quick Visual Studio 2010 project that creates a site column based on the custom field type you created earlier and uses that site column in a custom content type.

As always, start a Visual Studio 2010 and create a new solution based on the empty SharePoint project template. Choose it to be a sandbox solution this time because all the changes that you will do will go in the content database. Name this project "Album".

In this project, add the new SharePoint item and choose to add a content type. Name this content type "Track". Since every content type must have a parent, Visual Studio will prompt you to pick the parent of this content type. Choose the parent to be the item content type, as shown in Figure 6-14.

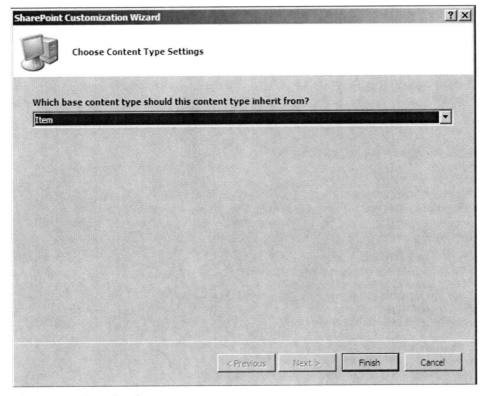

Figure 6-14. *Choosing the parent content type*

To keep your project clean, rename the elements.xml to TrackContentType.xml. The next step is to add some site columns into this content type. But you haven't set up any new site columns yet, especially a site column driven by the custom field type you just wrote. So, add another SharePoint item into the project, and this time choose to add an empty element. Name your element "TrackContentFields". By now, Visual Studio would have added a feature1 feature to your project. Rename that feature1 to "TrackContentType", and set its various properties appropriately.

This feature can either be scoped to web or site (collection). The way content type and site columns work is that you can declare them at any web level. All the child webs simply inherit all the created content types and site columns from the parent web. This technique can also be used to create look up columns that can work across sites. This is shown in an article I had written for SharePoint 2007, but is equally applicable to SharePoint 2010 as well. You can read the article at http://blah.winsmarts.com/ 2009-3-Using_Site_Lookup_Columns,_across_sites.aspx.

Coming back to this project, by now I assume that you have created a project structure that looks like Figure 6-15.

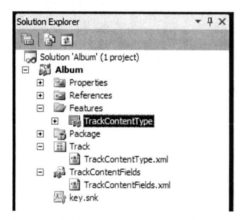

Figure 6-15. *Your content type project structure*

Your "TrackContentType" feature is scoped to web. Next, let's create site columns in the TrackContentFields.xml file. The code for TrackContentFields.xml can be seen in Listing 6-7.

Listing 6-7. *Creating Site Columns*

```xml
<?xml version="1.0" encoding="utf-8"?>
<Elements xmlns="http://schemas.microsoft.com/sharepoint/">
 <Field ID="{52d63c75-2b4e-41f2-9091-c92279c27f75}"
 Type="DateTime" DisplayName="ReleaseDate" Required="FALSE"
 Format="DateOnly" Group="Music"
 StaticName="ReleaseDate" Name="ReleaseDate"
 />
 <Field ID="{0eb47e64-4a6a-4fbf-b090-03d803967516}"
 Type="AutoCompleteField" DisplayName="Song Name" Required="FALSE"
 Group="Music" StaticName="Song_x0020_Name" Name="Song_x0020_Name"
 Hidden="FALSE" ReadOnly="FALSE"/>
</Elements>
```

As you can see from Listing 6-7, you have created two site columns, one that is called ReleaseDate based on that DateTime out of the box field definition and the second called SongName, based on the AutoCompleteField custom field definition that you wrote earlier. The weird looking Song_x0020_Name is simply "Song Name", with the unicode character for a space, %20 inserted in a special format typical to SharePoint. The ID you see in these Site Columns are GUIDs that I generated using GUIDGEN.exe. You can run GUIDGEN from Visual Studio under Tools\Create GUID.

Next, let's tie these site columns in a content type. The content type that you had added earlier, and had subsequently renamed the elements.xml to "TrackContentType.xml", already contains the bare bones structure information of the content type. Under the FieldRefs element, you need to reference various site columns that will be a part of this content type. Of course, there are many other things you can specify in a content type such as associated workflows, information management policies, document templates, and so forth. Shortly I will share a trick with you that will greatly ease your task of writing these XML files. But for now, edit the TrackContentType.xml file to reflect what is shown in Listing 6-8.

Listing 6-8. *Track Content Type Definition*

```
<?xml version="1.0" encoding="utf-8"?>
<Elements xmlns="http://schemas.microsoft.com/sharepoint/">
<!-- Parent ContentType: Item (0x01) -->
<ContentType ID="0x0100ce2744e3baea4734b2333d043aa5dd2c"
Name="Track" Group="Music"
Version="0">
 <FieldRefs>
  <FieldRef
  ID="{fa564e0f-0c70-4ab9-b863-0177e6ddd247}" Name="Title"
  DisplayName="Title" Sealed="TRUE" />
  <FieldRef ID="{52d63c75-2b4e-41f2-9091-c92279c27f75}"
  Name="ReleaseDate"/>
  <FieldRef ID="{0eb47e64-4a6a-4fbf-b090-03d803967516}"
  Name="Song_x0020_Name"
  Required="TRUE"
  Hidden="FALSE" ReadOnly="FALSE"/>
 </FieldRefs>
</ContentType>
</Elements>
```

Next, build and deploy your project. Create a new list instance based on the custom list definition and call it album. Inside album under advanced settings, choose to allow management of content types. Add the newly created Track Content Type to this list and delete the out of the box item content type. Now back in the list, choose to add a new track. You will see that your custom content type along with its custom site columns that build upon the custom field type are running, as shown in Figure 6-16.

You just saw a simplistic example of crafting up a content type from scratch. This ContentType had only structure in it, but content types can hold numerous other pieces of information as well. Also, a content type can then be used inside existing lists or existing list definitions. Writing all this requires you to write and remember gobs of XML, usually referred to as CAML. How do you craft up all that xml easily? You can easily reverse engineer that XML out of an existing SharePoint list as shown in this article http://blah.winsmarts.com/2008-2-Dev_Tip__The_SharePoint_University_of_Reverse_Engineering.aspx. The generated XML isn't perfect, but it gives you a big head start on writing all of the xml by hand. You also have schemas in Visual Studio to help you out, but between you, me, and the thousands of others who will read this book—that schema is far from accurate or complete.

So far you have written a custom field definition, site columns, and a content type. Next, let's write a list definition that uses this content type. Also, through the same Visual Studio solution, you will also create a provision a list instance based on this newly created list definition.

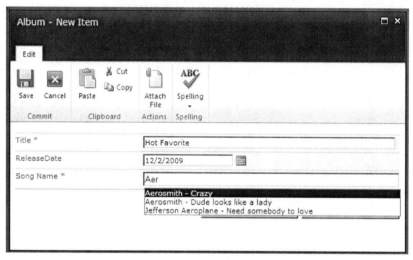

Figure 6-16. *Your custom content type using your custom field type*

Writing a List Definition and List Instance

Previously you just wrote and deployed a content type and all of its necessary facets. However, you then ended up creating a list that uses that content type through the browser. Obviously, music is such a common thing that you'd like to have many such lists. Perhaps you'd like to have a list called driving music, music to sleep to, or music to wake up to. Wouldn't it be nice if you were able to create a list definition for all such lists, based on which you can create many such lists easily? All of these lists would be exactly identical to each other. Also, perhaps through the same solution you're about to write, you could also create a starter list instance right through the .wsp?

Let's look at the process of authoring a list definition and list instance as a SharePoint solution. One thing I should point out, and perhaps you've already noticed, is that content types are not a lot of fun to work with in an iterative development environment. This is because as your content type is created and used at so many different places, its copies are made at all of these different places. Therefore, it becomes extremely difficult to reliably upgrade your content type by doing just a blind redeploy. You should use the feature upgrade mechanism built into SharePoint to update content types. Simply redeploying a new definition of a content type is not a reliable way of upgrading a content type, or anything that uses such a content type. A list definition is an example of something that uses a content type. Therefore, the steps I'm about to show that make use of the "Track" content type will be troublesome to operate in an iterative development environment. At this point, shut down and take a snapshot of your virtual machine, and then restart your virtual machine and follow the steps gingerly. If you mess up the steps, don't just edit your code and redeploy, instead revert the virtual machine snapshot, and refollow the steps.

As always, begin by starting Visual Studio 2010 and then create a new project based on the empty SharePoint project template. Call it "AlbumListDefinition". This project is to be deployed as a sandbox solution. You would note that there is also a List Definition project template. If you wish to use that instead, go for it! The end result is more or less the same. However, I will describe the steps using the Empty SharePoint Project template.

With your project created, add a new SharePoint item and choose to add a new list definition. Note that you could have also added a new list definition based on a content type. This would, however, require your existing project to have a content type. Since you are working with a brand new project, it is an option I can't use. Call your new list definition "AlbumList". Visual studio will next present you with a dialog box asking you a couple of questions about your list definition. Choose to name the list as "AlbumList", and base it on the "Custom List" definition. Also, choose to add a new list instance for this list definition, as shown in Figure 6-17.

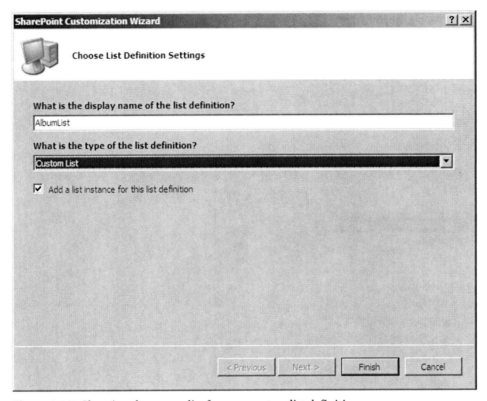

Figure 6-17. *Choosing the parent list for your custom list definition*

At this time, your project structure should look Figure 6-18.

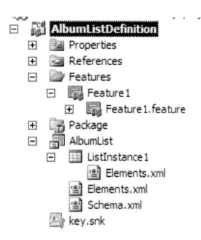

Figure 6-18. *Custom list definition project structure before renaming*

Next, rename the elements and various names all around the project, so your project structure now looks like Figure 6-19.

Figure 6-19. *Custom list definition project structure after renaming*

Now open the elements.xml file under the Driving Music List Instance and choose to edit it, as shown in Listing 6-9.

Listing 6-9. *List Instance elements.xml*

```xml
<?xml version="1.0" encoding="utf-8"?>
<Elements xmlns="http://schemas.microsoft.com/sharepoint/">
 <ListInstance Title="Driving Music"
        OnQuickLaunch="TRUE"
        TemplateType="10000"
        Url="Lists/Driving Music"
        Description="">
 </ListInstance>
</Elements>
```

As noted from Listing 6-8, you're choosing to create a list called driving music, which is based on template type 10000. Template type 10000 is declared in the elements.xml of my Album list definition itself. This can be seen in Listing 6-10.

Listing 6-10. *Elements.XML for the New List Definition*

```xml
<?xml version="1.0" encoding="utf-8"?>
<Elements xmlns="http://schemas.microsoft.com/sharepoint/">
  <ListTemplate
    Name="Album"
    Type="10000"
    BaseType="0"
    OnQuickLaunch="TRUE"
    SecurityBits="11"
    Sequence="410"
    DisplayName="Album List Definition"
    Description="My List Definition"
    Image="/_layouts/images/itgen.gif"/>
</Elements>
```

There are various attributes defined here, so I recommend glancing over MSDN for a full description of all possible attributes. The ones that you see describing this "Album" list definition will create lists that will appear on the quick launch bar. Also, their security bits are 11, which mean items created by a user are also editable by the user, and it has a certain description, display name, and sequence.

However, the structure of the lists resides in a file called schema.xml. Schema.xml gets deployed in a folder that has the same name as the "Name" attribute specified under the ListTemplate element in Listing 6-10. There are a number of things you can describe in your schema.xml. Starting from what columns will be in the list, what views will be in the list, what workflows will be associated with the created lists, and what content types get added in the list. All of this information and more goes into the schema.xml. To be honest, writing this schema.xml can be really painful. But if it is any consolation, it used to be worse in SharePoint 2007. Specifically, writing the views section in SharePoint 2007 was simply horrible. Since views in SharePoint 2010 are based on XSLT, they are a lot easier to write. In fact, you can literally craft up a view in SharePoint designer, and copy then paste the generated xml into your visual studio solution. You would also have to revert snapshots, especially if you are defining any content types in your schema.xml.

For this exercise, I'm going to demonstrate adding a new content type in your list definition. At the top of your schema.xml file, you will see the following code section.

```
<ContentTypes>
 <ContentTypeRef ID="0x01">
  <Folder TargetName="Item" />
 </ContentTypeRef>
 <ContentTypeRef ID="0x0120" />
</ContentTypes>
```

Delete this section and instead replace it with what you see in Listing 6-11.

Listing 6-11. *Content Types Section of the Schema.xml*

```
<ContentTypes>
 <ContentType ID="0x0100CE2744E3BAEA4734B2333D043AA5DD2C008CE532561D94F24791EB8149A5763927"
Name="Track" Group="Music" Version="0">
  <Folder TargetName="Track"/>
  <FieldRefs>
   <FieldRef ID="{fa564e0f-0c70-4ab9-b863-0177e6ddd247}" Name="Title" DisplayName="Title"/>
   <FieldRef ID="{52d63c75-2b4e-41f2-9091-c92279c27f75}" Name="ReleaseDate"/>
   <FieldRef ID="{0eb47e64-4a6a-4fbf-b090-03d803967516}" Name="Song_x0020_Name"
Required="TRUE" Hidden="FALSE" ReadOnly="FALSE"/>
  </FieldRefs>
 </ContentType>
</ContentTypes>
```

In Listing 6-10, you're creating another content type inside of your list definition that inherits from the content type "Track" you have already created in your site collection. You are also choosing to name this newly created content type as "Track", basically the same name as the parent content type. Where did you specify the ID of the parent content type? Review the ID of the content type in Listing 6-10:

```
0x0100CE2744E3BAEA4734B2333D043AA5DD2C008CE532561D94F24791EB8149A5763927
```

Now compare the ID of the parent track content type from Listing 6-8:
```
0x0100CE2744E3BAEA4734B2333D043AA5DD2C
```

Notice anything? Let's put them side by side.

```
0x0100CE2744E3BAEA4734B2333D043AA5DD2C
0x0100CE2744E3BAEA4734B2333D043AA5DD2C008CE532561D94F24791EB8149A5763927
```

The inherited content type simply attaches a GUID at the end of the parent content type with 00 as a separator. This is how SharePoint knows which content type is a parent of which. But, just inheriting the content type isn't enough. You explicitly have to specify the fields that will be used from the parent content type using the "FieldRef" element. If you choose to eliminate a field, you have to use the "RemoveFieldRef" element. Therefore, you have three FieldRef elements in Listing 6-11. Note that the ID's in the FieldRef elements are referring to the same site columns you have already created in this site. Since this track content type is a copy of the content type that exists in the site collection, this is an opportunity to also divert from the parent's definition without editing the parent itself.

Now that your content type has been created and associated with the list definition, you still need to do some more work to actually create the necessary fields of the content type in the list definition.

Right below the ContentTypes section in the scheme.xml file look for the Fields section should look like the following:

```
<Fields></Fields>
```

Change it to look like Listing 6-12.

Listing 6-12. *Fields Section of Your schema.xml*

```
<Fields>
<Field ID="{52d63c75-2b4e-41f2-9091-c92279c27f75}"
Type="DateTime" DisplayName="ReleaseDate" Required="FALSE"
Format="DateOnly" Group="Music"
StaticName="ReleaseDate" Name="ReleaseDate"
/>
<Field ID="{0eb47e64-4a6a-4fbf-b090-03d803967516}"
Type="AutoCompleteField" DisplayName="Song Name" Required="FALSE"
Group="Music" StaticName="Song_x0020_Name" Name="Song_x0020_Name"
Hidden="FALSE" ReadOnly="FALSE"/>
</Fields>
```

You're almost there! To make your life easier, you need to do one more step, which is optional, before deploying your list definition. Add the EnableContentTypes="True" attribute under the List element in Schema.xml. This is equivalent to allowing management of content types, so this will save you a few clicks later.

Your list definition is now complete. Therefore, build and deploy this list definition into your SharePoint site collection that already has a track content type created. This solution would now add a new list definition and a new list instance based on that list definition.

After deploying this sandboxed solution, visit http://sp2010 and you will see a list called "Driving Music" created for you. Go ahead and try to add an item into that list. You should see full functionality, as shown in Figure 6-20.

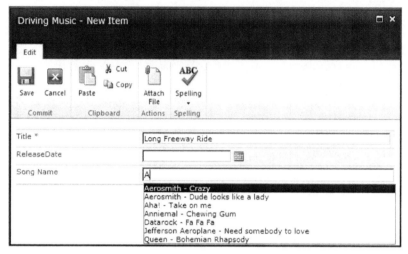

Figure 6-20. *A list created based on your custom list definition.*

Also, visit the list settings page. There you see that allow management of ContentTypes is turned on for you, because you added EnableContentTypes="true" in the List element of your schema.xml. You will see the track content type and the appropriate list columns are present in your list as well. This can be seen in Figure 6-21.

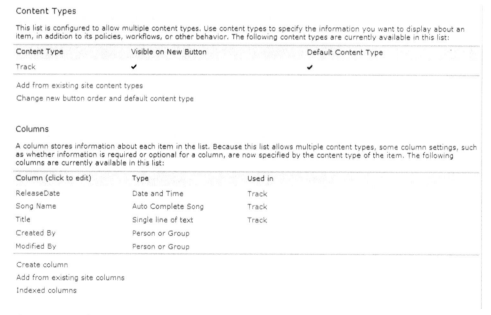

Figure 6-21. *The various content types and site columns present in your list*

Finally, click Site Actions\More Options, and you should see the ability to create more lists such as "Driving Music" (see Figure 6-22).

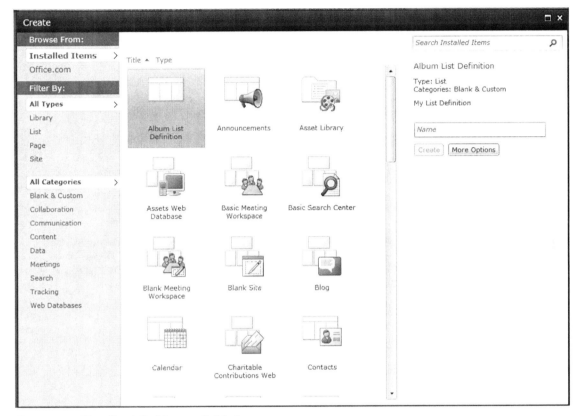

Figure 6-22. *Your list definition available for use*

Summary

Congratulations! You just wrote a list definition that uses a content type, which uses site columns, which uses a custom field type—you wrote everything and deployed it as a .WSP. You now understand the basics of authoring SharePoint objects that hold your data.

Management of this data obviously requires you to learn a lot more than just this.

- There is a whole event model around various objects in SharePoint.

- There is a science around querying SharePoint data stored in lists. This could be filtering (CAML) or searching via the built in SharePoint search facilities.

- When architecting SharePoint objects to hold your data, you also have to consider scalability concerns.

- There is a slew of enterprise content management features in SharePoint 2010.

- There is also an interesting SharePoint feature called business connectivity services (BCS) that allows you to assimilate and use external data in SharePoint.

Now that you have the ability to write the basic objects concerning SharePoint, the next chapter talks about the event model in SharePoint, querying facilities, and the scalability facilities and concerns around SharePoint lists. In subsequent chapters, I will talk about SharePoint enterprise content management features and business connectivity services.

■ ■ ■

CHAPTER 7

Managing SharePoint Data: Part 2

Reading Key: If you are familiar with SharePoint 2007, you will find this entire chapter interesting and with a lot of new information about SharePoint 2010.

In the previous chapter, you became familiar with writing the basic objects and structures in SharePoint that help you hold your data. Understanding the basic objects and structures is important, but you also need to have complete knowledge of what constitutes managing SharePoint Data.

In this chapter, I will talk about the various events available inside SharePoint that allow you to work on data as it changes within your SharePoint site. I will also talk about the various facilities available in SharePoint that allow you to query for store data. Finally, when architecting any system, you face a few issues. How much data can fit inside of one bucket? How much data can you put in a list? How many documents can you store in a document library? What happens if you go over that limit; can all this be managed? Are the boundaries somewhat extendable? You'll learn answers to these questions and learn more good stuff in this chapter.

Let's start by talking about the various events available in SharePoint.

SharePoint Events

Events are built into various places in SharePoint; for example, events are available on a list. Suppose that when an item is added into a list, you want to execute some code. Or maybe you want to execute some code right before the item is added so you can validate that item, and maybe even cancel the addition if it fails the validation. Could you also show a proper error message to the end user? Say, your item could not be added because "insert reason here"? Also, there could be events on objects other SharePoint list items. For instance, maybe you want to perform some action when a new subsite gets added into a site. All of these are good candidates for the implementation of events. And to satisfy this need, the SharePoint object model provides you with a rich event model infrastructure.

Events inside of .NET generally follow the "ed", "ing" design pattern. SharePoint does the same! Thus for instance, there is an ItemAdding event, and there is an ItemAdded event. As the name suggests, the ItemAdding event occurs right before the item has been added. This event is called synchronously, so you can set a property (e.Cancel = true) on a passed-in parameter in the event handler to cancel the addition. ItemAdded, however, occurs asynchronously right after an item has been added. Thus the user may see the data right before the event processing is complete. But if the computer's mood was better that day and it was quick in processing your post "ed" ItemAdded event, then the user may see half-cooked data. This is a problem, as you can tell, but it also has a new solution in SharePoint 2010, as you will see shortly. But before we go much further, let's write a very simple example of an event receiver and actions so we understand the basic concepts first.

I genuinely care about what everybody thinks about me (NOT!), so I intend to set up a SharePoint survey in which I will ask everyone what they think about me. To keep things simple, the survey will have only one question: "Is Sahil a good boy?". There are only two values as answers: "Yes" and "No". Now obviously the right answer is "Yes", so if users choose to answer "No", in the item added event receiver, I will change their answer to "Yes". Thus, first go ahead and create a new survey list, and call it "Sahil Feedback". If you created this list based on the survey list definition, immediately after creating the list, SharePoint will ask you to provide questions for the list. I'm going to add only one question: "Is Sahil a good boy?" of type "Choice", with possible values of "Yes" and "No". Yes is the default, and the user must provide a value (see Figure 7-1).

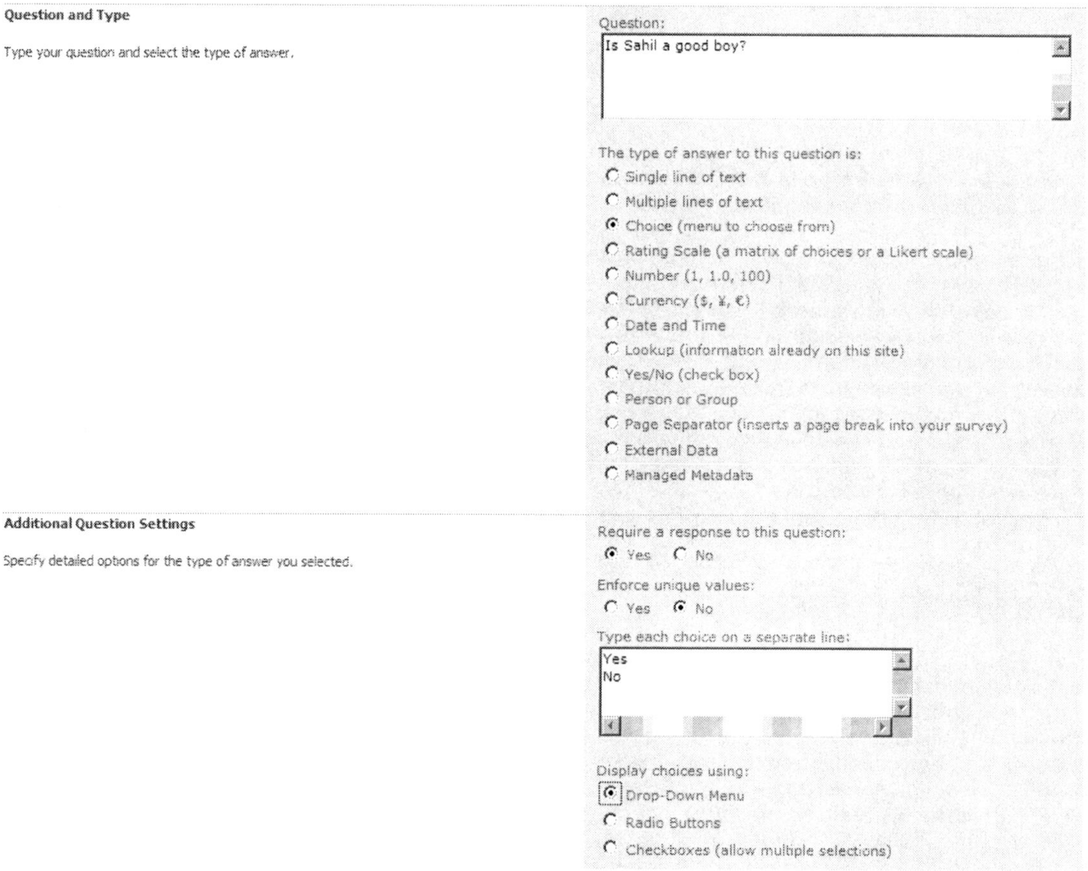

Figure 7-1. *Setting up the survey question*

Click Finish to complete the definition of your survey. Now don't take the survey just yet because I'm going to use an event receiver to rig the survey so all answers are "Yes".

Pop open Visual Studio 2010 and create a project based on the empty SharePoint project template. Call this project **EventReceivers** and choose it to be a sandbox solution. In this project, add a new SharePoint item and choose to add an event receiver. When adding an event receiver, Visual Studio provides you with a dialog box asking what kind of event you want to create. They are many choices and some of them are new in SharePoint 2010, as shown in Figure 7-2. Go ahead and look around the kinds of events you can add as an event receiver. When you're done looking, choose to add a "List Item Events" event receiver added to the survey item and choose to handle the "an item was added" event.

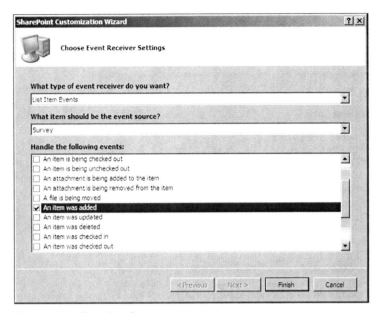

Figure 7-2. *Choosing the events*

Choose to call this newly added event receiver **Surveyrigger**. Adding this new event receiver adds a class that contains the actual implementation of the EventReceiver. This class inherits from the SPItemEventReceiver base class. Similarly, a ListEventReceiver inherits from SPListeventReceiver, an Email Event Receiver inherits from SPEmailEventReceiver, a Web event receiver inherits from SPWebEventReceiver, and a List Workflow Events event receiver inherits from SPWorkflowEventReceiver base class. Each one of these base classes provides you with suitable methods targeted to the target object you can attach this EventReceiver to. For instance, the Surveyrigger that you just created has suitable overrides for ItemAdding/ItemAdded, ItemDeleting/ItemDeleted, and many others. When I created this EventReceiver, I chose the "An item was added" check box for an item was added. Thus a default implementation for ItemAdded has been created for me in surveyrigger.cs. Go ahead and change this implementation, as shown in Listing 7-1.

Listing 7-1. *The ItemAdded Implementation to Rig the Survey*

```
public override void ItemAdded(SPItemEventProperties properties)
{
  base.ItemAdded(properties);
  SPListItem item = properties.ListItem;
  string fieldName = "Is_x0020_Sahil_x0020_a_x0020_goo";
  if (item[fieldName].ToString() == "No")
  {
    item[fieldName] = "Yes";
    item.Update();
  }
}
```

As you can tell from Listing 7-1, I'm getting a handle to the item that was just added to the list, and I'm checking to see whether the answer they provided was "No". If the answer they provided was "No", I'm changing the answer to "Yes".

So the logic of my survey EventReceiver is now complete. The next question over here is this: what list does this EventReceiver get attached to? Let's open the element.xml file. The current code for elements.xml should look like Listing 7-2.

Listing 7-2. *Unedited Code for elements.xml*

```
<Receivers ListTemplateId="102">
  <Receiver>
   <Name>SurveyriggerItemAdded</Name>
   <Type>ItemAdded</Type>
   <Assembly>$SharePoint.Project.AssemblyFullName$</Assembly>
   <Class>EventReceivers.Surveyrigger.Surveyrigger</Class>
   <SequenceNumber>10000</SequenceNumber>
  </Receiver>
</Receivers>
```

Listing 7-2 shows the CAML syntax for attaching an EventReceiver. But as it stands right now, the EventReceiver is getting attached to every list with TemplateID 102, which means that every survey list in the entire site collection will get this EventReceiver attached with it. That is certainly not what I intend to do! In fact, with every individual event, I may want to tie it to a specific site or even a specific web. Why not even a specific list? In the Receivers element, you can choose to specify three additional attributes:

- *Scope = Web, or Site*: Allows you to restrict the event receiver to the whole site collection or just an individual SPWeb.

- *RootWebOnly*: Allows you to specify that this event receiver is attached to lists with matching template IDs only on the root web of the site collection.

- *ListUrl*: Allows you to attach this event receiver to a specific list, which is what we would like to do. Also, because you are being so specific about the specific list you wish to attach this event receiver to, you will also need to delete the ListTemplateID attribute. Thus, go ahead and modify the Receivers element ,as shown following:

  ```
  <Receivers ListUrl="/Lists/Sahil%20Feedback/">
  ```

With your project complete, now go ahead and build and deploy this solution to your SharePoint site. Then visit the "Sahil Feedback" survey and respond to it. When asked "Is Sahil a good boy?", answer "No". Note that even though you answered "No", your answer was changed to "Yes" by the EventReceiver. You can choose to run the code in debug mode to verify that it was indeed the EventReceiver that is changing your answer for you.

So apparently my rigged survey is now working. This is good, but there's one big problem. The ItemAdded event handler executes after the item has been added. In other words, between the item being added and the event handler changing the user's response, the user is given control back on the page. Thus there is a finite probability that the EventReceiver will not execute fast enough, and the users might see the original response (although hitting Refresh will show them that changed response). This is obviously less than ideal. Is it possible that I can execute the item added EventReceiver synchronously instead of asynchronously? In other words, my post('ed) EventReceiver finishes execution, before the user's page is refreshed. This was not possible in SharePoint 2007 with post events (events that end in 'ed). But it is possible with SharePoint 2010 using post-synchronous event receivers. Let's enhance this example to see it in action, but first let's look at the various other SharePoint 2010 improvements in the event model.

SharePoint 2010 Improvements in the Event Model

SharePoint 2010 significantly enhances the event model of SharePoint. There is a concept of postsynchronous events, so the "ed" events can now be executed synchronously, thereby eliminating any chance of the user seeing uncooked data because the event finishes execution before the end user sees the rendered page. Also there is the ability to show custom error pages in case the event receiver chooses to cancel an event. Custom error pages are not possible in post-synchronous events, however.

Then there are various new events that have been added since SharePoint 2007, there are new registration capabilities allowing you to register events at SPSite or SPSite.RootWeb by defining the scope of an event registration.

Finally, it is common practice to start a workflow based on data changed in an item or the creation of an item. While the item was changed under the user's context, the workflow runs under the system account. This is usually a problem because if the workflow intends to change the item, and in certain situations say where the user had checked out an item to edit the item, the check-in, check-out mechanism of SharePoint may interfere with the updating. This is because technically you have two users (System and end user) trying to edit the same list item. SharePoint 2010 now adds the originating user and user token on SPEventPropertiesBase. Thus things such as workflows can now impersonate back to the originating end user to perform such updates. They are many other such situations in which you will find this facility useful. For instance, code that runs under timer jobs will also find this facility useful.

Let's look at a quick example of writing an event receiver that takes advantage of SharePoint 2010 capabilities. The specific example I intend to show here will enhance the previous Surveyrigger EventReceiver to run synchronously instead. This way, there is no danger of the user ever seeing half-cooked results. Changing an asynchronous event receiver to a post-synchronous EventReceiver is rather simple. You simply edit the element.xml of your EventReceiver, as shown in Listing 7-3.

Listing 7-3. *Post-synchronous EventReceiver element.xml*

```xml
<?xml version="1.0" encoding="utf-8"?>
<Elements xmlns="http://schemas.microsoft.com/SharePoint/">
 <Receivers ListUrl="/Lists/Sahil%20Feedback/">
   <Receiver>
    <Name>SurveyriggerItemAdded</Name>
    <Type>ItemAdded</Type>
    <Assembly>$SharePoint.Project.AssemblyFullName$</Assembly>
    <Class>EventReceivers.Surveyrigger.Surveyrigger</Class>
    <SequenceNumber>10000</SequenceNumber>
    <Synchronization>Synchronous</Synchronization>
   </Receiver>
 </Receivers>
</Elements>
```

Specifically the following element under the Receiver element was added:

```xml
<Synchronization>Synchronous</Synchronization>
```

That's basically it: compile, build, and deploy; but before you take the survey again, you will have to do two things:

- Delete your previous response because the survey will not allow the same user to respond to the survey multiple times.

- This time around, run the project in debug mode by hitting F5 in Visual Studio, which will launch the browser and point it to http://sp2010.

Now go ahead and take the survey once more and note that your EventReceiver executes before the page control is handed back to the user. In other words, the event executes synchronously.

Now that the rigged survey is running in production, people have begun to complain again! Basically they're saying that their responses should not be changed by the EventReceiver. I don't know why they are complaining, why can't they accept my Surveyrigger as a feature, not a bug?

Because I am a good consultant, instead of changing the responses from "No" to "Yes", I will instead make a little change to my EventReceiver next. Specifically if the user enters "No" as their choice, I will reject their answer and show them a custom error page. Because by now you are an expert in writing EventReceivers, I'll just give you the high-level steps to achieve this. You should go ahead and try to make this change yourself.

- Custom error pages can be shown by setting SPItemEventProperties.RedirectUrl. SPItemEventProperties is the parameter passed into your event receiver event handler method. However, custom error pages cannot work with "ed" events, synchronous or not. Thus you're going to have to tap the ItemAdding event handler rather than the ItemAdded event handler.

- In the item adding event handler, look for (SPItemEventProperties) properties.AfterProperties to check for the newly added survey response value. If the value is "No", you can cancel the event handler execution by setting properties.Cancel = true. If you have already set the properties.RedirectURL property, at this time a dialog box will pop open in the browser that will inform the user of the error. Provide a suitable error message such as "You nitwit, the right answer is YES!".

- The custom error message, in the RedirectURL, is actually an ASPX. This ASPX can be either a site page or an application page. I would be especially proud of you if you were to implement this as a SitePage and thus your solution remains a sandbox solution.

Go ahead and give this a try yourself. Also play with as many EventReceivers as you wish. Once you're done playing, come back and let's talk about list scalability in SharePoint.

Lists Scalability in SharePoint

If there is one topic that has generated more debate than anything else, it is the scalability of lists in SharePoint. You have as many opinions as there are people. Because I'm one of those people, allow me to express my opinions on this as well.

My opinion is that the SharePoint content database has been designed for low management overhead, not for ultra-extreme scalability. But where you need that extreme scalability, the architecture provides enough hooks and management infrastructure to satisfy almost any conceivable need to a real world project.

Now let's argue my opinion. First of all, what is this concept of scalability? Scalability is vastly different from performance.

Scalability versus Performance

Let's imagine a non–computer task. Let's say your business is to carry goods from point A to point B on the back of a donkey. Business is good, so you seem to be getting more and more requests to carry such goods. Soon enough, you realize that you need a donkey that performs better. So you kill your donkey and get a body builder donkey. As business grows, this body builder donkey is not enough, either. So you kill him, too, and replace him with a really expensive Sylvester Stallone donkey. Business is getting even crazier, so you kill the Sylvester Stallone donkey. You get an Arnold Schwarzenegger donkey and you pump him with steroids. By now, your donkey is really performing well, but also really expensive. And even this crazy donkey has limits. He is expensive, high maintenance, doesn't show up at work on time like a typical government worker, and some people say he has a funny accent.

The same goal could have been achieved by numerous cheaper donkeys, by scaling your operation among the numerous cheaper donkeys. This means that a scalable architecture breaks down its tasks into equivalent activities that any cheaper donkey can pick.

The process of finding a stronger and stronger donkey is aiming for better *performance*. The equivalent in the computer world is replacing weaker servers with stronger servers. The process of distributing distributable loads across multiple servers is referred to as *scaling out* your operation.

As you can see, scalability is a very different animal (no pun intended) from performance. The end result is perhaps the same; you can support more business and more users hitting your system. It is how you solve the problem by providing better performance or better scalability that what differentiates the cost. Numerous less-powerful servers are almost always cheaper than a single very high performance supercomputer/superdonkey.

Now let's leave the donkeys behind and come back to SharePoint. In SharePoint, you can distribute your application across different site collections and different sites. Within all these sites and site collections your data will eventually live inside of lists or document libraries. As an architect of the SharePoint project, the first thing you should do is to attempt to distribute the logical layout of your applications among sites and site collections just as you would solve the scalability problem in any other project.

However, in every project the system can be scaled out only to a point where the distributed load is identical. In other words, the overall throughput of a system depends both on scalability and performance. So performance is important, too! And we cannot talk about lists scalability in SharePoint while turning a blind eye to performance. So let's talk a little bit about performance, too.

Because you're a developer, I'd like you to sit back and think of the most complicated project you've ever worked on. Chances are that project involved some sort of database. In that complicated database, how many tables had more than 10,000 or 20,000 rows? I would say that ignoring reporting databases, in most scenarios 80% of your tables don't have that many rows. This number of 10,000 or 20,000 rows is something that SharePoint lists can very comfortably handle. But you also have to consider that when developing for a system and marking an architecture as scalable, you must also consider all sorts of operations that may perform on that data. These may be inserts, updates, deletes, or queries. Also SharePoint lists give you a ton of infrastructure on top that lets you create sophisticated user interfaces and permissioning models on top of your data. All that doesn't come for free!

But despite all the infrastructure and toppings you get on top of your data with SharePoint, I can very confidently say that when targeting that 80% scenario, SharePoint 2010 lists are more than capable of handling all sorts of operations at that number. In fact, there are built-in mechanisms such as indexing that in reality let SharePoint go much beyond this number for query operations quite comfortably.

The 20% Scenario

Now let's consider the 20% scenario. It consists of cases in which you have a very large number of items in a list (let's say millions), extremely large documents inside a document library, or a large number of smaller documents in a document library.

Let's discuss the 20% scenario of document libraries first. Document libraries accentuate scalability and performance concerns because SharePoint by default stores its documents inside the content database. Is storing documents as blobs inside a database a good idea?

Perhaps the best and the worst thing about databases is that there is no black or white answer. A lot of people argue that storing blobs in a database is not recommended. Nothing could be further from the truth. There are very significant advantages of putting blobs in a database; for instance, you don't have any file name overwrite issues, you don't have virus issues, backups are easy, transactions are possible, and so on. One argument I have heard against using blobs in a database is that performance may suffer. Again, such a black-or-white argument can be very misleading, especially when talking about databases. In fact, performance depends on how often the blobs get updated and the size of those blobs. Databases tend to get fragmented more easily than file systems. And as they get more and more fragmented, their performance gets worse.

File systems, on the other hand, tend to defragment themselves in downtimes. Also, new advances in solid state drive technologies make defragging a problem of the past. While file systems have the advantage of being less susceptible to fragmentation, they suffer from some significant disadvantages as well. Given the restricted cluster size of the file and the effort required to read the position off the file before the file itself can be read, the performance and overhead for extremely small files may suffer. With smaller file sizes, you can actually get better performance by putting the smaller files in a database rather than on a file system.

Tip As a rough rule of thumb, files between zero KB and 256 KB will almost always perform better when placed in the database. Files between 256 KB and 10MB are a gray area and depend upon how often those files get updated. Files larger than 10 MB are better stored on the file system.

As a result, when storing blobs inside the SharePoint content database, you as the architect have to make a conscious decision based upon the file size and the update frequency of those blobs. By default, the blobs will go in the content database. However, with SharePoint 2010 you have the ability to leverage Remote Blob Storage (RBS). Using an RBS provider, you can choose to store the actual file in an alternate store without affecting the SharePoint object model at all. In other words, the storage location of the document be it the content database or an RBS store is invisible/transparent to the SharePoint object model and thus to your applications.

Note If you want to read more about the inner details of this topic, read the "To Blob or Not to Blob" white paper from Microsoft research at `http://research.microsoft.com/apps/pubs/default.aspx?id=64525`.

Next, let's talk about the 20% scenario, with lists that contain millions of items. If you reverse-engineer the SharePoint content database structure (which you should do only for learning purposes), you see some significant changes between SharePoint 2007 and SharePoint 2010. Queries and tables now use indexes that are integers in addition to GUIDs, queries now provide NOLOCK hints and ask the execution plans to use those integer-based indexes. Connection strings use ENLIST=FALSE, thus preventing distributed transactions and isolation levels escalating to serializable. There are many such under-the-cover improvements that allow a SharePoint content database to be much more scalable than before. However, the SharePoint content database has been designed so they can be managed with least overhead. Your custom applications usually will find a database administrator updating statistics at 2:00 AM, which is something that a SharePoint content database does not have the luxury for. So with auto updating statistics and clustered indexes, you still have the ability to easily query millions of items in a single list and return the results in a very short time. Such really fast queries can be done using the object model. However, the user interface has been designed more for the 80% scenario. In other words, if you generate HTML that is going to show you millions and millions of rows as one query result, obviously that page will load more slowly. And to be honest, I'd rather have a system that works well for 80% and not have the 20% tail wag the 80% dog.

Still, the 20% scenario is important. And to prevent even this problem, SharePoint comes with numerous management features that prevent average users from querying more than a certain number of items or creating projections of lists with numerous columns and them. These are commonly referred to as *list throttling scenarios*.

Thus, with extremely large lists querying is never a problem. What can become a problem, however, is inserting or updating items.

So suppose you have a borderline scenario of a table with millions and millions of items, and these millions and millions of items are changing very frequently. First, I would argue that this is a very borderline scenario. Second, this being a borderline scenario, it is reasonable to expect organizations to hire a database administrator to manage such a crazy table. And finally, even such a table can be used inside of SharePoint using business connectivity services. So it is really not such a problem after all.

Thus with all this background behind us, let me restate my opinion.

Note In my opinion, the SharePoint content database has been designed for low management overhead, not for ultra-extreme scalability. But where you need that extreme scalability, the architecture provides enough hooks and management infrastructure to satisfy almost any conceivable need to a real-world project.

I made some interesting allusions to various facilities inside SharePoint 2010 that let you satisfy the 20% extreme scenarios:

- List column indexing

- List throttling and management scenarios

- SharePoint 2010 RBS storage

We'll look into each one of them one by one. Also I will talk about Business Connectivity Services (BCS), which lets you work with external data in SharePoint, in Chapter 9.

List Column Indexing

SharePoint 2010 allows you to create unique columns. Unique columns are indexed and help run queries faster. In any list, you can add a column and choose to make it unique. When making it unique, SharePoint will ask you if you would like to make the column index simple as well. A unique column has to be made indexable, as shown in Figure 7-3.

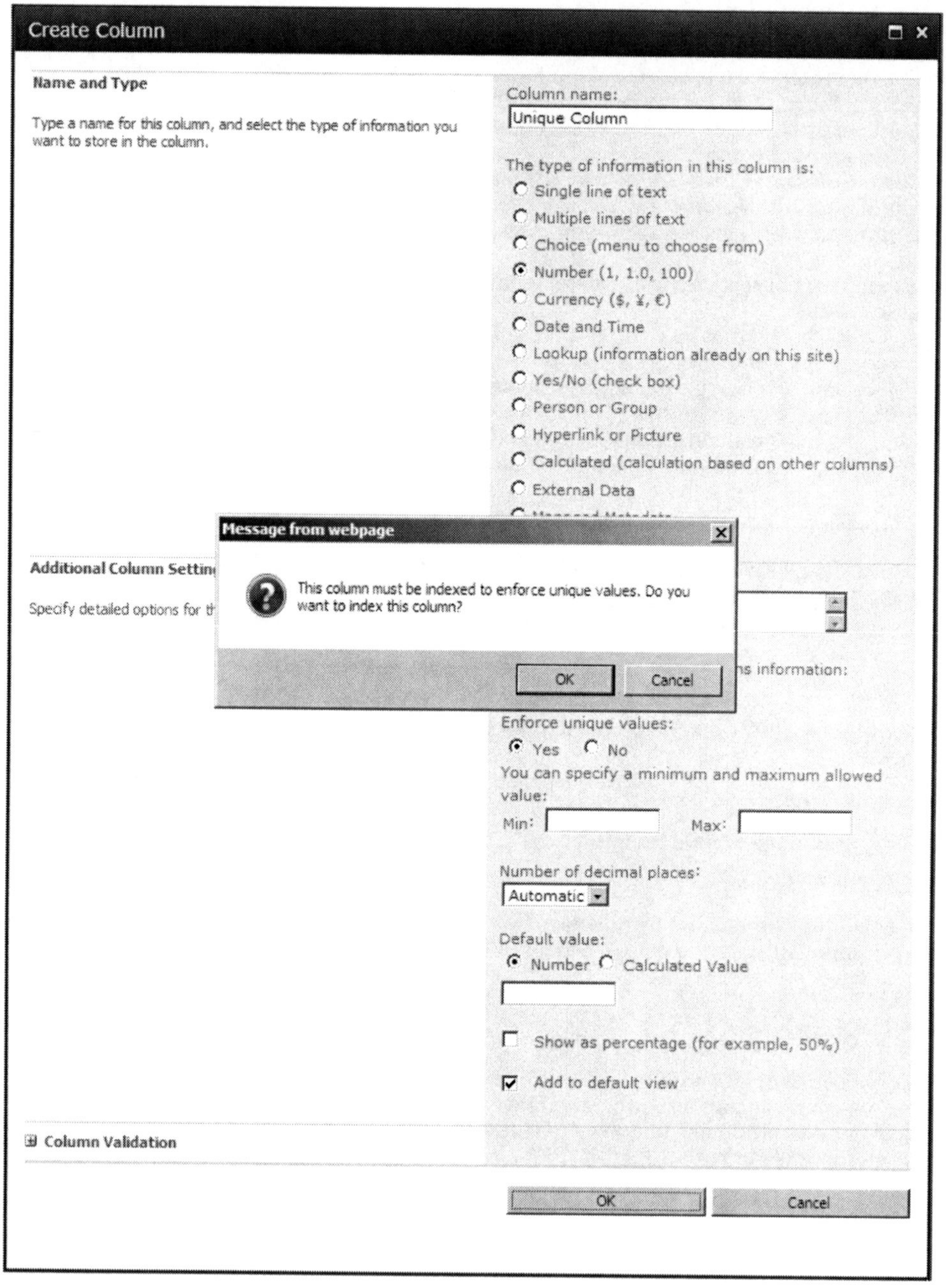

Figure 7-3. *SharePoint prompts you to index a column.*

You can choose to make a column not indexed at a later date, but before you remove a column from being indexed you have to remove its uniqueness first. You also have the ability to create indexes that use multiple columns. In order to do so, go to List Settings and click the indexed columns link under the "Columns" section. On this page, specifically at _layouts/IndexedColumns.aspx?List=<<listGUID>>, you should be able to see all the existing indices on the list. There is a maximum of 20 indices you could create on any particular list. Also from here you can click the Create a new index link, and choose to create an index that uses a primary column and a secondary column. Do note that not all sorts of columns can be used for indexing purposes. Specifically, the following types of columns are allowed for indexing purposes:

- Single line of text
- Choice field, but not multichoice
- Number
- Currency
- Date/time
- Look up, but not a multivalue look up
- Person or group, but not multivalue
- Title, except in a document library

Also it is important to note that uniqueness and indexing are case insensitive. While indexing will make queries faster, it will also increase the size of your database, and it does not help the inserts and updates on any particular list. Also while indexing can help speed up queries, they are still numerous facilities available in SharePoint 2010 that allow the administrator to police what queries can be run. This is commonly referred to as list throttling.

List Throttling

List throttling in SharePoint 2010 has been designed to give IT administrators a tool to manage and police their servers. Using the list throttling capabilities built inside of SharePoint 2010, IT administrators can define some maximum limits at the web application level. Using list throttling, you can configure and control the number of items fetched as a result of a query. There are warning levels, different levels for administrators, and the ability to configure time windows for expensive queries or the ability to request throttle overrides in the object model. Also, the administrators can choose to block all possible throttle overrides on a per-web application limit.

Let's use a real example. Go ahead and write some code in a SharePoint console application, as shown in Listing 7-4. Do note that a SharePoint console app is slightly different from a regular console app (see Chapter 3 for an example of a SharePoint console app).

Listing 7-4. *Sample Code for Checking Web Application Level List Throttling Settings*

```
using (SPSite site = new SPSite(siteUrl))
{
  Console.WriteLine("MaxItemsPerThrottledOperation:{0}",
    site.WebApplication.MaxItemsPerThrottledOperation);
  Console.WriteLine("MaxItemsPerThrottledOperationOverride:{0}",
    site.WebApplication.MaxItemsPerThrottledOperationOverride);
  Console.WriteLine("MaxItemsPerThrottledOperationWarningLevel:{0}",
    site.WebApplication.MaxItemsPerThrottledOperationWarningLevel);
}
```

In Listing 7-4, queries for various properties are available on the web application. If you run the previous console application, you should see the following output:

```
MaxItemsPerThrottledOperation:5000
MaxItemsPerThrottledOperationOverride:20000
MaxItemsPerThrottledOperationWarningLevel:3000
```

This output has three components. What MaxItemsPerThrottledOperationWarningLevel is telling you is that you will be given a warning on the list settings page if a list has more than 3000 items in it, and the list is throttled. This warning can be seen on the list settings page shown in Figure 7-4.

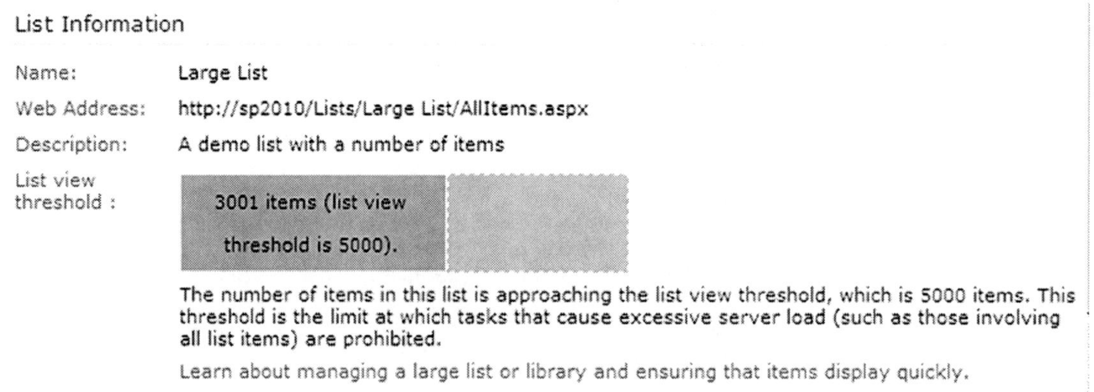

List Information

Name:	Large List
Web Address:	http://sp2010/Lists/Large List/AllItems.aspx
Description:	A demo list with a number of items
List view threshold :	3001 items (list view threshold is 5000).

The number of items in this list is approaching the list view threshold, which is 5000 items. This threshold is the limit at which tasks that cause excessive server load (such as those involving all list items) are prohibited.

Learn about managing a large list or library and ensuring that items display quickly.

Figure 7-4. *Large list warning*

In order to enable throttling on any particular list, you have to set the SPList.EnableThrottling property to "true".

MaxItemsPerThrottledOperation tells you that if the list contains 5,000 to 20,000 items , and if the administrator queries the list, the administrator will be given all the lists items requested. However the administrator will be shown a warning on the list settings page, telling the administrator that even though his query was successful, nonadministrative users will not be able to query more than 5,000 items. This warning can be seen in Figure 7-5.

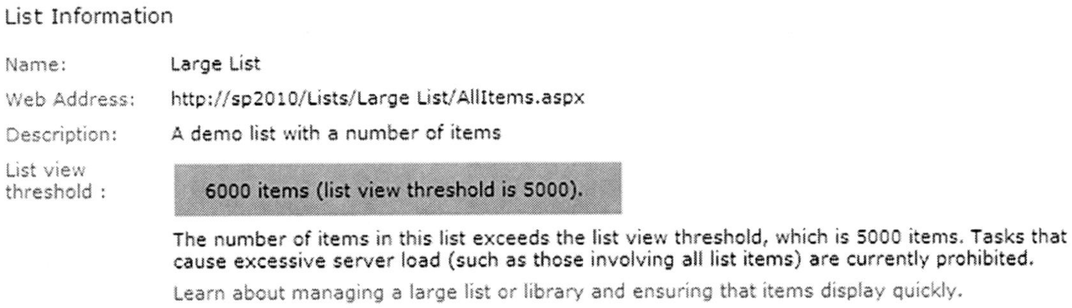

List Information

Name:	Large List
Web Address:	http://sp2010/Lists/Large List/AllItems.aspx
Description:	A demo list with a number of items
List view threshold :	6000 items (list view threshold is 5000).

The number of items in this list exceeds the list view threshold, which is 5000 items. Tasks that cause excessive server load (such as those involving all list items) are currently prohibited.

Learn about managing a large list or library and ensuring that items display quickly.

Figure 7-5. *A large list you're over the maximum limit*

This is great, but in certain instances you want throttling to be disabled. For instance, you may have a legitimate need to query for all items in the list. Such querying can be done in off hours, and that time window can be set by using the SetDailyUnthrottledPrivilegedOperationWindow method on the WebApplication Object. Also, such a time window can be disabled or enabled by setting the UnthrottledPrivilegeOperationWindowEnabled property on the WebApplication object.

What if you want to execute an expensive query during business hours? You can do so in code by using the SPQuery.RequestThrottleOverride and SPSiteDataQuery.RequestThrottleOverride methods. Also, the IT administrator can globally disable all such override requests at the WebApplication level by using the WebApplication.AllowOMCodeOverrideThrottleSettings property.

Yet another important property on the SPWebApplication object is the MaxQueryLookupFields property. As I will talk about later in this chapter, SharePoint 2010 now lets you perform joins between lists that have lookup columns. However, the total number of joins in a single query cannot exceed the value of the MaxQueryLookupFields defined on a web application. The default value of MaxQueryLookupFields is 8.

SharePoint 2010 RBS Storage

RBS stands for Remote Blob Storage. In SharePoint, any document that you upload into any SharePoint site, all the metadata and the actual blob are both stored in SQL Server, specifically in the content database. As I mentioned earlier, there are many situations in which you might want to change this behavior, and allow a SharePoint installation to store its binary blobs outside of the SharePoint server database:

- You may want to separate out large blobs, say video files, and store them on a non–database file store for performance reasons.

- SQL storage is generally expensive when compared with simple file stores.

- Larger blobs also mean longer backup and recovery times for the SharePoint content databases.

- Blobs generally hold files that are sometimes very critical. They may need to be "shredded" when they are deleted, or maybe (depending upon the need they need to be immutable) only new versions can be created. Shredding individual files as they are stored in the databases is not an easy thing to do, but is more manageable on a file store.

- Databases store blobs using varbinary(max) column types. This means that the maximum file size is limited to 2GB. Blob stores have no such limitation.

All these problems are solved by RBS. In order to use RBS, you will have to use SQL Server 2008 R2 or better with SharePoint 2010. With SharePoint 2010, you have the ability to make the BLOB store externalizable at a per–content database level. By specifying a SQL RBS provider, you choose to redirect the actual blobs to some external storage, but the metadata continues to live in the content database. Thus, the SharePoint object model doesn't know the difference between whether your content database is storing the blobs within itself or redirecting the blobs to an external blob store.

As the third-party marketplace develops, there will be many third-party RBS providers. From Microsoft, however, RBS for SQL Server 2008 R2 is a downloadable stand-alone component. You can download this provider from http://go.microsoft.com/fwlink/?LinkId=177388.

Go ahead and download this provider. Before you can install it, however, you need to configure your SQL Server installation to work under Filestream. If you did not enable Filestream on your SQL Server installation during setup, you can still do so by going to SQL Server configuration tools, finding the service running your SQL Server, choosing right click\properties on the service, and going to the FILESTREAM tab. Configure to run Filestream as shown in Figure 7-6.

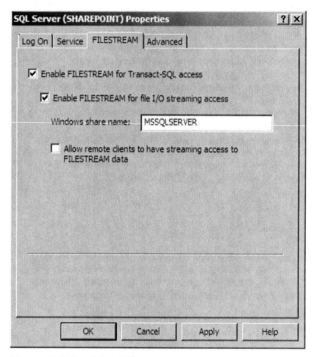

Figure 7-6. *Enabling Filestream*

Then, in SQL Server Management Studio, execute the following command:

```
EXEC sp_configure filestream_access_level, 2
RECONFIGURE
```

Next, execute the TSQL script shown in Listing 7-5 in SQL Server Management Studio to create a master encryption key and to set up the blobstore file group in the WSS_Content database.

Listing 7-5. *TSQL Script for Configuring Filestream support on WSS_Content*

```
use WSS_Content

if not exists (select * from sys.symmetric_keys where name =
N'##MS_DatabaseMasterKey##')create master key encryption by password = N'Admin Key Password
!2#4'

if not exists (select groupname from sysfilegroups where
groupname=N'RBSFilestreamProvider')alter database WSS_Content
 add filegroup RBSFilestreamProvider contains filestream

alter database [WSS_Content] add file (name = RBSFilestreamFile, filename = 'c:\Blobstore') to
filegroup RBSFilestreamProvider
```

You may verify at this point that a directory called c:\Blobstore has been created for you, and an RBSFilestreamProvider Filegroup has been created for you under the WSS_Content database. This can be seen as shown in Figure 7-7.

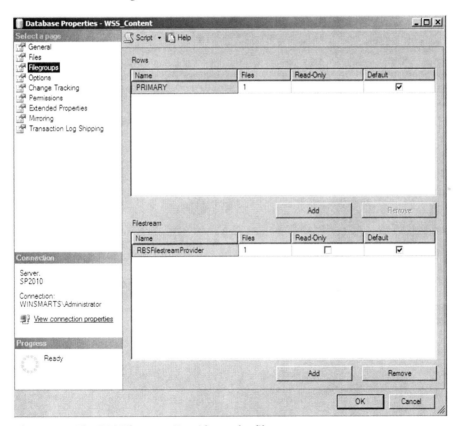

Figure 7-7. *The RBSFilestreamProvider under filegroups*

You are now ready to install and configure your RBS provider. Once the provider is downloaded, go ahead and install it by executing the following command from DOS Prompt, in the same directory where the RBS blob provider you downloaded earlier is saved:

```
msiexec /qn /lvx* rbs_install_log.txt /i RBS_X64.msi TRUSTSERVERCERTIFICATE=true
FILEGROUP=PRIMARY DBNAME="WSS_Content" DBINSTANCE="SP2010"
FILESTREAMFILEGROUP=RBSFilestreamProvider FILESTREAMFILEGROUP=RBSFilestreamProvider
FILESTREAMSTORENAME=FilestreamProvider_1
```

Give the previous command about a minute to run. It should produce an output in a file called rbs_install_log.txt. Open that file, and look for the following line toward the end of the log file.

```
Product: SQL Remote Blob Storage -- Installation completed successfully.
```

This line indicates that the RBS provider was successfully installed. At this point, changes have been made to the content database. You should verify that by opening the content database, and looking for numerous tables that start with "mssqlrbs".

If you are doing this in a production environment, it will need to be installed on all web servers and application servers; install the RBS Provider on each web front end. You can do so using this command:

```
msiexec /qn /lvx* rbs_install_log.txt /i RBS_X64.msi DBNAME="WSS_Content" DBINSTANCE="SP2010"
ADDLOCAL="Client,Docs,Maintainer,ServerScript,FilestreamClient,FilestreamServer"
```

Next, you need to enable and test RBS. In order to do so, launch the SharePoint 2010 management shell (which is a customized power shell for SharePoint and can be found under Programs\Microsoft SharePoint 2010 products\SharePoint 2010 management shell). In that shell, execute the following script:

```
$cdb = Get-SPContentDatabase -WebApplication http://sp2010
$rbss = $cdb.RemoteBlobStorageSettings
$rbss.Installed()
$rbss.Enable()
$rbss.SetActiveProviderName($rbss.GetProviderNames()[0])
$rbss
```

Next, visit your SharePoint site and create a new document library there. In this document library, go ahead and upload a file. It would be rather nice if you can upload an image file instead. I have included a sampleimage.jpg with the source code for this purpose. Note that the image file gets uploaded into the document library as you expected SharePoint to do.

Now things get interesting. Visit the C:\Blobstore directory and sort by Date Modified. Look for the GUID looking directory that was modified last. Inside it you will find another directory that looks like a GUID. Strangely enough, these GUIDs correspond to the Site Collection GUID and the Document library GUID. Keep drilling down until you see a file sitting on the file system (see Figure 7-8).

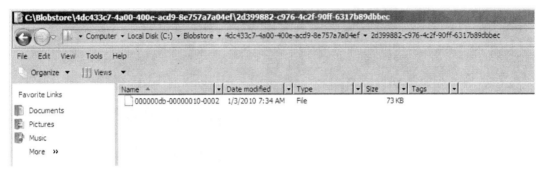

Figure 7-8. *Stored file on the file system, thanks to the RBS provider*

Drag and drop that file into Internet Explorer. What do you see? You should see the same image you had uploaded load up Internet Explorer (see Figure 7-9).

Figure 7-9. *It's the same image you put in the document library.*

Thus as you can see, the RBS storage mechanism redirected the blob to the filestream. The SharePoint object model is blissfully ignorant of this redirection, so your applications continue to function as-is.

Querying SharePoint Data

Now that you've been putting a lot of data into your SharePoint server, what are the facilities available to you that allow you to query this data from SharePoint?

There are many ways to pull data out of SharePoint. You can use the object model and get hold of the SPList object, and run a for/each over SPListItems. Of course, that isn't the smartest way to filter for data, though. Filtering via iteration can be extremely resource-expensive.

You could use Search, even programmatically. You can do so by using the FullTextSqlQuery object as demonstrated in an article you can read at http://blah.winsmarts.com/2008-2-SharePoint_Search_ranking_rules_and_running_it_programatically.aspx. While that will provide you with results quickly, it may or may not provide you with accurate results, and certainly has an external dependency on crawl schedules and algorithms. Given the nature of search, you also have limited control over the sorting mechanisms. The sorting is controlled generally by the rank, which is dependent on an algorithm that you can influence, but not fully control. Filtering or querying is more definitive, results are more accurate, and they appear instantaneously. Search requires indexing, may not pinpoint the actual results, but it's less accurate nature, allows the user to execute a search, without knowing exactly what they're looking for. Specifically here we will be talking about querying filtering, not search.

Querying Using CAML

CAML, the Collaborative Application Markup Language, is used for many purposes within SharePoint, one of which is extracting the very data you need and striking an excellent balance between speed, dependability, and accuracy.

Within SharePoint, there are a number of objects that make use of CAML and can help you query for data. You would define your CAML query using a syntax as follows:

```
<Query>
  <Where>
  <And ...
                                <BeginsWith ..
                                <Eq ..
                                <Contains ..
                                <Geq ..
        ... etc.
  <Or ...
  </Where>
</Query>
```

You can find a full reference to the CAML syntax at http://msdn.microsoft.com/en-us/library/ms467521.aspx.

Once you do write the CAML query, there are numerous ways to execute this query on your SharePoint server. You can choose to execute this query using the lists web service available at /_vti_bin/lists.asmx. Listing 7-6 shows an easy way to filter out all rows modified by a given user id, using the lists.asmx web service.

Listing 7-6. *Using lists.asmx to Filter Out Rows Modified by a Certain User*

```
XmlDocument camlDocument = new XmlDocument();
camlDocument.LoadXml(
  @"<Query>
    <Where>
      <Or>
        <Eq>
          <FieldRef Name='Author' />
          <Value Type='User'>
          Winsmarts\Administrator
          </Value>
        </Eq>
        <Eq>
          <FieldRef Name='Editor' />
          <Value Type='User'>
          Winsmarts\Administrator
          </Value>
        </Eq>
      </Or>
    </Where>
  </Query>");


using (SP2010.Lists ws = new SP2010.Lists())
{
  ws.Credentials =
   System.Net.CredentialCache.DefaultCredentials;
  ws.Url = "http:// SP2010/_vti_bin/lists.asmx";

  XmlNode xView =
   camlDocument.CreateNode(
    XmlNodeType.Element, "ViewFields", "");
  XmlNode xQryOpt =
   camlDocument.CreateNode(
    XmlNodeType.Element, "QueryOptions", "");

  //query the server
  XmlNode xNode =
   ws.GetListItems(
    "Announcements", "",
    camlDocument.ChildNodes[0], xView,
    "", xQryOpt, "");
}
</div>
```

Web services have their advantages, but performance and XmlSerialization isn't one of them. So it is reasonable to expect that you have very rich support for CAML in the object model as well. At the heart of it are the SPQuery object and the SPSiteDataQuery object. The SPQuery object and SPSiteDataQuery object are quite similar to each other, except that the SPSiteDataQuery object has the capability to query over an entire site collection. Starting with SharePoint 2010, you can also perform joins between various lists using CAML.

I'll illustrate this with the help of a simple example. (You can find the associated code in the QueryData example in the associated code download for this chapter.) You first need to set up some sample data. To set up the sample data, find the "Raw Data.wsp" solution package in your associated code download and then upload and activate it in the solution gallery. Activating the solution will give you a new site definition called "Raw Data". Go ahead and create a subsite at http://sp2010/sampledata based on the "Raw Data" site definition. This newly created site will give you two lists: Artists and Songs. Specifically, the Songs list will have a lookup column pointing to the artist list. This lookup column will allow me to demonstrate the capability of CAML to perform joins between lists.

The sample data for the artist's lists can be seen in Figure 7-10.

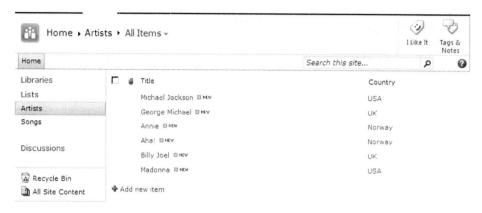

Figure 7-10. *Artists list*

And the sample data for the Songs list can be seen in Figure 7-11.

Figure 7-11. *Songs list*

As you can see, I'm pulling in both the Title and the Country column from the artist's list into the Songs list. Next, create a simple SharePoint console application using Visual Studio 2010. I will first demonstrate the ability to query using the SPQuery object without doing a join. What I intend to do is return every song whose artist's name contains a specified input parameter. Because the Artist.title has been pulled into the Songs list, I can perform such a query on the Songs list. Also I will project this data back into a custom business object. Start by adding a class into your console application project, called **Song**. This class can be seen as –follows:

```
public class Song
{
  public string SongName { get; set; }
  public int SongID { get; set; }
  public string Country { get; set; }
}
```

Next, add a method in your console application, as shown in Listing 7-7.

Listing 7-7. *Querying on a Single List Using CAML and SPQuery*

```
public static List<Song> GetSongsByArtist(string artistContainsText)
{
  List<Song> songs = new List<Song>();

  XmlDocument camlDocument = new XmlDocument();
  camlDocument.LoadXml(
    @"<Where>
      <Contains>
        <FieldRef Name='Artist' />
        <Value Type='Lookup'>[artistContainsText]</Value>
      </Contains>
    </Where>".Replace("[artistContainsText]", artistContainsText));

  using (SPSite site = new SPSite(siteUrl))
  {
    SPWeb web = site.OpenWeb();

    SPQuery query = new SPQuery();
    query.Query = camlDocument.InnerXml;

    SPListItemCollection items = web.Lists["Songs"].GetItems(query);

    IEnumerable<Song> sortedItems =
      from item in items.OfType<SPListItem>()
      orderby item.Title
      select new Song { SongName = item.Title, SongID = item.ID };

    songs.AddRange(sortedItems);
  }

  return songs;
}
```

As you can see from Listing 7-7, I'm executing a CAML query and I'm using a "contains" clause to filter out all items where the Artist column contains the specified input word "artistContainsText". I then execute this query on the Songs list using the GetItems method. Finally I execute a LINQ query to create a projection of this data in my custom business object, which I return from this method.

Thus the usage of this method becomes really simple:

```
List<Song> songsMichael = GetSongsByArtist("Michael");
foreach (var song in songsMichael)
{
  Console.WriteLine(song.SongName);
}
```

Running this code should show an output as shown in Figure 7-12.

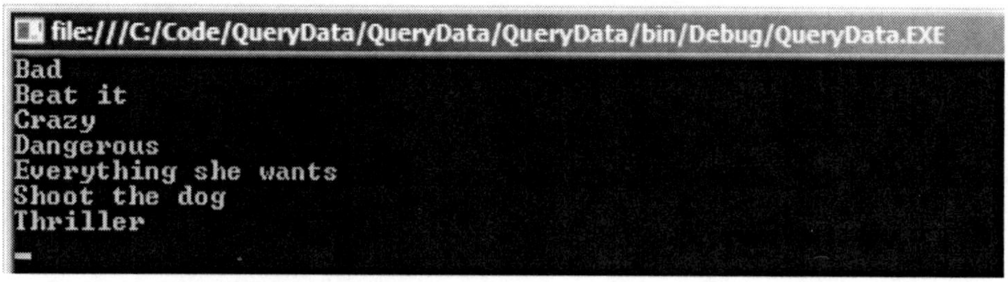

Figure 7-12. *Results of a Simple CAML Query*

As you can see, all the songs are either from Michael Jackson or George Michael. Both of them have the word *Michael* in their name, so both of their songs are matched.

This is great, but sometimes you do not have the projected fields available in the related lists. In those scenarios, it is very useful to be able to perform joins between these lists. The ability to create joins is a little bit different from joins in an SQL server. Joins in SharePoint are driven off of lookup-based columns. In order to support joins in CAML queries, CAML queries in SharePoint 2010 and their associated objects have been enhanced to support these:

- <Joins> element in CAML and the SPQuery.Joins property

- <ProjectedFields> element in CAML and the SPQuery.ProjectedFields property

Next let us look at an example, in which I will query the Songs list for all songs whose title contains an input string. Then I will use joins and create projected fields from the Artist list to show which song comes from which country. You can achieve this by using the code shown in Listing 7-8.

Listing 7-8. *Ability to Create Joins Using the SPQuery object and CAML*

```
public static List<Song> GetSongsByName(string titleContainsText)
{
  List<Song> songs = new List<Song>();

  XmlDocument camlDocument = new XmlDocument();
  camlDocument.LoadXml(
    @"<Where>
      <Contains>
        <FieldRef Name='Title' />
        <Value Type='Text'>[titleContainsText]</Value>
      </Contains>
    </Where>".Replace("[titleContainsText]", titleContainsText));
```

```
  using (SPSite site = new SPSite(siteUrl))
  {
    SPWeb web = site.OpenWeb();

    SPQuery query = new SPQuery();
    query.Query = camlDocument.InnerXml;
    query.Joins =
      @"
       <Join Type='LEFT' ListAlias='Artist'>
        <Eq>
          <FieldRef Name='Artist' RefType='Id'/>
          <FieldRef List='Artist' Name='ID'/>
        </Eq>
       </Join>
        ";

    query.ProjectedFields =
      @"
        <Field Name='Country' Type='Lookup' List='Artist' ShowField='Country'/>
        ";

    SPListItemCollection items = web.Lists["Songs"].GetItems(query);

    IEnumerable<Song> sortedItems =
      from item in items.OfType<SPListItem>()
      orderby item.Title
      select new Song { SongName = item.Title, SongID = item.ID, Country =
item["Country"].ToString()};

    songs.AddRange(sortedItems);
  }
  return songs;
}
```

As you can see from Listing 7-8, I'm embellishing a simple CAML query with a specified join and specified projected fields. Then, as before, I'm executing a LINQ query to create a projection of this data into my custom business object, and I am returning that custom business object from this method. This code can be executed as shown here:

```
List<Song> songsA = GetSongsByName("A");
foreach (var song in songsA)
{
  Console.WriteLine("{0} is from {1}", song.SongName, song.Country);
}
```

Executing the preceding code should show the output shown in Figure 7-13.

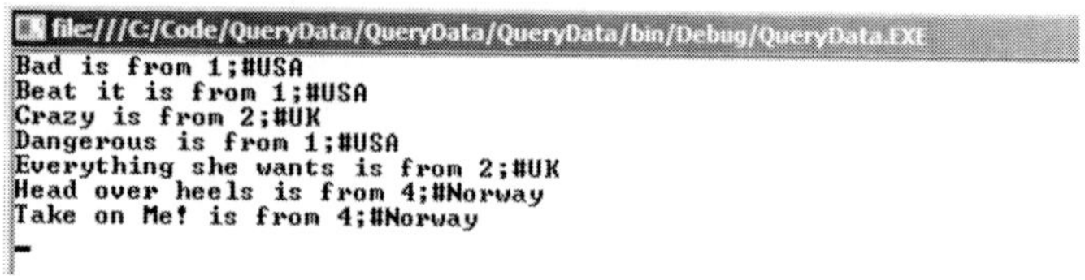

Figure 7-13. *Results of a CAML join*

As you can see, not only are you showing the titles of the songs but you can also perform a join with the artist's lists and show which country the song came from. Nevertheless, there are some things I don't like about this code. For one, it shows that weird ID that looks like 1;#. Then the CAML queries aren't a lot of fun to write, and the errors I make in CAML queries will be caught at runtime, not compile time. Is there a better way?

Querying Using LINQ

The CAML join syntax is not the easiest to write or read. Let me complicate the picture a little bit further. What if you want it to not just query data but also to query the data and update the queried objects? While updating the queried objects, you want to take care of things such as concurrency. Not only that, most CAML queries are embedded in your code as strings. What if you want it to do compile time checking; in other words, strongly type code to represent your SharePoint site collection? All these things are not possible to do with pure CAML. But with SharePoint 2010, you have the ability of using LINQ to SharePoint, to address all these problems. Thus, SharePoint supports yet another way of interacting with its data, and that is LINQ to SharePoint.

For those of you who have worked with LINQ to SQL, LINQ to SharePoint is very similar. Just like LINQ to SQL, LINQ to SharePoint ships with a command-line utility called SPMetal that allows you to create a data context to interact with your SharePoint site. You can create such a data context on your sample data site using this command:

```
"%14%\bin\spmetal" /web:http://sp2010/sampledata /code:sampledata.cs
```

Note that 14 is an environment variable I have created that points me to the SharePoint root. If you followed the instructions to set up your development virtual machine as outlined in Chapter 1, you should have such a variable created as well.

Executing the preceding command will create the data context in a file called "sampledata.cs". Go ahead and create a SharePoint console application and add this newly created file, and thus add your data context into your SharePoint console application. Also go ahead and add a reference to Microsoft.SharePoint.LINQ.dll. You can find Microsoft.SharePoint.LINQ.dll in the %14%\ISAPI folder.

With the data context ready, I'm going to show you three examples of using LINQ with SharePoint. I will demonstrate querying using a simple LINQ query, changing data using LINQ, and performing joins using LINQ. You can find the associated code for this example in the LINQDemo project in the associated code download for this chapter.

First, let's see the example of a simple LINQ query. You can see the code for a simple LINQ query in Listing 7-9.

Listing 7-9. *A Simple LINQ Query*

```
private static void SimpleLINQQuery()
{
  Trace("Simple LINQ Query", true);
  using (SampledataDataContext context = new SampledataDataContext(siteUrl))
  {
    var artistsMichael = from artist in context.Artists
            where artist.Title.Contains("Michael")
            select artist;

    foreach (var artist in artistsMichael)
    {
      Trace(artist.Title);
    }
  }
}
```

As you can see from the listing, I create an instance of my SampleDataContext. I always do so in a using block because it'll automatically dispose the data context for me. With the data context ready, I can then execute a LINQ query as shown here:

```
var artistsMichael = from artist in context.Artists
        where artist.Title.Contains("Michael")
        select artist;
```

Executing the LINQ query then allows me to work with my queried objects in a very easy-to-read fashion, as shown here:

```
foreach (var artist in artistsMichael)
{
  Trace(artist.Title);
}
```

Note that the trace methods are simply helper methods I have written in the associated code. This code is much easier to read and deal with than the CAML code. It is strongly typed, thus my errors are caught during compile time and not at runtime, and I can code more effectively using intellisense. The biggest disadvantage of LINQ, however, is that after your data context has been generated, changing the schema of the target site can potentially invalidate this generated data context.

Later on, I will show the best of both worlds, in which you have the resiliency of CAML-based code and the ease of writing of LINQ-based code.

Now let's say you have this data queried, how would you update the changes to this data back into SharePoint? When it comes to updating data, LINQ to SharePoint and LINQ to SQL, both work in a similar fashion.

▓**Note** If you are interested in reading more about LINQ to SQL, I recommend that you read the articles found here: `http://blah.winsmarts.com/2006/06/02/demystifying-dLINQ-part1--an-introduction-to-dLINQ.aspx`. LINQ to SQL used to be called DLINQ.

In Chapter 5, I described the concept of object identity, which guarantees the identity of an object over repeated queries from the original data source. The data context for both LINQ to SharePoint and LINQ to SQL builds upon that concept. There is, however, a method on the data context called RefreshData, which allows you to explicitly specify that you wish to overwrite you're in-memory objects with the latest representations from the original data source.

Excluding the case of calling RefreshData, usually all disconnected update models would appear to work as follows:

1. Query data.

2. Disconnect from the underlying data source

3. Change some data.

4. Submit the changes back to the data source.

Things get a little tricky at number 4 because while you were executing steps 2 and 3, someone else could have changed the data that you had queried. Thus in step 4 you need to perform concurrency checks before your data was written into the server. Similar to LINQ to SQL, step 4 is encapsulated in the SubmitChanges method of the DataContext. Also, there are various options you can specify to SubmitChanges to control the concurrency behavior. You can also use System.Transactions to control the transactional behavior on such updates.

You can see an example of transactional updates on LINQ to SQL concepts in an article I had written at http://www.developer.com/net/net/article.php/3613531/DLINQ-Submitting-Your-Changes.htm.

But this is where LINQ to SharePoint and LINQ to SQL slightly bifurcate. Specifically, there are two things you need to be careful of when you call SubmitChanges in LINQ to SharePoint.

- Try not to treat SharePoint like a high-volume transactional database. As mentioned previously, the SharePoint content database in SharePoint 2010 has undergone significant improvements from SharePoint 2007. This means that the database is less prone to issues such as locks and transaction isolation levels being elevated. However, it is probably still more prone to such issues than a highly optimized and customized SQL database.

- Do not use transactions that span more than one content database. System.Transactions will work as long as you stick with a single content database because to prevent serializable isolation levels in transactions, SharePoint stores all its internal connection strings with "Enlist=False". This means databases are explicitly precluded from enlisting in distributed transactions a rather good idea. But it prevents cross-content database transactions from succeeding.

Now updating data using LINQ to SharePoint is extremely simple. You simply change the queried objects and then call the SubmitChanges method. THATS IT! No really, it is that simple. Thus in Listing 7-9, if you add the following two lines, you would change the data in the SharePoint list:

```
artist.Title = "Some new title";
dataContext.SubmitChanges() ;
```

Adding new items is slightly more involved but not difficult, either. You can see an example of adding a new artist in Listing 7-10.

Listing 7-10. *Adding a New Artist Using LINQ to SharePoint*

```
private static void ChangeDataUsingLINQ()
{
  Trace("Update Data Using LINQ", true);
  using (SampledataDataContext context = new SampledataDataContext(siteUrl))
  {
    ArtistsItem duranduranArtist =
      new ArtistsItem() { Country="USA", Title="Duran Duran" };
    context.Artists.InsertOnSubmit(duranduranArtist);
    context.SubmitChanges();
    Trace("Item Added");
  }
}
```

As you can see from Listing 7-10, I create a new instance of the ArtistsItem. I then use the InsertOnSubmit method to mark the newly created artists item to be persisted in the next SubmitChanges call. This causes my newly created artist to get added into the SharePoint list. Go ahead and execute the code shown in Listing 7-10 and verify that Duran Duran is actually added to the list.

Can you author an example of adding songs to the Songs list where the artist = Duran Duran? If you do, shoot me an email from http://www.winsmarts.com/contact.aspx. The first successful example will be posted on my blog with full credit to you.

Next, let's look at an example of performing joins using the LINQ to SharePoint. This is where LINQ to SharePoint truly shines! Go ahead and author a method as shown in Listing 7-11.

Listing 7-11. *Performing Joins Using LINQ to SharePoint*

```
private static void JoinUsingLINQ()
{
  Trace("LINQ Query with a Join", true);
  using (SampledataDataContext context = new SampledataDataContext(siteUrl))
  {
    var songs = from song in context.Songs
          where song.Artist.Title.Contains("Michael")
          select song;

    // context.Log = Console.Out;

    foreach (var song in songs)
    {
      Trace(song.Title);
    }
  }
}
```

As you can see, performing a join using LINQ to SharePoint is a matter of simply dereferencing the appropriate object in the generated object model, as I am doing with song.Artist.Title. Because I was using look up columns, SPMetal.exe had enough information to create the object model to reflect the structure of my site, including all relationships defined by lookup columns. Executing the code shown in Listing 7-11 will show you an output as shown in Figure 7-14.

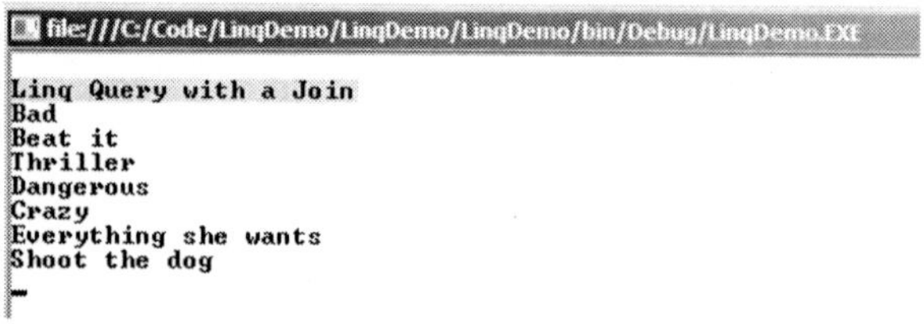

Figure 7-14. *Results of a LINQ Join*

As you can see, all songs that contain the word "Michael" in the artist name match in this query.

Earlier I mentioned that writing CAML queries by hand can be a little cumbersome. That problem is solved using LINQ to SharePoint. But LINQ to SharePoint introduces its own additional challenge of restricting the schema changes of the site after the DataContext has been generated. Is there a best of both worlds? Yes!

From Listing 7-11, uncomment the following line:

```
// context.Log = Console.Out;
```

Execute the code one more time. You should see an output shown in Figure 7-15.

Figure 7-15. *Results of a LINQ Join with the Associated CAML Query*

The LINQ query that LINQ to SharePoint was executing for you has been written out for you on the console. This query after cleanup is shown in Listing 7-12.

Listing 7-12. *Automatically Generated CAML Query by the Data Context*

```
<View>
 <Query>
  <Where>
   <And>
    <BeginsWith>
     <FieldRef Name="ContentTypeId" />
     <Value Type="ContentTypeId">0x0100</Value>
    </BeginsWith>
```

```xml
      <Contains>
       <FieldRef Name="ArtistTitle" />
       <Value Type="Lookup">Michael</Value>
      </Contains>
     </And>
    </Where>
  </Query>
  <ViewFields>
   <FieldRef Name="Artist" LookupId="TRUE" />
   <FieldRef Name="ID" />
   <FieldRef Name="owshiddenversion" />
   <FieldRef Name="FileDirRef" />
   <FieldRef Name="Title"/>
  </ViewFields>
  <ProjectedFields>
   <Field Name="ArtistTitle" Type="Lookup" List="Artist" ShowField="Title" />
  </ProjectedFields>
  <Joins>
   <Join Type="LEFT" ListAlias="Artist">
    <!--List Name: Artists-->
    <Eq>
     <FieldRef Name="Artist" RefType="ID" />
     <FieldRef List="Artist" Name="ID" />
    </Eq>
   </Join>
  </Joins>
  <RowLimit Paged="TRUE">2147483647</RowLimit>
</View>
```

You're executing nothing but just a simple CAML query with joins. You could take the same query and get the same results if you wished. But then, of course, you will be restricted to doing updating using the regular SharePoint object model.

So you have an option here: you can either lean toward developer productivity and restrict schema changes, or you can have a very flexible system with resilient code, but have the developer work a bit harder, while borrowing such queries generated LINQ. As an architect, it is good to have choices!

Summary

In this chapter, you added to your understanding of managing data inside of SharePoint. I talked about the events available inside of SharePoint. I talked about all necessary information that allows you to scale and size your SharePoint lists appropriately or to store data in external stores using RBS. Finally, I talked about various mechanisms you can use to query data out of your SharePoint server.
Everything I've talked about in this chapter and the previous chapter is applicable to both SharePoint foundation and SharePoint server. Managing data, however, is a big science. In fact, there is a whole field of work based on it: enterprise content management. Therefore in SharePoint foundation and especially SharePoint server, there are rich facilities for enterprise content management. In the next chapter, I will discuss many such ECM facilities.

■ ■ ■

CHAPTER 8

Enterprise Content Management

Reading Key: If you are familiar with SharePoint 2007, you will find this chapter interesting.

For a couple of reasons, I had a very difficult time picking the right title for this chapter. First, there are many distant cousins to enterprise content management, for example, document management and web content management. Second, this is one of those terms sometimes used inappropriately. And third, once you master the enterprise content management (ECM) concepts as they apply to SharePoint 2010, you'll be well equipped to handle document management and web content management as well. Trying to write this chapter was like fitting a Saint Bernard through a cat door! Although this topic is simply too big to cover in a single chapter, I hope it gives you a good start in digging up further information. So let's start by finding out what ECM is all about.

What Is ECM?

Modern organizations produce a lot of information these days. Think about all the information that is consumed and produced in your job: in meetings, in documents, e-mail, videos, discussions, audio, video, marketing information, the stuff that is on the web site, product catalogs, support documents, consulting reports, RFPs, expense reports, travel logs, and so on. Now think about what most organizations get sued about these days! What almost always gets them in trouble is mishandling of information! If an unruly customer breaks equipment at a fast food restaurant, don't you wish you had your surveillance videos archived? But most modern surveillance video equipment lets you store only a certain amount of days before it is overwritten! Wouldn't it be nice if somehow that information was backed up onto less expensive storage? Maybe even automatically deleted 18 months from when it was created?

What about e-mail? Chances are that e-mail sent by the CEO is probably more important than the ones I sent! So e-mail should be more discoverable than mine. Thus, depending upon the content type (uh oh, did I just use a SharePoint term here, or is this a business term, or both?) and the necessary metadata fields in that content type, different rules may apply to any content.

Consider one more thing: how do you collect such information in the first place? The funny thing is that organizations are producing, and perhaps even collecting, some of this information already. Don't project managers create project plans? Don't people e-mail each other anyway, and don't IT administrators run backups on your exchange server? So, do we ask people to update yet another system just to capture this information? Good luck implementing that! The reality is that people are not going to do any extra work than they already do. So you must capture all this information without changing people's workflows.

Thus, a good enterprise content management system is pervasive, not invasive.

■**Note** A good enterprise content management system is pervasive, not invasive.

Pervasive means that this information should be captured, stored, and maintained as part of the usual work processes people already follow! Thus, if you use SharePoint as your enterprise blogging engine, or if you have SharePoint workflows enforcing document routing, then by virtue of using the tools that people use to perform their daily tasks, you are able to apply enterprise content management principles to it readily.

So, before we go forward, let's clearly define Enterprise Content Management, per AIIM[1].

■**Note** Enterprise content management (ECM) refers to the technologies, strategies, methods, and tools used to capture, manage, store, preserve, and deliver content and documents related to an organization and its processes.

A similar but often confused term is *web content management (WCM)*. This technology addresses the content creation, review, approval, and publishing processes of web-based content. Key features include creation and authoring of tools or integrations, input and presentation template design and management, content re-use management, and dynamic publishing capabilities. In that sense, WCM is a subset of ECM. And when you have the same platform (hopefully SharePoint 2010) doing both WCM and ECM, your headache is greatly reduced.

But then what is document management? *Document management (DM)* technology helps organizations better manage the creation, revision, approval, and consumption of electronic documents. It provides key features such as library services, document profiling, searching, check-in, check-out, version control, revision history, and document security.

But doesn't that make DM pretty much the same as ECM? DM is similar to ECM, but not the same! Both DM and ECM facilitate information lifecycle management, encourage collaboration, and help manage information. But similarities aside, there are some key differences between ECM and DM:

- ECM can manage more than just documents, including videos and even hard copies. Thus ECM's scope is much wider than that of DM.

- ECM brings a larger science of records management and formal records management. DM is purely the management of the documents, with or without any records management.

What is Records Management?

Did I just introduce yet another term? I know, so far this chapter doesn't feel like it belongs in a SharePoint book, but trust me—this background is helpful for both understanding this chapter and sounding impressive to the records manager of a Fortune 100 firm. Yes indeed, there is such a formal job as a records manager because companies feel it is very important.

Records management, or RM is the practice of maintaining the records of an organization from the time they are created up to their eventual disposal. Duties may include classifying, storing, securing, and destroying (or in some cases, archiving) records.

This brings up a whole bunch of interesting associated concepts. The classification of the information largely depends on the associated metadata collected. The associated metadata in SharePoint terms is the structure of your content types.

The storage of these content types is preceded by another relevant concept, referred to as the file plan. The *file plan* is a hierarchical structure that allows the management of various content types organized throughout the tree. One item can appear at multiple locations within the file plan. But rules

---

[1] http://www.aiim.org/What-is-ECM-Enterprise-Content-Management.aspx

can be specified on each one of these nodes within the file plan. These rules are also referred to as *retention policies* and *disposition workflows.*

Retention policies refer to rules that define how content moves from one bucket to another. For instance, when I get a bill in the mail, after I am done cursing, I place it on my table until I have paid it. Once I pay it, I put it in the drawer. When I am sure that the payment has gone through, I move it from the drawer to a little brown box. Finally, at the end of the year I move that brown box into the garage. A few years later, I burn that brown box along with all the memories of the bill I paid. Burning that brown box is the equivalent of disposition, and all the rules I associated in moving the content from one store to another are retention policies. Organizations find these policies very important, because in moving the content from one box to another, they are reducing their storage costs by a *huge* amount, while making the content less discoverable. Thus as content is moved to cheaper storage or is destroyed, organizations can save huge sums of money. And you know organizations love to do that, but they need to manage what gets destroyed and when.

Finally, there are various other relevant concepts, such as physical records management, which refer to the science of managing non-electronic assets by using electronic systems. Unique document IDs which give every document in an organization a configurable and meaningful document ID. Tiered storage models reduce costs of storage within the organization by successively moving content from one store to another. By default, SharePoint will store every uploaded document in SQL Server. When was the last time you saw a content database that was petabytes in size? And what was the cost of running it? I can assure you that the fans on that petabyte server will keep Washington D.C. warm without all the politicians' hot air.

All these concepts, were supported by SharePoint 2007, but are vastly improved in SharePoint 2010.

This chapter feels a bit like squeezing a Saint Bernard through a cat door. So with this background behind us, I will start describing each of these concepts as they apply to SharePoint 2010. I should mention that there are two site definitions that ship with SharePoint 2010: the document center and the records center. Those two site definitions are a quick start on all these features, but the reality is that most organizations need much more flexibility in the actual implementation of their ECM strategy than those two site definitions provide.

In SharePoint 2010, every feature you see in the records center and document center can be broken up and used individually as features in any site you want. As a result, there is this whole new concept of *in-place records management,* in which users or automated processes can mark records right where they use and produce them. In this chapter, we will cover all these concepts. So let's start examining the various facilities in SharePoint 2010 that address these scenarios.

Document IDs

Organizations need to identify documents uniquely. In the last chapter, I talked a bit about scalability and performance in SharePoint 2010. Scalability and performance may be reasons why you would want to separate out your logical topology of SharePoint installation into various site collections and maybe even multiple web sites. There can be other reasons however, such as security, navigation, or simply the process of moving a document between various audiences. As a document moves through all these various site collections, how do you give it a unique ID that ensures the document is always guaranteed to be found?

List items in SharePoint have an ID column, which is an integer that would constantly increase. It is unique across a document library, but not unique across an organization. Also, using the document ID only, it is difficult to tell the document ID to be anything else, except an integer. In reality, organizations have their own schemes for numbering documents, and especially when you have documents spread across many sites and site collections, you want the document IDs to be more meaningful and unique as they move across the system. Also, you want these document IDs to be more permanent and binding if they are to be useful.

A document ID in SharePoint 2010 is a pluggable identifier for a document or a document set (described later). It also provides a static URL or a permalink that opens the document or document set associated with the ID, regardless of the location of the document.

Thus, you can reference documents as *permalinks*—links that don't change or break as the location of the document changes. And also, the format and generation logic of the generated document IDs is customizable. Let's see how this actually works! In order to use document IDs, you have to first activate the Document ID Service under site collection features as shown in Figure 8-1.

Figure 8-1. *Activating the Document ID Service*

Activating the previous feature will schedule a timer job that will configure the feature. After the Document ID Service feature is configured, add a document in a document library in the site collection. As you will see, the document now gets a unique document ID (see Figure 8-2).

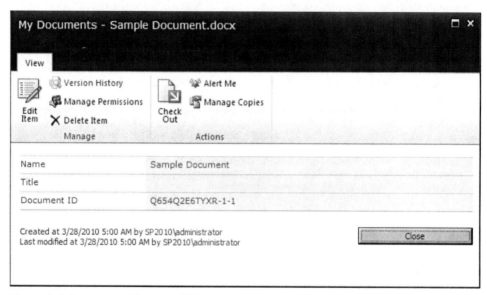

Figure 8-2. *Document IDs created for you*

Note the URL for the document ID. It looks like as shown in Figure 8-1: `http://sp2010/_layouts/DocIdRedir.aspx?ID=ZKUNP6SFESZK-1-2`

This URL has no bearing on the document's location; it relies on the document redirection service to remember where that document is. And because the ID never changes, you can always count on that permalink to work.

Also, with the document ID service now activated, visit the document ID settings area, which can be accessed under the Site Collection Administration area under Site Settings. The specific URL for document ID settings is at `http://sp2010/_Layouts/DocIdSettings.aspx`. This page will allow you to specify custom prefixes to your document IDs, and thus ensure that the documents in different site collections do not get conflicting document IDs.

Document Sets

In a typical project in which documents are being produced frequently to accomplish one task, you may have not a single document, but instead a set of documents that need to be treated as one. This is where document sets come into the picture. A *document set* is implemented as a site collection feature. Activating it gives you a special content type that allows you to group together multiple documents as a "set of documents."

  This gives you many interesting new options. For instance, a document set can have its own welcome page that can tell users what the specific document set is all about. Because document sets are implemented as a content type, they get everything that a content type gets: versioning, workflows, policies, and so on. Only this time around, the entire document "set" (i.e. multiple documents together) can participate in the business processes defined on the document set. Let's see how this works.

  To use document sets, activate the site collection level feature called Document Sets. Then in a document library, allow management of content types and add Document Set as an allowed content type. This can be seen in Figure 8-3.

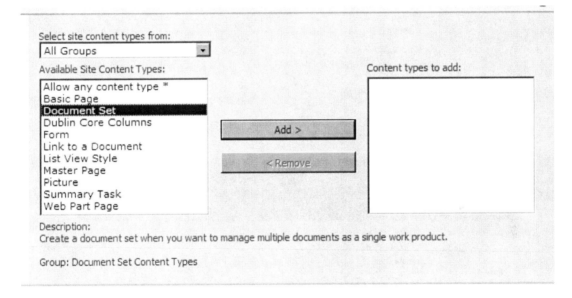

Figure 8-3. *Document sets available as a content type to add*

  With this new content type added to the document library, you will be able to create a new document set from the New button under the Documents ribbon. Creating a new document set will simply ask you for a name and description. In the welcome page, you can begin to add new documents in the document set (see Figure 8-4).

Figure 8-4. *Document sets cover/welcome page*

The welcome page is customizable to anything you want. But for now, click the View All Properties link. You should see a popup shown in Figure 8-5.

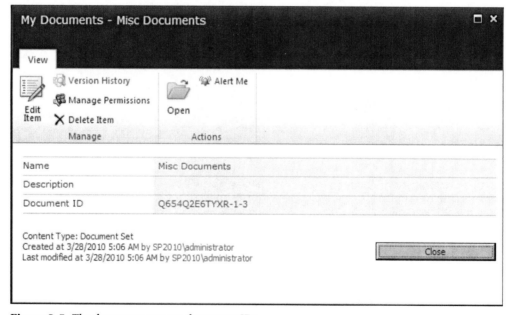

Figure 8-5. *The document sets get document IDs*

As you can tell, everything that you are used to seeing at a document level is now available at a document set level. Interestingly, the document set participates in the document ID numbering as well. This truly lets you treat a set of documents as one entity.

It is important to realize, however, that a document set is nothing but just another content type. This means all the facilities that are applicable to a content type are also applicable to document set. Let's examine this in further detail. Because you have a content type called Document Set in your site collection already, create a new content type called **My Document Set** and have it inherit from the Document Set content type. Now visit the content type management page for this new My Document Set content type that you created. You will see that just like any other content type you have all the facilities, but you have a new link called Document Set settings. This can be seen in Figure 8-6.

Figure 8-6. *The Document Set settings link*

Clicking Documents Set settings allows you to customize a number of things about the My Document Set content type:

- Under the Allowed Content type section, you can pick and choose the content types that are allowed inside this document set.

- Under the Default Content section, you can choose to prepopulate this document set to include certain specific items. Not only that; you can also choose to specify those default items as certain associated content types. For instance, a document set called Client Interaction may by default include a company overview, welcome letter, and proposal outline.

- Under Shared Columns, you can choose to synchronize the value of a column from the document set onto all the constituent documents.

- Under the Welcome Page Columns section, you can choose to show all columns from the documents that will appear on the welcome page.

- Under the Welcome Page section, you can choose to customize the welcome page of the documents set. You would note that the welcome page for the My documents at content type lives at `http://sp2010/_cts/My%20Document%20Set/docsethomepage.aspx`. "_cts" is a special folder in any site collection that contains all the files necessary to support a content type. You can choose to edit the welcome page right through the browser because this is just a WebPart page. But you also have the option of performing serious customizations through SharePoint Designer or even Visual Studio.

Managed Metadata, Keywords and Tags

Conventionally, users have used folders for ages to organize their content. Folders give you a rich hierarchical view of the organization of your data. Where they fall short, however, is that in the real world sometimes one piece of content may belong in two or more folders. For instance, is buying a diamond ring for your girlfriend a financial decision or a romantic decision? The answer: it is both! (Of course, she doesn't think so, though!)

Another issue with folders is that they are somewhat inflexible. For instance, when a number of folders are set up, and they are populated with content, sometimes it becomes hard to reorganize them and the content between them. Think about this: when was the last time your organization was completely shuffled around? To get around all these challenges, the concept of tagging was invented. *Tagging* simply refers to marking your content with strings that are pertinent to the nature of the content. What is special, though, is that one piece of content can have as many strings as you want. For instance, rather than putting the diamond ring transaction in either the romantic folder or the financial folder, you simply mark it with both romance and finance tags; that way, it is findable under both.

Of course, these tags in any organization also need their own structure. The world of tagging usually is not black or white. On one end of the spectrum, the *dictionary* of all these tags (perhaps a better word is *terms*) is maintained by a committee locked in a room in the basement somewhere! On the other end, users who are actually familiar with the content that they're working on need to have the ability to add to this dictionary of tags. The first instance in which the dictionary of these terms is controlled hermetically is commonly referred to as *metadata taxonomy*. The second instance, when participants of an organization who are familiar with the content type they're working on add terms to this dictionary, is referred to as *folksonomies*.

Also it is reasonable to expect that as the dictionary of terms, both formal and informal, grow, over time you would want to mark synonyms or even delete or deprecate terms.

In addition, between the range of committee-managed tags and completely open folksonomies, you might have a midrange in which you might want to assign administrators for certain terms sets. The bottom line is that such flexibility in tagging categorization of your data makes your data much more discoverable.

The good thing is that SharePoint 2010 allows you to address all these scenarios! Let's see how. At the heart of the tagging and metadata management infrastructure inside of SharePoint is the managed metadata service, which you can find in central administration. If you visit /_admin/ServiceApplications.aspx, you will see an instance of the managed metadata service provisioned for you (see Figure 8-7).

| Managed Metadata Service | Managed Metadata Service | Started |
| Managed Metadata Service | Managed Metadata Service Connection | Started |

Figure 8-7. *The Managed Metadata Service link in central admin*

The managed metadata service also works in conjunction with the facilities in SharePoint used to synch content types across site collections. (I will talk about that facility later in this chapter.) In addition to synching content types across site collections, the managed metadata service also allows you to publish and consume keywords from other metadata service instances as necessary. The other metadata service could potentially be located on a completely different SharePoint farm. While you could use the out-of-the-box instance of the managed metadata service, I'm going to demonstrate the process of setting up your own metadata service instance from scratch. Thus, select the out-of-the-box managed metadata service instance, and choose to delete it. In the ensuing dialog box that pops up, also choose to delete data associated with the service applications (see Figure 8-8).

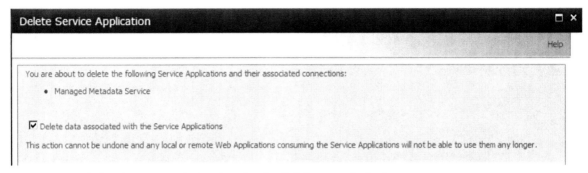

Figure 8-8. *Deleting the Managed Metadata Service link in central admin*

Next, on the same screen choose to create a new managed metadata service. Choosing to create a managed metadata service will ask you a few basic questions: the name of the new managed metadata service, the database location in which the terms will be stored, an application pool, among other such questions. I choose to call my managed metadata service **Winsmarts**. Use the following settings for this service instance:

- Name: Winsmarts
- Database Name: Winsmarts_DB
- Leave the failover server blank
- Pick sp_admin as the application pool
- Leave the content type hub dialog box blank

At the bottom of Create new managed metadata service is an interesting question, shown in Figure 8-9.

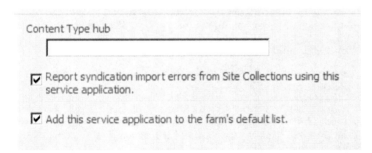

Figure 8-9. *Creating a new managed metadata service asking a question*

As I will describe later in this chapter, with SharePoint 2010 you now have the ability to share and synchronize content types across site collections. For now, just leave the content type hub as blank and leave the two check boxes checked for now. I will describe the content type hub functionality later in this chapter.

Once the managed metadata service is created, click it to access the term store management tool. Go ahead and add a few terms, as shown in Figure 8-10.

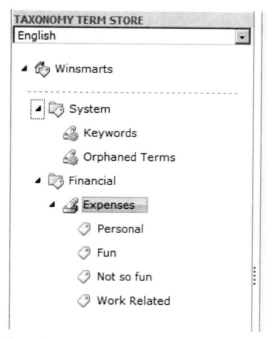

Figure 8-10. *My Taxonomy*

As you can see from the figure, I have set up a new group of terms called Financial. At a group level (Financial), I can choose to assign group managers or contributors. Contributors have the ability to edit terms and term set hierarchies within this group, and group managers can appoint other contributors as well.

At an individual term set level, you can specify a number of things:

- You have the ability to appoint an owner of a term set. The owner of the term set has the eventual responsibility of maintaining the term set.

- You have the ability to specify a contact e-mail address for the term set. Usually term sets that are locked down will need some ability for end business users to be able to contact the person who can accept suggestions for the term set. This contact e-mail address would be the person who receives all these suggestions.

- You have the ability to define stakeholders, who will be notified if any changes are made to the term set.

- You have the ability to define a close or open submission policy. A closed submission policy would restrict the ability to make changes to only owners of this term set. While this would keep the term set cleaner, it would put more responsibility on the term set owner to maintain the term set as it grows.

- Finally you have a simple check box that makes the term said available for tagging existing content.

I set up the expenses term set settings to look as shown in Figure 8-11.

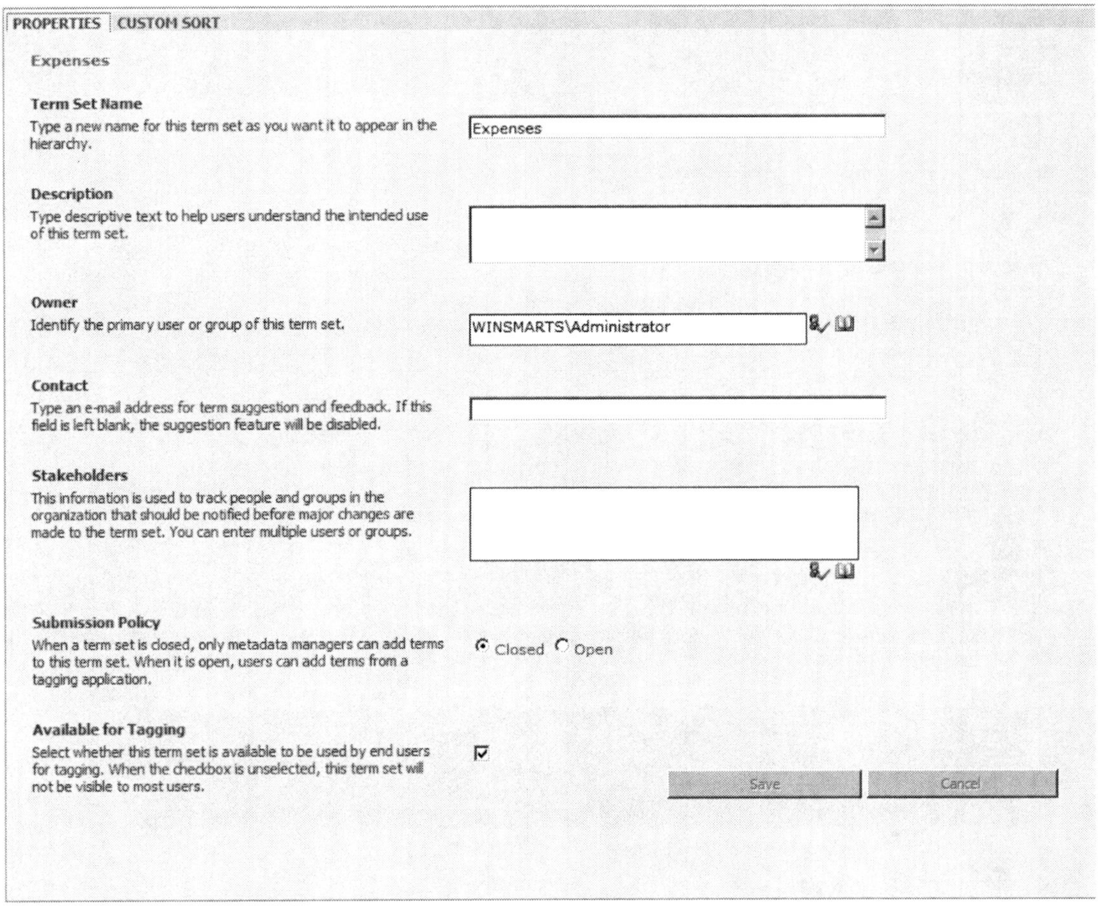

Figure 8-11. *Managing the Expenses term set*

With your term set now set up, start using this term set in your SharePoint application. At http://sp2010, set up a list called **My Expenses**. This list will be based on the custom list site definition. Add another column in this list called **Amount**, which will be based on type currency. Now the idea is that as I start making expenses and documenting them in this list, I want to be able to tag them with the Expenses term set, which makes my content more discoverable. In order to be able to be able to tag the content, I need to add a managed metadata site column to my list. Most ECM features have been designed so they can be turned on or off in any site as a feature. In order to use managed metadata in a blank site definition site, run the following command:

```
stsadm -o activatefeature -url http://sp2010 -id 73EF14B1-13A9-416b-A9B5-ECECA2B0604C
```

Once the feature is added, go ahead and add a new managed metadata column called **Category**, allow it to have multiple values, and point it to the managed term set Expenses. This can be seen as in Figure 8-12.

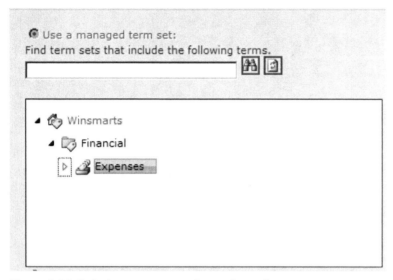

Figure 8-12. *Pointing your managed metadata column to a term set*

Now I'm going to add a new item to this list. You will see that as you start typing in the category from the metadata, SharePoint will prompt you with appropriate synonyms of the matching terms in the term set (see Figure 8-13).

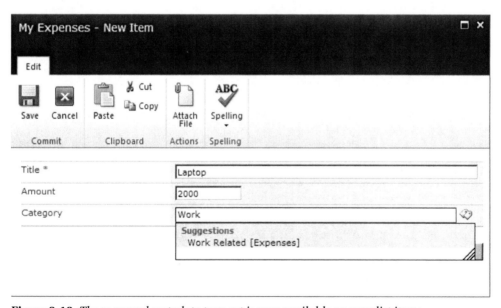

Figure 8-13. *The managed metadata term set is now available on your list items*

Notice that I said synonyms! Back in central administration, add another term called **Office Related**. Then click Work Related and choose to merge the Office Related and Work Related terms. Now try adding another item into the My Expenses list. SharePoint is smart enough to prompt you with the actual tag even if you were trying to type the previous tag. This can be seen in Figure 8-14.

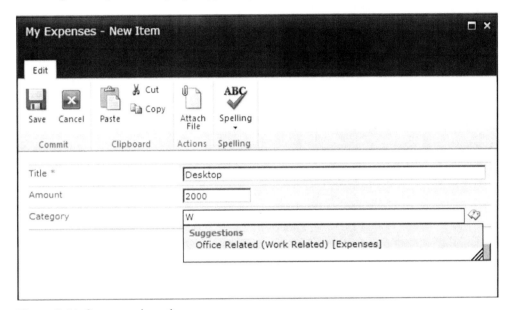

Figure 8-14. *Synonyms in action*

There are numerous other facilities in the metadata management of SharePoint 2010, including the ability to delete terms, mark terms as orphans, deprecate terms, or even visit the term store management tool under the site collection settings of http://sp2010.

Now assume that you have added a few items into your overall expense. How did metadata tagging make your content more discoverable? Under the site features, activate the Metadata Navigation and Filtering feature. Back in the My Expenses list, visit Metadata Navigation Settings under List Settings. Choose to configure the Navigation Hierarchies and the Configure Key Filter section to navigate and filter using the Category column, as shown in Figure 8-15.

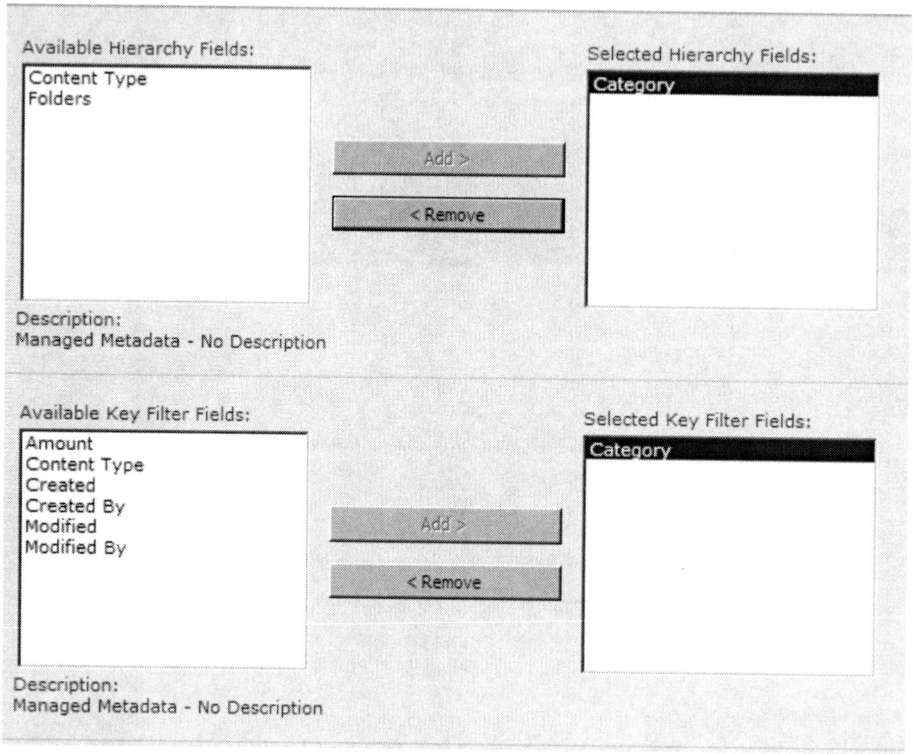

Figure 8-15. *Metadata navigation settings*

Now visit the My Expenses list once again. Note that you now have the ability to browse for content using the tags that you specified earlier. This can be seen in Figure 8-16.

Home ▸ My Expenses ▸ All Items
Home
Libraries
My Documents
Lists
My Expenses
Discussions
My Expenses
Category
Fun
Not so fun
Office Related
Personal
Title
Desktop NEW
Laptop NEW
Add new item

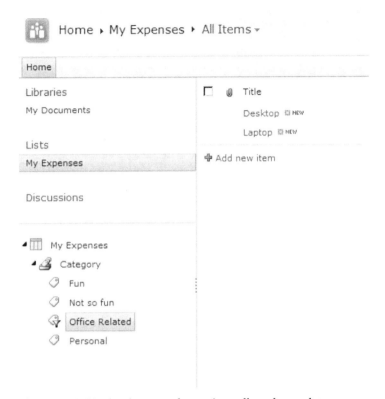

Figure 8-16. *Navigating your data using collected metadata*

The Key Filters section enables you to specify multiple tags as your filtering criterion (see Figure 8-17).

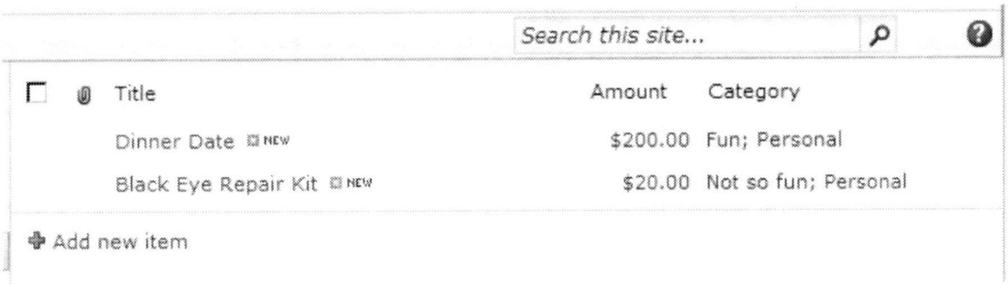

Search this site...
Title
Amount
Category
Dinner Date NEW
$200.00
Fun; Personal
Black Eye Repair Kit NEW
$20.00
Not so fun; Personal
Add new item

Figure 8-17. *Navigating your data using collected metadata: multiple tags*

What is really compelling about this set up is that you can combine the metadata navigation and filtering with folders. Those folders can have unique permissions on them, and metadata navigation and filtering will start to present security trimmed content.

This is great, but one big downside of this approach was that the metadata term set was very tightly controlled by the metadata administrators. Sure, the metadata administrator could potentially delegate the term set administration to other users, but users who are familiar with the content will eventually want to suggest more terms. In other words, they will want to specify their own keywords to content all over SharePoint and perhaps filter by using those keywords as well.

The SharePoint metadata architecture allows for a loosely controlled metadata setup commonly referred to as *folksonomies*. You can set up any of the term sets to be open; then users can add their terms to an existing term set. One common example of this is the Enterprise keywords functionality that is built into SharePoint 2010 out of the box. To examine this, add a new document library and call it **My Documents**. Under Document Library settings, visit the Enterprise Metadata and Keywords Settings link, and choose to add Enterprise Keywords to this list and enable Metadata Publishing. Now choose to add a new document. You can add keywords to this newly added document using both the Document Information Panel (DIP) and the Edit Properties button on the ribbon in SharePoint 2010. The keywords will also surface under the Enterprise Keywords section of backstage view in Office applications. Figure 8-18 shows this view.

Properties ▾	
Size	25.0KB
Pages	1
Words	171
Total Editing Time	7 Minutes
Title	Add a title
Comments	Add comments
Enterprise Keywords	USA; Germany;

Figure 8-18. *Backstage view in an Office application*

Figure 8-19 shows the DIP in an Office application.

ⓘ Document Properties - Server ▾

Title:

Enterprise Keywords:
USA; Germany;

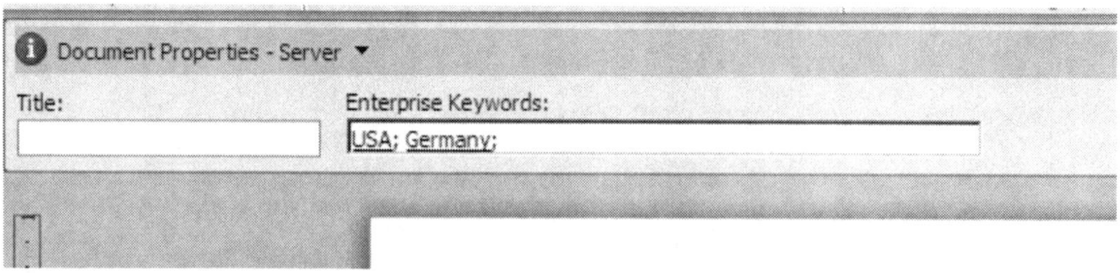

Figure 8-19. *Document Information Panel in an Office application*

Figure 8-20 shows Enterprise Keywords in a web browser.

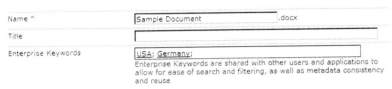

Figure 8-20. *Enterprise Keywords in Document Properties in the web browser*

Curiously, these keywords seem to underline themselves as you type them. Not only that; as you try and reuse a keyword that you previously used, SharePoint will prompt you to pick from an existing keyword to let you create a new one (see Figure 8-21).

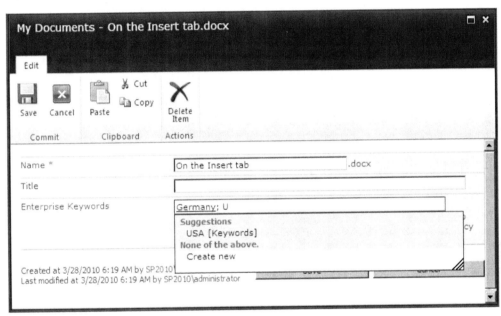

Figure 8-21. *The interface prompting you to pick existing keywords before typing in a new one*

What is happening behind the scenes is that whenever SharePoint encounters a new keyword, it adds it to the database behind the scenes, gives it an ID, and ties it to the document that you are editing in your site. But if you are typing in a keyword that SharePoint has already seen, then SharePoint will prompt you to pick from an existing keyword. Because the keywords are also built on the managed metadata infrastructure, all the metadata concepts such as hierarchies of keywords, synonyms, or deprecated or orphaned keywords. You can verify that by visiting the Keywords section under the System group of the Winsmarts metadata service in central administration, as shown in Figure 8-22.

Figure 8-22. *Entered keywords being captured in the same taxonomy*

In addition to such keywords, you also have the ability of tagging the content specifically for your needs. For instance, select the document that you just added and from the ribbon click the Tags and Notes button. You can now add some tags, as shown in Figure 8-23.

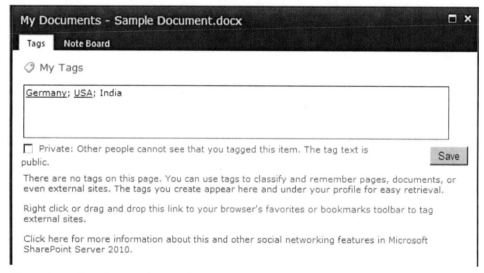

Figure 8-23. *Entering new keywords*

Interestingly, these tags are also driven from the same keywords group that the managed keywords are being driven from. One of the most interesting tags is the I Like It tag. There is an I Like It button on every single page and content inside of SharePoint, so clicking that button will simply add the I Like It tag to the associated content. As you tagging, rating, and liking the content all over SharePoint, this also surfaces in the activity feed in your site. My activity feed is shown in Figure 8-24.

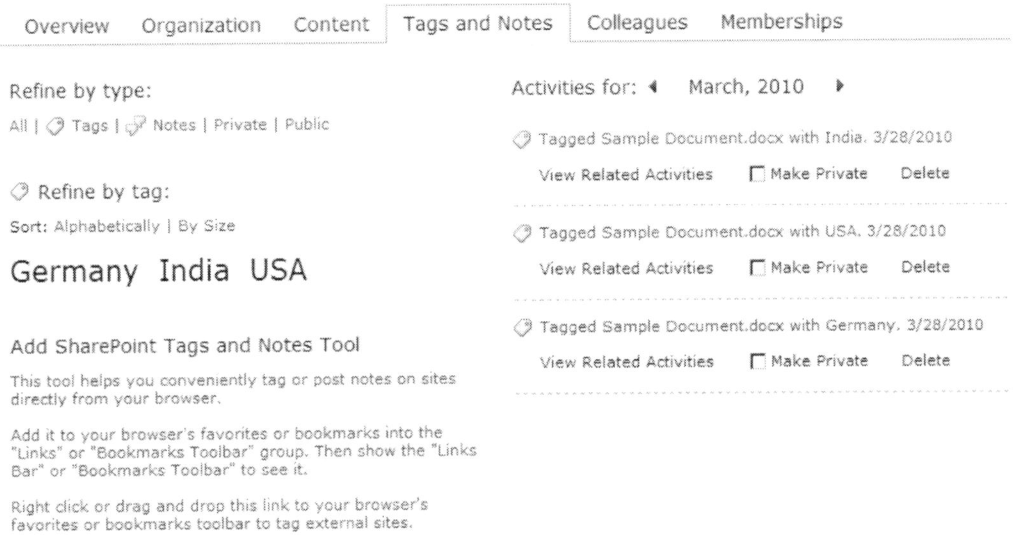

| Overview | Organization | Content | Tags and Notes | Colleagues | Memberships |

Refine by type:

All | ⬧ Tags | ⬧ Notes | Private | Public

Activities for: ◄   March, 2010   ►

⬧ Tagged Sample Document.docx with India. 3/28/2010

    View Related Activities   ☐ Make Private   Delete

⬧ Refine by tag:

Sort: Alphabetically | By Size

Germany India USA

⬧ Tagged Sample Document.docx with USA. 3/28/2010

    View Related Activities   ☐ Make Private   Delete

Add SharePoint Tags and Notes Tool

This tool helps you conveniently tag or post notes on sites directly from your browser.

Add it to your browser's favorites or bookmarks into the "Links" or "Bookmarks Toolbar" group. Then show the "Links Bar" or "Bookmarks Toolbar" to see it.

Right click or drag and drop this link to your browser's favorites or bookmarks toolbar to tag external sites.

⬧ Tagged Sample Document.docx with Germany. 3/28/2010

    View Related Activities   ☐ Make Private   Delete

Figure 8-24. *My activity feed*

Now others in the organization can choose to subscribe to the activity feed, and keep on top of the content that is interesting to me.

Content Organizer

By now, you are familiar with numerous facilities in SharePoint 2010. As exciting as these features may be individually, they truly shine when used with each other. For instance, in the last chapter, I talked about scalability versus performance. I talked of how you can scale SharePoint, and how SharePoint 2010 is so much better at performance than SharePoint 2007 ever was! What I am about to describe in this section of content organizer is applicable in many ways, and can be used with many other facilities in SharePoint 2010. But, as a classic example, let me talk about the scalability perspective.

I talked in the last chapter that in order to deliver a solution to the end business user, the business user really cares about the following questions:

- Can the system support X users?

- Can the system support X users in Y response time?

- Can you build this system and keep it under the Z cost/price point?

Thus, as I am architecting a system, I use both scalability and performance of the underlying platform to try and meet the X, Y, and Z of the end business user's requirement. Sure, the straightforward way of meeting the Y response time is to increase performance, but performance becomes expensive very quickly, and frankly any system in the world will perform only so well; at some point you have to scale it.

Let's talk about this in SharePoint 2010. I mentioned that SharePoint 2010 lists are a *lot* more performant than SharePoint 2007. I wasn't lying; they indeed are! But even with better performing lists, you will at some point hit a limit. Even if the limit is in millions of list items or tens of thousands of documents, there is a limit—trust me, there is! Thus, beyond a certain point, you will have to scale. But how exactly do you scale in SharePoint? You can create more folders, more document libraries, more lists, and maybe even more sites. Heck, you can create even more site collections in more content databases, depending on your scalability needs. Honestly, with the facility to scale using more and more such containers, you can scale to almost infinity.

Sounds good on paper! But this creates a unique challenge. Guess how many sites, site collections, or even document libraries the average business user wants. Usually the answer is *one*. Think about it—even if you are producing millions of documents, wouldn't it be nice if there were a single place for you to input and discover *all* your content? (Seriously, if these customers didn't pay me so well, I'd never work for them!)

The good news is that SharePoint can help! While SharePoint allows you to scale to infinity for all practical purposes, it also has facilities to make the content easily collected and easily discoverable, no matter how big your store is. Discovering the content can be done easily using document IDs. Thus, if you provision a document center or records center site, you can easily find any document using the document ID facility of SharePoint that I described earlier. If the document IDs are difficult to remember, you can also discover content by using search. So imagine this, you have content being tagged using metadata, you can instantly filter documents within a single document library using metadata, or you can find them with a crawl period delay using search. Using advanced search, you can also slice and dice all such collected content across whichever store you prefer—a store that can span multiple web applications or even farms! So discovery of content is possible, no matter how big your store is. SharePoint gives you all the necessary facilities that you as an architect can use to build a system suitable for a small or large store. Content can remain discoverable using CAML filtering (small store) or search (large store). In most projects, you will end up using a combination of both.

Now let's talk about putting content into SharePoint. Content that is being produced may need to be collected at a different place from where it is being stored. Here are two different and diverse examples:

- Content may be produced all across the farm or even multiple farms. But content, especially important content that you care about (based upon its metadata, perhaps?) may need special treatment. For instance, you could create a tag called Important, and all such content may get aggregated in a central document library from all SharePoint farms in the organization. Or content might be automatically routed to a central records center, perhaps to a humungous document library with a well-defined structure of folders, so that there is a common place to go and discover all content that the organization cares about! As you will see later, this humungous document library in a records center, that I talked of, a more appropriate and fancy sounding name for this is called as the file plan. (I will talk about that later in this chapter.) Thus, there may be a need to "aggregate" important content from all over the place into a central place. I call this the "All roads lead to Rome" scenario.

- The second and perhaps just as important scenario is completely opposite. Imagine that there is a central document library, okay let me use the right term: the file plan of a records center. And users have the ability to manually submit content into this file plan. You probably don't want all the content to sit at the root level of the document library. Imagine this: an e-mail–enabled document library, with each "reply" to the e-mail seeming to have the same subject. Does each reply overwrite the previous reply? Well obviously not! Similarly in a records center, you probably want centrally submitted content to be "fanned out" to appropriate folders (or maybe even separate stores), so appropriate retention policies or storage facilities can be applied on such content. I refer to this scenario as "fanning out of content".

Both of these ("All roads lead to Rome" and "fanning out of content" or any combination thereof) can be used in SharePoint 2010 using a facility called content organizer. Also, as I said earlier in this chapter, the best thing about SharePoint 2010's ECM facilities is that all that I talked of can be activated as features on any site collection, and these features can be taken advantage of in any site collection. Let me illustrate the usage of content organizer in SharePoint 2010 in the blank site definition.

Content organization in SharePoint 2010 is implemented as two features that need to be activated on a site.

The first feature is called DocumentRoutingResources, with FeatureID 0c8a9a47-22a9-4798-82f1-00e62a96006e. This feature adds the necessary field types, and a new content type called Rule under the Content Organizer Content Types. Go ahead and activate this feature on http://sp2010 using the following command:

```
stsadm -o activatefeature -id 0c8a9a47-22a9-4798-82f1-00e62a96006e -url http://sp2010
```

Activating this feature will give you a new content type in the Content Type Gallery as shown in Figure 8-25.

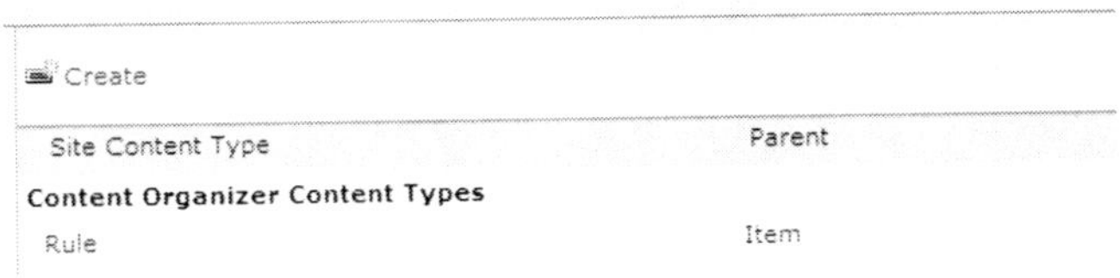

Figure 8-25. *Content organizer rules*

In this content type are various fields that define the structure of a content organization rule, such as priority, the details of the rule, the destination of matched content etc. Next, you need a facility to make use of these rules. Something to store the rules, and something to act upon these rules.

Those facilities are implemented as the DocumentRouting feature with feature id 7ad5272a-2694-4349-953e-ea5ef290e97c. This feature has an ActivationDependency on the DocumentRoutingResources feature, thus if you try activating the DocumentRouting feature before the DocumentRoutingResources feature, you will get the following error message:

```
Dependency feature 'DocumentRoutingResources' (id: 0c8a9a47-22a9-4798-82f1-00e62a96006e) for
feature 'DocumentRouting' (id: 7ad5272a-2694-4349-953e-ea5ef290e97c) is not activated at this
scope.
```

Go ahead and activate the DocumentRouting feature on the http://sp2010 site. Activating this feature will give you the following:

- It will give you two new custom actions under the site settings\site administration area:

- Content Organizer Settings

- Content Organizer Rules

- It will give you a new list called RoutingRules, which can be accessed by clicking the Content Organizer Rules custom action created under the site settings\site administration area.

- It will give you a new document library called the Drop Off Library, where users should drop off content so it can be routed to various locations per the rules defined in Content Organizer Rules.

Now before I dive into setting up a rule and routing new documents, let's first visit the Content Organizer Settings custom action under site actions\settings first. This is a layouts page (also known as an application page) at /_layouts/DocumentRouterSettings.aspx. Over here you can see various settings as applicable to content organizer within this site. Following are the settings you can configure for content organization in SharePoint 2010.

- Redirect users to the Drop Off Library. If this setting is checked, all the document libraries that the content organizer rules know about will see the message shown in Figure 8-26.

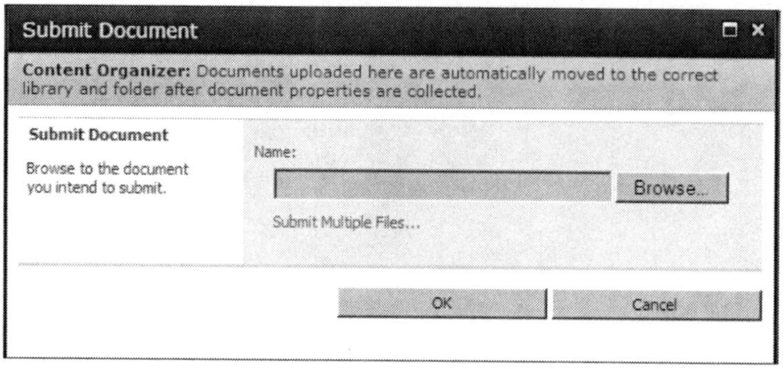

Figure 8-26. *Dropping off a document in the Drop Off Library*

- Now this must not be confused. Content organizer isn't magic and it won't show you this message that the rules have no idea about. This is generally useful for organizing content that participate in content organizer rules.

- Sending to another site: By default, the content organizer is limited to moving content within a site. In fact, when setting up a content organizer rule, the browse button only shows you navigation within the current site collection. However, by checking this check box, you can send the content anywhere you wish.

- Folder partitioning: Folder partitioning in content organizing is an important tool. As I mentioned earlier, frequently different documents may have the same file names. Thus in specifying the rule itself, you can set up such de-duplication rules and individual files can be named differently. However, as a global setting you can create folders based on the number of documents collected. This ensures that no single folder gets so large that the views on it become a performance hassle. Also, to keep your storage costs low, you can now also set retention policies to perhaps archive out content other than say the last 2500 most recent documents, and so on.

- Duplicate submissions: The content organizer rules give you facilities to ensure unique naming. However, if the content organizer administrators were sloppy and didn't envision a particular case that caused a duplicate submission, SharePoint 2010 can allow you to de-duplicate content by using either SharePoint versioning (default) or by making the file name unique.

- Preserving context: Sometimes in records management projects, it is important to preserve audit log histories and various properties. For example, if an insurance company is being sued for privacy information being leaked, you probably want to use audit logs to find out who viewed that information. Just because content was reorganized, you probably don't want to lose this information. However, preserving audit log information can significantly increase the size of your content databases, thus the default value of this property is false.

- Rule managers: This is one or more individuals responsible for managing the content organization rules within a site collection.

- Submission points: By default, a document library called the Drop Off Library is set up for you that allows you to drop content for organization. However, using this setting you can enable more drop-off points, notably a web service at /_vti_bin/OfficialFile.asmx, and an e-mail address for e-mail–enabled document libraries. This facility can thus be used to perform records management on e-mail within SharePoint.

Thus, as you can see, content organizer is quite powerful. Let's see it in action. Set up a document library called **Target**. My intent is that any document with the word *Important* dropped in the Drop Off Library will end up in the target document library. Using the Content Organizer Rules custom action under site actions\site administration, set up a new content organizer rule with the following values:

- Name: Important

- Priority: 5. Priority is important because sometimes you may want to control which rule runs before which rule. You can also choose to inactivate any particular rule by choosing the inactive option.

- Submission Content Type: I choose to target the Document content type, but as you can see, you can choose to use content organizer based on different content types. Depending on the content type, you may also have different properties available to you to set up the content organization rules. Also, content organization can span site collections. Also as you will see later in this chapter, content types can also be shared across site collection boundaries. This section also lets you specify in the rule if the given content type has different names in other site collections.

- Conditions: This is where you specify the rule conditions. All these conditions are "And"-ed with each other. If you're wondering why Or is not an option, remember that you can always set up multiple content rules to simulate Or. The condition I set up was Name "contains all of" Important.

- Target location: If the rule matches, the content is moved to the specified target location. The target location I specified is a document library called Target. You can also choose to prevent accidental overwrites of documents by separating them into their own folders based on property.

Okay, good! So far you have set up a content rule and a Target document library. Now drop a document called Important.docx in the Drop Off Library. Note that soon as you upload the document, the content organizer shows you the message shown in Figure 8-27.

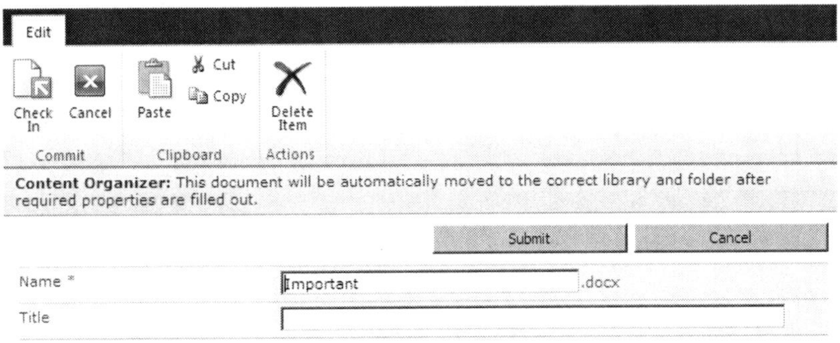

Figure 8-27. *Message prompted to the user after the user drops off a document*

Because you just uploaded the document, the document at this point is effectively checked out to you until you hit the Submit button. The user at this point could just close the browser and leave the document checked out, but if you noted in the content organizer settings, the content administrator can be notified after a configurable number of days if any stray unorganized content is left in the drop off document library. Later in the chapter you will also see the possibility of writing custom information management policies to automatically check in or discard such stray content using custom code.

Now, as soon as you fill out the other properties, and hit the Submit button, the document is effectively checked in for you and is routed to its final destination as shown in Figure 8-28.

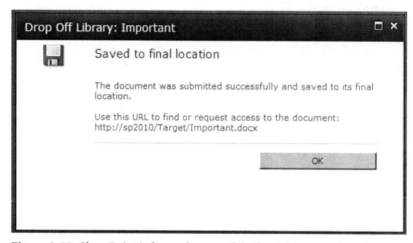

Figure 8-28. *SharePoint informs the user of the final document location*

As you can see, the content organizer rule was run on the newly created document. And per the rule settings, the document was saved to the Target document library, and the final location is communicated to you. The sucky thing here, however, is that because the documents are now flowing all over SharePoint, how will the user remember that URL? Can you guess!?? Simple! Activate the Document ID Service, and you are presented with a dialog box as shown in Figure 8-29.

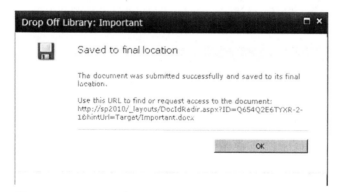

Figure 8-29. *Drop Off Library and Document ID Service in action together*

So as you can see, as more and more of these features are used together with each other, they become increasingly compelling. Next, let's look at a feature that truly adds a lot of value: ECM, content type synchronization.

Enterprise Content Types

Content types are probably some of the most important things you need to master for literally any SharePoint project. They let you attach so much manageability with your data that you cannot really even think of managing your data in SharePoint without leveraging content types. As awesome as content types are, historically speaking, using them consistently across your entire farm has been very troublesome. Not just using them, but also updating them, and synchronizing them all across your farm has been nothing but a pain in the neck! Historically, smart developers have found out ways to push down content type updates using carefully crafted solution packages (or should I say craftily careful solution packages?). Traditionally, out of the box, the boundary for a content type has been the site collection! How limiting, really!

Starting with SharePoint 2010, this is changing! Content types are now free to break the boundaries of the site collection and can freely roam around the farm. Also the way it is implemented is quite easy to manage! It is built on top of the managed metadata service and a hub and spoke model! The idea is that you the architect can decide which site collection gets to be the hub (i.e. the boss of content types) that every other participating site collection listens to. Then from this site collection, you can choose to publish content types and decide which content types get published! Other "spoke" site collections will simply reflect the updates to their content types as they were published from the hub. And in the background, this synchronization of content types occurs with the help of SharePoint jobs.

Let's see this in action. In the example that I am about to set up, I will set up the site collection at root as the hub and another site collection at /sites/receiver as one of the spokes. Then I will create a content type in the hub (i.e., the root site collection), and you will see the process of the content type being made available in the spoke (i.e., in the /sites/receiver site collection). Thus, start by ensuring that you have two site collections: one at root and the other at /sites/receiver. Then, in the root site collection, activate the Content Type Syndication Hub feature. And in the spoke (i.e. receiver/listener) site collection, activate the following feature:

```
stsadm -o activatefeature -url http://sp2010/sites/receiver -id 73EF14B1-13A9-416b-A9B5-
ECECA2B0604C
```

Then visit central administration, under the managed services area. You can create many instances of the managed metadata service, but if you have been following this chapter, you should have an instance by the name of Winsmarts set up. It is in a managed metadata service instance that you would specify which site collection gets to be the hub of the content type synch. Choose the Winsmarts instance, and select Properties from the ribbon. In the ensuing dialog box, point this service to use the root site collection as the Content Type hub, as can be seen in Figure 8-30.

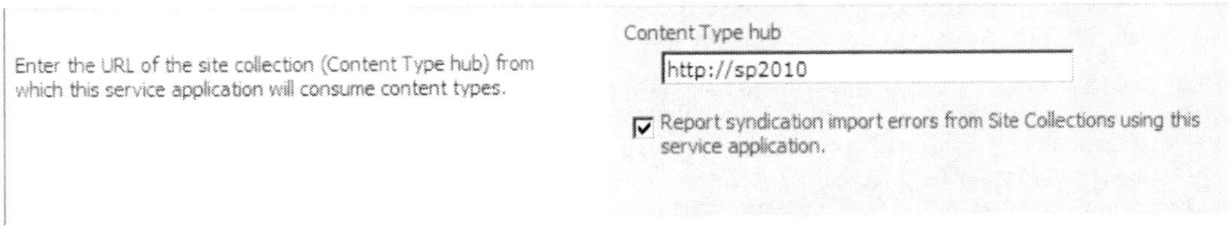

Enter the URL of the site collection (Content Type hub) from which this service application will consume content types.

Content Type hub

http://sp2010

☑ Report syndication import errors from Site Collections using this service application.

Figure 8-30. *Specifying a Content Type hub*

Next, right below the instance of the Winsmarts managed metadata service, click the proxy/connection of the Winsmarts managed metadata instance, and select the check box next to "Consumes content types from the Content Type Gallery at http://sp2010," as shown in Figure 8-31.

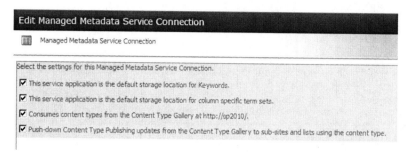

Figure 8-31. *Editing a managed metadata service connection*

Next, go ahead and create a content type in the hub/root site collection. I am going to create a content type called Winsmarts Document that inherits from Document. You can play with a number of settings in the content type, such as the document template, associated workflows, columns, and do on. But as a general rule, as a content type gets synched over to the spoke site collections, you will see that while the content type and all its reusable settings do get synched, the actual supporting artifacts do not. In other words, let's say you have a content type with a workflow associated. The content type along with the workflow associations will get synched, but the workflow itself will have to be deployed and activated on the target site collections.

Now, once you have created the Winsmarts Document content type, visit the content type settings page and look for the Manage Publishing for this content type link. Clicking that link will take you to a page that shows you the various publishing options associated with this content type, and the previous publishing history. The various publishing options are as follows:

- *Publish*: As the name suggests, this option will make the content type available for publishing. If this content type has never been published before, it will be the only option enabled. Do note that published content types in target/spoke site collections are available as read-only/sealed.

- *Unpublish*: Unpublishing a content type as the name suggests will stop publishing further changes to this content type. Note that I said "further" changes—the changes done so far will remain in the target/spoke site collections, and going forward the content types in the target/spoke site collections will become unsealed, and thus available for changes. But future changes will not be applied.

- *Republish*: If for any reason the target/spoke site collections are showing you incorrect content types, you can choose to republish them and thus push the content types afresh!

Now, as I mentioned, the only option available to you at this time will be Publish because this content type has never been published. Thus go ahead and publish this content type. Immediately after you publish this content type, visit the /sites/receiver site collection's Content Type Gallery. What do you see? Unless you are *really* lucky, you shouldn't see the Winsmarts Document content type synched down just yet because this synch runs as a job that is set to run every 15 minutes. To run this job immediately, visit the Job Definitions page in central administration\monitoring, and look for the Content Type hub job definition. Clicking that job definition will show you that this job is set to run every 15 minutes. Also, you will see a Run Now button as shown in Figure 8-32.

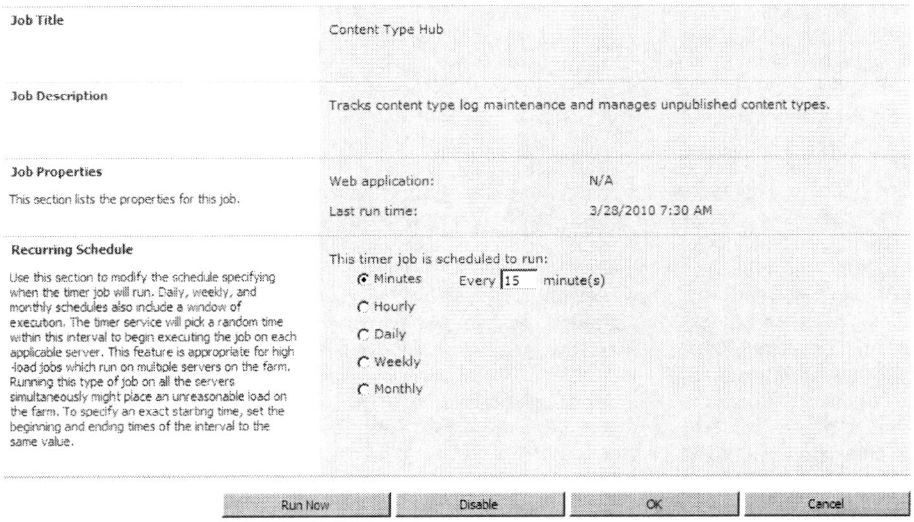

Job Title	Content Type Hub
Job Description	Tracks content type log maintenance and manages unpublished content types.

Job Properties	Web application:	N/A
This section lists the properties for this job.	Last run time:	3/28/2010 7:30 AM

Recurring Schedule	This timer job is scheduled to run:
Use this section to modify the schedule specifying when the timer job will run. Daily, weekly, and monthly schedules also include a window of execution. The timer service will pick a random time within this interval to begin executing the job on each applicable server. This feature is appropriate for high -load jobs which run on multiple servers on the farm. Running this type of job on all the servers simultaneously might place an unreasonable load on the farm. To specify an exact starting time, set the beginning and ending times of the interval to the same value.	⦿ Minutes Every [15] minute(s) ○ Hourly ○ Daily ○ Weekly ○ Monthly

[Run Now]   [Disable]   [OK]   [Cancel]

Figure 8-32. *Timer job schedule and the Run Now button*

Go ahead and click the Run Now button to run the job immediately. Now, visit the Winsmarts Document publishing settings under the root/hub site collection, and under publishing history, you should hopefully see Last successful published at ... This can be seen in Figure 8-33.

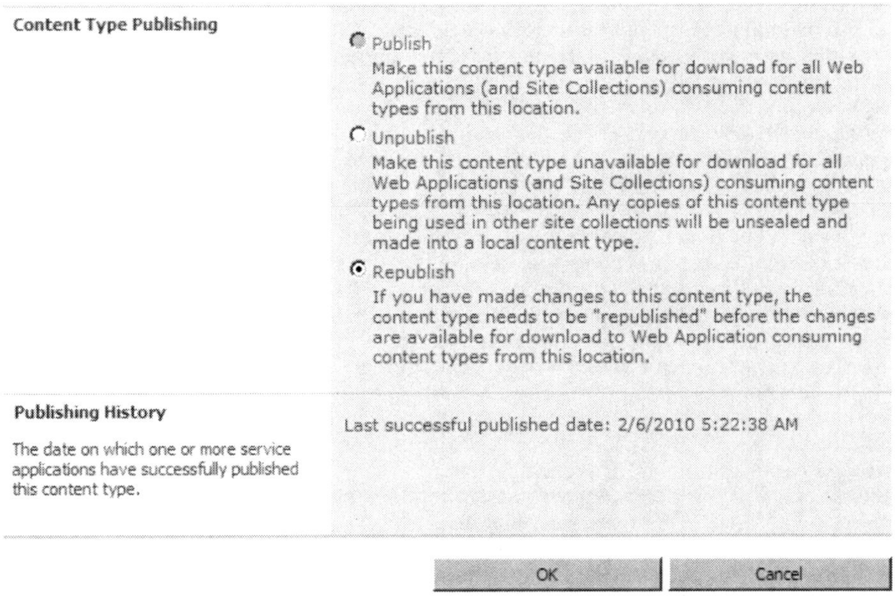

Content Type Publishing	○ Publish Make this content type available for download for all Web Applications (and Site Collections) consuming content types from this location. ○ Unpublish Make this content type unavailable for download for all Web Applications (and Site Collections) consuming content types from this location. Any copies of this content type being used in other site collections will be unsealed and made into a local content type. ⦿ Republish If you have made changes to this content type, the content type needs to be "republished" before the changes are available for download to Web Application consuming content types from this location.
Publishing History The date on which one or more service applications have successfully published this content type.	Last successful published date: 2/6/2010 5:22:38 AM

[OK]   [Cancel]

Figure 8-33. *Various choices under content type publishing*

Now check in the spoke site collection at /sites/receiver. You still wouldn't see the newly created content type propagated here. What you need to do is go back into the jobs area in central administration, and run the Content Type Subscriber job. Now, in the receiver/spoke site collection, under site settings, visit the content type publishing hubs link. Here you should see all the subscribed content types. You should also see the Winsmarts Document content type show up here now. Visit the Content Type Gallery of the receiver/spoke site collection. You should see the Winsmarts Document content type available here. Now click this content type in the receiver site collection. You will note that this content type is read-only. This makes sense because the content type is being published from the root/hub site collection, so any changes being done to this content type must be done in the root/hub—not in the listener/spoke site collection.

Now I'd like you to try out a few experiments on your own! I'd like you to try out the process of unpublishing the content type from root. The content type will become unsealed, but it will not be deleted from the spoke. Also, before you unpublish it, make some further changes to the content type and see its effect on the subscribing/spoke site collections. You will see that subsequent changes are also pushed down to the site collections.

Now let me ask you a question: can one site collection receive content types from more than one hub? Think it over. Let me give you some pointers. I declared a particular site as a content type syndication hub in a managed metadata service instance. Can I have multiple managed metadata service instances pointing to the same hub? Try it out!

In-Place Records Management

Large organizations these days must manage their information properly, so they know who to point a finger at when they are sued. And when they are sued, they need to freeze a current state of all relevant content. In order to freeze relevant content they need to be able to discover relevant content that needs to be frozen.

The previous paragraph covers three important aspects of enterprise content management. To manage information, you need to have proper records management. To freeze documents, you need to be able to place certain documents on hold. And to identify which documents need to be frozen, you need to perform eDiscovery.

SharePoint 2010 allows you to do all these tasks and gives you flexibility to perform each one. Let's start with records management.

Records management can be done in-place, or centralized. Centralized records management will involve the creation of a records center, which is something you can either craft yourself, or you can use an out-of-the-box site definition called Records Center. In contrast, in-place records management will allow you to perform records management tasks right where the content is. Thus you will be able to select a document in a document library and choose to declare it as a record for instance. There are many other ways to declare a document as a record, though. Documents can be declared as records automatically, based on preset information management policies, or they can be declared as records via workflows. In fact, there is even a SharePoint designer workflow activity that will allow you to declare a document as a record. This truly allows you to make the process of recordization truly ingrained into your existing business processes.

Once a document has been declared as a record, you will be able to apply various rules to it, such as its editability, and perhaps you have a centralized records center in which such content can be routed at a later date, perhaps using a retention policy or similar.

There is no right or wrong approach between the two, and most organizations will end up using a mixture of both in-place and centralized records management.

Holds and eDiscovery work in a similar fashion. Let's say I am this huge multibillion-dollar organization in the business of giving legal advice to my clients. One of my clients ends up losing a lot of money and believe they lost that money because of bad advice I gave them. So they are now suing me for giving them bad advice. So I need to prove that my advice was good. In doing so, I (or my lawyers) will need to freeze a state of all pertinent content that deals with this client. Thus, I need to place all this content on hold, which obviously has a downside: current work that requires editing on the content grinds to a halt. So maybe I want to make a copy of the content and freeze the copy instead. As I will show you shortly, SharePoint 2010 allows you to address all these scenarios easily.

And finally because a document has been declared as a record or has been placed on hold, I need to be able to click any document and view its current compliance details. In other words, I can find out whether a current document is on hold or not. If so what are the details of the hold? Is the current document a record? If it is a record, what are the details of this record?

So you have in-place records management eDiscovery, and Hold. There are two other concepts I need to talk about before I dive into showing all this in action. One is auditing and reporting; the second is retention and expiration.

Auditing and reporting refers to the ability to produce per-item level audit log reports. You can keep tabs on events such as who saw what information! Also part of reporting is an overall file plan report. Fileplan is something that is perhaps more pertinent to centralized records management, though it can be applied to in-place records management as well. But in short, it refers to a folder-like structure you would create, and the various information management policies can be hierarchically applied. Content can then be routed using content organizer rules into appropriate folders. A fileplan report allows you to see an overview of all your content management policies. As you may guess, file plan is one of the most critical and evolving decisions you will take in any serious ECM project.

Finally, there is retention and expiration. Retention and expiration is a concept that can apply to both in-place records management and centralized records management. The whole idea here is that you have certain metadata with any collected SharePoint content. This metadata can be normal columns or metadata columns. Based on that metadata, and perhaps even other rules, you can create policies that move content from one basket to another. In moving content from one basket to another, you can treat the content differently; you can make the content less or more discoverable, you can make it less or more searchable, you can permanently freeze it for further changes, or you can even destroy it (commonly referred to as *disposition of content*).

Good! With the theory behind us, let's see all this in action.

But before I start, I should mention once again that everything you are seeing here is available as a centralized preset site definition (records center or documents center), or as features you can activate in any site you want.

Okay, so let's start! Create a site definition using the blank site definition. In this site definition, create a document library called **MyDox**, and another Wiki library called **MyWiki**. Go ahead and put some random content in both of them. Also, for the site collection, go ahead and activate the in-place records management site collection level feature.

Now, go to the MyWiki document library and access Library Settings; you should see a link for Information Management Policies. Clicking that link will show you all the existing content types in the document library and whether any retention policies are associated with the content type. One thing to note is that when you are creating information management policies, you should first create your own relevant content types and then create those information management policies on those content types! This makes sense because for example Winsmarts sends invoices to clients; those invoices are in many document libraries; each invoice needs to have a retention policy applied to it; and so I should attach such a policy to the content type invoice, not to the various document libraries where such content appears.

To keep things simple for now, click the Wiki Page content type, and you will be taken to a page where you can set up various information management policies on the given content type:

- *Barcodes and Labels*: These are used for physical records management. Imagine that you have some old printouts from the 1970s sitting organized by cardboard boxes in a temperature-controlled room; you can still organize those boxes in your document library, and the document library can generate the barcode or appropriate label, which can then be stuck to those boxes.

- *Auditing*: Auditing allows SharePoint to keep a log of a history of certain events performed on the document. These events can be seen in Figure 8-34.

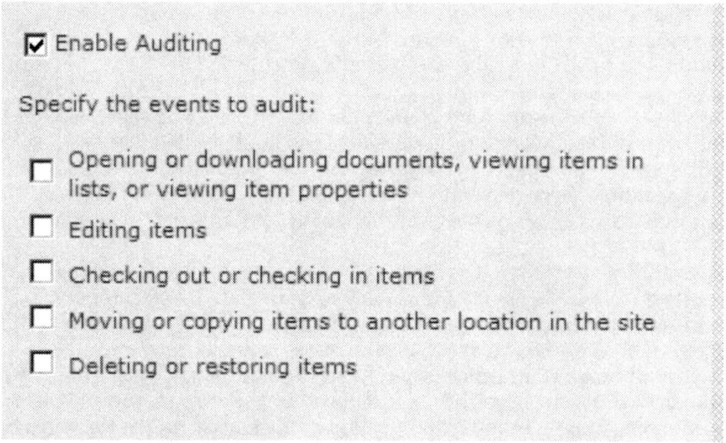

☑ Enable Auditing

Specify the events to audit:

☐ Opening or downloading documents, viewing items in
lists, or viewing item properties

☐ Editing items

☐ Checking out or checking in items

☐ Moving or copying items to another location in the site

☐ Deleting or restoring items

Figure 8-34. *Enabling auditing*

- *Retention*: Retention policies allow you to specify how content is moved between different buckets/containers within your SharePoint installation and is eventually deleted. You can specify how exactly the content gets moved based on various conditions you can add. The combination of the condition (formula) with the appropriate action together forms a retention policy. You also have the ability to treat records and nonrecords differently. I will talk about records shortly, but you care about records more than nonrecords, so you probably want to apply different retention policies to them. Check the Enable Retention check box Click the Add a retention stage link, which will allow you to add a retention stage (see Figure 8-35).

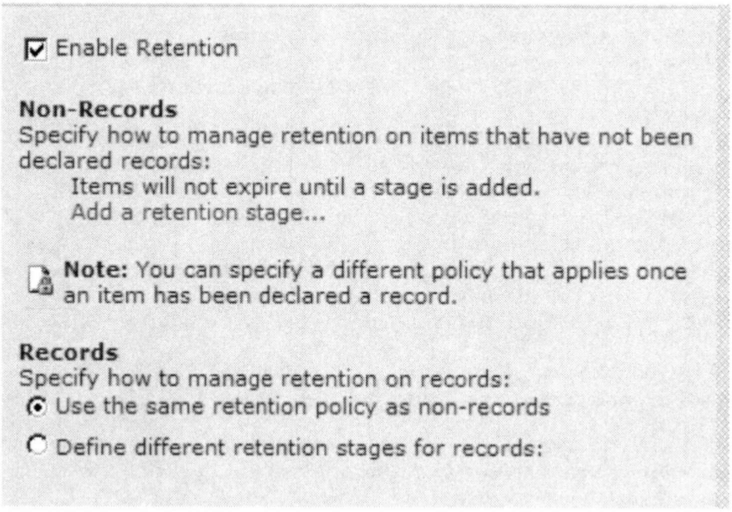

☑ Enable Retention

Non-Records
Specify how to manage retention on items that have not been
declared records:
    Items will not expire until a stage is added.
    Add a retention stage...

   Note: You can specify a different policy that applies once
an item has been declared a record.

Records
Specify how to manage retention on records:
  ◉ Use the same retention policy as non-records

  ○ Define different retention stages for records:

Figure 8-35. *Adding retention stages*

Click the Add a retention stage link, choose to add a retention policy, and set up a new retention policy as shown in Figure 8-36.

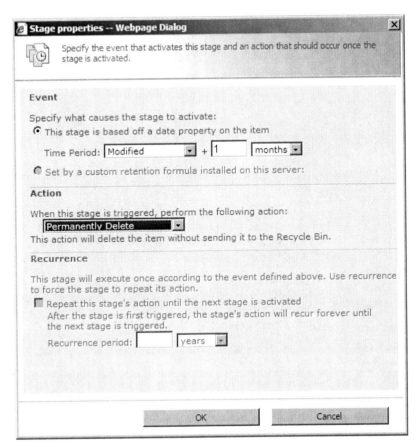

Figure 8-36. *Details of a retention stage*

Remember that a retention policy is based on a formula and an action. Well there you have it! The formula here is Modified + 1 month, so any document whose modified date > 1 month will match this formula. Then if something matches, what action do I want to perform on it? Well, I want to permanently delete it. You can also write your own expiration formula by implementing the IExpirationFormula interface and your own custom action by implementing the IExpirationAction interface as shown here: http://blah.winsmarts.com/2008-10-Authoring_custom_expiration_policies_and_actions_in_SharePoint_2007.aspx. Poke around a bit and see what other formulas and actions you can specify. You will see that one of the actions you can specify is the ability to declare an artifact as a record. Thus, you have the ability to declare records through retention policies just in case your end business users are too lazy to declare records manually (which they probably will be!). As soon as you add the information management policy, you will also note that you can add many stages to the same retention policy. This is very useful because you can specify things such as running a document through seven stages, after which you assume that this is a useless document and delete it to save on storage costs.

Also, while you're at it, set an auditing policy that enables auditing for opening and viewing of the content as shown in Figure 8-37.

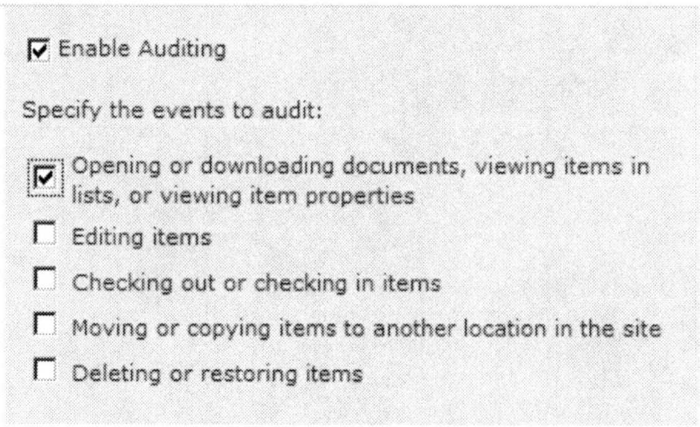

☑ Enable Auditing

Specify the events to audit:

☑ Opening or downloading documents, viewing items in lists, or viewing item properties

☐ Editing items

☐ Checking out or checking in items

☐ Moving or copying items to another location in the site

☐ Deleting or restoring items

Figure 8-37. *Enabling specific events to be audited*

Go ahead and save this newly created information management policy. You've just set up a retention policy and an auditing policy! Now the wiki page you created, if left untouched for > 1 month, will get deleted automatically. However, everyone who has viewed this page will be logged as a part of your auditing policy.

But before I show you how, I'd like you to do one more thing! Go ahead and activate one more feature in the site, called Holds and eDiscovery. Once this feature is activated, a new section will become available under site settings called Holds and eDiscovery. In this section, you will see three links:

- *Hold reports*: Tells you what content has been placed on hold.

- *Holds*: Allows you to create one or more holds. Each hold is managed by a hold administrator.

- *Discover and Hold content*: Allows you to execute search queries and places all matched documents on hold.

Thus, before you can start placing stuff on hold, you need to make sure your search is running. I will talk about search in much further depth elsewhere in the book, but for now just go into Managed Services under central administration, and click Search Service Settings. On the settings page for Search Service Settings, look for the Content Sources link on the left side. When you see a content source called Local SharePoint Sites, issue a full crawl on that content source. This page will look like Figure 8-38.

Use this page to add, edit, or delete content sources, and to manage crawls.

🖳 New Content Source   📄 Refresh   ■ Stop all crawls   ‖ Pause all crawls

Type	Name	Status	Current crawl duration	Last crawl duration
🗐	Local SharePoint sites	Starting		00:02:00

Figure 8-38. *Crawling your content and making it available for search*

Once the crawl is finished (i.e., your content is now searchable), come back to the site collection settings of the root site collection at port 80 where you had created the MyDox and MyWiki document libraries, and click the Discover and Hold Content link.

- *Search Criteria*: Lets you pick search criteria; all content matching search criteria will be placed on hold for you.

- *Local Hold or Export*: Allows you to either hold and freeze the content where it is or copy the content to a specified destination location and place the hold there. This will allow the content to be continued to work upon, and a snapshot is placed a hold on in an alternate location.

- *Relevant Hold*: Allows you to specify the specific hold, along with its administrator that you intend to place these documents under.

In my case, I had the word *Random* appear on my wiki, so I searched for the keyword *random*. I decided to place a hold on the content directly where it was, and I created a hold called Random Hold whose administrator was Winsmarts\administrator. After specifying all these details to your hold content form, click the Add results to hold button at the bottom of the page. The message shown in Figure 8-39 appears

Figure 8-39. *Confirmation of placing a hold*

In the background and using a job, SharePoint will place a hold on all content that matches your search query, and it will send you an e-mail when the hold is complete!

Note that you also have the option of selecting a document individually and placing it on hold. For instance, in this case, go to the MyWiki document library, and using the Library tab in the ribbon, choose to view all pages in the MyWiki document library. Then in the ECB menu of any wiki page, choose to view Compliance Details; you will see the dialog box shown in Figure 8-40.

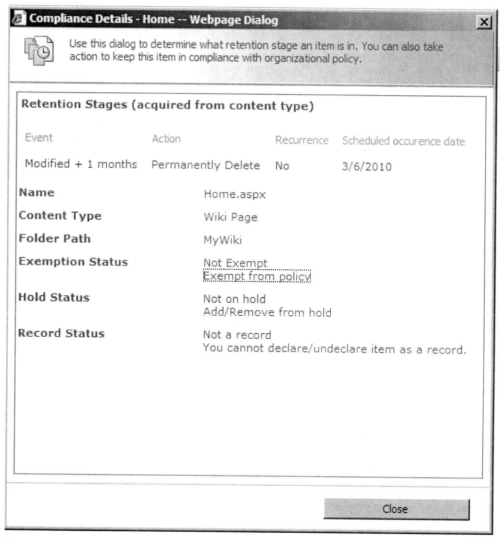

Figure 8-40. *Marking a document as exempt from a policy*

The Compliance Details dialog box shows you a number of things. It shows you the retention stages on the item; whether or not the item is exempt from any information management policies, such as auditing; and right from here you can choose to place an individual document on hold or remove a hold on an individual document! Go ahead and place a document on hold or wait for the timer job to place all searched documents on hold. After a document has been placed on hold, the wiki page shows clearly that the document is on hold and is thus unavailable for further changes. This can be seen in Figure 8-41.

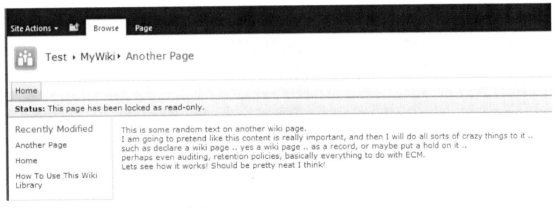

Figure 8-41. *A wiki page placed on hold*

Now there is one other interesting thing I want to show you! Look at the Compliance Details dialog box one more time. What do you see? There is a choice at the bottom that tells you that this particular document is not a record. Not only that, it tells you that this "item" cannot be declared as a record. Bummer! I thought I had turned the In-Place Records Management feature on in this wiki page library. Well, simply activating that feature isn't enough! You also need to specify where in the site collection the ability to declare records is available. There are two places where you can specify it.

The first place is under site collection settings under a link called Record Declaration Settings. This page allows you to specify three things.

1. You can choose record restrictions: to have no restrictions on records, block deletes on records, or block edits and deletes on items that have been declared as records.

2. You can choose to make available where the ability to declare records is available. From here, you can either turn it on globally within the site collection or turn it off globally. But if you turn it off globally, you can still turn it on a per-location basis on individual lists and document libraries. Note that I said, lists *and* document libraries, so starting with SharePoint 2010, all sorts of SharePoint content can participate in the RM lifecycle. How exciting! To access that section, you may visit any list or document library, go to list or document library settings, and look for a link called Record Declaration Settings. On this page, you can choose to inherit the site collection's record declaration setting, override the site collection's setting and always allow the facility to declare records, or override the site collection's setting and never allow the facility to declare records. You can also choose to automatically mark all added items or documents into this list as records.

3. Finally, back under the site collection record declaration settings, under Declaration Rules, you can choose to specify who can declare records and who can undeclare records. This setting can be seen in Figure 8-42.

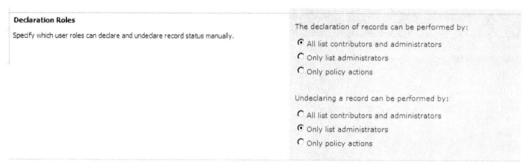

Declaration Roles

Specify which user roles can declare and undeclare record status manually.

The declaration of records can be performed by:

- ⦿ All list contributors and administrators
- ○ Only list administrators
- ○ Only policy actions

Undeclaring a record can be performed by:

- ○ All list contributors and administrators
- ⦿ Only list administrators
- ○ Only policy actions

Figure 8-42. *Who can declare and undeclare records*

Now you know how to make record declaration available! So, go ahead and make declaration of records available in the wiki library. Choose to mark a few documents as records, and you will see that the wiki pages icons show little locks by them (see Figure 8-43).

☐	Type	Name
		Misc Documents
		On the Insert tab
		Sample Document

✛ Add document

Figure 8-43. *Locks visually identifying which items are records*

As you will see, declaring any item or document as a record also trims the ECB menu, the ribbon, and appropriately reflects the details in the Compliance Details dialog box.

Hierarchical File Plans and Folder-Based Retention

In the previous section, I talked about retention policies that you can apply to individual content types in lists or document libraries. The reality is that usually the amount of content and categories of content generated in a typical organization will require a better manageability of retention policies. For instance, the policies would sound something like this: "If this e-mail is more than six months old, go ahead and archive it, but if the CEO sent it, don't archive it." This sounds very much like the ability to set retention policies and then be able to override certain retention policies under special conditions.

Now, you also saw the content organizer in action earlier in this chapter. So think of it this way: if you were managing e-mail or documents, then based on sender or creator of the document, the content could be routed to an appropriate document library. Even better, if you had a centralized place for managing all records, the document could be routed to an appropriate folder. Thus, there could be a folder called Documents that are Records, but if the CEO created such a document, you could have a subfolder called CEO's Documents. Then by using appropriate content organizer rules, you could theoretically route the documents to the appropriate location. This is the beginning of the formation of your hierarchical file plan!

Now, wouldn't it be nice if in this file plan you could apply hierarchical retention policies? And that you can! Usually you would take such an approach in a records center or centralized records management, but nothing stops you from using this feature right inside your site collections. Simply activate the Library and Folder Based Retention feature at the site collection level and then visit the MyDox document library you created earlier. Under MyDox, create a folder called **Child**, put some documents in it, and create a folder called **GrandChild** and put some documents in it, too. Now, go into the information management policy settings of the MyDox document library, and you should see Library Based Retention Schedule option. This can be seen in Figure 8-44.

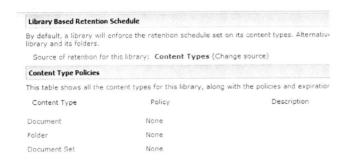

Figure 8-44. *Specifying retention schedules on a document library*

On this screen, choose to change source for the retention for this document library. You will be able to change the retention policy source from content types to library and folders. By changing the retention source to Library and Folders, you will now be able to add retention stages at the library level. Go ahead and add a retention schedule specifying that if a document has a created date > 1 year, it is moved to the Recycle bin (see Figure 8-45).

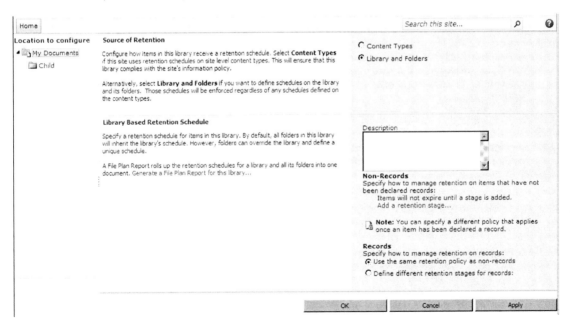

Figure 8-45. *Specifying a retention policy*

Now, I'd like to draw your attention to the left side of the preceding figure You can see the folder structure shown as a tree view! Hmm, I wonder what happens if I click the Child folder? The UI changes to that shown in Figure 8-46.

Figure 8-46. *Children inherit retention policies from the parent*

By default, child folders inherit from the parent's retention policies, but you have the ability to configure retention stages at the child level different from the parent. This is referred to as a hierarchical file plan and retention policies specified in your hierarchical file plan.

One final thing I'd like to mention before I shift my focus to the Records Center is the availability of a list definition called Records Library that has automatic records declaration and such relevant features preconfigured for you. Go ahead and create a list based on the Records Library and examine its facilities. You will find that it is simply a document library with automatic declaration of records turned on, among other things.

Records Center

You know the funniest thing about this entire chapter? I've told you everything that the Records Center does without actually talking about it! So let's talk about it.

The Records Center is a site that puts together all the features I described previously as a single site. It is available to create as a child site or as a site collection. But in order to be able to create the Records Center as a child site, you must activate the content organizer features first. This has been described in this chapter earlier, so I won't go over the instructions again. But whether you create the Records Center as a site or as a site collection, the feature set is the same. But what creating the Records Center as its own site collection does give you is the ability to segregate that site collection as its own content database and thus be able to use RBS capabilities of SharePoint to store all those documents in an alternate storage. Believe me, you will need it.

Through central administration, create a site collection based on the Records Center template called Records at /sites/Records. When you create the Records Center you will notice the following:

- This is a site collection with the content organizer turned on. There is a Drop Off Library and you can set up various content organizer rules to route the documents accordingly.

- There is a records library created for you.

- There is a facility to submit new records or to query for an existing record using the unique document ID facilities in SharePoint, as described earlier in this chapter.

- You will find a custom action under site settings called Manage Records Center that takes you to a page at http://sp2010/sites/Records/rcconsole.aspx. This page puts together all the convenient facilities in a SharePoint records center (nothing that you haven't already seen in this chapter), activated as individual features.

The Records Center is intended to be that gargantuan centralized location where all records for the organization are ingested. There is another site definition called the Document Center, which is again a site definition with features turned on that are described in this chapter. There are some additional search- related facilities in both the Document Center and the Records Center that I didn't describe in this chapter, but they, too, are just features that can be turned on in any site collection.

Summary

As I said at the start of this chapter, enterprise content management in SharePoint 2010 is a big topic. We discussed a number of facilities in SharePoint 2010 that makes both ECM and document management better and easier. I talked about document IDs, document sets, and the whole managed metadata infrastructure. I also discussed the concept of enterprise content types, which now allow content types to break free of the site collection boundary and freely roam around the farm. Then we took a deep dive into various records management features such as recordization, auditing, eDiscovery, holds, and retention policies. I also discussed the concept of hierarchical file plans, and retention policies work within that. Perhaps the biggest takeaway here is that all these facilities are available for you in any site collection. Or you can use them in a centralized form in the shape of a Records Center.

CHAPTER 9

■ ■ ■

Business Connectivity Services

In the past few chapters, I've been talking about managing data in SharePoint 2010. A discussion on managing your data without the mention of BCS, or Business Connectivity Services would be incomplete. However, BCS isn't as much about Data inside SharePoint, it's more about SharePoint acting as the medium (or as I like to say, the "goo") that binds all your disparate systems and different kinds of data together. BCS is a set of out of the box features, services and tools that enhance SharePoint by streamlining the creation of solutions with deep integration of external data and services into SharePoint. The idea here is that SharePoint is not the only system you will have in your organization. There will be many other systems that contain valuable data in an enterprise. It is bringing those systems into SharePoint so all relevant data from various systems can be presented on the same canvas is what makes BCS so compelling.

BCS can be viewed as three major components.

- The back-end systems where the data resides. These maybe LOB systems, systems exposing WCF services, databases, web 2.0 sources, or basically anything that is programmable in some way or another.

- The BCS layer, which includes the BCS runtime, external content types (described in this chapter), and external lists that make use of external content types.

- The client side, which includes a BCS runtime, or you can use your favorite Office applications, including InfoPath to interact with BCS data.

Note that there used to be a similar technology in SharePoint 2007 called BDC. If you wish to read more about BDC, please see http://blah.winsmarts.com/2007-4-Sharepoint_2007__BDC_-_The_Business_Data_Catalog.aspx. But BDC was much more primitive compared to BCS. Following are the major architectural differences between BCS and BDC.

- BCS has a much richer feature set when it comes to presentation of the data. The data is now available in SharePoint workspace, Office Clients etc. I will demonstrate some examples in this chapter.

- BCS has a much wider choice when it comes to connectivity. You have the ability to communicate with WCF services, SQL Server or .NET components. BDC could communicate with only Web Services or ADO.NET data providers. Also, the architecture is designed for both read and write.

- BCS has much better tooling support in both SharePoint designer, and Visual Studio.

External Content Types

Data in an organization can live in various back-end systems. An external content type is a content type available in SharePoint 2010, that describes the schema, and data access capabilities of an external data source and its behavior within Office and SharePoint 2010.Thus, the external content type in BCS is the logical equivalent of what used to be called the Entity in BDC. But, External Content Types contain much more information than a BDC entity.

Once you have described all the above information in an external content type, you then have the capability of leveraging the external data as external lists or through the object model directly in the SharePoint thin client, i.e., your web browser, or you can use it in thick clients such as Office apps.

You have the ability to describe such External content types, and the various usages of external content types using the full gamut of Office tools. For instance, power users can create a full no-code BCS solution using tools such as SharePoint Designer. Using SharePoint designer they have the ability to bring in external data, and be able to connect the external data to Outlook or SharePoint workspace. Then you have the ability to customize interaction with the BCS data using InfoPath forms, Outlook task pane and ribbon, and Word templates using Quick Parts. BCS data can also be used in workflows, and WebPart pages. These approaches can be simple, or complex, and may or may not require a developer depending upon what you are doing with the usage of BCS data. Finally, you have the ability to use Visual Studio to define custom connectivity and aggregation of your entity information, embed logic inside forms, create reusable UI elements, and basically anything you desire. Let's look at each one of these one by one.

BCS and SharePoint Designer (No Code)

The datasource I will use throughout this chapter is the NorthWind database. You will find an .sql script to setup the NorthWind database in the associated code download, or you can download it from Microsoft's website. Thus, at this time, go ahead and run that script and setup NorthWind database on a SQL Server you can access. I set it up on the same SQL Server that is on my development virtual machine. The process of using BCS in SharePoint involves setting up an External Content Type and then using that content type inside of an external list. Thus, start SharePoint designer 2010, and open the http://sp2010 site. Once the site is opened, the various categories of artifacts of the site are shown in a navigation bar on the left side. One of those is "External Content Types", go ahead and click it. Because, as of now you have no external content types setup in this SharePoint site collection, you will see an empty pane on the right. Now, in the ribbon, go ahead and click on the "New External Content Type" button.

What I intend to do is, setup an external content type that shows all NorthWind customers. But these customers are very similar to an existing content type in SharePoint called "Contacts". Is it possible perhaps to show these customers as contacts, and thus be able to do with NorthWind Customers (which are also my contacts), and operate upon them like a regular SharePoint contact? Let's see!

After you click on the "New External Content Type" button, SharePoint designer will show you a form that will let you customize various properties of the new External Content Type you are setting up. In this form, go ahead and specify the name to be "NorthWind Customer", and choose to base it on the Office Item Type "Contact". Also glance over the other choices available to you there. Do these seem like something you might be able to use in Outlook?

When you have filled out the form, click on the "Click here to discover external data sources and define operations" link as shown in Figure 9-1.

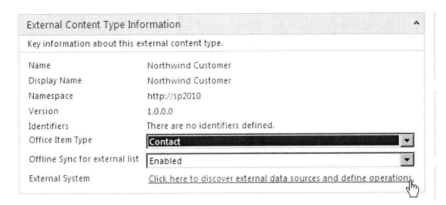

Figure 9-1. *Defining external sources and operations*

Clicking on that link will bring you to a screen where you can add one or more data sources for this content type. Clicking on the "Add connection" button will pop open a dialog box asking you, what kind of data source you wish to add. There are three choices.

- .NET Type: Allows you to use a .NET component as your data source.

- SQL Server: Allows you to use a backend SQL Server database as your datasource. This is the choice we will use for this example.

- WCF Service: Any WCF service can also act as a data source, this means existing web services will also work, because they are effectively WCF Services with basicHttpBinding.

In this example, choose SQL Server as the back-end datasource. In the dialog box that pops up, you can specify the datasource details along with the authentication mechanism used. As you can see, there are three choices for SQL Server based connections. You can choose to connect using the user's identity which is great for development purposes but in production will cause a new connection pool to be created for every user who uses this external content type - hardly a good choice! Later on, once your external content type datasource is setup, if you poke through the UI, you will discover a checkbox that lets you completely disable connection pooling as well. Bad or disabled connection pooling will severely negatively affect your performance. If you are interested in reading more details on connection pooling and application performance, you should see another book I wrote, "Pro ADO.NET 2.0", specifically Chapter 4, example #4.3 illustrates that eliminating connection pooling will cause a performance impact of 20 times! Not 20 percent, 20 times! Not to mention, this would mean effectively securing logical database objects at the database level, something we usually don't do! We like to control SQL Server security for SQL Server objects such as stored procedures, but logical business logic security is implemented in the queries as where clauses. The other two choices, allow you to use either windows based identity or a custom identity such as a claims aware identity, while leveraging the secure store API in SharePoint. This is very much like SSO used to be in SharePoint 2007. I will describe this technique in depth in Chapter 12, where I talk about security, but for now, go ahead and choose to connect as the user's identity and make sure you, the logged in user, have access to the backend NorthWind database you are trying to connect to.

Once the connection has been added, look for the "Customers" table under NorthWind, right click on it, and choose to create all operations. You would note that BDC was designed to be read-only, but in BCS you can create all sorts of read/write operations. Also, from this screen you can choose to create associations. Once you choose to create all operations, a dialog box will pop-up, which will prompt you with any unresolved issues, both warnings and errors, in your newly created operations. On this screen, you should map a queried column to an Office Property. For instance, I mapped CustomerID to Account, Customer Address to Business Primary Address etc. Not everything needs to be mapped, but the identifier fields do need to be mapped. Also, on this screen you should pick a column or two that will show up in the picker in SharePoint. The picker will otherwise show all columns, which is not such a great user experience. I choose to show the ContactName in the picker.

The last screen in adding operations allows you to add filters. Not adding filters will cause a large amount of data to be fetched into SharePoint. Unlike BDC, BCS External Lists do not store the information in the content database - they leave the information in the back-end store, and bring it into SharePoint when it is needed. As a result, very large amounts of data being brought into SharePoint may not be too good for performance. It isn't as bad as it sounds though, because BCS does have bulk load operation routines, so unless you are fetching thousands of items, this shouldn't be such a problem. For the NorthWind customers, I choose to not add any filters. Click on Finish to complete adding the operations. You can double click on any operation to further tweak the operations as necessary.

Now, glance at the ribbon! You will see two more interesting buttons. First of all, both of these buttons will require you to save the external content type first. So go ahead and save the external content type first. You might wonder where this entity was stored. If you visit central administration\manage service applications, and click on the "Business Data Connectivity" service application, you should see the NorthWind Customer saved as shown in Figure 9-2.

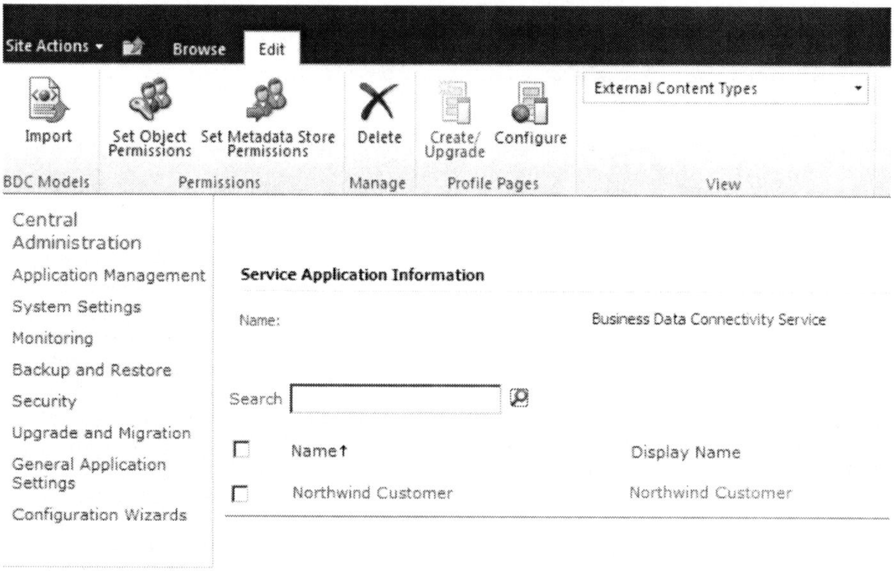

Figure 9-2. *Newly created external content type*

Once your entity is saved, come back to SharePoint designer and look at those two buttons enabled on the ribbon.

The first button deals with creating the profile page! A profile page is what shows a single entity. This is a concept carried over from BDC, behind the scenes you need a method instance of "SpecificIdentifier" for the profile page to be created. Since you have a "Read Item" operation created in the NorthWind Customers External Content Type, you are able to create a profile page. But if you click on this button, you will get the error shown in Figure 9-3.

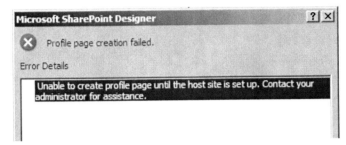

Figure 9-3. *Can't create the profile page*

While this looks like an error, it is a huge improvement over BDC. In BDC, the profile page ended up getting created in the SSP - you are not going to give end users access to the SSP! So in the real world, you ended up deleting that profile page, then creating a new one. What a pain! In SharePoint 2010, you first specify the profile page host URL, so you choose where the profile pages get created! Thus go ahead and specify the host URL for profile pages. You can do so by visiting the newly created external content type under central administration\manage service applications\business data connectivity, and clicking on the "Configure" button in the ribbon as shown in Figure 9-4.

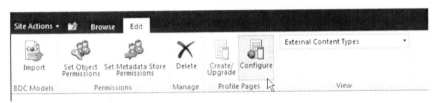

Figure 9-4. *The Configure button on the ribbon*

Once you have setup the profile page host URL, come back to SharePoint designer, and click on the Create Profile page once more time! Profile pages are also what the end user's will see as search results when these external content type entities get crawled.

The second button is prompting you to create lists and forms. Lists will be based on external content lists, and forms will be the user interface through which you will be able to interact with this external content type. Both of these can be done through the browser, or from SharePoint designer. If you decided to create the external list using the browser, you would create a new list using a list definition called "External List". You would then specify which External Content Type this external list is to be based upon. But for now, in SharePoint designer, go ahead and click on this button to create the external list. This will pop up a dialog box as shown in Figure 9-5. Fill the dialog box, and choose to not create an InfoPath form yet.

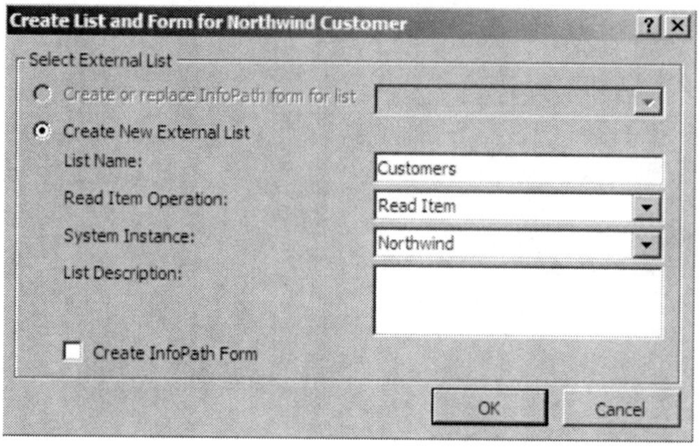

Figure 9-5. *Creating an external list based on an existing external content type*

Next, give yourself all permissions to the "NorthWind Customers" BCS external content type in central administration. All permissions are not required to simply use the object, but at least one user should be given all permissions to the BCS external content type. Do note that the BCS metadata is cached for a minute, so if you don't see the results of your permission changes immediately, try after a minute.

Finally, visit the list at http://sp2010/Lists/Customers. You should see all NorthWind Customers pulled into the list. You are probably looking at a lot of columns, but you can always modify the view to show a subset of columns! Now go ahead and edit the first database row, uhhh, I mean list item, with CustomerID "ALFKI". You would note that editing the list item updates the SQL database row! Now in the ribbon, click on the "Connect to Outlook" button under the "List" tab, and SharePoint will generate a vstopackage at runtime and prompt you to install it as shown in Figure 9-6.

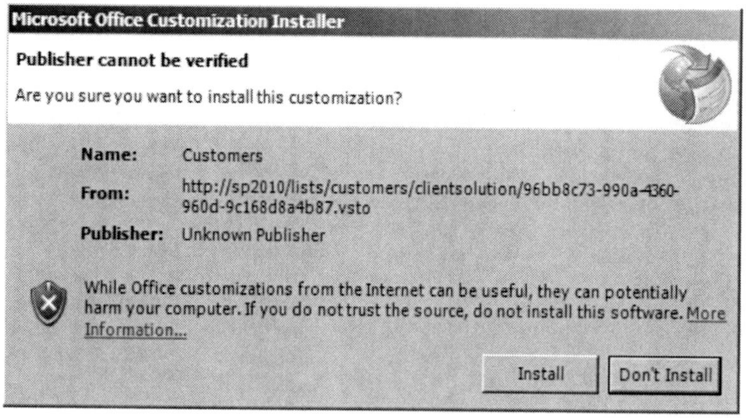

Figure 9-6. *Prompt to download and install a package*

Choose to install the package, and then start Outlook. You would note that all your NorthWind customers are now available as "Contacts" in a separate .pst. This can be seen in Figure 9-7.

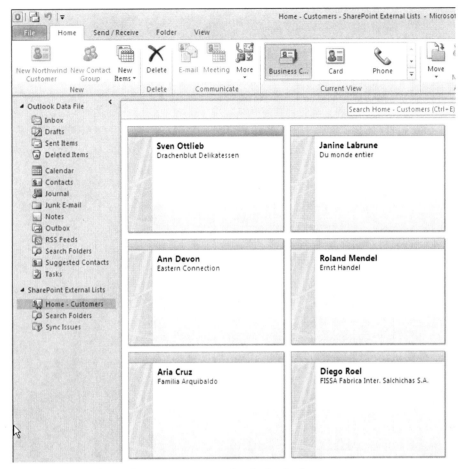

Figure 9-7. *NorthWind Customers appearing in Outlook as contacts*

Remember when you had setup this external content type, you had based it on the "Contact" Office type? What do you think would happen if you had based this external content type on "Task" or "Appointment" Office type?

Having content available as external content types, and in external lists also opens up some other interesting possibilities. For instance, you can use external content types as data sources in your Word templates! Lets imagine that you want to compose a Word document to a NorthWind customer. While you could start by typing up a fresh document, it would be nice if such a document was based on a template. Also, now that you have contact information available as an external content type in your SharePoint site, it would be nice if somehow my Word template was smart enough that typing in the CustomerID would fill in all the rest of the details, such as their full name, and their address.

All this is possible with BCS and external content types. Let's see how! Start by creating a new document library called "Customer Communication". In this document library, go ahead and add a column based on the "External Data" column. Choose to import the information as shown in Figure 9-8.

Additional Column Settings
Specify detailed options for the type of information you selected.
Description:
Require that this column contains information:
Yes No
External Content Type:
Northwind Customer (Northwind)
Select the Field to be shown on this column:
CustomerID
Display the actions menu
Link this column to the Default Action of the External Content Type
Add a column to show each of these additional fields:
Select all fields
Address
City
CompanyName
ContactName
ContactTitle
Country
CustomerID
Fax
Phone
PostalCode
Region
Add to default view

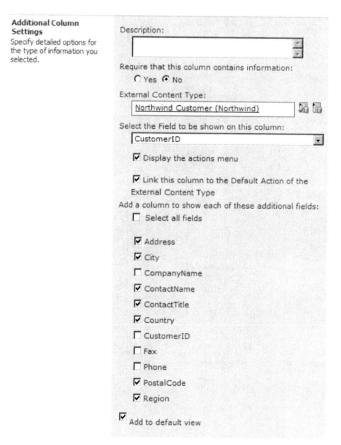

Figure 9-8. *External Data Column settings*

Now, visit the document library settings, and under "Advanced settings" look for the document template. Click on the link to "Edit Template", and Word should pop up allowing you to edit the Template. Now, go ahead and craft up the template as shown in Figure 9-9.

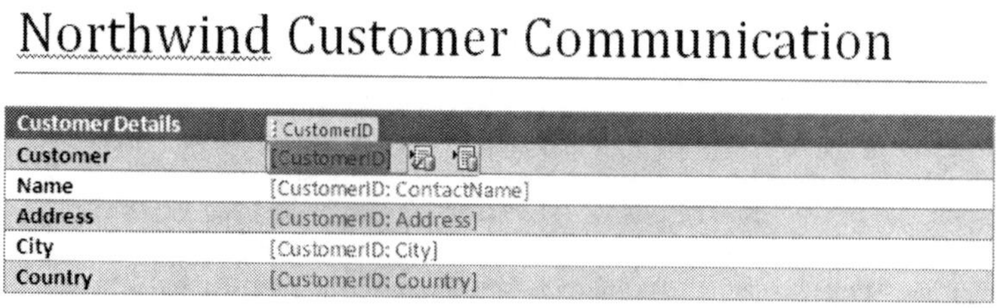

Northwind Customer Communication
Customer Details
CustomerID
Customer
[CustomerID]
Name
[CustomerID: ContactName]
Address
[CustomerID: Address]
City
[CustomerID: City]
Country
[CustomerID: Country]

Figure 9-9. *Placeholders in your Word document*

Those placeholders you see in the right column have been picked from the Document Properties under Quick Parts under the Insert Tab of the Word ribbon. This can be seen in Figure 9-10.

Figure 9-10. *Inserting Document Quick Parts*

Particularly speaking, the first Quick Part you see is "CustomerID". This will be editable in the final Word template, allowing you to pick an individual customer; the other Quick Parts will be read-only. To be sure that you dropped the right quick part, the customer quick part will show two icons right next to the Quick Part as shown in Figure 9-11.

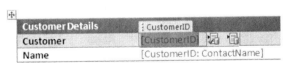

Figure 9-11. *The two icons right next to the quickpart*

Okay good, now go ahead and save your template, close Word, and come back to the "Customer Communications" document library. Choose to create a new document in the document library, and once a new document is created for you using the template that you just created. Use the picker icon (the second icon in Figure 9-11), and which should bring up a picker as shown in Figure 9-12.

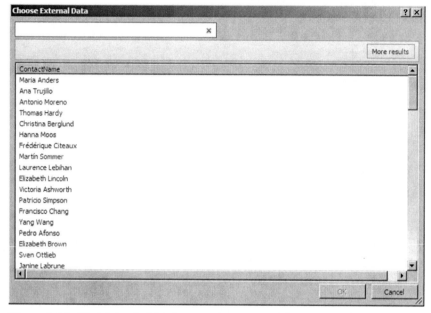

Figure 9-12. *The picker in Word prompting you to pick a customer*

You would note that the rest of the fields get populated for you as shown in Figure 9-13.

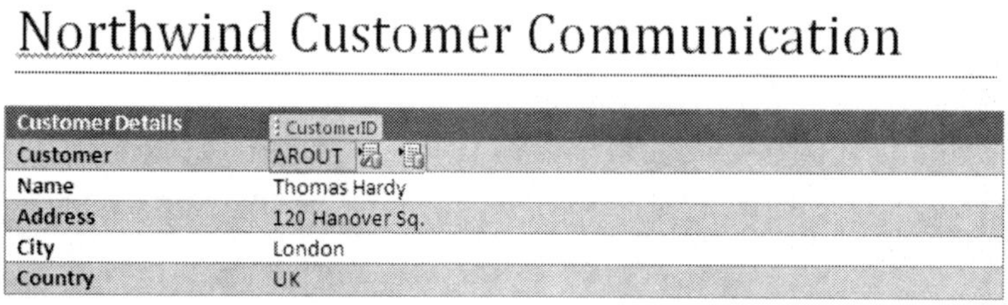

Northwind Customer Communication

Customer Details	: CustomerID
Customer	AROUT
Name	Thomas Hardy
Address	120 Hanover Sq.
City	London
Country	UK

Figure 9-13. *The BCS Entity fills the customer information out for you*

BCS with Visual Studio 2010

As you just saw, you can author BCS external content types using SharePoint designer. These external content types can be used in various scenarios as you just saw, but if you truly want to go beyond those limits, BCS in SharePoint 2010 also has a very compelling Visual Studio story. Let's begin by writing and using simple BCS external content type in Visual Studio.

Start Visual Studio 2010 and create a new project based on the "Business Data Connectivity Model" project template, and call it "BDCDemo". This project is going to generate a collection of BCS external content types. An out of the box entity is created for you, which gives you an identifier and two methods. This entity represents the bare minimum definition that you need to create to be able to create an external list from. Once you have created a project based on this project template you will notice three different sections in your Visual Studio project. On the left you will see a graphical representation of your entity. If you have multiple entities with associations between them they will appeal over here as well. On the right under BDC explorer you will see the definition of the model with the different entities sorted as a tree view. This can be seen in Figure 9-14.

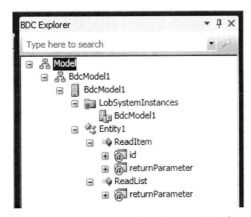

Figure 9-14. *Your Visual Studio BDC Explorer structure*

And at the very bottom you should see a pane called BDC method details. In this pane you will see the various methods and other details that help you design this entity. You will probably end up spending a lot of time in this pane. You would also note that all these three panes are connected with each other. Editing one will reflect the changes in the other two panes. Behind the scenes you're really editing an xml file. The xml file in this case is the BdcModel1.bdcm file. You could edit the xml file directly as well, but this is a huge improvement over SharePoint 2007, where you didn't have good tools to edit your xml file that defined the application definition. So chances are that I won't be editing the xml file manually too much. Also behind each entity there's a code behind that is being maintained for you. To view the code-behind select the Entity1 and press the F7 button. You would note in the code-behind that there are methods created for you for both read item and read list. The ReadItem is the equivalent of the specific finder method; it returns a single instance of an entity. ReadList on the other hand returns a number of instances of the entity. The generated code can be seen in Listing 9-1.

Listing 9-1. *The out of the box code for ReadList*

```
public static IEnumerable<Entity1> ReadList()
{
    // TODO: This is just a sample. Replace this simple sample with valid code.
    Entity1[] entityList = newEntity1[1];
    Entity1 entity1 = newEntity1();
    entity1.Identifier1 = "0";
    entity1.Message = "Hello World";
    entityList[0] = entity1;
    return entityList;
}
```

As you can see from Listing 9-1 I'm returning an IEnumerable<Entity1>. Also the out of the box code is creating a single instance of the entity, and stuffing it into the return value. Thus if you were to deploy this external content type and create an external list based on that, that external list will contain a single list item, with two columns, named Identifier1, and Message, with values 0, and "Hello World" as shown in Figure 9-15.

Figure 9-15. *A basic hello world external content type in action*

Also note that by pressing F5 on your project to run your project, Visual Studio will package up the BDC entity as a .wsp, deploy it, and since this is a farm solution modify the web.config to enable debugging, and even allow you to step through breakpoints in your code behind.

Thus now if you wanted to offer something more powerful, example entity instances been generated on the fly based on some intelligent logic, you would simply have to modify that code-behind! That's all.

And when I say, modify the code-behind that really involves two steps,

1. The first step is to define the structure of Entity1, maybe perhaps give Entity1 a decent meaningful name. This is done by describing something called as a TypeDescriptor.

2. The second step obviously is to define the details of the ReadList method, so that it fills your custom entity structure.

So turning my HelloWorld example into a more real world example, let's say that I intend to create an external content type, which when dropped into an external list, will always return the calendar for the current month. This calendar will have three columns: the identifier, the day, and the date. So let's make this happen!

As I mentioned the first step is to define the structure of Entity1, which I am going to rename to "MonthDay". Also, I will rename Identifier1 to DayNumber, and in the properties, I will change its type to System.Int32. At this point, my graphical view of my BDC Model looks like as shown in Figure 9-16.

Figure 9-16. *Entity Structure in your BDC Model*

So far so good, now, click on the ReadItem method. In the bottom pane, you would see the Method Details. Look for the ReadItem method, and see what parameters it accepts, and what parameters it returns! It seems to accept "id", direction "In", and its Type Descriptor to be "Identifier1". Well that's obviously incorrect!

First of all, what is a Type Descriptor? As the name suggests, it describes a type! A type that is independent of WCF, SQL Server, or .NET connector data types - it is a type that is defined purely in BCS terms, so it is reusable across all those sources. Thus instead of Identifier1, change the input parameter to DayNumber. Also ensure that its data type is now a System.Int32.

Now look at the second parameter called "returnParameter". Its direction is "Return", but its Type Descriptor is "Entity1". Again this is incorrect, and you need to ensure that the return type is represented by a Type Descriptor that represents the structure of the information you wish to return. Thus go ahead and set up TypeDescriptor as your return parameter as shown in Figure 9-17.

Figure 9-17. *The TypeDescriptor for MonthDayEntry*

In this figure, Date is of type System.DateTime, Day is System.String, and DayNumber is System.Int32.

This basically sets up the ReadItem method structure, you still need to provide details of the code-behind! I'll get to that in a minute, but first let's also set up the structure for ReadList. For ReadList, create a return type descriptor called "MontyDayEntries", and copy paste the "MonthDayEntry" type descriptor under it. Your BDC Explorer should look like as shown in Figure 9-18.

Figure 9-18. *The TypeDescriptor for MonthDayEntries*

Finally, you need to create a class that represents the structure of MonthDayEntry. I am going to rename Entity1.cs, to MonthDayEntry.cs, and put code in as shown in Listing 9.2.

Listing 9-2. *Structure for MonthDayEntry*

```
public partial class MonthDayEntry
{
    public int DayNumber { get; set; }
    public string Day { get; set; }
    public DateTime Date { get; set; }
}
```

Great, now all that's left is to populate the code-behind's of ReadItem and ReadList methods, and you will be ready to use this entity within SharePoint. You can find the new code-behind in Listing 9-3.

Listing 9-3. *Your custom ReadList and ReadItem methods.*

```
public class MonthDayService
{
    public static MonthDayEntry ReadItem(int id)
    {
        MonthDayEntry oneDay = newMonthDayEntry();
        DateTime oneMonthFromNow = DateTime.Now.AddMonths(1) ;
        int maxDaysInCurrentMonth =
            (newDateTime(oneMonthFromNow.Year, oneMonthFromNow.Month, 1)).AddDays(-1).Day;
        if (id > maxDaysInCurrentMonth) id = maxDaysInCurrentMonth;
                oneDay.Date = newDateTime(DateTime.Now.Year, DateTime.Now.Month, id);
        return oneDay;
    }

    public static IEnumerable<MonthDayEntry> ReadList()
    {
        int currentMonth = DateTime.Now.Month;
        int currentYear = DateTime.Now.Year;
        DateTime oneMonthFromNow = DateTime.Now.AddMonths(1) ;
        int maxDaysInCurrentMonth =
          (new DateTime(oneMonthFromNow.Year, oneMonthFromNow.Month, 1)).AddDays(-1).Day;
        MonthDayEntry[] entityList = newMonthDayEntry[maxDaysInCurrentMonth];

        for (int i = 1; i <= maxDaysInCurrentMonth ; i++)
        {
            MonthDayEntry oneDay = newMonthDayEntry();
            oneDay.Date = newDateTime(currentYear, currentMonth, i);
            oneDay.Day = oneDay.Date.DayOfWeek.ToString();
            oneDay.DayNumber = i;
            entityList[i - 1] = oneDay;
        }
    return entityList;
    }
}
```

Now, go ahead and build and deploy your project. Then, create an External List called "Days", and use the above created external content type as the source external content type for this list. Also, through central administration, give yourself access to this BCS external content type. You should see the list created as shown in Figure 9-19.

	DayNumber	Day	Date
☐	1	Monday	1/31/2010 7:00 PM
	2	Tuesday	2/1/2010 7:00 PM
	3	Wednesday	2/2/2010 7:00 PM
	4	Thursday	2/3/2010 7:00 PM
	5	Friday	2/4/2010 7:00 PM
	6	Saturday	2/5/2010 7:00 PM
	7	Sunday	2/6/2010 7:00 PM
	8	Monday	2/7/2010 7:00 PM
	9	Tuesday	2/8/2010 7:00 PM
	10	Wednesday	2/9/2010 7:00 PM
	11	Thursday	2/10/2010 7:00 PM
	12	Friday	2/11/2010 7:00 PM
	13	Saturday	2/12/2010 7:00 PM
	14	Sunday	2/13/2010 7:00 PM
	15	Monday	2/14/2010 7:00 PM
	16	Tuesday	2/15/2010 7:00 PM
	17	Wednesday	2/16/2010 7:00 PM
	18	Thursday	2/17/2010 7:00 PM
	19	Friday	2/18/2010 7:00 PM
	20	Saturday	2/19/2010 7:00 PM
	21	Sunday	2/20/2010 7:00 PM
	22	Monday	2/21/2010 7:00 PM
	23	Tuesday	2/22/2010 7:00 PM
	24	Wednesday	2/23/2010 7:00 PM
	25	Thursday	2/24/2010 7:00 PM
	26	Friday	2/25/2010 7:00 PM
	27	Saturday	2/26/2010 7:00 PM
	28	Sunday	2/27/2010 7:00 PM

Figure 9-19. *The newly created external content type in action*

As you can tell, at the time of writing this chapter, I was in February 2010, and the days of February 2010 are laid out very neatly in this list!

You would also note that since you have not created all the Methods on this external content type, the user interface is appropriately trimmed. You would note that the "New Item", "Edit Item", and "Delete Item" buttons are grayed out.

At this time, for your own practice. go ahead and create some other interesting external content types using Visual Studio 2010. If there is a sample challenge for you, why don't you create an external content type that returns NorthWind customers that were returned using plain ADO.NET. Once you have written and deployed this external content type, create a list just like before, and try to connect that list to Outlook! SharePoint will give you an error as shown in Figure 9-20.

Figure 9-20. *I can't seem to connect the external content type to Outlook.*

This error is to be expected, and this is one of those errors that gives you a good description of exactly what you need to do, to get rid of this error. What you need to do here is open the "Customers" external content type in SharePoint designer, and define the various mappings between your external content type and Outlook types, just like you have already done in this chapter using the external content type you created using SharePoint designer.

The BCS Object Model

By now in this chapter you have learned how to create an external content type using both SharePoint designer and Visual Studio. But the real question over here is what makes external content type so compelling? Sure they let me bring in data from external systems into SharePoint, but I could've done that by writing a simple WebPart! Why bother with the complications that BCS brings? Other than the fairly obvious benefits such as BCS entities become searchable, you have the ability to use these entities like SharePoint lists, and you can use certain WebParts and other facilities such as associations and actions on these BCS entities, there's one big huge advantage that BCS brings.

And that huge advantage, is the ability to represent any back-end system, in a consistent object model that can be programmed against. This object model is the BCS object model. What this means is that as the back-end systems change and upgrade over time, as long as their equivalent BCS external content types are kept up to date, all existing systems can continue to leverage the same object model, and existing systems will continue to work with changing newer versions of back-end systems without even the need of a recompile. This is because, as long as you update the BCS external content types, the actual BCS object model won't change, and will continue to work and will simply reflect the updated external content types.

Let's look at a quick example. Earlier in this chapter you set up an external content type that represents the days of the current month. Next let's write a simple console application that has the ability to work with that BCS external content type.

The sample that I am about to show assumes that you have the "NorthWind Customer" external content type setup in your system. The BCS object model provides you with functionality to both query and maintain the catalog, or to execute methods on individual external content types.

Start Visual Studio 2010 and create a .net 3.5 console application. Make sure the target platform is AnyCPU, and add the following references.

- C:\Program Files\Common Files\Microsoft Shared\Web Server
  Extensions\14\ISAPI\Microsoft.Sharepoint.dll

- C:\Program Files\Common Files\Microsoft Shared\Web Server
  Extensions\14\ISAPI\Microsoft.BusinessData.dll

- Microsoft.Sharepoint.BusinessData.Administration.Client.dll from the GAC

In your console application add a static variable pointing to your SharePoint site as shown below:

```
privatestaticstringsiteUrl = "http://sp2010";
```

The you can browse through the existing catalog by using the AdministrationMetaDataCatalog object in the Microsoft.Sharepoint.BusinssData.Administration.Client namespace. This can be seen in Listing 9-4.

Listing 9-4. *Browsing through the catalog on your Sharepoint installation.*

```
private static void BrowseCatalogDetails()
{
    Console.WriteLine("Now Browsing the details of the catalog:");
    AdministrationMetadataCatalog catalog =
    AdministrationMetadataCatalog.GetCatalog(siteUrl);
    EntityCollection entities = catalog.GetEntities("*", "*", true);
    Console.WriteLine("\nEntities in the system:");
    foreach (Entity entity in entities)
    {
        Console.WriteLine(entity.Name);
    }

// Lets pick the first entity
    var entityEnum = entities.GetEnumerator();
    entityEnum.MoveNext();
    Entity firstEntity = entityEnum.Current;
    Console.WriteLine("\nMethods on the first Entity:");
    foreach (var method in firstEntity.Methods)
    {
        Console.WriteLine(method.Name);
    }
}
```

As you can see from Listing 9-4, you have access to all the entities and all the details of all the entities in the catalog. In fact if you poke around the object model, you will be able to find that purely through the object model you can create the new entities in the catalog as well. This is very similar to what used to be able to do in SharePoint 2007 using the BDC object model. However there is one big difference that may not be very apparent! Note that the Microsoft.Sharepoint.BusinssData.Administration.Client namespace is actually part of the client stack. In other words, the code shown above does not need to run on the server! In SharePoint 2007 you were required to run this code on the machine that was running the SSP and then expose it as a web service. That is no longer necessary.

Next let us look at an example of actually executing a method on an entity, and writing the results out. This can be seen in Listing 9-5.

Listing 9-5. *Executing a method and writing the results out.*

```
private static void ExecuteMethod()
{
    Console.WriteLine("\nNow Executing methods");
    using (SPSite site = newSPSite(siteUrl))
    {
        using (newSPServiceContextScope(SPServiceContext.GetContext(site)))
        {
            BdcService service = SPFarm.Local.Services.GetValue<BdcService>();
            IMetadataCatalog catalog =
                service.GetDatabaseBackedMetadataCatalog(SPServiceContext.Current);

            IEntity entity = catalog.GetEntity(siteUrl, "Northwind Customer");
            ILobSystemInstance LobSysteminstance =
                entity.GetLobSystem().GetLobSystemInstances()[0].Value;

            IMethodInstance method =
                entity.GetMethodInstance("Read List", MethodInstanceType.Finder);
            IEntityInstanceEnumerator ieie =
                entity.FindFiltered(method.GetFilters(), LobSysteminstance);

            Console.WriteLine("\nCustomers in Northwind:");
            while (ieie.MoveNext())
            {
                Console.WriteLine(ieie.Current["ContactName"].ToString());
            }
        }
    }
}
```

As you can see from Listing 9-5, I'm able to use a consistent object model, irrespective of the details of the external content type, or the back-end system, and be able to execute methods on the back-end system. Thus as the back-end system changes, and the external content type is maintained, the code shown in Listing 9-5 will remain unchanged. This is the value that BCS offers! Also if you poke through the object model further, you will see significant enhancements in the object model over the SharePoint 2007 equivalent. For instance in SharePoint 2010, you now have support for bulk operations, and for reading blob types with streaming support.

Summary

This chapter covered a rather important part of SharePoint 2010, called as the business connectivity services. As you saw in this chapter, business connectivity services is vastly improved over business data catalog from SharePoint 2007. The improvements include, much better tooling support, much better support in the presentation of the content, and enhancements in the object model. Perhaps the most compelling example of a much more mature platform than SharePoint 2007, is that all through this chapter I never had to show you the xml that defines the external content type. You almost never have to touch that xml manually in SharePoint 2010, whereas in SharePoint 2007, editing that xml manually was the only choice at least when SharePoint 2007 was released. Then overtime third party products were introduced that help you maintain that xml application definition.

But still due to various other limitations including licensing restrictions of business data catalog, business connectivity services most probably will be a widely used feature of SharePoint 2010. At this time you should have a solid understanding of how you can manage data in your SharePoint installation. In this chapter, I showed you how to write BCS applications through SharePoint designer, Visual Studio, and how to interact directly with the BCS object model. The one topic related to BCS that I was not able to cover in this chapter, is the ability and almost a requirement for real world scenarios, for BCS applications to work with the secure store service. In working with the secure store service, BCS applications are able to offer alternate credential mechanisms and leverage claims based identities. I will cover this in detail in Chapter 12. But, for now, in the next chapter I will talk about SharePoint workflows.

CHAPTER 10

■ ■ ■

Workflows

Reading Key: If you are familiar with SharePoint 2007, you will find this chapter interesting

These days organizations have two possible ways to get ahead of each other. One is by working harder and the other is by working smarter. Now we all know how much working hard gets you ahead, not much! So it all boils down to working smarter. Working smarter simply means achieving more by doing less. This means finding someone else to do your work, so you don't have to do it, conventionally referred to as outsourcing. Interestingly, we know that doesn't go too far either! Therefore, the only long term and viable alternative that organizations have discovered to better productivity is to automate. Automate more and more processes. Automation in an office environment means creating software that supports business processes that involve numerous roles, people, and perhaps, even external systems.

As a result of following those automated processes, there is never a confusion on whose turn it is next to approve a certain project proposal so it can be efficiently routed to a customer. In contrast, when a serious exception occurs based on predefined rules, appropriate people can be emailed so human intervention can be involved where necessary. By following these processes in a system setup, you can be assured that no particular step was missed. There is no need to double check, because the computers are doing that double-checking for you. Finally, by working through the process defined in a computer system, you are also collecting historical information that can be looked at later or archived using one of the many ways to manage SharePoint data as you have already seen in this book.

To support this endeavor, a new player was introduced in .NET 3.0 called as the Workflow Foundation! SharePoint 2007 and SharePoint 2010 leverage Workflow foundation to provide the capability of authoring and running workflows in SharePoint as well. In other words, SharePoint can act as a workflow host.

Now you might argue that everything I described so far about creating automated business processes in software can be hand-coded from scratch. You'd find me agreeing with you—not everything needs workflow foundation. In fact, using workflow foundation introduces some additional complexity and also ties you down to a certain way of doing things. But, it gives you so much other stuff on top, that maybe in some instances it makes sense to represent complex long-running business processes using workflow foundation. In terms of SharePoint 2010, the following interesting facilities become available to you should you choose to author your business processes in SharePoint Workflows.

- Everything that workflow foundation gives you, such as the reliability of long-running processes to last across machine reboots, is made available to you, if you represent your business processes as workflows in SharePoint.

- Ability to visualize the workflow graphically, so the end users can view the current flow. The running progress of a workflow is made available using Workflow Visualization using Visio if you use Workflow in SharePoint 2010.

- Business users can craft up workflows in tools such as Visio or SharePoint Designer in a very easy-to-use graphical way. These graphical views of the workflow can then show running workflows in SharePoint; reporting analysis tools can be written on the log history of the running workflow instances which can allow you to perform improvements on the running workflow.

- The same workflows that have been written by business users can then be exported to Visual Studio, where developers can extend the workflows and integrate them with custom logic, third party products, and make them interact with proprietary algorithms or systems. Of course, you do have the capability of writing a workflow from scratch in Visual Studio as well.

Given an enterprise processes problem, when should you choose to implement it as a workflow and when should you just write custom code representing that business process? I hope once you have examined all of the preceding scenarios in this chapter, you will be able to answer this question very well.

In this chapter, I will start by demonstrating out of the box workflows that come with SharePoint, so you get an idea of what workflow foundation in SharePoint gives us. Once you have a solid understanding of the basics, then I will enhance it further by involving tools such as Visio and SharePoint Designer. Finally, I will wrap up by involving Visual Studio in authoring complex logic that SharePoint Designer and Visio are unable to express. Let's get started with using out of the box workflows in SharePoint 2010.

Out of the Box Workflows

SharePoint 2010 comes with several workflow templates out of the box. These are generally installed as features, and are available for you to associate with lists or at the site level. In SharePoint 2007, you could only associate workflows with lists. Therefore, step one of having a workflow available for use is for it to be installed as a feature. Once it is available for use, you can then create "Associations" of the workflow with existing lists or sites. At this point, you can optionally ask the user associating the workflow some questions, usually presented as an "Association Form". An association form is what allows the workflow to interact with the user when the workflow is first associated with a list.

Once you have created an association of a workflow template, you can then choose to run the workflow on individual list items (or run it on the site if you had chosen to associate it). When you start a workflow, it can ask more questions by showing yet another form called as the initiation form. Thus, the "initiation form" is what allows the system to ask questions when a workflow is first initiated/instantiated.

As the workflow is running, it can ask further questions of the users. In asking those questions, the workflow can create tasks for users, and those tasks can then be performed by the end users. Those tasks go in a list, and can be represented as yet another kind of form, called as the "Task Form". Note that a workflow can have zero or one association forms, it can have zero or one initiation forms, but it can have many task forms.

Similar to task forms, the workflow can also be altered midcourse by end-users by using yet another kind of form called a "Modification form". Just like the task form, there can be zero or many modification forms on a workflow.

Let's pick an out of the box workflow and understand the usage of all these forms and the workflow lifecycle in general. The workflow I intend to use here is the "Approval" Workflow, which comes out of the box in paid versions of SharePoint.

In your SharePoint site, go ahead and create a new list based on the Custom List Template and name it "Items to be Approved". Then visit the list settings page of this list and view the versioning settings. Under versioning settings, choose to "require content approval for submitted items". By choosing this option, you just enabled the ability to have draft items available in the list. Draft items mean items that are currently a work in progress and should not be seen by everyone. They can be seen only by the author or by people who have the ability to view and approve draft items. This is controlled by the "manage lists" permission, which is one of the permission settings that you can give any particular SPPrincipal. An SPPrincipal can be an SPGroup or SPUser. I will talk more about security in Chapter 12 where these object names will make more sense.

Next, back under lists settings visit the workflow settings link. Here you will find the various workflow associations you can create with this particular list. If you are using the enterprise version of SharePoint, the various workflow associations available to you are the following:

- Disposition approval

- Three state

- Collect signatures

- Approval

- Collect feedback

For this example, you will use the approval workflow. Therefore, select the approval workflow template and give it a name of "Approval". Then, click the next button. Clicking the next button brings up the association form, which is an out of the box InfoPath form. If you have used this workflow in SharePoint 2007, you would note that this form has been redone. Fill out the form as shown in Figure 10-1.

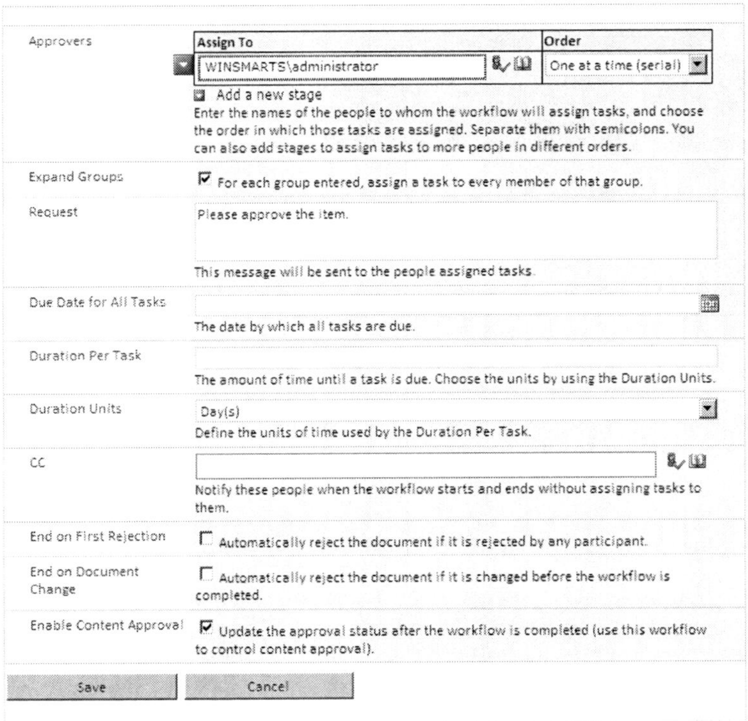

Figure 10-1. *The Association form created in InfoPath*

Notably, I have checked the check box for "Enable Content Approval". This means that the completion of this workflow will approve the associated list item that this workflow is running upon. Once you've filled out the form, click the save button. You will then be presented with a screen, as shown in Figure 10-2.

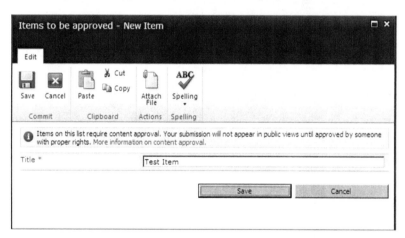

Figure 10-2. *The associated workflows with a list*

This screen informs you of all the associated workflows with this particular list. If you have used workflows in SharePoint 2007, you would note a notable difference here. Even within a list, you now have the ability to configure to run a particular workflow with a particular content type.

Now add an item into the list and put "Test Item" in the Title. Note that SharePoint informs you that the items in this list require content approval, and that your items will not appear in public views, unless they are first approved by someone with proper rights. This can be seen in the Figure 10-3.

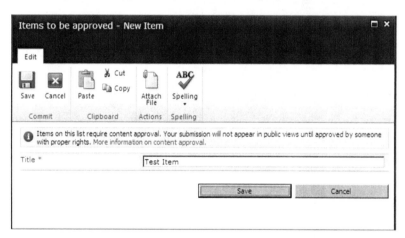

Figure 10-3. *You are being informed that items on this list will require content approval.*

Once you have created this item you would also note that the default view now contains a column called "Approval Status" and the approval status as of now is "Pending". Select the item and from the ribbon under the items click the workflows button. Alternatively, you can also choose to access the workflow screen from the ECB menu. Click the approval workflow association that you had created earlier to initiate the workflow. Initiating the workflow will present you with the initiation form. This form can be seen in Figure 10-4.

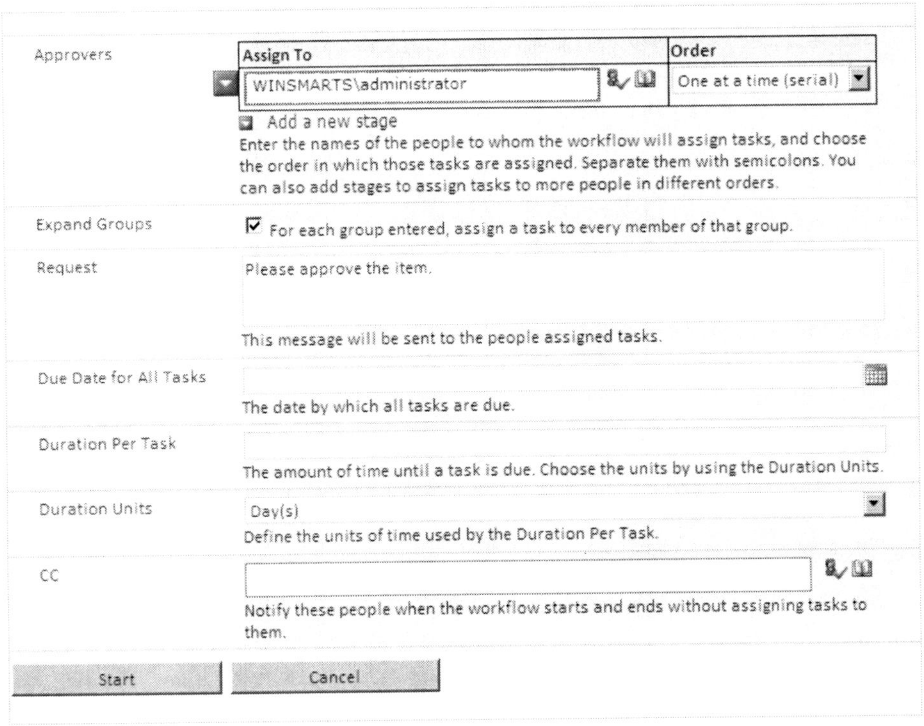

Figure 10-4. *The initiation form for the workflow*

Click the start button to start the workflow. By starting the workflow, the specified approver will be sent an e-mail message, and a task will be created for them requesting to come and approve the item. This task presents itself as yet another InfoPath form and can be accessed directly from either their e-mail or from the SharePoint site. In the SharePoint site, the task is created in a list called "Tasks". You specified this list name right before association form. There is another list you specified when creating this association, called "Workflow History". This is a hidden list and will store all the history activities of the running workflows.

Now visit the tasks list at http://sp2010/Lists/Tasks, and you will see a task created for the administrator. Clicking on this task brings up another form, which is the task form. This can be seen in Figure 10-5.

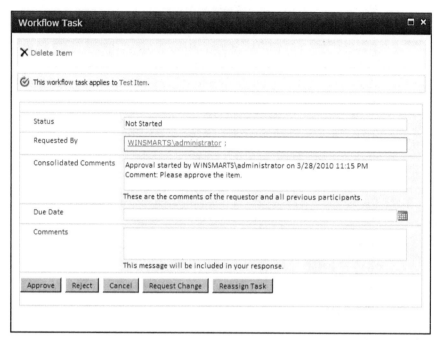

Figure 10-5. *Task form for the workflow*

At this point, clicking on the request change or reassigned task will bring up the necessary modification forms as well. For now, go ahead and click the approve button and then visit the "items to approve" list one more time. You would note that the item that the workflow was running upon has now been approved. This can be seen in Figure 10-6.

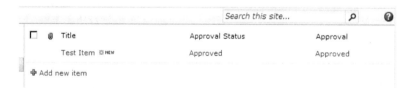

Figure 10-6. *Approval Status and Workflow Status on the list item*

Now, let me show you something really cool! Click the "Approved" link under the "Approval" column. This should take you to a page that informs you of the status of the current workflow. Assuming that you have office web applications installed in the current site collection you're working in, and you have activated the "SharePoint Server Enterprise Site Collection features", and that Visio Services of configured on your web application, you should see a graphical view of the current workflow instance as shown in Figure 10-7[1].

---

[1] Note that in Figure 10-7, I took the screenshot on a machine with domain name "SP2010", your domain will be "Winsmarts" or whatever you choose.

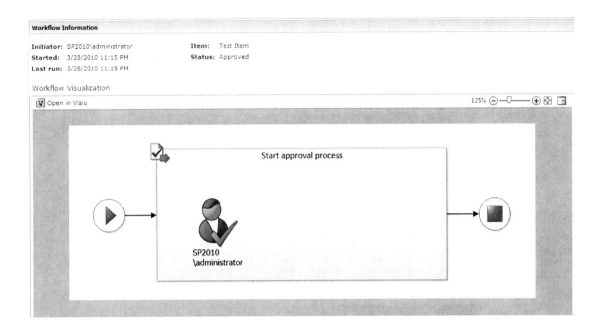

Figure 10-7. *Visio Visualization of your workflow*

This is really amazing because it gives the user a friendly graphical view of the current workflow instance with the necessary values populated. On the same page, you would also see the historical tasks, and the workflow history associated with this instance of the workflow. This is information that most organizations would find extremely helpful.

Now that Visio services picture was pretty cool! Wouldn't it be helpful if end user's could also craft up a Visio diagram to display their workflow, and perhaps that same visio diagram could be used to give life to an actual running workflow in SharePoint 2010? Exactly this scenario is possible.

Customizing Out of the Box Workflows

Out of the box workflows are great, and the biggest reason they are so great is because you don't have to write them. However, if you have business users like the ones I deal with, there will always request a minor tweak to an out of the box workflow, and then they give me puzzled looks when I give them a time estimate in weeks. In SharePoint 2007, out of the box workflows were pretty much sealed. They were what they were and you could not change them. In SharePoint 2010, however, you have the ability to tweak out of the box workflows and change them to your heart's content.

Let's take the example of the out of the box workflow. Say that you want to perform a minor tweak to an out of the box workflow. Specifically, the tweak you wish to do is that you don't want to display the CC Field in the initiation form. Also, since I'm not too fond of the colors used on the initiation form let's also change the colors of the inititiation form.

You have the ability of customizing out of the box workflows using SharePoint Designer. Open your site collection in SharePoint Designer and look at all the workflows available within this site. You should see the "Approval - SharePoint 2010" workflow available and you can double-click it and start editing it right through SharePoint Designer. What I like to do is to right-click an existing out of the box workflow definition, choose to make a copy, and then modify the copy. This way the original workflow definition remains intact, so someone else can use it later.

Therefore, right-click the "Approval - SharePoint 2010" workflow template and choose "Copy and Modify". By doing so, SharePoint Designer will ask you for a name of the copy, call it "Approval Copy". Also, SharePoint Designer will ask you which content type you want to limit this workflow to. This can be seen in Figure 10-8.

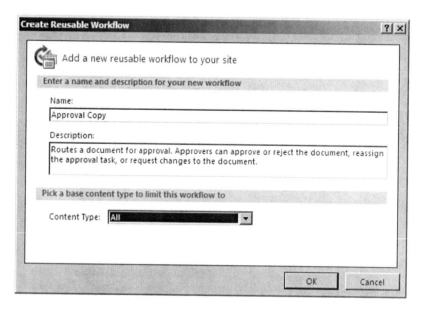

Figure 10-8. *Associating the workflow to a particular content type*

What you're doing here is creating a reusable workflow. This reusable workflow can be exported as a solution package. It can be imported into Visual Studio for further tweaking or it can be deployed across various other farms. When you create a reusable workflow through SharePoint Designer, you associate it with a content type. By associating a reusable workflow to a content type, you are essentially defining the structure of information that this workflow can always assume will be present. Therefore, if you associate the workflow with announcements, you can be sure that there will be a field called "Expires" because every announcement has an "Expires" field in it.

Any content type that inherits from announcement will be able to use your reusable workflow. Therefore, in order to create a globally reusable workflow, you should associate with the item content type. By doing so, you can be guaranteed that only the title field is present. This workflow can then be associated with any content type, since every content type eventually inherits from the item content type.

For this example, choose the content type to be "All" and click OK. The next screen will show you the workflow logic written out as a series of logical steps and conditions. This can be seen in Figure 10-9.

Figure 10-9. *Workflow design in SharePoint Designer 2010*

Let's say that at the very end of this workflow you wish to log to the history list that the workflow has finished executing. If you pay close attention to this logic tree, you will see an orange horizontal blinking cursor. By either using your cursor keys or by clicking the mouse left button, you have the ability to move that orange cursor. Take that cursor to the very end of the workflow, as shown in Figure 10-10.

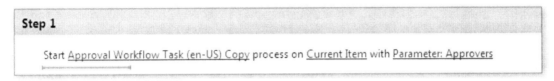

Figure 10-10. *I just moved my cursor to the end of the workflow.*

With the cursor double-click it using the left button of your mouse. After a text box appears prompting you to start typing to search. Start typing "Log" and you will see that SharePoint Designer has narrowed your search to the Log to History list activity, as shown in Figure 10-11.

Figure 10-11. *Picking a workflow activity in SharePoint Designer 2010*

As prompted, hit enter to insert the necessary activity and then configure it to log a suitable message into the workflow history list. This can be seen in Figure 10-12.

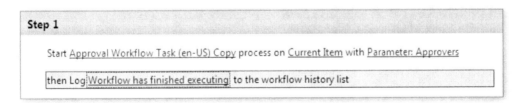

Figure 10-12. *A configured workflow activity in SharePoint Designer 2010*

Go ahead and save this workflow. Now draw your attention to the ribbon, which shows a button that says "Export to Visio". Clicking on this button will allow you to export a .vwi file. Save this .vwi file at a convenient location on the disk.

Next, start Visio and create a new diagram under the flowchart category, based on the "Microsoft SharePoint Workflow" stencil. This visio diagram allows a business analyst to craft up an entire workflow from scratch entirely in Visio. This can be imported/exported back and forth from SharePoint Designer as many times as you please. You can experiment by creating a brand new workflow yourself using the Visio stencil, but I'm going to import the .vwi file you had exported from SharePoint Designer earlier. In Visio, go to the flowchart category and create a new diagram based on "Microsoft SharePoint Workflow". Once the diagram is created, in the ribbon under the process tab, look for the import and export buttons, as shown in Figure 10-13.

Figure 10-13. *The import/export buttons for the SharePoint workflow*

Click import and choose to import the .vwi file you had exported from SharePoint Designer earlier. You should see a graphical representation of your workflow in Figure 10-14.

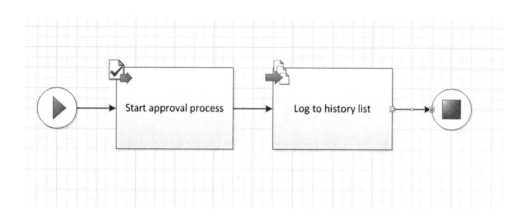

Figure 10-14. *Your created workflow depicted graphically in Visio*

For a moment, I'd like you to stop here and compare this graphical representation with the Visio Services representation you saw earlier. You will see that the log to history list block is new. Therefore, this diagram accurately reflects my intent.

Again, I leave it up to you to experiment with this Visio stencil and the various workflow actions and conditions you can use in Visio and give those SharePoint flowcharts life as SharePoint workflows with SharePoint Designer.

Now come back to SharePoint Designer and let's make some additional tweaks to the approval copy workflow you were working on. There are two additional things I'd like to do to this workflow. I'd like to tweak the look of the infopath form and I'd like to eliminate the CC Field from the initiation form. In order to do so, open the approval copy workflow in SharePoint Designer and click the Initiation Form Parameters button in the ribbon. This form will allow you to add, modify, or remove various parameters for the workflow, and also choose which ones appear in the initiation form, association form, and which appear in both. Select the CC variable and choose to modify it by having it appear only in the association form. This can be seen in the Figure 10-15.

Modify Field
Field name:
CC
Description:
Notify these people when the workflow starts and ends without assigning tasks to them.
Information type:
Person or Group
Collect from parameter during:
Association (attaching to a list)
< Back
Next >
Cancel

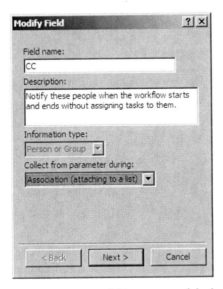

Figure 10-15. *Modifying an out of the box workflow*

The variables specified over here will also automatically generate the necessary InfoPath forms for you. Now double-click the InfoPath form under the "Forms" section of the workflow and make some modifications to the InfoPath form. Your modified infpath form should look like Figure 10-16.

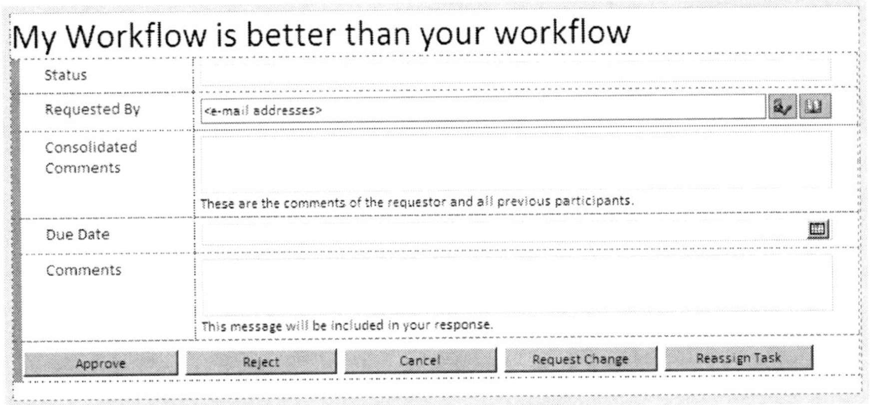

My Workflow is better than your workflow
Status
Requested By
<e-mail addresses>
Consolidated Comments
These are the comments of the requestor and all previous participants.
Due Date
Comments
This message will be included in your response.
Approve
Reject
Cancel
Request Change
Reassign Task

Figure 10-16. *Modified InfoPath form*

Save this infopath farm anywhere on your machine. Then, publish it by clicking on the quick publish button next to the save button in the title bar of InfoPath.

Your modifications to the workflow are now complete. Click the edit workflow link one more time and from the ribbon choose to save and publish. Publishing the workflow will process all the necessary files, including the workflow visualization and the solution package, and will make the workflow available on the SharePoint site.

Just like before, create a new association to the "Approval Copy" workflow and run the workflow. Note the following:

- The CC Field is no longer being asked for in the initiation form.

- The workflow visualization now shows a log to history list activity at the end of the workflow.

- The task form reflects the changes you had made previously.

- In the workflow history, you should see a new comment saying "Workflow has finished executing", as shown in Figure 10-17.

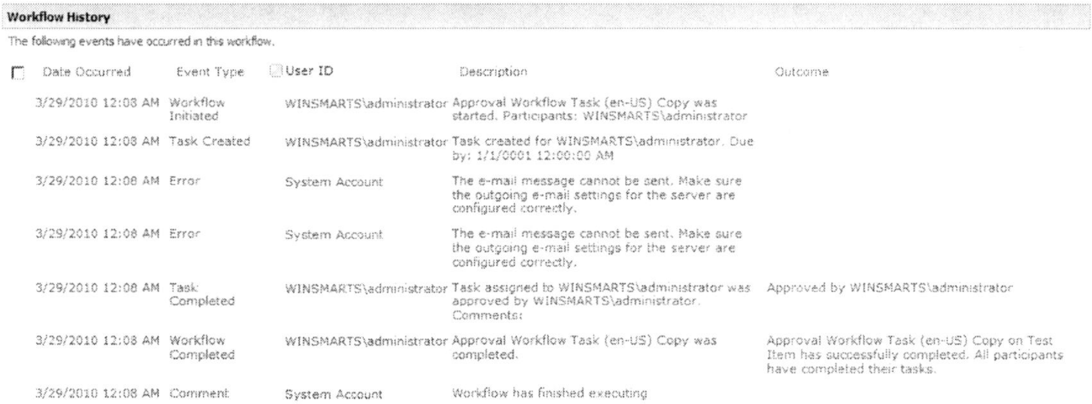

Workflow History

The following events have occurred in this workflow.

	Date Occurred	Event Type	User ID	Description	Outcome
	3/29/2010 12:08 AM	Workflow Initiated	WINSMARTS\administrator	Approval Workflow Task (en-US) Copy was started. Participants: WINSMARTS\administrator	
	3/29/2010 12:08 AM	Task Created	WINSMARTS\administrator	Task created for WINSMARTS\administrator. Due by: 1/1/0001 12:00:00 AM	
	3/29/2010 12:08 AM	Error	System Account	The e-mail message cannot be sent. Make sure the outgoing e-mail settings for the server are configured correctly.	
	3/29/2010 12:08 AM	Error	System Account	The e-mail message cannot be sent. Make sure the outgoing e-mail settings for the server are configured correctly.	
	3/29/2010 12:08 AM	Task Completed	WINSMARTS\administrator	Task assigned to WINSMARTS\administrator was approved by WINSMARTS\administrator. Comments:	Approved by WINSMARTS\administrator
	3/29/2010 12:08 AM	Workflow Completed	WINSMARTS\administrator	Approval Workflow Task (en-US) Copy was completed.	Approval Workflow Task (en-US) Copy on Test Item has successfully completed. All participants have completed their tasks.
	3/29/2010 12:08 AM	Comment	System Account	Workflow has finished executing	

Figure 10-17. *The workflow history of the approval copy workflow*

Writing Workflows with SharePoint Designer

Just like you have the ability to edit out of the box workflows, using SharePoint Designer you can also craft up brand new workflows. In order to do so, open your site collection and SharePoint Designer and click the workflows section. From the ribbon, you will see three possibilities as shown in Figure 10-18.

Figure 10-18. *The kinds of workflows you can create*

A list workflow is associated with an individual list. This is very similar to how it used to be authoring workflows in SharePoint Designer 2007 with the concept of association when an initiation was merged. Compared to SharePoint Designer 2007, SharePoint Designer 2010 offers significant improvements such as a completely redesigned workflow editor, the ability to export workflows as .wsp's, and so forth.

The second button, "Reusable Workflow", is very similar to the customization of the out of the box workflow that you just did in the previous section of this chapter. Creating a reusable workflow simply means that you're targeting the workflow to a particular content type. Once you have crafted up such a workflow definition, you can then associate this workflow with the source content type or any content types that inherit from the source content type.

The last button is rather interesting. It allows you to target the workflow to the site. This is something you were not able to do in SharePoint 2007. Frequently, you will be presented with enterprise processes that don't really tie to a list item. In fact, they don't even tie to a document set. In those instances, it is helpful to run the workflow on a container that is not exactly an individual list item. SharePoint 2010 allows you to run workflows on a site collection. These are referred to as site workflows. Let's create a site workflow.

The workflow I am about to set up adds the facility of users being enabled to add simple reminders for themselves in the site. Similar to a calendar, by starting a workflow, the user would be able to enter a title, a description, and a date and time at which an e-mail would be sent to the user with the title and description with a reminder.

Start SharePoint Designer, and under workflows, click site workflow in the ribbon. Call your new Workflow "Remind Me". Add the following initiation form parameters to this workflow:

- *Remind title*: Single line of text, visible on the initiation form only.

- *Remind description*: Multiple Lines of text, visible on the initiation form only.

- *Remind time*: Date and Time. The form should ask for both date and time, visible on the initiation form only.

Next, craft up the workflow, as shown in Figure 10-19.

Figure 10-19. *Your workflow structure in SharePoint Designer 2010*

Now go back to the main workflow page within SharePoint Designer and check the check box for "Show workflow visualization on status page". Save and publish the workflow. If you get any errors during publishing, make sure that you followed all the previous steps, including populating the subject and body of the email.

Next, visit your site collection in the web browser and visit all site content and click the "Site Workflows" link. Here you should see the option to start the "Remind Me" workflow. Start this workflow but note that by starting up this workflow SharePoint prompts you with the initiation form, as shown in Figure 10-20.

Remind Title	Eat Lunch
Remind Description	Don't forget to eat!
Remind Time	3/29/2010 12:30:15 AM

Start   Cancel

Figure 10-20. *The initiation form for your workflow*

Fill out the form as shown and click the start button. Note that the workflow visualization clearly tells you exactly where the workflow is at the given point. This can be seen in Figure 10-21.

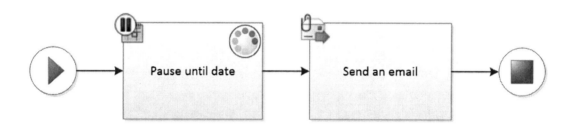

Figure 10-21. *Visio Visualization of your workflow*

Once the workflow has finished, and assuming that you have your SMTP server configured, you should receive an e-mail with the necessary reminder.

Writing Workflows with Visual Studio

So far you have seen that you can take a workflow between Visio and SharePoint Designer multiple times, and allow the business user to express their workflow desires to a great length. However, there will be situations where you will need to involve a developer. The situations are twofold, either you need to use an activity that you cannot find in SharePoint Designer, in which case you will have to author a custom activity in Visual Studio 2010 and use it in your workflows. Alternatively, your workflow involves crazy proprietary calculations or integration with external systems, stuff that you cannot expect SharePoint to provide out of the box.

In either of these scenarios, you have the ability to use Visual Studio. Visual studio has the ability to import a .wsp package, which was in turn exported from SharePoint Designer, and could contain workflow definitions. Or you can use Visual Studio to craft up a brand new workflow from scratch!

In order to write a brand new workflow in Visual Studio, start Visual Studio and create a new project called "RollOfDiceWF" based on the empty SharePoint project template. Since this project will contain workflow templates, you need to make this a farm solution. What I intend to do in this workflow, is begin by rolling dice. Rolling dice should give me a random number between one to six and that randomly generated number will be updated in the title of the list item the workflow is running upon.

Thus, right-click the project and choose to add a new SPI of type "Sequential Workflow". You could also choose to add a state machine workflow. Any process can be represented as either a sequential workflow, or a state machine workflow. However, it is generally easier to represent machine involving tasks that you can easily think of as flowcharts as sequential workflows. It is generally easier to represent workflows that go through various states have long pauses between them and involve human being or external system interaction as state machine workflows.

As soon as you choose to add a new sequential workflow, Visual Studio will ask you a couple of questions.

- It will ask if this is supposed to be a site workflow or a list workflow. In this case, choose to make it a list workflow.

- The second and optional step here is to automatically associate this workflow to a list and also specify a tasks and workflow history list. This is a convenience that Visual Studio provides you which facilitate easy debugging; you could assign a workflow yourself manually if you wished. However, associate the workflow with a list called "Test" based on the custom list template. Also, if your site collection currently doesn't have a tasks and workflow history list, just create an association to any out of the box workflow through the browser, and that will give you an option to create the tasks and workflow history list.

As you will note, once the sequential workflow has been added the first activity in the workflow is the onWorkflowActivated activity. This can be seen in the Figure 10-22.

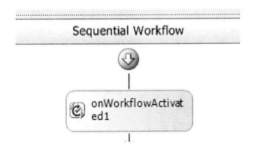

Figure 10-22. *The onWorkflowActivated activity*

The first activity in any SharePoint workflow has to be the onWorkflowActivated activity. The responsibility of this activity is to set the various context variables, such as the list item you are operating upon, the user that started the workflow, etc. Therefore, when you're adding more activities into your workflow you must always ensure that your activities fall below the onWorkflowActivated activity.

Also, note that in the toolbox you have the ability to add activities from workflow foundation 3.0, workflow foundation 3.5, and SharePoint workflow activities. .NET activities are also usable within SharePoint workflows, but you must be careful of not using certain activities in SharePoint workflows such as TransactionScope activity, CompensatableTransactionScope activity, SynchronizationScope activity etc.

At this point, drag and drop a code activity and place it below the onWorkflowActivated1 activity in your sequential workflow. As soon as you drag and drop the activity, you would see a red exclamation mark on the code activity, which is informing you that further work needs to be done before this workflow is complete. Double-click the code activity to create its MethodInvoking event handler, and add the code shown in Listing 10-1 into this event handler.

Listing 10-1. *MethodInvoking event handler for codeActivity*

```
private int diceRoll = 0;
private void codeActivity1_ExecuteCode(object sender, EventArgs e)
{
    Random rnd = new Random();
    diceRoll = rnd.Next(1, 6);
    workflowProperties.Item["Title"] = diceRoll;
    workflowProperties.Item.Update();
}
```

As you can see from Listing 10-1, you're generating a random number between one and six and updating the items title with the generated number. Next, build and deploy your workflow, and then run the workflow on a new list item that you create in the test list you created earlier. Note that the title of the list changes at random between one to six.

Since you're rolling dice, let's make this a little bit more interesting. The idea here is that anytime you get a number greater than two, a task should be created for you allowing you to win a prize. In order to do so, drop an ifElseActivity under the code activity. This ifElseActivity will have two ifElse branches. You need only one, so go ahead and delete one of those branches. Inside the ifElse branch that is left, drag and drop the createTask activity from under the SharePoint workflow, workflow activities category. Your newly added section in the sequential workflow should look like Figure 10-23.

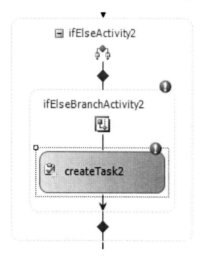

Figure 10-23. *Red exclamation marks on my activities. I have more work to do.*

The red exclamation marks signify that there is some additional work that needs to be done on those activities to properly configure them. Specifically, the if else branch activity needs a condition supplied on it. Select the if else branch activity and in its properties choose to specify a declarative condition. Give the condition name as "isWinner", and the Expression as "this.diceRoll > 2".

By specifying the condition in this manner, you will cause the create task activity to be called whenever the diceRoll value is greater than two. The next thing you need to do is to configure the create task activity.

The createTask activity requires a correlation token. Correlation tokens are an integral concept to workflows. Workflows run in a workflow host, and a number of instances of the workflow are multiplexed in a single running instance of an in-memory workflow class. Between various activity executions the workflow can be paused and persisted back to the persistence database, in this case the content database, and then rehydrated as necessary in the future. For the workflow host to keep everything straight between multiple workflow instances but a single in-memory instance of the workflow, workflow foundation relies on correlation tokens. Note that you already have a correlation token for the entire workflow. Since there can be many tasks within a single workflow, you need to create a new correlation token for the task. Therefore, edit the properties of the create task activity, and under the correlation token, type the new correlation token and call it "taskToken". You will also have to specify an owner activity name. At this point, you can really pick any other activity name that is at the parent level of the createTask activity, but choose to make the workflow itself as the owner activity name.

The next thing you need to do is to specify values for the TaskID and TaskProperties of the create task activity. To do so, click the ellipse by each one of these, and go to the "bind to a new member" tab then choose to create a field, as shown in Figure 10-24.

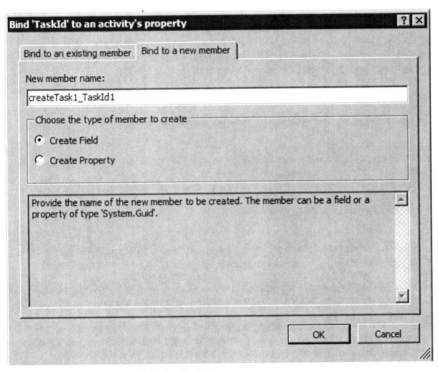

Figure 10-24. *Creating a field for TaskID*

Repeat this procedure for TaskProperties. Once you have configured the create task activity, the properties pain should look like Figure 10-25.

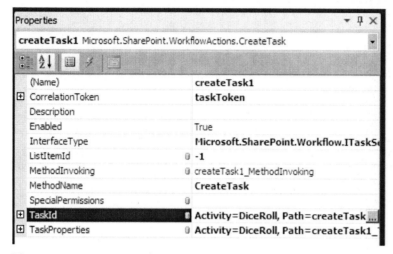

Figure 10-25. *Properties of my CreateTask activity*

Next, double-click the create task activity to create a MethodInvoking event handler for it. The MethodInvoking event handler is a great opportunity for you to set properties on the task before the task actually gets created. In this event handler, put the code as shown in Listing 10-2.

Listing 10-2. *Code for the createTask MethodInvoking Event Handler*

```
private void createTask1_MethodInvoking(object sender, EventArgs e)
{
    createTask1_TaskId1 = Guid.NewGuid();
    createTask1_TaskProperties1.AssignedTo = workflowProperties.Originator;
    createTask1_TaskProperties1.Title = "Congratulations!!";
    createTask1_TaskProperties1.Description =
        "You have won!!! Now go and claim your prize";
    createTask1_TaskProperties1.SendEmailNotification = true;
}
```

As you can see in the MethodInvoking event handler for the create task activity, you're specifying the task title to task descriptions and sending an e-mail and and assigning the task to the user that originated the workflow.

Rebuild and redeploy this workflow and execute it on a list item again. Run the workflow a couple of times, until you get a value greater than two. Note that whenever you get a value greater than 2, a task is created for you in the tasks list.

Now let's make this workflow even more interesting. What if at the beginning of each workflow you could pick, "On whose behalf I'm playing this game". In other words, when the workflow is started you could present an initiation form with a dropdown prepopulated with the list of users in the site.

In order to add an initiation form in the workflow, first add the layouts mapped folder in your project. Once the layouts folder has been added, right-click your project and choose to add the new SPI. When prompted to pick the kind of SPI you're adding choose to add a workflow initiation form. Add this workflow initiation form at _layouts\RollOfDiceWF\WFInitiationPlayer.aspx.

Your workflow initiation form has been added to the project. It will now be deployed with the project. But you need to do three things to actually make it work with your workflow.

1. You need to edit the initiation form so it presents the user with a dropdown with the list of users in the site.

2. You need to tell the workflow that the workflow needs to present an initiation form to the end user whenever the workflow is instantiated.

3. Finally, in the MethodInvoking event handler off your createTask activity, instead of assigning the POS to the workflow originator you need to assign the task to whoever the user picked in the initiation form.

Let's go implement the previous three steps one by one. Step one is to edit the initiation form so it presents the user with the dropdown list of users in the site. In order to do so in the placeholdermain ContentPlaceHolder of your initiation form, add the code shown in Listing 10-3.

Listing 10-3. *Code Necessary to Present the User with the Dropdown with a List of Users*

```
<asp:Content ID="Main" ContentPlaceHolderID="PlaceHolderMain" runat="server">
    <SharePoint:SPDataSource runat="server" ID="usersList" DataSourceMode="List"
    SelectCommand="<Query><OrderBy><FieldRef Name='Title'
Ascending='true'/></OrderBy></Query>">
        <SelectParameters>
            <asp:Parameter Name="ListName" DefaultValue="User Information List" />
        </SelectParameters>
    </SharePoint:SPDataSource>

    On whose behalf are you playing?

    <br />
    <asp:DropDownList ID="userName" runat="server" DataSourceID="usersList"
        DataTextField="Title" DataValueField="Account">
    </asp:DropDownList>

    <asp:Button ID="StartWorkflow" runat="server" OnClick="StartWorkflow_Click" Text="Start
Workflow" />
          
    <asp:Button ID="Cancel" runat="server" OnClick="Cancel_Click" Text="Cancel" />
</asp:Content>
```

As you can see from Listing 10-3, you're creating an SPDatasource object bound to the "User Information List". The "User Information List" is a hidden list present in any site collection that gives me a list of users in the site collection. You're then data binding that data source to a simple DropDownList.

The second thing you need to do is to tell your workflow that the initiation form needs to be popped up whenever the workflow is instantiated. To do so, you need to edit the workflow element in the element.xml that defines your workflow. The workflow element in the elements.xml is shown in Listing 10-4. Note that my workflow name is DiceRoll, and you need to appropriately reflect the CodeBesideClass attribute in your code.

Listing 10-4. *The Edited Workflow Element*

```
<Workflow
    Name="RollOfDiceWF - DiceRoll"
    Description="My SharePoint Workflow"
    Id="05b3d065-ad8a-4a9b-b808-aa32eab22057"
    InstantiationUrl="/_layouts/RollOfDiceWF/WFInitiationPlayer.aspx"
    CodeBesideClass="RollOfDiceWF.DiceRoll.DiceRoll"
    CodeBesideAssembly="$assemblyname$">
```

As you can see from Listing 10-4, you have added a new attribute called InstantiationUrl. At this point, play with the intellisense offered by the xml schema for elements.xml and try to discover how you will specify an association form a modification form and a task form. Note that all of these details are specified in a manner similar to InstantiationURL.

You've done the first two steps, which will pop open an instantiation form and show the appropriate drop down. The last thing you need to do is to assign the picked value from the dropdown in the create task MethodInvoking method handler. This last step actually involves two steps. The first step is to populate the initiation data. This is done in the code behind of the initiation form in a method called GetInitiationData. The code for this method is as follows:

```
private string GetInitiationData()
{
    return userName.Text;
}
```

You're simply returning the picked username text. If you add multiple initiation variables perhaps it is a good idea to return an xml formatted string.

Next, in MethodInvoking event handler of the create task activity comment out the following line:

```
// createTask1_TaskProperties1.AssignedTo = workflowProperties.Originator;
```

Instead, replace it with the following code line:

```
createTask1_TaskProperties1.AssignedTo = workflowProperties.InitiationData;
```

As you can see, instead of assigning the task to the user that originated the workflow, you are assigning the workflow to the user that was picked in the drop down list.

Your workflow changes are now complete so go ahead and rebuild and redeploy the workflow. Run a workflow instance on a list item, and you will note that an initiation form, as shown in Figure 10-26.

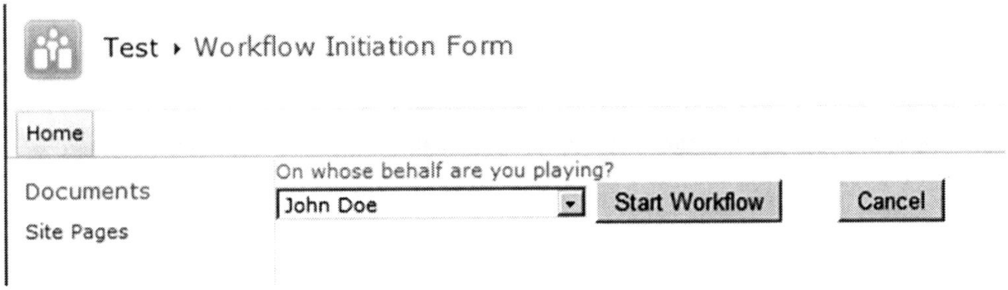

Figure 10-26. *Your inititiation form shows up at the start of the workflow.*

Pick a user other than the logged in user and click the start workflow button. Keep playing this game until you get a value greater than two. Once you get a value greater than two, visit the tasks list and look at the task created by this workflow. Note that the task has been created for the user that you picked in the dropdown in the initiation form. This can be seen in Figure 10-27.

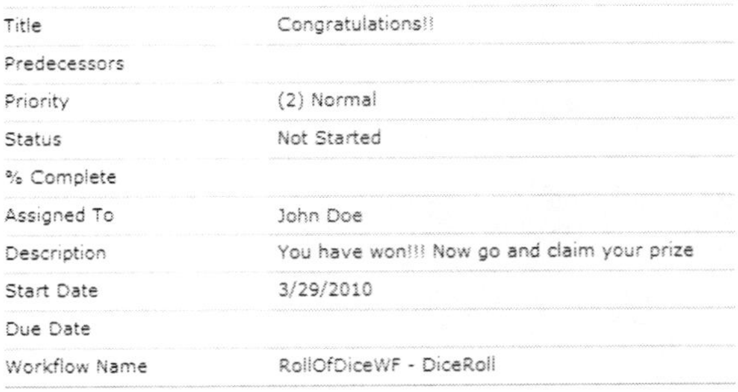

Title	Congratulations!!
Predecessors	
Priority	(2) Normal
Status	Not Started
% Complete	
Assigned To	John Doe
Description	You have won!!! Now go and claim your prize
Start Date	3/29/2010
Due Date	
Workflow Name	RollOfDiceWF - DiceRoll

Figure 10-27. *Task created if you win the dice roll.*

This is how you can write workflows in Visual Studio 2010 and add forms into those workflows allowing them to interact with the user.

Summary

Workflows are an important topic of SharePoint. In this chapter, you familiarized yourself with the basic concepts of authoring and using workflows in SharePoint. You saw that there are certain out of the box workflows. You saw that those out of the box workflows can be visualized using Visio visualizations or they can be tweaked further using SharePoint Designer. You also saw that business users can author the workflows directly inside Visio by using the SharePoint sequential workflow stencil. Also, workflows can be imported and exported back and forth between SharePoint Designer and Visio as many times as you wish.

A huge improvement over SharePoint 2007 workflows is that SharePoint Designer workflows are now much more usable and they can be exported as solution packages. Therefore, they can be moved between farms and environments. Also, when they are exported as solution packages they can be imported right inside Visual Studio and a project can be created out of them.

You can then choose to customize such a workflow in Visual Studio, or you can write a workflow from scratch in Visual Studio, including various kinds of forms associated with the workflow. Obviously when you begin customizing a workflow using Visual Studio, your customizations can include anything, and therefore such highly customized workflows cannot be imported back into SharePoint Designer. Therefore, the move from SharePoint Designer to Visual Studio is one way!

Business Intelligence

Today organizations use computers for all sorts of processes. Chances are if you work in one of these modern organizations your day starts by logging into a computer. Once you are logged in, you use various Software Systems all throughout the day to perform the various information worker roles particular to your job.

As the software developer, what tool do you use most? Visual Studio! If you look at the various other tools to use besides Visual Studio, chances are you use a system to input timesheet information. You probably use Exchange Server. In your projects, you use some sort of bug tracking software. Something to manage feature requests. However, now imagine if youare an investment consultant, finance specialist, or an insurance broker, your reliance on all this data would be even more important.

Using these various systems, organizations collect a lot of valuable data. Smart organizations look back into this data and use the collected data to run reports. These reports help improve existing business processes. That is really what business intelligence is all about.

Business intelligence is a set of concepts, methods, and processes to improve business decisions using information from multiple sources and applying experience and assumptions to develop an accurate understanding of business dynamics. It is the gathering, management, and analysis of data to produce information that is distributed to people throughout the organization to improve strategic and tactical decisions.

Business intelligence involves the integration of core information with relevant contextual information to detect significant events and illuminate cloudy issues. It includes the ability to monitor business trends, to evolve and adapt quickly as situations change, and to make intelligent business decisions on uncertain judgments and contradictory information. It relies on exploration and analysis of unrelated information to provide relevant insights, identify trends, discover opportunities, take proactive decisions, and create value.

In short, business intelligence means leveraging the organizations' internal and external information assets for making better business decisions.

Microsoft has many products to support the BI initiative. Some of these products are the following:

- Microsoft dynamics

- Excel

- Project

- SharePoint

- SQL server

- Visio

Particularly, SharePoint is central to Microsoft's BI offering. Since this is a SharePoint book, we will look at Microsoft's BI offerings from a SharePoint point of view. In SharePoint, there are three major offerings from Microsoft in the BI spectrum.

- Visio Services

- Excel Services

- PerformancePoint services

Some people also consider BCS as a BI offering. Since I have already described BCS in Chapter 9, I won't be describing BCS in this chapter. It is important to understand that frequently SQL server is central to all of these. However, SQL server doesn't necessarily have to be the engine powering BI reports through SharePoint. Reports that are surfaced through SharePoint can have any backend data source; it can be any database or it doesn't even have to be a database.

In this chapter, I will evaluate each of these one by one.

Visio Services

Visio is a tool that ships with Microsoft office and allows users to create diagrams. We have been creating diagrams since we were kids and since we were prehistoric apes. Diagrams are an excellent way to communicate a complex concept. Even though high-level languages have evolved, sometimes a picture does speak a thousand words.

Visio helps you create beautiful looking diagrams, but until the last version of SharePoint these diagrams were mostly static pictures. That is about to change starting this version. In SharePoint 2010, there is a component of SharePoint called as Visio Services. Visio Services allows you to view any of your diagrams created in Visio, right through the browser. Also, it allows you to give that diagram life. In other words, the diagram can show live data by formatting itself in different ways or presenting indicator icons depending upon the state of the data. The data can come from various sources. Let's look at an example.

I am a really busy guy, so I like to maintain all my tasks in a tasks list in SharePoint. Figure 11-1 shows my tasks list in SharePoint after I populated some tasks in it.

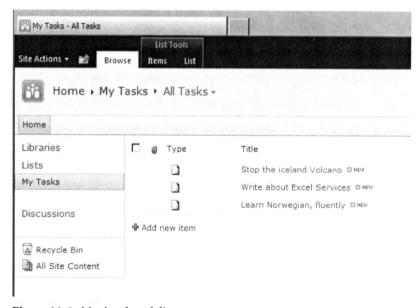

Figure 11-1. *My simple task list*

Let's say I intend to communicate to everyone in a graphical way the percent complete on all these tasks. What I intend to do is present these tasks using a web browser interface served in SharePoint. To do this, create a blank Visio diagram in Visio 2010, and start by inserting a new container under the insert button from the ribbon. Inside this container drag and drop three "To do" shapes which you will find under the Schedule\Calendar stencil. If you can't find the "To do" shape, just drag and drop any other shape. You're just learning here, so you don't need to be all artsy about it. At this point, your Visio diagram should look like Figure 11-2.

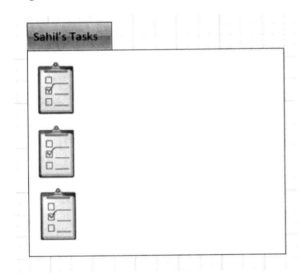

Figure 11-2. *My Starter Visio Diagram*

Next, click the data tab then click the link data to shapes button in the ribbon. In the ensuing wizard that pops open, choose to import data from the tasks list using "Microsoft SharePoint foundation list" as your choice data source.

At the bottom of your Visio window, you should see the various rows that have been pulled from the linked data source. This can be seen in Figure 11-3.

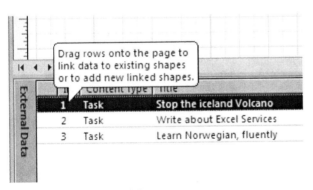

Figure 11-3. *The linked datasource*

As the tooltip prompts you, drag and drop each one of the three rows onto the three "to do" icons you had placed earlier. Dragging and dropping each one of these three rows one by one will link the row to the target shape that you drag drop the row to. It will also create a default data graphic for you, as shown in Figure 11-4.

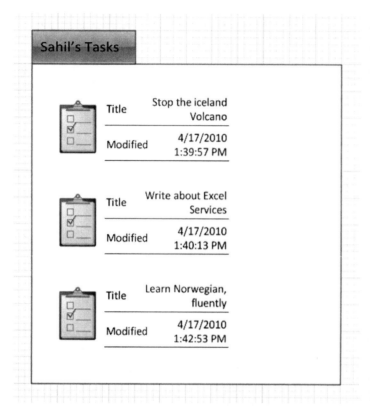

Figure 11-4. *The linked datasource showing data in the visio diagram*

The default data graphic shows the title and start date. The default data graphic is fine, but I'd like it to be little bit more interesting. For example, let's show some decent formatting. Therefore, maybe the text should be a little bit wider and also show the percent complete as a progress bar.

In order to do so, click the data graphics button in the ribbon and choose to create a new graphic. In the new data graphic window that pops open, click the new item button. Choose to specify the new item being driven from the data field percent complete, displayed as a data bar, in the style of progress bar. This can be seen Figure 11-5.

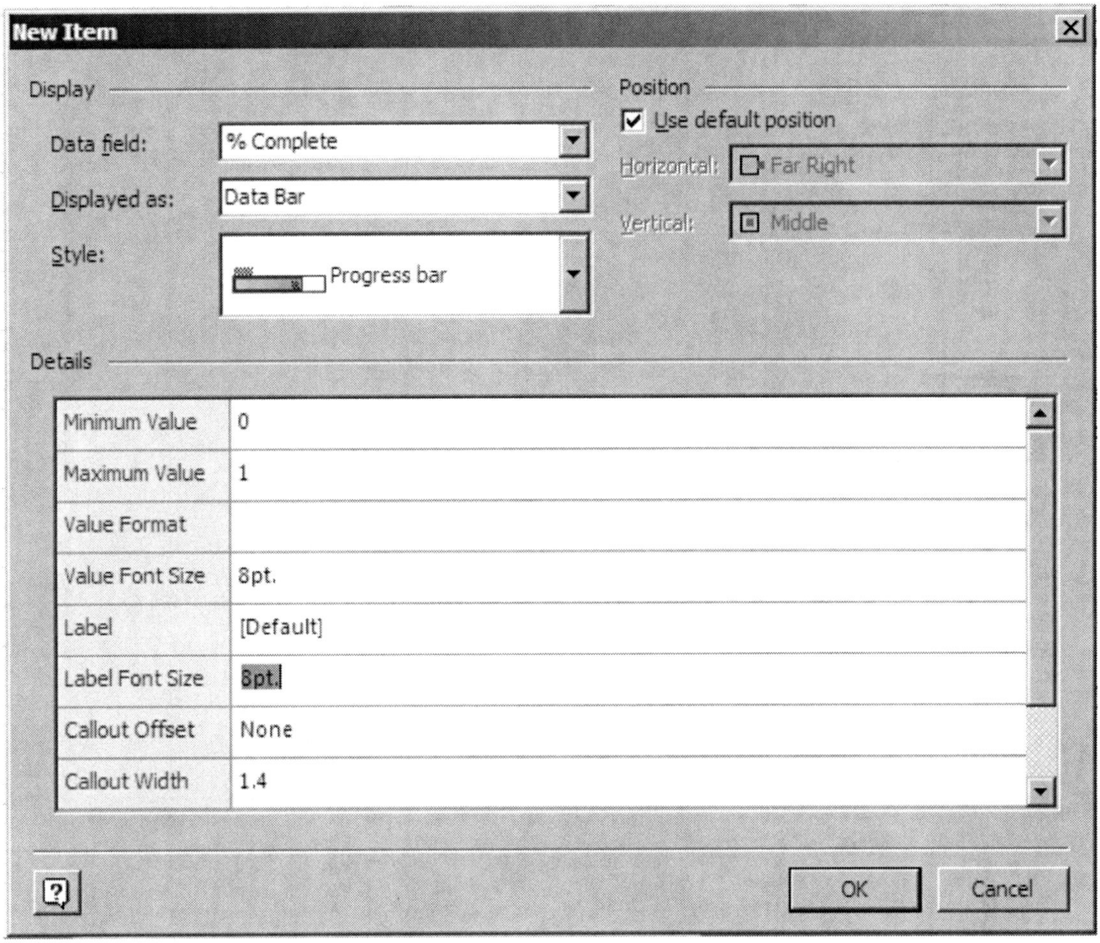

Figure 11-5. *Customizing the data graphic*

Repeat the previous step for the title and start date columns as well. The title and the start date columns are to be shown as text. You will also have to play a bit with the width. The final changes are shown in Figure 11-6.

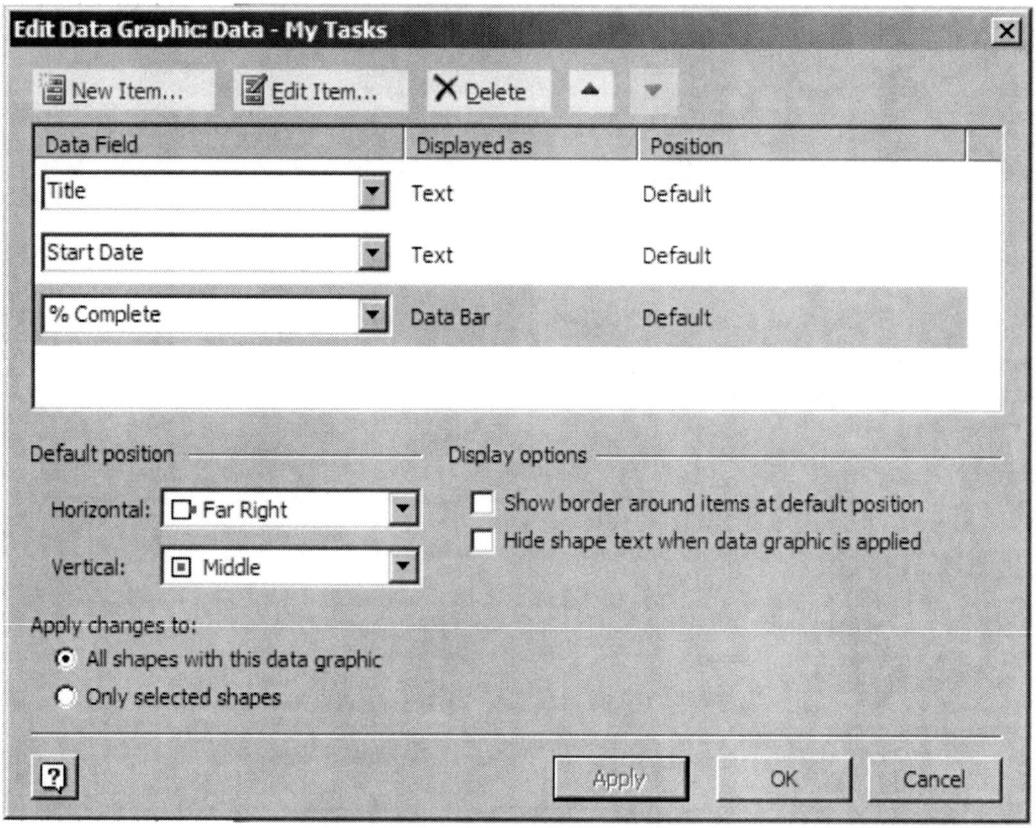

Figure 11-6. *Customizing the data graphic*

Finally, click OK and apply this newly created data graphic to the three shapes that you had earlier on the screen. After some formatting, aligning, and final touches on color, your Visio diagram should look like Figure 11-7.

Figure 11-7. *Your final visio diagram*

Go ahead and save this on your disk. Next, you need to make some changes to your SharePoint site collection. Activate the SharePoint enterprise features under site collection because Visio Services is a part of those enterprise features. Also, create a document library called "Visio diagrams".

Next, in the backstage view of Visio 2010, click on Save and Send\Save to SharePoint\Save as Web Drawing (Data-refreshable drawing for use with Visio Services on SharePoint). Choose to save it at http://sp2010/Visio Diagrams. Save the file as "Sahils Tasks.vdw". Saving the file will immediately open this Visio diagram in the web browser. If it doesn't, you need to activate the SharePoint enterprise features on your site collection, and you should have created a document library called "Visio Diagrams".

On the default.aspx page of your site collection, choose to drop a "Visio Web Access" WebPart. Configure this WebPart to point to the http://sp2010/Visio Diagrams/Sahils tasks.vdw file. Also, you may need to configure the height width, etc., of this WebPart. Once the WebPart is configured, you should see it running in the web browser.

This looks very good! So let's say that I've started on task one, and let's say that I'm only 25% complete with that task. Therefore, I go to the tasks list and update the percent complete of this task to 25%. Now I come back to Visio Services diagram running in the browser. Note that the percent complete is beautifully reflected on the diagram, as shown in Figure 11-8.

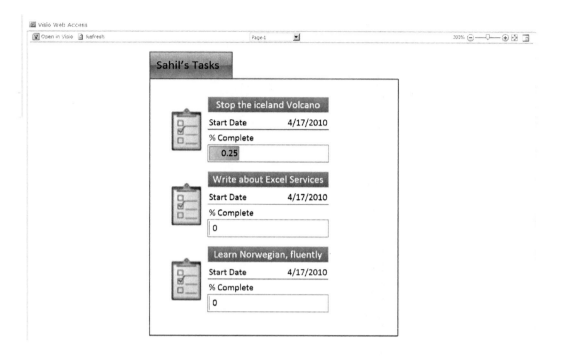

Figure 11-8. *My task list in a visio diagram running in SharePoint*

As you can see, I've barely started stopping the Icelandic volcano that is disrupting European air travel at the moment. But, hopefully, that problem will figure itself out. Let me start talking about Excel Services.

Excel Services

Excel services is yet another important pillar in Microsoft's business intelligence offering. Business users really like Excel. This is because Excel for them is easy to use and they are able to add complex formulas to Excel to express their logic. They can do so without involving the IT guy. The problem with this scenario, however, is that it becomes very difficult to share this Excel sheet with their coworkers. Usually they would e-mail the sheet around, but sometimes these sheets are too large to be emailed, sometimes they have backend data connections, and sometimes emailing causes version confusion hell.

Excel services solves all of those problems. In short, Excel services allows you to publish an Excel sheet in a document library, the Excel sheet is then calculated on the server, and is then presented to one or more clients. In the calculation, Excel sheets can involve external datasources or even custom UDF's (user defined functions) written in .NET. Once this Excel sheet has been published, it can be consumed directly through the browser by using the Excel web application component, Excel web access webpart, or Excelservice.asmx web service. The Excel sheet functionality is also available over REST based APIs and thus can be exposed as atom feeds or JSON.

Let's look at a practical example. Start by setting up the Northwind database in a SQL server. You will find the script to set up the Northwind database in the associated code download of this chapter.

Next, you're going to craft up an Excel sheet that displays orders information from this database as a pivot table and pivot chart.

Then, start Excel 2010, and click on the data tab in the ribbon. In the data tab, click "From other sources", and choose to import data from SQL server. You would note that you have the ability to import data from various other sources as well. When prompted to import data from SQL server, choose to import the data from the "Orders" table in the Northwind database using windows authentication. You have the ability to use either windows authentication, SQL server authentication, or to provide a secure store service ID and get credentials at runtime. Once you have finished importing the data from SQL server, choose to save the .odc file in a SharePoint "Data Connections Library" that you will need to create beforehand.

At this point, Excel will prompt you to import the data as either a table, a pivot table, or a pivot table and pivot chart. Choose to import the data as a pivot table and pivot chart.

Now in the pivot table make the following changes:

- Make ShipCountry the Report Filter

- Make ShipCity

- and ShippedDate as Row Labels

- Show sum of freight values

Choose to make it filtered by selected country. Your pivot table should look like Figure 11-9.

	A	B
1	ShipCountry	USA
2		
3	Row Labels ▾	Sum of Freight
4	⊞ Albuquerque	2134.21
5	⊞ Anchorage	983.53
6	⊞ Boise	6683.7
7	⊞ Butte	129.96
8	⊞ Elgin	207.08
9	⊞ Eugene	1087.61
10	⊞ Kirkland	70.01
11	⊞ Lander	558.67
12	⊞ Portland	341.95
13	⊞ San Francisco	202.11
14	⊞ Seattle	1353.06
15	⊞ Walla Walla	19.4
16	Grand Total	13771.29
17		

Figure 11-9. *My PivotTable*

Note that the pivot chart has been updating itself and is showing you a graphical view of the data you see in the pivot table. Thus, the pivot chart and pivot table are connected with each other. Format the chart a bit, like choosing to show a line graph instead of a bar chart, and your pivot chart looks like Figure 11-10.

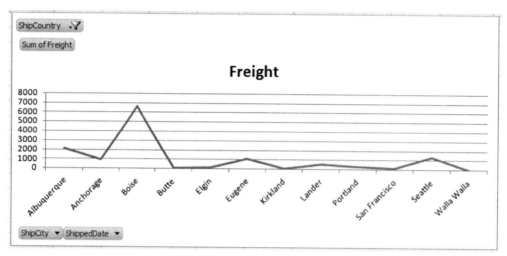

Figure 11-10. *My PivotChart*

Next, add a column next to the pivot table and give it a heading of "Difference from Avg.". Give it a formula of "=B4-AVERAGE(B4:B15)" and choose to repeat this formula on all available cells. Also, apply conditional formatting to this cell, so it graphically shows you all cities have freight less than average and which cities have freight greater than average. The pivot table now looks like Figure 11-11.

ShipCountry	USA	
Row Labels	**Sum of Freight**	**Difference from Avg.**
⊞ Albuquerque	2134.21	986.6025
⊞ Anchorage	983.53	-113.834167
⊞ Boise	6683.7	4463.26
⊞ Butte	129.96	1644.154
⊞ Elgin	207.08	-1749.717778
⊞ Eugene	1087.61	1087.9025
⊞ Kirkland	70.01	-2260.917143
⊞ Lander	558.67	-2149.076667
⊞ Portland	341.95	2795.612
⊞ San Francisco	202.11	3634.355
⊞ Seattle	1353.06	-3694.856667
⊞ Walla Walla	19.4	6875.945
Grand Total	**13771.29**	

Figure 11-11. *DataBars added within each cell in my pivot table*

Finally, select the A1 cell in the pivot table to make the options tab in the ribbon visible. With the options visible, click on insert slicer, and then choose to make shipregion available in the slicer. This will allow you to slice the data at runtime and subsequently affect the pivot table and pivot chart.

The final Excel sheet looks like Figure 11-12.

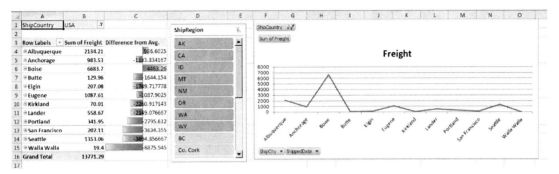

Figure 11-12. *The final Excel sheet*

From the backstage view of Excel 2010, click save and send\Save to SharePoint\Browse for a location. For now, publish this sheet to a document library called sheets. You will have to pre-create this document library in your site collection. Also, you will need to pre-activate the enterprise features in your site collection. If you have used Excel services with SharePoint 2007, you would remember that you would also have to go into central administration and add a trusted file location. This is no longer necessary in SharePoint 2010. By default, all SharePoint sites are available as trusted file locations. You can verify this by going to central administration, clicking on manage service applications, and choosing to manage the Excel services service. In there, click on trusted file locations and you should see an entry similar to Figure 11-13.

Add Trusted File Location

Address	Description	Location Type	Trust Children
http://		Microsoft SharePoint Foundation	Yes

Figure 11-13. *Trusted file locations within SharePoint for Excel Services*

This entry makes the entire SharePoint farm available as a trusted file location.

With the Excel sheet published, drop the Excel web access WebPart on the homepage of your SharePoint site collection and configure it to show your newly published Excel sheet. You should see your Excel sheet running with full interactivity in both the pivot table, pivot chart, the slicer, and showing live data from the Northwind database. This can be seen in Figure 11-14.

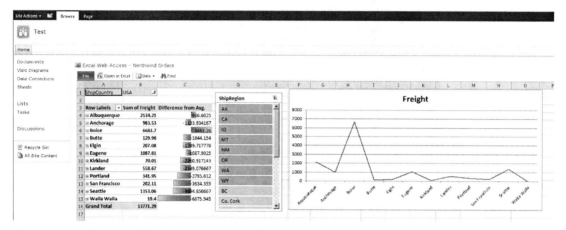

Figure 11-14. *The Excel Sheet running in Excel Services*

This is a very compelling example, because the end business user can craft up such sheets talking to real data and publish them for the world to see. However, it gets even more interesting than this. For the current web session, these sheets can be edited in the browser and can recalculate themselves and present new data. In Excel services, you also have the ability of parameterizing certain sheets. Finally, the logic of the sheets is exposed over a web service and REST API.

Accessing Excel Services Over REST

Here is the best news. The Excel sheet that you have so far been working with is already being exposed over the rest based API. Don't believe me? Assuming that your filename was "Northwind Orders.xlsx", Visit the following URL:

```
http://sp2010/_vti_bin/ExcelRest.aspx/Sheets/Northwind%20Orders.xlsx/model¹.
```

As you will note, the URL provides you with all the details embedded in your Excel sheet over an atom feed. Now visit the following URL:

```
http://sp2010/_vti_bin/ExcelRest.aspx/Sheets/Northwind%20Orders.xlsx/model/Charts('Chart%201')
?$format=image.
```

You would note that your Excel sheet chart is being exposed as a simple image. This is really useful. I'm going to show a practical demonstration of this. Imagine that your task is to craft up a document that shows the graph of the freight cost for USA. Usually, you would copy then paste such a chart from an existing web site and embed it in the document. That is not a perfect approach because sooner or later the chart will become out of date. However, you can use Excel services to create a chart that updates with live data every time the document is opened. To do so, start Word 2010 and under the insert tab click quick parts. Choose to include a new field and in the ensuing dialog box choose to "IncludePicture", which provides the appropriate URL as shown in Figure 11-15.

---

¹ Note that the URL contains the name of the Excel sheet. If you named your sheet something else, your URL would be different.

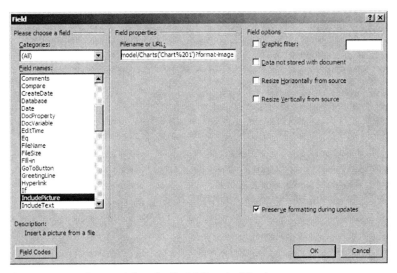

Figure 11-15. *Customizing the QuickPart in Word*

This will immediately insert a chart from the web-based URL, and every time the Word document is opened this chart will automatically be refreshed. This can be seen in the Figure 11-16.

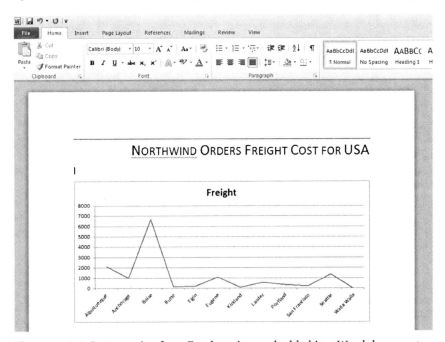

Figure 11-16. *Data coming from Excel services embedded in a Word document*

It goes without saying that you can embed this chart in any web-based content, such as a content editor WebPart, blog post, or even a non SharePoint application. What is really compelling is that this functionality of Excel service being exposed as atom-based feeds is also available on sky drive in the cloud as well. Therefore, you can technically host Excel sheets in your sky drive, and have those generate graphs that can be embedded in your blog posts or anywhere else.

Not only can you embed charts, but you can embed truly any content being exposed from an Excel sheet into any other consumer. For example, now try visiting the URL:

```
http://sp2010/_vti_bin/ExcelRest.aspx/Sheets/Northwind%20Orders.xlsx/model/PivotTables('PivotT
able1')?$format=html.
```

Note the end of the query string parameter in the previous URL. By default, the content is exposed as atom feeds, but you can choose to request JSON or even HTML.

The previous URLs renders an HTML table, as shown in Figure 11-17.

ShipCountry	USA
Row Labels	**Sum of Freight**
Albuquerque	2134.21
Anchorage	983.53
Boise	6683.7
Butte	129.96
Elgin	207.08
Eugene	1087.61
Kirkland	70.01
Lander	558.67
Portland	341.95
San Francisco	202.11
Seattle	1353.06
Walla Walla	19.4
Grand Total	13771.29

Figure 11-17. Data coming from Excel services available as an HTML table

Now this HTML table can be embedded into any container that can render HTML. This can be your browser, Word or Excel, or something else. For example, to insert this content into Word again choose to insert a quick part, but this time choose to insert using "IncludeText".

Accessing Excel Services Over SOAP

Just as you're able to access Excel sheets over REST based APIs, they are also exposed over SOAP based APIs. The previous sheet that I was working with involved a pivot table and pivot chart. Pivot tables and pivot charts are extremely powerful, but since their data is being driven by an external data source, they do not lend themselves to be changed easily from the front end.

For this section, let's craft up a slightly different and perhaps simpler Excel sheet. Let's say the sheet that I want to create reflects my daily activities for the day. This sheet can be seen in Figure 11-18.

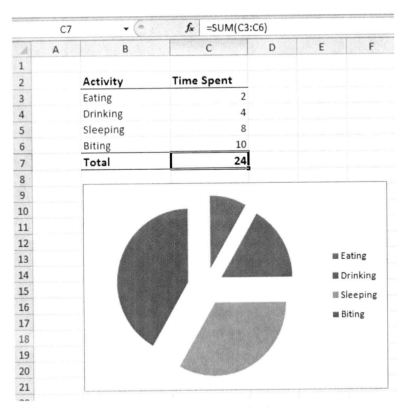

Figure 11-18. *An Excel sheet with various activities*

If you note closely, C7 is filled with a formula, whereas the other rows in the C column are static values. Also, there is a pie chart being driven from the same data. Anytime I change the number of hours spent in any activity, the pie chart automatically redraws itself to show the updated data.

Publish this to Excel services and choose to also display this in the Excel web access WebPart. When choosing to display the sheet in the Excel web access WebPart, look for a check box called "All Workbook interactivity" under "General Interactivity Settings" when the webpart is in edit mode. Check that checkbox. The Excel sheet running in the browser looks like Figure 11-19.

Let's say that people are complaining that I was spending too much time drinking others. So, I need to reduce the time spent in biting and perhaps increase the time spent in eating. Go ahead and edit the Excel sheet, and change cell C6's value to eight. At the same time, click on cell C3 and change its value to four. You would note that the chart immediately reflects your changed values and also the formula at C7 immediately reflects your changed values in the browser. I wish my parents that easily reflected my changed values.

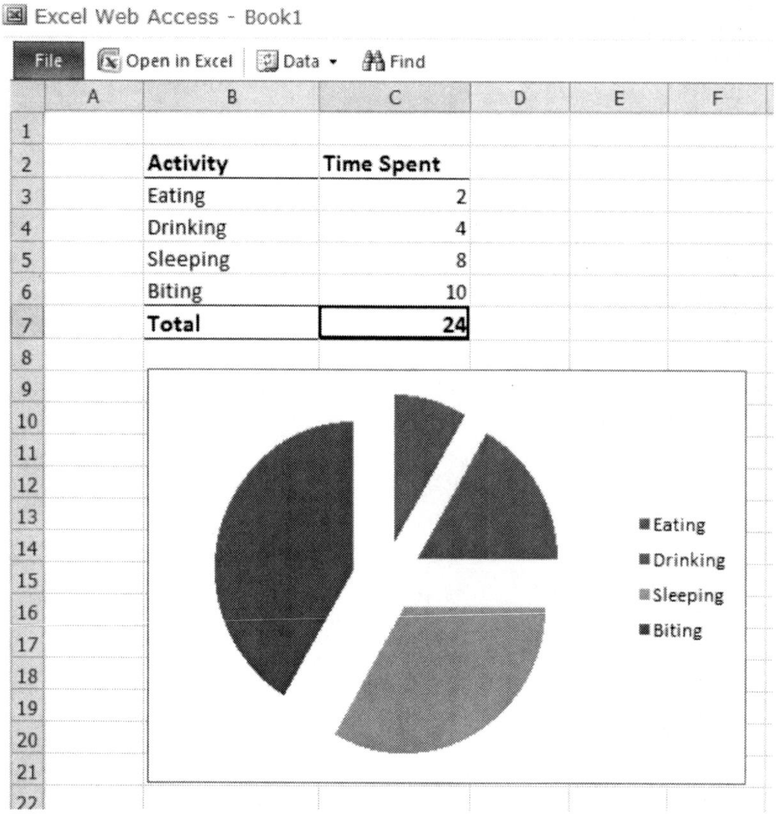

Figure 11-19. *The Excel sheet running under Excel web access*

There is one important thing to note here though. All the changes that you're doing from the Excel web access WebPart are being changed only for your current web session. In other words, if you were to close your browser and come back to the Excel web access WebPart, all the changes you had done previously would be lost. To make the changes permanent, you need to edit the source Excel sheet using thick client Excel or using Excel web applications.

Interestingly, all these embedded formulas and intelligence are a sheet that is exposed over a soap based API. Let's see this in action. Start Visual Studio 2010 and create a console application. In this console application, you will add a reference to /_vti_bin/excelservice.asmx, so this can be any version of .NET that can consume a web service. Since WCF can consume web services using basicHttpBinding, you're going to go with the .net 3.5 application. Call your console application ExcelSvcClient. In this console application, choose to add a service reference to http://sp2010/_vti_bin/ExcelService.asmx in the namespace ExcelService. After you have added the service reference, quickly examine the app.config for your client application. You should see a section that specifies the security settings for the client WCF application and you should change it to the following code:

```
<security mode="TransportCredentialOnly">
  <transport clientCredentialType="Ntlm" proxyCredentialType="Ntlm" realm="" />
  <message clientCredentialType="UserName" algorithmSuite="Default" />
</security>
```

This section now ensures that the client sends the NTLM identity to the server with all its requests. This is necessary since your SharePoint installation is protected behind active directory authentication.

Now modify the source code for your console application, as shown in Listing 11-1.

Listing 11-1. *Source Code for Your ExcelService As WCF client*

```
private static string workbookURL = "http://sp2010/sheets/Book1.xlsx";
static void Main(string[] args)
{
  ExcelService.ExcelServiceSoapClient client =
    new ExcelService.ExcelServiceSoapClient();
  client.ClientCredentials.Windows.AllowedImpersonationLevel =
    TokenImpersonationLevel.Impersonation;
  ExcelService.Status[] outStatus;
  string sessionID =
    client.OpenWorkbook(workbookURL, "en-US", "en-US", out outStatus);
  ExcelService.RangeCoordinates rc = new ExcelService.RangeCoordinates()
  {
    Column = 3,
    Row = 6,
    Height = 1,
    Width = 1
  };
  client.SetCell(sessionID, "Sheet1", 4, 2, 10);
  outStatus = client.Calculate(sessionID, "Sheet1", rc);
  Console.WriteLine(
    client.GetCell(
      sessionID, "Sheet1", 6,2, false, out outStatus).ToString());
}
```

At this time, if you compile and run your console application, you would note that the total which is calculated out of a formula is written out to your console. Again, it is important to note that you interact with Excel services using the sessionID and these changes are specific only to your sessionID. The actual sheet itself is unchanged. You should further explore the various other methods available to you in ExcelService.asmx. Some of the interesting methods allow you to export binary data out of the sheet, or to export a snapshot of an edited sheet as a byte array.

PerformancePoint Services

There used to be a product called Microsoft Office business scorecard manager. It had some compelling monitoring and analytic capabilities. As a successor to that product, Microsoft released a product called Microsoft Office PerformancePoint server in November 2007.

PerformancePoint server 2007 included Monitoring and Analytics features, which include Dashboards, Scorecards, Key Performance Indicators (KPIs), Reports, Filters, and Strategy Maps are delivered via a Monitoring Server. They were primarily two client user interfaces to the monitoring server, namely the dashboard designer and various SharePoint webparts. The dashboard designer was a thick client application downloaded from the monitoring server, which allowed power users to do the following:

- Create data source connections
- Create views that use those data connections

- Assemble the views in a dashboard

- Deploy the dashboard to Microsoft Office SharePoint Server 2007 or Windows SharePoint Services

All of this information was stored to a SQL server 2005 database that was managed directly through the monitoring server. Note that I'm still talking about the PerformancePoint server available with SharePoint 2007.

Once a dashboard had been published to the monitoring system database, it could then be deployed to Microsoft Office SharePoint Server 2007 or Windows SharePoint Services. Therefore, in that sense PerformancePoint server was a product that worked in parallel with SharePoint. Yet another portion of the PerformancePoint server was the planning center operation. PerformancePoint planning server supported a variety of management processes which included the ability to define, modify, and maintain logical business models integrated with business rules workflows and enterprise data.

Finally, there was the management report which was a component designed for financial reporting.

That is all history! The product Microsoft Office PerformancePoint server was discontinued in April 2009. Before you feel sad or shed any tears for the loss, the product was instead reincarnated as PerformancePoint Services for SharePoint 2010. It is available as a part of non-free versions of SharePoint 2010. Plus it is envisioned to be quite disruptive to the marketplace that it is entering, because it is indeed a highly reengineered and well thought out product.

What is PerformancePoint Services for SharePoint 2010? PerformancePoint Services for SharePoint 2010 is that part of SharePoint that allows you to create rich context-driven dashboards that aggregate data and content to provide a complete view of how your business is performing at all levels. In other words, it is the easiest way to create and publish business intelligence dashboards in SharePoint 2010. At the heart of PerformancePoint services is the dashboard designer. The dashboard designer is a thick client that you can launch directly from the browser, and it allows you to create KPIs, scorecards, analytic charts and grids, reports, filters and dashboards.

Compared to PerformancePoint server 2007, they are many enhancements in PerformancePoint services 2010. Some of these enhancements include the following:

- *Enterprise level scalability.* Built upon the new services infrastructure in SharePoint 2010, PerformancePoint Services has the ability to scale a lot more than PerformancePoint server 2007.

- *SharePoint repository.* There is no longer a separate monitoring server database. All objects created are now stored in the content database. This has numerous advantages, centered around security, administration, backup and restore, and even the end user experience.

- *All PerformancePoint features are now SharePoint features:* There is a business intelligence repository available as a site definition or you have the ability to create new sites based upon other site definitions and enable certain features to make use of PerformancePoint features in any site collection.

- PerformancePoint filters can now be connected with standard SharePoint webparts, because they build upon the standard WSS WebPart connection framework.

- Integration with SharePoint also makes it possible for PerformancePoint to work with every other SharePoint feature such a search, indexing, workflows Excel Services, Visio Services and so on so forth.

- There are some significant improvements in the various SharePoint WebParts, chart types, and the dashboard designer.

With this theory, let's start with the process of administrating configuring and using PerformancePoint services in SharePoint 2010. Configuring PerformancePoint services is split into two halves: one that you would need to do in central administration and one that you would need to do in the site collections you intend to use PerformancePoint services.

PerformancePoint Central Administration Settings

If you used the farm wizard to configure your SharePoint installation, chances are PerformancePoint services ready to go for you. Let's look at the specific configuration necessary to use PerformancePoint services on any particular farm. Visit central administration for your farm. Under central administration click on manage service applications. PerformancePoint services is yet another shared services application within SharePoint. Look for PerformancePoint service application within central administration, if one isn't here choose to create one in central administration using the page at /_admin/ServiceApplications.aspx. If you click on properties for PerformancePoint service application, you should see a screen shown in Figure 11-20.

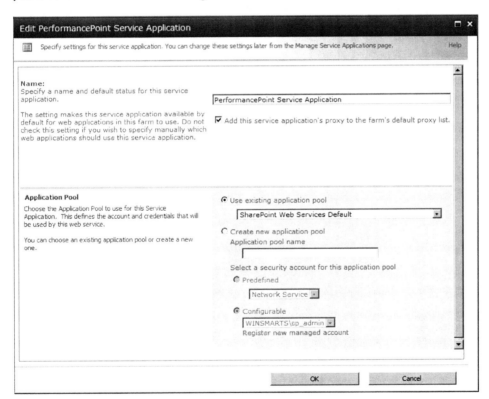

Figure 11-20. *PerformancePoint Service Application settings*

The check box that you see next to the name of the PerformancePoint service application is telling SharePoint that all new web applications by default would use this particular instance of PerformancePoint service application. Therefore, for any web site to use a different instance you would have to explicitly go into the web site settings and allow a certain web site to use a different application instance. This is an important consideration from a planning and scalability point of view.

There is yet another very important service available on SharePoint called as the secure store service. The secure store service is the evolution of what used to be single sign-on in SharePoint 2007. Single sign on in SharePoint 2007, and the secure store service, provide a secure mechanism to store various credentials for various application IDs. Specifically, if the PerformancePoint Services application was not associated with a secure store service, you would not been be able to set an unattended service account for PerformancePoint services to connect to datasources with. As a result, the only mechanism you would be able to use to connect to data sources would be where the identity of the logged in user is used to connect to the backend data source. This means that Kerberos must be running properly on your network. For practical reasons though, you need to configure Kerberos on your network anyway, so this is not such a big deal.

One other thing I should mention here is that PerformancePoint services is claims aware. However, in today's world, a lot of backend datasources are not claims aware. As a result, even though the identity being passed within the PerformancePoint infrastructure is a claims based identity, the identity acquire to talk to backend datasources as of today usually is a Kerberos identity.

Next choose to manage the PerformancePoint Service application. You will then see a screen with four options as shown in Figure 11-21.

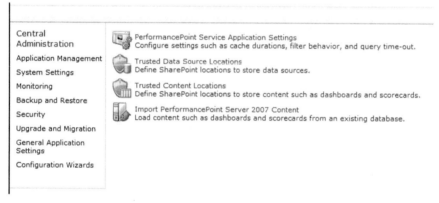

Figure 11-21. *Managing the PerformancePoint Service Application*

Starting from the bottom, the "Import PerformancePoint server 2007 content", as the name suggests allows you to import content from previous versions of PerformancePoint to PerformancePoint services for SharePoint 2010.

Trusted content locations and trusted datasource locations work in a manner very similar to Excel services. By default all SharePoint locations are trusted. This is a setting similar to Excel Services.

The setting at the top "PerformancePoint service applications settings" is where all of the other settings go. At the very top of this page is a section for secure store and the unattended service account. In Central Administration, under Manage service applications, if you use the farm configuration wizard to set up your farm, you should see an instance of the secure store service already created for you. If it isn't created for you go ahead and create one.

Back in the PerformancePoint services application settings page, provide the name of the secure store service application name and provide an unattended service account. The unattended service account is what will be used to authenticate with backend data sources. Thus, you want to ensure that this account is not a highly privileged account and is different from your farm account or any application pool accounts. Not doing so may inadvertently give access to data sources that you didn't plan on giving access to. Also, before you're able to specify the unattended service account, you will first have to visit your secure store service application settings page and ensure that you generate a new key first. This generated key requires you to specify a password using which the database will be encrypted. Try not to lose this password.

The one final setting that you do not have to perform, but you should know about is that under manage web applications, select your port 80 web application and choose "Service Connections" from the ribbon. This should pop open a dialog box that lets you associate various service application instances with existing web applications. This can be seen in Figure 11-22.

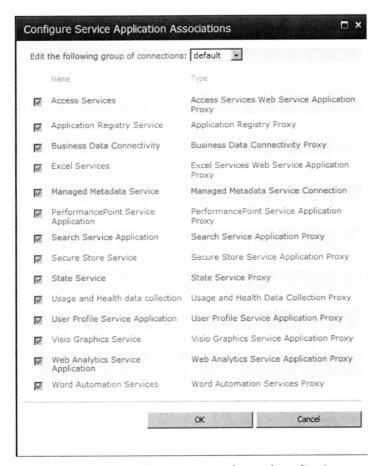

Figure 11-22. *Service application settings for a web application*

PerformancePoint Site Collection Settings

Let me start with a bit of good news first! If you have installed SharePoint enterprise, you do not need to do anymore farm level or web application level configurations. The various webparts, web services, and the dashboard designer are already there for you. All you need to do now is to activate the appropriate features on the sites and site collections to start making use of PerformancePoint services.

Now I'm in the laziest guy you'll ever meet. I like to take the simplest possible way to get my work done. Right out of the box there is a site definition called the business intelligence center provided for you, which makes use of all the necessary features. But just like as I had described in the enterprise content management chapter earlier, all those features that make up that site definition can also be individually activated in other site collections so you can use PerformancePoint services anywhere you wish. This truly gives you immense flexibility, and even though I'm the laziest guy you'll ever meet, I will demonstrate the use and configuration of PerformancePoint services in a blank site collection. Start by creating a blank site collection at the root level in your port 80 web application.

Configuring your site collection is a matter of activating a few features. You need to activate the following site collection features in the following order:

- SharePoint Server Enterprise Site Collection Features.

- SharePoint Server Publishing Infrastructure.

- PerformancePoint Services Site Collection Features.

- Then, under the "Site Features" (not Site Collection), activate the "PerformancePoint Services Site Features" feature.

Note that SharePoint server publishing infrastructure is a prerequisite for PerformancePoint services site collection features. This is because the dashboard publishing uses the SharePoint server publishing infrastructure.

Once the above features are activated, also activate the "PerformancePoint services site features" at the site level.

Using PerformancePoint

Earlier in this chapter, I had mentioned that PerformancePoint server 2007 used a separate database to store all of its necessary information. That has changed, because all the necessary information is now stored inside of lists and document libraries; lists that contain dashboards definitions, reports, scorecards, filters, KPIs, and indicators as well as document libraries that contain exported dashboards and datasources.

Now that you have properly configured PerformancePoint both in central administration and in the site collection you now have available all the list definitions and the necessary content types to get started.

1. Create a new list based on the "PerformancePoint Content List" list definition and call it "PerformancePoint Content".

2. Create a new document library called "Dashboards" based on "Dashboards Library" list definition.

3. Create another document library called "Data Connections" based on the "Data Connections for PerformancePoint" list definition.

In the PerformancePoint content list, you would see all the necessary content types as shown in Figure 11-23.

One thing is clear, the driving force behind PerformancePoint services are nothing but content types. Therefore, anything that applies to content types, reusability, queryability, structure, information management policies, all of that can be used with PerformancePoint content.

Click on any one of them and that should launch a click once application which is your dashboard designer. Once the dashboard designer is launched, you can then work entirely in the dashboard designer to create various artifacts. Start by saving your dashboard as MyDashBoard.ddwx on your local disk before you add any new items in the workspace. At this point, your workspace in the dashboard designer should look Figure 11-24.

Figure 11-23. *The various choices available within the PerformancePoint content list*

Figure 11-24. *Your Dashboard designer*

Before you can start creating any artifacts in PerformancePoint, let's first set up the database that you will use. PerformancePoint services is very versatile and can work with various backend sources such as Excel services, analysis services, a regular SQL table, or even reporting services. For this chapter, I will demonstrate the usage of PerformancePoint services using analysis services.

To begin, set up the adventure works sample databases downloaded from http://msftdbprodsamples.codeplex.com/releases/view/24854.

1. Once you have downloaded and installed the adventure works sample databases, open the
    C:\Program Files\Microsoft SQL Server\100\Tools\Samples\AdventureWorks 2008R2
    Analysis Services Project\enterprise\Adventure Works.sln project in the BI Studio of SQL
    Server 2008.

2. After opening the solution, in the Solution Explorer double-click the "Adventure Works.ds"
    data source. Click the Edit...button just below the Connection String box. Supply your SQL
    Server (database engine) server and instance name (if it's a named instance). Click the Test
    Connection Button. If the test succeeds, click OK to save the changes.

3. Right click the solution in Solution Explorer, choose Properties. On the Adventure Works
    DW 2008 SE Property Pages dialogue, choose the tree item for Deployment. Change the
    Target ~TRA Server property to your Analysis Services server name and instance name (if it
    is not a default instance).

4. In the solution explorer, right-click the solution (Solution 'Adventure Works') and click
    Deploy.

Once the project is deployed, right-click the data connections document library in your dashboard
designer and choose to create a new data source. Create a new Analysis services based project, using the
"Adventure Works DW 2008R2" database and use the "Adventure Works" cube. This can be seen in
Figure 11-25.

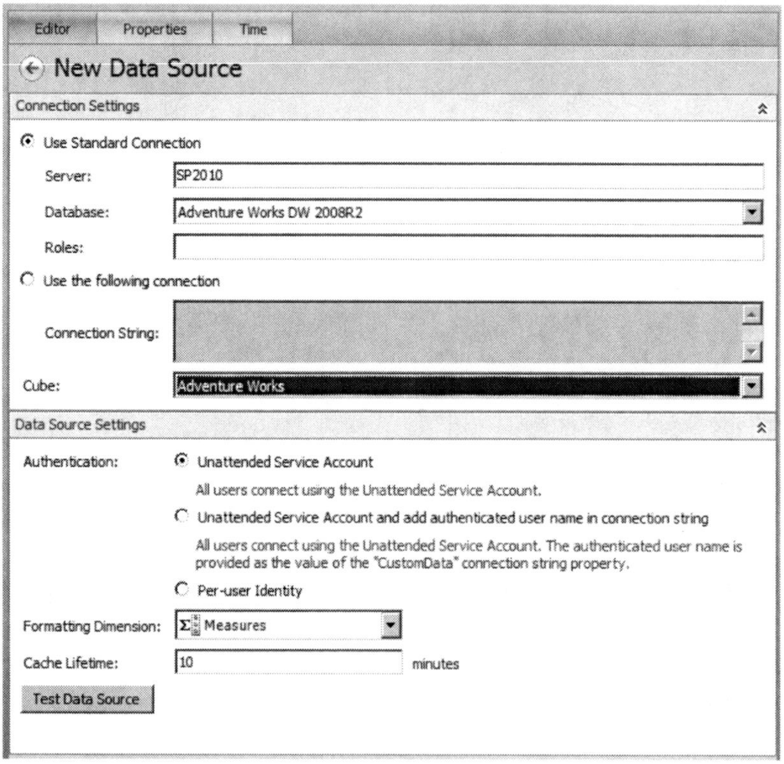

Figure 11-25. *Defining a new datasource*

Choose to save this data connection as "AdventureWorks".

Next, right-click the PerformancePoint content list and choose to add a new report. When prompted, choose to add a new analytic chart. Choose the new AdventureWorks Data connection you have just created as the data source for this analytic chart. In the new report, drag and drop product categories in the Series and in the bottom axes drag drop geography. This can be seen in Figure 11-26.

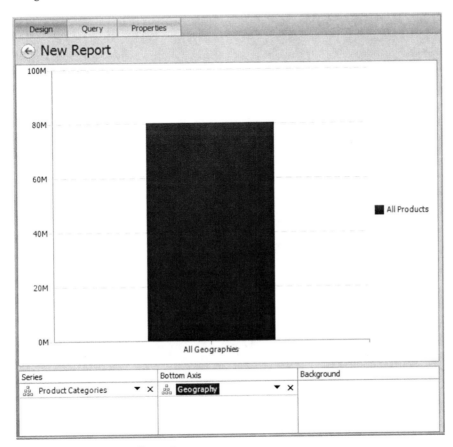

Figure 11-26. *Your configured report*

Save this report as "AdventureWorks Products". Once this report is saved in your list, note that it is saved as a certain content type. I'd like to point out here that if you were to add that content type in any other list, you would be able to save your reports in any list in SharePoint you wished. This really gives you the maximum flexibility you need.

Back on your SharePoint site on the default page, put the page in edit mode and drop the PerformancePoint report WebPart. Then, point this WebPart to this newly created report that you've just uploaded in your SharePoint site. You would note that the report is running in full interactivity on the SharePoint site. You should see a big blue bar called all geographies. Go ahead and click on the big blue bar, and the report should update giving you the various products available. This can be seen in Figure 11-27.

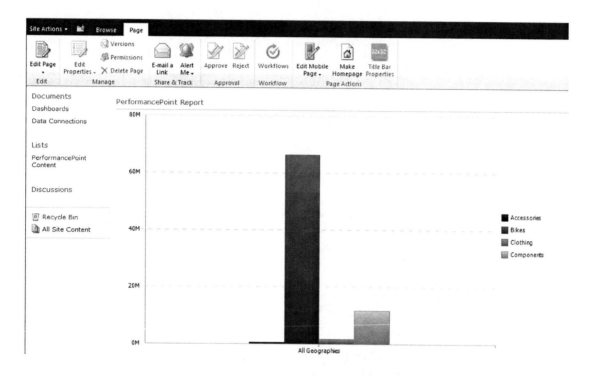

Figure 11-27. *The report running in SharePoint*

So far, so good. Why is it that my bike sales are so high? I'm not asking this, but I know my business users will. When you see the bright red bar, right-click it and choose decomposition. This would bring up a decomposition tree for the underlying data source, and it would immediately tell you that you are selling a lot of road bikes (see Figure 11-28).

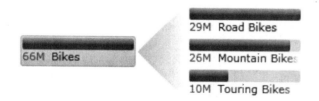

Figure 11-28. *The decomposition tree*

Why are you selling so many Road bikes? As an analyst now, you can click on it and easily choose the dimension you wish to expand upon (see Figure 11-29).

Figure 11-29. *Picking a dimension to decompose upon*

Let's expand on Geography, which reveals that you are selling a lot of bikes in California. Expanding further by city reveals that you are selling a lot of bikes in Carson City, and especially in the months of May, November, August, and February. This is a pattern that repeats every year! This can be seen in Figure 11-30.

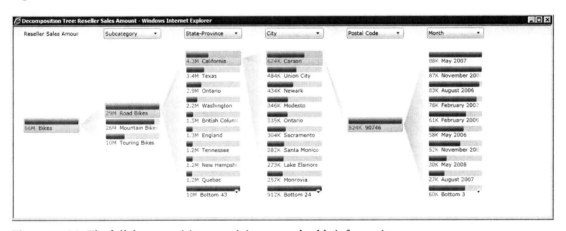

Figure 11-30. *The full decomposition tree giving you valuable information*

This clearly tells you that the Carson City market is pivotal to your company's success! And, you were able to know this without bothering a developer. How nice!

Summary

Business intelligence is a very important part of any organization. It is certainly a very important part of SharePoint. There are numerous features in SharePoint 2010 that fall in the BI spectrum. In this chapter, I talked about Visio Services, which allows you to take a Visio diagram connected to data and show it on a browser. I then talked about Excel services, which allows you to render a rich Excel sheet with some interactivity directly through the browser. Finally, I talked about the kingpin of the business intelligence offering from Microsoft which is PerformancePoint services.

In the next and last chapter off this book, I will talk about security, which is central to everything we have talked about in this book so far.

CHAPTER 12

Security

Security is one of those things that adds no features to your application, but at the same time is impossible to ignore. Security isn't a problem until you get hacked, and while business users may not appreciate the value of investing in this insurance, believe me they will appreciate it as soon as they get hacked.

As a result, you as the system architect cannot ignore security. This means you need to think of security from the ground up; from the very point you start your system, not slapped on towards the end.

One of the ways to describe security is that security is the opposite of convenience. When you leave your home you put a lock on the door. When you come back with a coffee in your hand, your briefcase, and your laptop, it is rather inconvenient to open that lock. Inconvenient but you still deal with it, because you never leave your home unlocked. So, security is the enemy of convenience.

Lucky for us we are working with SharePoint. In SharePoint 2010, there have been significant improvements on the security side of things which seem to strike a good balance between convenience and security. That's the good news. The bad news, of course, is that you need to learn even more. Let's dive in.

The security architecture of SharePoint is comprised of three major things.

- The authentication model that SharePoint works under. In SharePoint 2007, this used to be active directory by default or you could replace it with a custom membership provider. Starting with SharePoint 2010, you have the ability to use claims based authentication.

- The second part is the secure store service built into SharePoint 2010. This allows for a convenient and safe storage of credential information that can be used across various applications in your farm. This is a much better and improved replacement for the SSO service in SharePoint 2007.

- Finally, there's the object model which enforces the security inheritance and role permissions within SharePoint.

Let's examine each one of these one by one.

Claims Based Authentication

A core part of Microsoft.NET is the windows identity foundation (WIF). In essence, WIF enables .NET developers to externalize identity and authentication logic from their application. This means as your authentication models change, your application doesn't have to change. Also, to your application an identity is an "identity". Therefore, it doesn't matter if it came from a windows identity, a Live ID identity, or anything else.

WIF revolves around the concept of claims based identity. Claims based identity is a very simple idea and revolves around some simple concepts such as claims, tokens, and identity providers.

For a moment stop thinking about technology and think of what an identity really means. Let's say you met me at the conference before. Then, one fine day, you find me homeless on the streets of San Francisco begging for donuts. You would probably look at me and try to recognize some of my features that you think I cannot fake and find features that you can trust such as my eyes, my height, or voice, and I'll probably be talking about SharePoint. These features will allow you to establish an identity of me in your mind. Given that identity you will probably give me $5.00 to go buy donuts. However, if with that identity I requested to see your driver's license you would probably turn me down. Unless perhaps, I provided additional claims about myself that you can trust, like my proving that I'm really an undercover police officer.

At that point, I would be establishing my identity with you by providing claims about myself in a way that you can trust those claims. Also, as the needs of my access change, you can query me for additional claims. Therefore, my identity can be augmented as I work through your system; something you could not do with a pure authentication only model.

In this case, however, you are requesting the claims and you yourself are validating the claims. Let's think of an example where the party validating the claims is different from the party requesting the claims.

Say I was caught speeding on some freeway in California. I don't live in California, but chances are if I presented my home state's drivers license to the police officer, that is an identity that the police officer trusts. In other words, the California police trusts the issuing authority of my driver's license. In this scenario, as long as the California police officer is convinced that my claims are valid and untampered, my identity can be established in the mind of the California police officer. This is an example where the relying party (California policeman), relied on an external secure token service (my home state driver's license issuing authority) to provide the user (me) with some service.

Therefore, in terms of computers, as long as you can transfer an untamperable token with one or more claims about who you are, service providers will grant you the necessary access. Also, within the same application as you need further levels of elevated access you can simply continue to provide more claims about who you are. These claims can represent anything about a user. But, if in fact the server requested the exact age of the user then a new claim can be presented, perhaps from the driver's license issuing authority. Therefore, claims can represent pretty much any information about the user and applications can continue to ask further claims, without worrying where the claims are coming from—as long as they are not tampered.

In a computer system how exactly does this work? Typically, when a user makes a request to a server, and if the server is protected behind some sort of authentication, the user through their web browser or another client would ask an Security Token Service (STS) for a token containing claims for this user. Such a request is made using the standard protocol WS-Trust. This request is authenticated in some manner such as providing a kerberos ticket or maybe a password. Once such authentication has been done by the STS, it would then generate the token and return it to the requestor. The requester can then present that token, usually encoded as Security Assertion Markup Language (SAML) and present it to the service provider server.

Imagine if your SharePoint site was protected behind windows live ID. As the user, you would try accessing the SharePoint site; SharePoint would inform your browser that it requires a certain kind of token and where you can get such a token from. You would then reach out to the STS of windows live ID and then present that token to SharePoint in order to be able to gain access to the SharePoint site.

Now let's say your SharePoint site could accept two kinds of claims. It could accept the windows live ID or it could accept a windows identity. In either case, you would reach out to the appropriate STS and provide SharePoint with the appropriate identity. What is most interesting is that the actual application, SharePoint itself, doesn't really care where you got the token from as long as you have a valid token that SharePoint trusts. This means that one single web site can now support multiple authentication mechanisms; there is no difference between authentication mechanisms, so things such as client integration will continue to work no matter what kind of authentication you're using.

Compare this with what you used to have to do in SharePoint 2007. In SharePoint 2007, in order to support multiple authentications, you had to extend your web application on multiple web sites. Then each one of those applications could be configured to use a different kind of authentication mechanism. This meant that you had multiple URLs for the same content which caused a lot of confusion. Also, this meant that depending upon the kind of authentication you're using certain features did not work.

Another corollary of this problem was that sometimes you would have the same user accessing a system both from inside the firewall and outside the firewall over different kind of authentication mechanisms. To SharePoint in SharePoint 2007, this would appear as two separate identities. This was a huge functionality problem. Claims based identity also allows you to do identity reconciliation. However, in SharePoint 2010, identity reconciliation is something that is not built as a part of SharePoint. You could perform identity reconciliation outside of SharePoint in the claims based identity framework.

Claims Based Identity in SharePoint

With the basic theory of claims based identity behind you, now let's see how claims based identity works inside of SharePoint. Deep inside the depths of the SharePoint object model, any authenticible entity in SharePoint is represented with the SPPrincipal object. The two classes that inherit from SPPrincipal are SPGroup and SPUser. At the end of the day, as long as either a windows identity or a claims based identity can be normalized to a SPPrincipal, the rest of the object model doesn't have to worry about the kind of identity you're using.

When you create a new web application under the authentication section, you can pick from either claims based authentication or classic mode authentication. This can be seen in Figure 12-1.

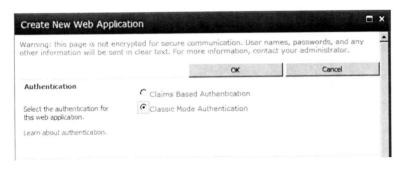

Figure 12-1. *Choosing the authentication type*

Assuming that you have picked and configured claims based authentication in your web application, accessing a protected resource within SharePoint is illustrated in Figure 12-2.

Identity Provider

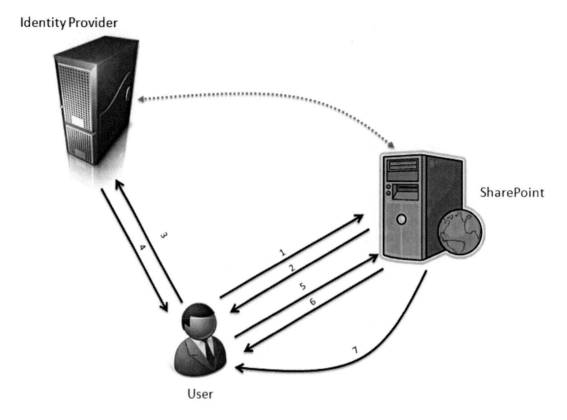

Figure 12-2. *Claims based authentication steps*

The steps being followed in sequence are described as follows.

1. *Resource request*: It all starts at the resource request. The user makes a request through a client. The client can be a web browser, or a thick client, such as the office client. A resource request can be as simple as a "GET" request, asking for something like a Word document for example.

2. *Authenticate redirect*: SharePoint tells the user that the user is not yet authorized to get the resource, but replies with a URL that the client can go to in order to authenticate.

3. *Authenticate request*: At this point, the user makes an authentication request to the separate identity provider security token service (IP-STS).

4. *Security token*: Once you have provided your credentials, the IP-STS will validate you against the internal store. The internal store can be Active Directory, ASP.NET Membership Provider database, Live ID, or anything else. Assuming that your credentials are valid, you will then be provided with a security token.

5. *Service token request*: With a security token provided to the client, the client then provides that token to the SharePoint STS.

6. *Security token response*: The SharePoint STS decides if it wishes to trust the provided security token. Assuming that a trust relationship has previously been defined between the SharePoint STS and the IP-STS, SharePoint internally will talk to a number of other claims providers and see if there are any additional claims that can be added to the trusted security token. For example, if you have logged in as "smalik", a claims provider to my ERP system may authorize me as a person who has the ability to approve invoices and may add that claim into my token. At this point, the token is repackaged, and a new SAML token is issued by SharePoint, to be used within SharePoint, which is the security token response. This is also sometimes referred to as augmented claims token.

7. *Request resource with service token*: Finally, a request is made with the final package and augmented security token response and a resource request is repeated with the security token response. At this point, the request is converted into an SPUser object and is passed on to the SharePoint authorization infrastructure.

As you can see, all the complexity of actually identifying the user is completely separate from the authorization portion. This means that you can have multiple identity providers, and these multiple identity providers can potentially also be in different organizations. As long as they trust each other, this SAML-based token can be passed across firewalls or even across the Internet. This means that you can have multiple hop of the user's identity all across the Internet. This user's identity can also be used to authenticate to systems such as web services, and the user can use his own organization's identity to authenticate with any other organization's system as long as a trust relationship has previously been established between the two organizations.

All of these are scenarios were previously somewhere between impossible and very difficult to implement in SharePoint 2007.

Next, let's see the specific steps you need to take to enable claims based identity on a SharePoint site. You will create a web application in the SharePoint installation that uses two kinds of authentication. One is based on windows authentication and the second is based on forms based authentication. Both of these authentications are normalized to an SPUser identity as I described earlier, but this is done using claims based authentication.

1. The first thing you need is a membership provider. You can use any membership provider as long as it implements the ValidateUser() method, because the claims based infrastructure in SharePoint relies on this method to tie in an ASP.NET identity with a claims based identity. The membership provider I intend to use in this example is the AspNetSqlMembershipProvider, which is an out of the box membership provider with .NET 2.0. For this membership provider, you need a membership provider database. Therefore, create that ASP.NET DB membership provider database by running the following command:
C:\Windows\Microsoft.NET\Framework\v2.0.50727\aspnet_regsql.exe.

2. Running this command will pop open a wizard-like interface which will guide you through the steps of creating such a database on a SQL server. Choose to use SQL authentication over windows authentication because the SharePoint installation will also need to talk to the server, and the various configuration changes are a lot easier if you choose to use SQL authentication over windows authentication.

3. Once you have created such a database, the next thing you need to do is to populate this database with some users. Therefore, in Visual Studio create a blank ASP.NET application and add a connection string section, as shown in Listing 12-1. Note you need to specify the proper user credentials in the connection string.

Listing 12-1. *The ConnectionStrings Section for the ASP.NET web.config*

```
<connectionStrings>
<remove name="LocalSqlServer"/>
<add connectionString="Data Source=SP2010;Initial Catalog=aspnetdb;User
ID=sa;Password=p@ssword1" name="LocalSqlServer"/>
</connectionStrings>
```

4. You can populate the users inside the membership provider using numerous ways. The simplest way to do this is to launch the web site administration tool. You can launch the tools by visiting the project menu and choosing ASP.NET configuration. Be careful as the project menu is available only when you have an ASPX open and not when you have the web.config open.

5. When the ASP.NET website administration tool opens, click the security link, and click "Select Authentication Type" to choose to authenticate users from the Internet.

6. Next, click the create user link and add a new user, as shown in Figure 12-3.

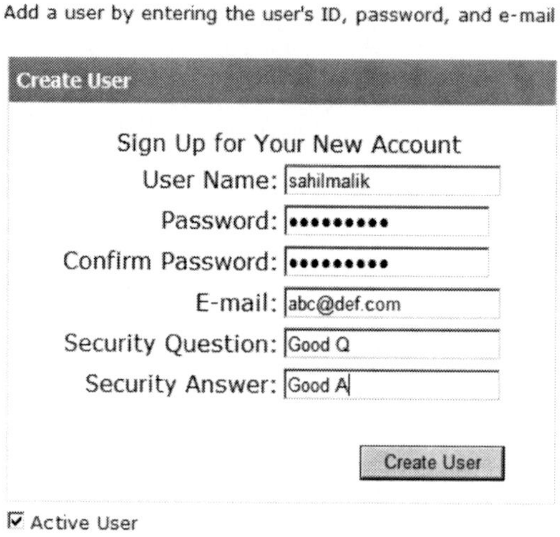

Add a user by entering the user's ID, password, and e-mail

Create User

Sign Up for Your New Account

User Name: sahilmalik

Password: •••••••••

Confirm Password: •••••••••

E-mail: abc@def.com

Security Question: Good Q

Security Answer: Good A

Create User

☑ Active User

Figure 12-3. *Setting up a user in your membership provider database*

7. Your database is now set up. Next, you need to provision a new web application from central administration that will use claims based authentication. In order to do so, visit central administration and under applications settings\manage web applications, choose to create a new web application. If you need to switch the authentication type on an existing web application, you may follow the instructions here *http://blah.winsmarts.com/2010-3-Enable_Claims_based_Auth_on_a_SP2010_website,_after_it_has_been_provisioned.aspx*. As you create a new web application, choose to use claims based authentication instead of classic mode authentication. Choosing claims based authentication will make a new section visible that will allow you to pick the different authentications you wish to use within this web application. Choose to configure it, as shown in Figure 12-4.

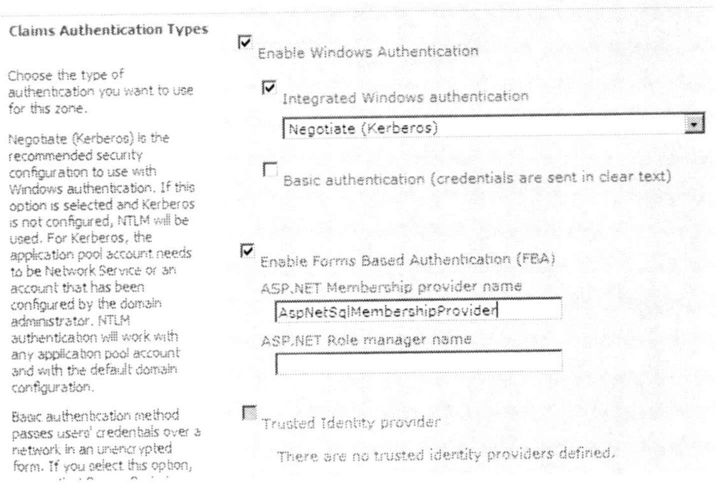

Figure 12-4. *Specifying authentication types*

8. Your database setup and your web application are now set up. (I created my web application on Port 80.) Next, you need to make three web.config changes within SharePoint. The first two changes configure the membership provider properly inside the port 80 and central administration web sites. Therefore, open the web.config for central administration and for your port 80 web application add the same ConnectionStrings section you see in Listing 12-1 into these web.configs.

9. The other web.config you need to change is for the SharePoint STS. This needs to know about the membership provider as well, so open the web.config for the SharePoint STS, which you will find at {SharePointRoot}\WebServices\Root\web.config, and add the same ConnectionStrings section to this web.config. Now, scroll to the top of this web.config and look for the system.web\membership section. Note that this web at config chooses to clear all membership providers defined in the machine.config. Over here you need to read the AspNetSqlMembershipProvider. This can be seen in Listing 12-2.

Listing 12-2. *The Entry for the AspNetSqlMembershipProvider*

```
<add name="AspNetSqlMembershipProvider"
 type="System.Web.Security.SqlMembershipProvider, System.Web, Version=2.0.0.0,
Culture=neutral, PublicKeyToken=b03f5f7f11d50a3a"
 connectionStringName="LocalSqlServer" enablePasswordRetrieval="false"
enablePasswordReset="true" requiresQuestionAndAnswer="true"
 applicationName="/" requiresUniqueEmail="false" passwordFormat="Hashed"
maxInvalidPasswordAttempts="5" minRequiredPasswordLength="7"
 minRequiredNonalphanumericCharacters="1" passwordAttemptWindow="10"
passwordStrengthRegularExpression=""/>
```

10. You're all set, with one exception. You haven't yet created a site collection. In your port 80 web application, create a site collection and mark two different site collection administrators, one coming from the membership provider and another using windows identity. This can be seen in Figure 12-5.

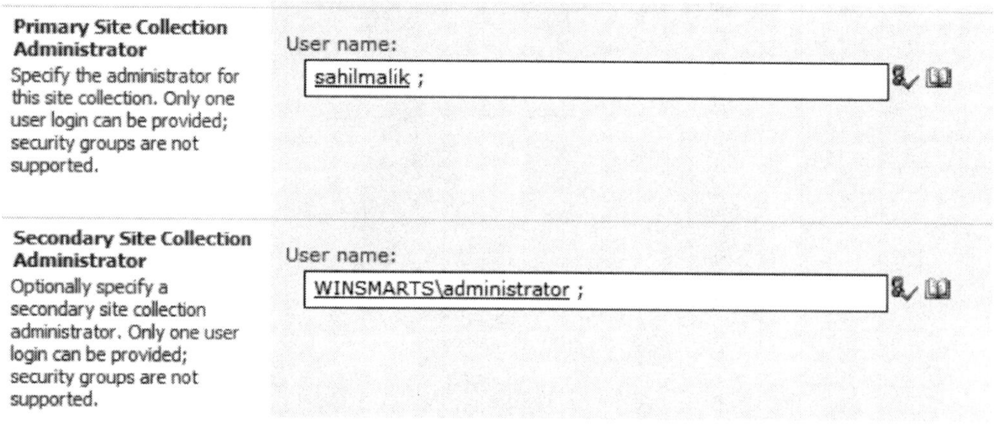

Primary Site Collection Administrator

Specify the administrator for this site collection. Only one user login can be provided; security groups are not supported.

User name:

sahilmalik ;

Secondary Site Collection Administrator

Optionally specify a secondary site collection administrator. Only one user login can be provided; security groups are not supported.

User name:

WINSMARTS\administrator ;

Figure 12-5. *Specifying site collection administrators*

Perfect! Now open your web browser and visit your port 80 web application. Note that you are prompted to pick the authentication mechanism in a dropdown, as shown in Figure 12-6.

Sign In

Select the credentials you want to use to logon to this SharePoint site:

Figure 12-6. *Claims based authentication, asking you to pick authentication type*

Sign in using windows authentication. Note that the browser automatically signs you in using your windows identity. Now choose to sign out (not just close the browser). You can sign out by clicking your name on the right-hand top corner in your browser and choosing the sign out menu item.

Next, try and login using forms authentication. When you login using forms authentication, you would note that your forms based identity is available on the same site, and the same URL as you had logged in using windows authentication earlier. Therefore, all SPPrincipals are available in all zones. While you're signed in, create a document library and put in a sample document in that document library. I created a document at http://sp2010/My%20Documents/Test%20Document.docx.

Next, sign out once more and start Word 2010. Choose to open a new document and in the file name type http://sp2010/My%20Documents/Test%20Document.docx. Note that Word 2010 prompts you with a claims based identity login dialog box, as shown in Figure 12-7.

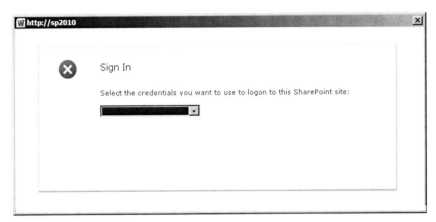

Figure 12-7. *Claims based authentication, asking you to pick authentication type in an office application*

Sign in using either forms based identity or windows based identity and Word will be able to open the document using your claims based identity. Therefore, you can see that the experience across different kinds of clients does not change no matter what kind of authentication you're using.

When using FBA in SharePoint 2010, you should keep the following in mind:

- FBA identities are now claims based identity instead of generic ASP.NET identities.

- It is the STS that calls the membership provider to validate users and issues claims tokens. This is done using standard hooks in the windows identity framework.

- ValidateUser() must be implemented in the membership providers.

- Roles are also converted to claims and can be used as SPUsers inside SharePoint.

- All SPPrincipals are available in all zones.

Secure Store Service

In SharePoint 2007 there used to be a service called a single sign on. Single sign on wasn't exactly like single sign on as you would consider it in the case of live ID or kerberos tickets. Instead of being a ticket based single sign on, it was more like a credential policeman. In other words, the application would supply an application ID and the SSO service would give you with the credentials that you would need to log into the backend system. Other than the fact that this SSO feature was misnamed, there was another big problem with SharePoint 2007's SSO feature. The problem was that it would rely on the office single sign on service which would rely on the windows single sign on service, so configuring SSO on a server required you to have many accounts with a lot of elevated privileges. Many organizations would have a problem setting up so many accounts with so many elevated privileges. To get around all these issues, you did have the ability to implement a custom SSO provider and register it with SharePoint. This technique is demonstrated in this article http://blah.winsmarts.com/2007-8-Using_BDC_with_RdbCredentials_-_when_you_have_no_ Domain.aspx. You can still implement custom SSO providers, but hopefully the need to do so will reduce a lot with the introduction of the secure store service.

In SharePoint 2010, the SSO service is being replaced with a secure store service (SSS). It is a shared service that provides the storage and mapping of credentials such as account names and passwords to individual applications. It allows you to securely store this data in an encrypted database and these credentials can then be queried for at runtime by running applications.

For example, if you are trying to create a Visio visualization that talks to a SQL server database, you could use the identity of the logged in user and pass that identity all the way back to the backend system. While that approach will work, it will require you to manage permissions at the backend system level, and it will not allow you to use connection pooling effectively. Therefore, using the SSS Service, you can provide credential mapping on a per user, per application basis.

Before you can start using the SSS Service, you need to configure it inside central administration first. Therefore, visit central administration and under the application management section click manage service applications. If you haven't already provisioned an instance of the secure store service, provision it using the new button in the ribbon. If you have provisioned a secure store service, select it and choose manage from the ribbon. The first thing you will need to do in a newly provisioned SSS Service instance is to generate a new key. This key will be used to encrypt the backend database that will store all the credentials. So, pick a key that you're not going to forget. Once you have generated the key, you can then click the new button to create a new target application. Before you create a new target application, let me explain a practical scenario that you will use here.

Using SSS with BCS

In Chapter 9, I talked at length about business connectivity services. Business connectivity services allow you to query an external system and bring that data into SharePoint as an external content type. This external content type can then be used as external content lists. If you examine that chapter, the external content type that I had created included the authentication information that SharePoint would use to query the backend system. In Chapter 9, I had simply used the user's identity to be passed onto the backend system. This approach worked, but it has a few problems.

- If the user's identity is used to query the backend system, this means that you're adding your headache of managing user identities in every backend system.

- You're also defeating the purpose of connection pooling because a new pool will be set up for every user identity that SharePoint runs across. These connection pools will be maintained on the server so the effects are greatly accentuated.

- Perhaps a bigger problem is the double hop issue. Your identity will be sent to the IIS server that is running SharePoint. Since SharePoint doesn't really have your password, it only has your identity, there will be a problem sending that identity to a backend system. Classically, this problem has been sorted out by enabling and configuring kerberos. Kerberos, however, is a beast that is difficult to configure, and it will work only with windows identities. Ideally, you should be able to send a claims based identity all the way to the backend system and you should be able to solve the multiple hop issue with such a claims based identity. Of course beyond two hops, you also have to consider if back-end systems accept a claims based identity.

The secure store service solves all of the preceding problems. Before you dive into creating a new target application in the secure store service, first create an external content type that talks to the northwind database and brings the customers table into a SharePoint external list. When asked for the connection details, ensure that you intend to connect using the user's identity to the backend system. This can be seen in Figure 12-8.

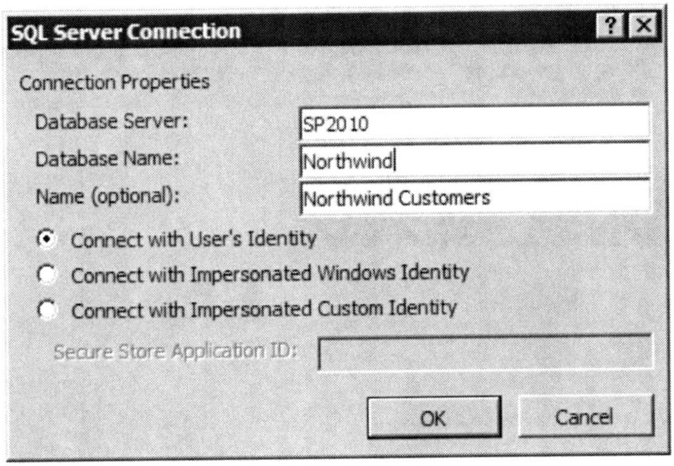

Figure 12-8. *Creating a new BCS External Content Type and specifying authentication*

If you are unclear on exactly how to set up this external content type, please refer the steps mentioned in Chapter 9 on business connectivity services. The steps are exactly the same here, so I will skip mentioning them. Once you have set up this external content type, create an external list called customers that uses this external content type. When logged in as administrator, and assuming the administrator has access to the backend northwind database, you would see that SharePoint is able to bring external data into the external list, as shown in Figure 12-9.

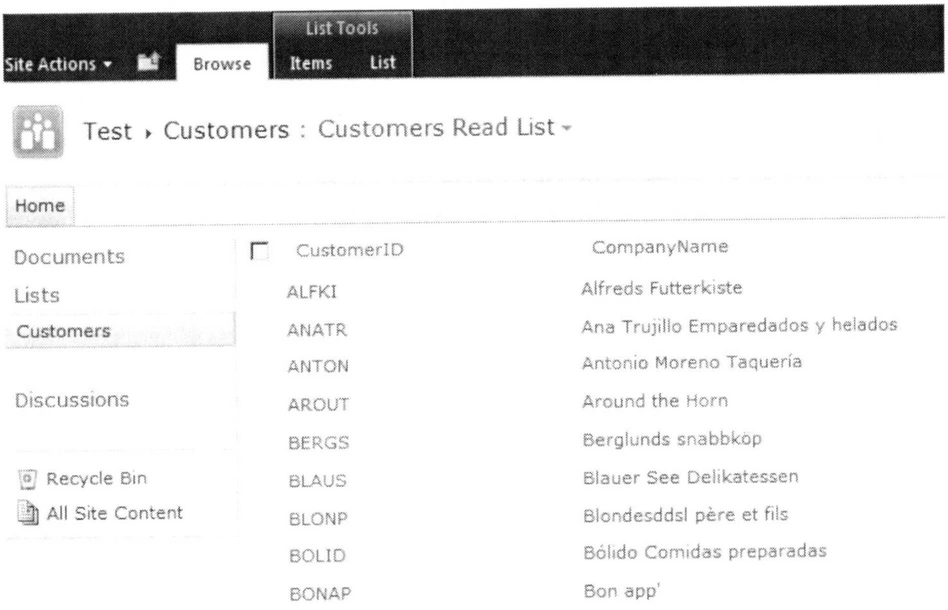

Figure 12-9. *The External List based on the external content type*

Now in the same site, add two new users called "John Doe" and "Jane Doe". You will have to create these users in your active directory first. Both of these users are restricted users in that they do not have access to the backend SQL Server system. When logged in as John Doe into your SharePoint site, try accessing the customers list again. Note that John Doe is unable to query data from the backend system. This can be seen in Figure 12-10.

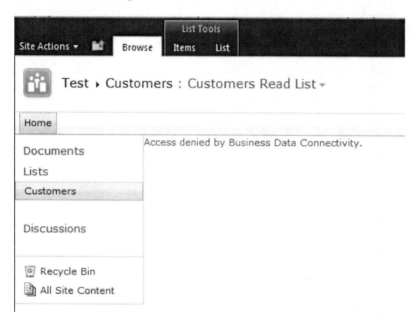

Figure 12-10. *BDC denied you access.*

Let's try and diagnose what's going on here. Start SQL server profiler and begin by looking at failed login attempts to the northwind database. At this point, you would note that John Doe's request is not even making it to the backend database. This makes sense because the BCS external content type you have created hasn't yet given John Doe permission to use that content type. Back in central administration, under manage service applications, click manage for the business connectivity services application associated with your web application. Select the customer's external content type, and click set object permissions button from the ribbon. Ensure that you give John Doe and Jane Doe appropriate rights to this external content type. This can be seen in Figure 12-11.

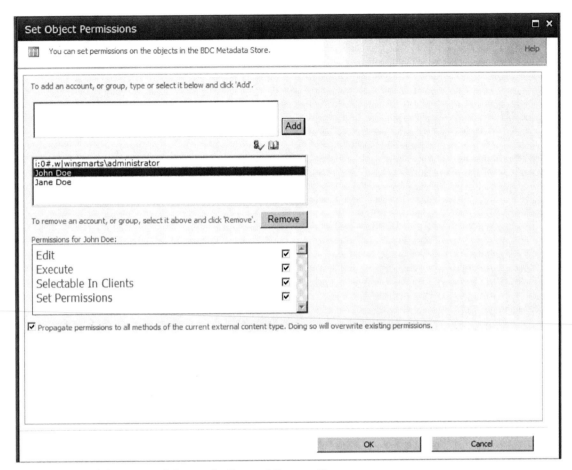

Figure 12-11. *Fixing access rights on the External Content Type*

Now that you have given access to the external content type, you need to make some changes to your external content type. The changes are twofold.

- You need to configure your external content type to use the SSS Service.

- In the SSS Service, you need to create a new target application ID.

Back inside SharePoint designer, open the Northwind Customers external content type, and click the "External System" link. Ensure that your external system now chooses to use an authentication mode that "Impersonates custom Identity", and it uses a secure store application ID of Northwind. This can be seen in Figure 12-12.

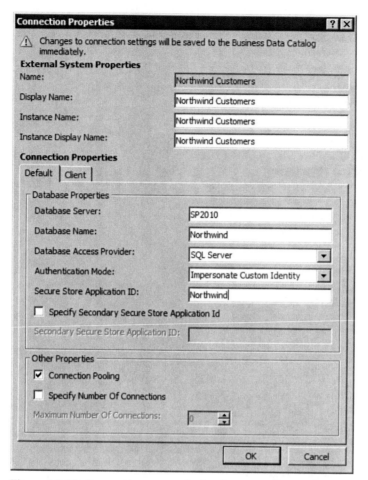

Figure 12-12. *Connection properties for the external content type*

Now that you have told your external content type to use a secure store application ID of Northwind, inside of the secure store service itself you need to create a new target Application ID with the same id of "Northwind". Back in central administration, under manage service applications choose to manage the secure store service and create a new target application ID. Fill in the details as shown in Figure 12-13.

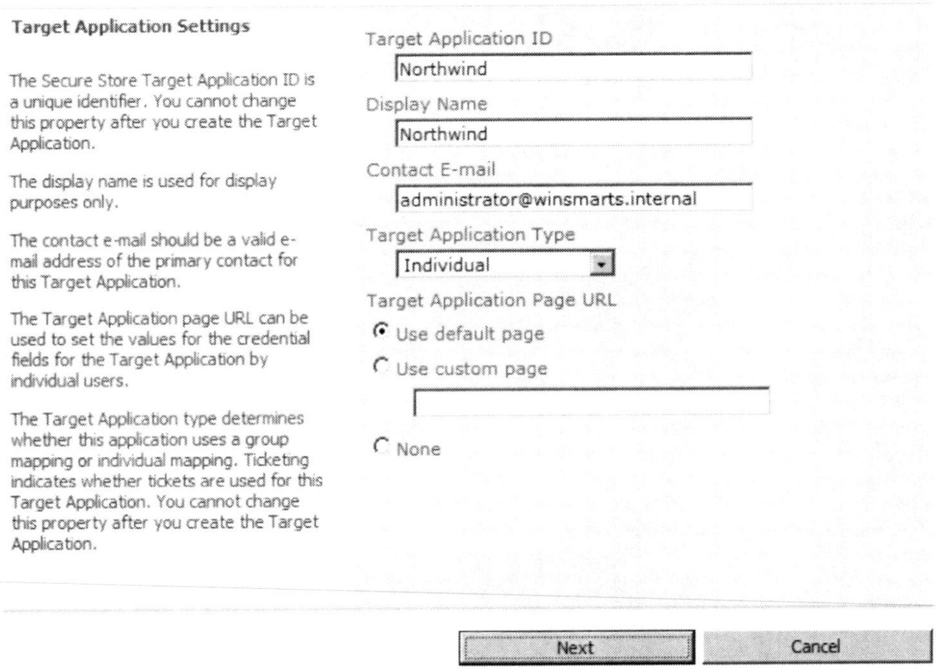

Target Application Settings

The Secure Store Target Application ID is a unique identifier. You cannot change this property after you create the Target Application.

The display name is used for display purposes only.

The contact e-mail should be a valid e-mail address of the primary contact for this Target Application.

The Target Application page URL can be used to set the values for the credential fields for the Target Application by individual users.

The Target Application type determines whether this application uses a group mapping or individual mapping. Ticketing indicates whether tickets are used for this Target Application. You cannot change this property after you create the Target Application.

Target Application ID

Northwind

Display Name

Northwind

Contact E-mail

administrator@winsmarts.internal

Target Application Type

Individual

Target Application Page URL

(•) Use default page

( ) Use custom page

( ) None

[Next]   [Cancel]

Figure 12-13. *Target application settings in the SSS*

Once you have specified the basic details of your target application ID, you need to specify what information this target application ID chooses to store. In this case, you intend to store a SQL server username and password, so go ahead and specify the details, as shown in Figure 12-14.

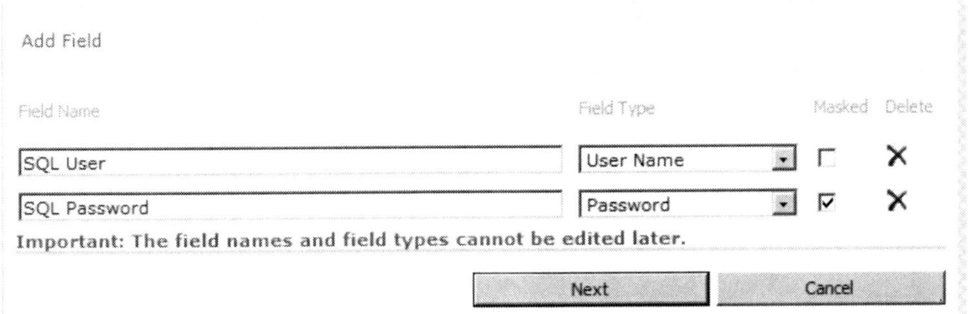

Add Field

Field Name	Field Type	Masked	Delete
SQL User	User Name	☐	✕
SQL Password	Password	☑	✕

Important: The field names and field types cannot be edited later.

[Next]   [Cancel]

Figure 12-14. *Specifying the structure of your credentials in the SSS*

In the final screen of creating a target application ID, you need to specify the application administrators for this target application. Choose to specify the administrator as the target application administrator, as shown in Figure 12-15.

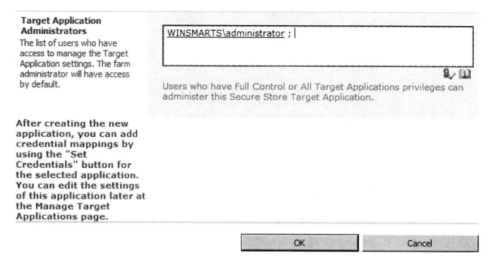

Target Application Administrators
The list of users who have access to manage the Target Application settings. The farm administrator will have access by default.

WINSMARTS\administrator ;

Users who have Full Control or All Target Applications privileges can administer this Secure Store Target Application.

After creating the new application, you can add credential mappings by using the "Set Credentials" button for the selected application. You can edit the settings of this application later at the Manage Target Applications page.

OK   Cancel

Figure 12-15. *Specifying the target application administrators*

Your target application is all set! Now you need to add some credentials into it.

You might be wondering why I created two users John Doe and Jane Doe? I did that to illustrate an important difference which you're getting into next. Once you have created the target application ID of Northwind, you need to set credentials inside this target application ID. You can do so by selecting the appropriate target application ID, and then choosing to set credentials either by accessing it by the ECB menu or through the set credentials button in the ribbon. This can be seen in Figure 12-16.

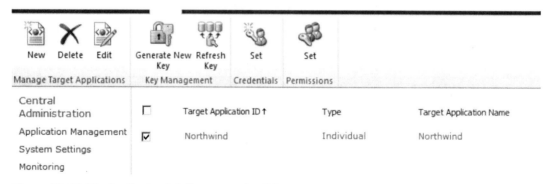

Figure 12-16. *The Set Credentials Button on the ribbon*

Here you should set credentials only for John Doe. In other words, when John Doe tries to access the customers list and, therefore, the external content type, his request will automatically be mapped to a SQL server username and password. Specify new credentials for John Doe, as shown in Figure 12-17.

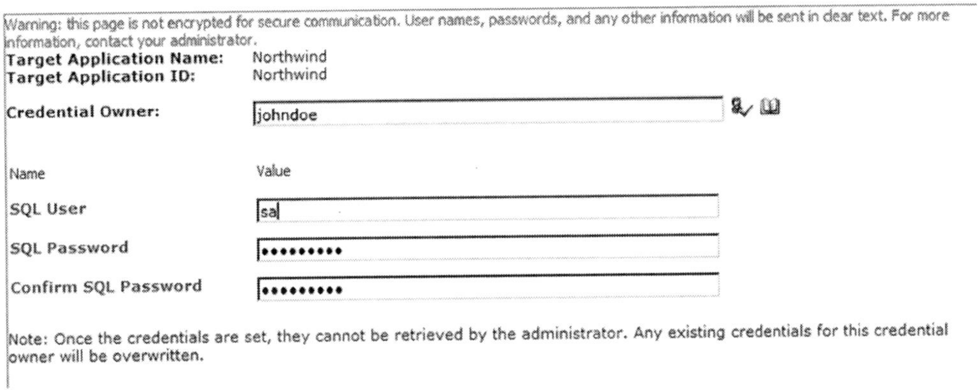

Warning: this page is not encrypted for secure communication. User names, passwords, and any other information will be sent in clear text. For more information, contact your administrator.

| Target Application Name: | Northwind |
| Target Application ID: | Northwind |

Credential Owner: johndoe

Name	Value
SQL User	sa
SQL Password	••••••••
Confirm SQL Password	••••••••

Note: Once the credentials are set, they cannot be retrieved by the administrator. Any existing credentials for this credential owner will be overwritten.

Figure 12-17. *Specifying credentials for John Doe*

As far as Jane Doe goes, do not specify any credentials for her. Back in your SharePoint site, while logged in as John Doe, access the customers external list. You would note that John Doe is now able to seamlessly access the external list. If you were to run SQL profiler to check and see who exactly is accessing the backend list, you would note that his requests are being converted to the "sa" account, as shown in Figure 12-18.

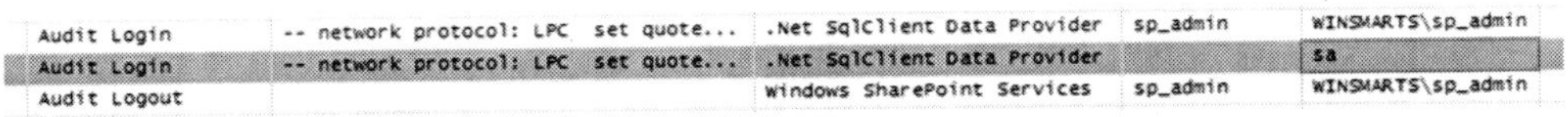

Audit Login	-- network protocol: LPC set quote...	.Net SqlClient Data Provider	sp_admin	WINSMARTS\sp_admin
Audit Login	-- network protocol: LPC set quote...	.Net SqlClient Data Provider		sa
Audit Logout		Windows SharePoint Services	sp_admin	WINSMARTS\sp_admin

Figure 12-18. *SQL Server audit log. The sa account is making the request.*

As you may have guessed, the SharePoint BCS infrastructure has queried the northwind target application ID in the secure store service, and it is using the credentials supplied from the secure store service to authenticate to the backend system.

John Doe was lucky because you went ahead of time and set credential mapping for him. What happens if users who don't have set credentials try accessing this external list? Such a user would be poor and neglected Jane Doe. Try accessing the same external list while logged in as Jane Doe. SharePoint will now present you with a user interface, as shown in Figure 12-19.

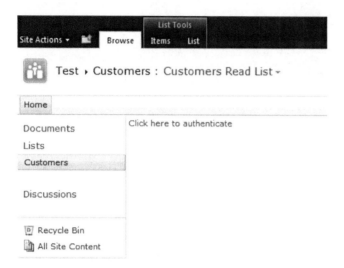

Figure 12-19. *Jane Doe being prompted to enter credentials*

SharePoint was smart enough to understand that this external content type relies on a target application ID called Northwind. However, credential mapping has not been set in advance for Jane Doe, but since the target application ID and the structure of credentials has already been set, SharePoint will present you with a user interface to try and authenticate you to the backend system. Clicking that link will present you with the user interface, which will prompt you to enter a SQL username and password. This can be seen in Figure 12-20.

Figure 12-20. *Jane Doe entering her credentials.*

Supplying the correct username and password will now allow Jane Doe to access the backend system as well.

The SharePoint Security Object Model

The SharePoint object model also implements security all the way through. If you have been working with this chapter, so far you should have a site collection with three users, namely the administrator, John Doe, and Jane Doe set up in your SharePoint environment. John Doe and Jane Doe are restricted users in your site collection. If you do not have such a site collection, please create such a site collection.

Now examine the class diagram shown in Figure 12-21.

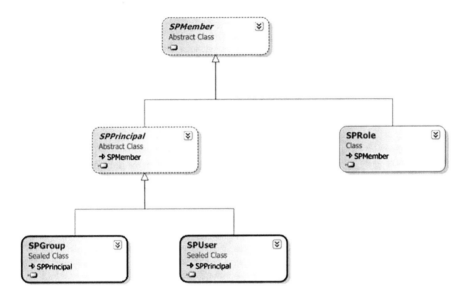

Figure 12-21. *SPMember based objects in the SharePoint object model*

This is a class diagram of some standard SharePoint objects available inside the SharePoint object model. As you can see from this object model, there are two internal classes, namely SPMember and SPPrincipal. SPPrincipal inherits from SPMember. In short, anything that can be given a security right within SharePoint in one way or the other inherits from the SPMember base class. Therefore, there are SPGroup, SPUser, and SPRole. These three objects are what can be given permissions inside of SharePoint. As you will see shortly, SPRole has been deprecated since SharePoint 2007.

Now examine the class diagram shown in Figure 12-22.

At the heart of this class diagram is an internal abstract base class called SPSecurableObject. Anything inside of SharePoint that be given a permission is an SPSecurableObject. Any SPSecurableObject implements the ISecurableObject interface. Examples of such object are SPWeb, SPSite, SPList, and SPListItem. Let's take the example of SPWeb. SPWeb inherits from SPSecurableObject. Therefore, it is an object that permissions can be given to. The next question is how exactly do you give permissions to this object? The SPWeb object has different properties on it. These properties represent the roles (SPRole), the group's (SPGroup), and the user's (SPUser) that have access to this particular SPWeb. Note that I haven't talked about what level of access yet. I'll discuss this shortly.

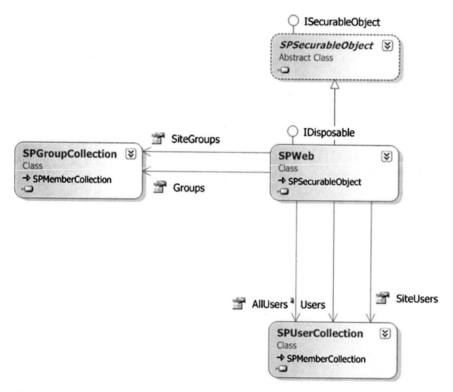

Figure 12-22. *SPSecurableObject based objects in the SharePoint object model*

Let's take the example of users. There are three properties representing the users that have access to this particular SPWeb. They are SiteUsers, Allusers, and Users.

- *Users*: Users explicitly added to the SPWeb.

- *AllUsers*: All users that have anything to do with the SPWeb. Users plus users SharePoint saw through Groups.

- *SiteUsers*: Aggregation of AllUsers at the SiteCollection level.

The SiteUsers is a superset of AllUsers is a super set of Users. And all three of these are a collection of the SPUser object. This can be seen in Figure 12-23.

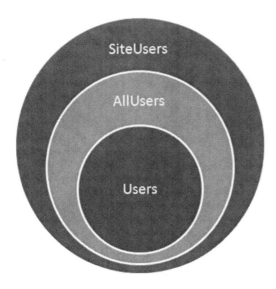

Figure 12-23. *The relationship between Users, AllUsers, and SiteUsers*

Obviously, it is the SiteCollection which is the eventual security boundary. All SPWeb inherit the users from SiteCollection, unless of course such inheritance has been broken. Similarly, there are two properties representing groups, which are Groups and SiteGroups. You can probably guess what these are: the groups are also inherited from parent to SPWeb. As before, both Groups and SiteGroups represent collections of the SPGroup object.

Finally, there is also a property called Roles. This is a collection of type SPRole. However, as mentioned earlier, that SPRole has been deprecated since SharePoint 2007. To replace these, two new objects have been introduced, namely SPRoleDefinition and SPRoleAssignment, which can be seen in the class diagram in Figure 12-24.

In order to understand these two objects, visit your site collection. In your site collection, go to site settings, and then under users and permissions click site permissions. You should see the various groups and users added to this SiteCollection, along with their associated permission levels. This can be seen in Figure 12-25.

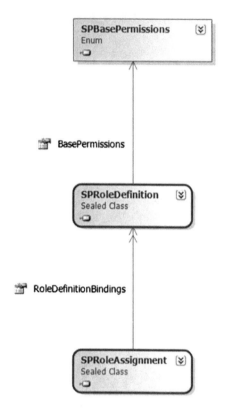

Figure 12-24. *The permissioning model in SharePoint 2010*

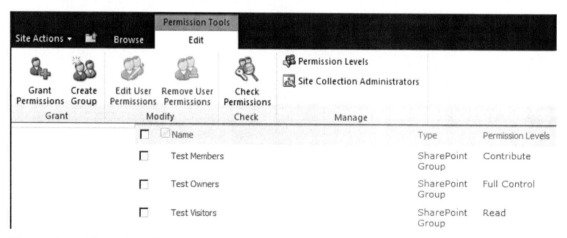

Figure 12-25. *The various SharePoint groups*

In the ribbon, you will also find a button called permission levels, so click that button. Clicking this button will show you the defined permission levels inside a SiteCollection, as shown in Figure 12-26.

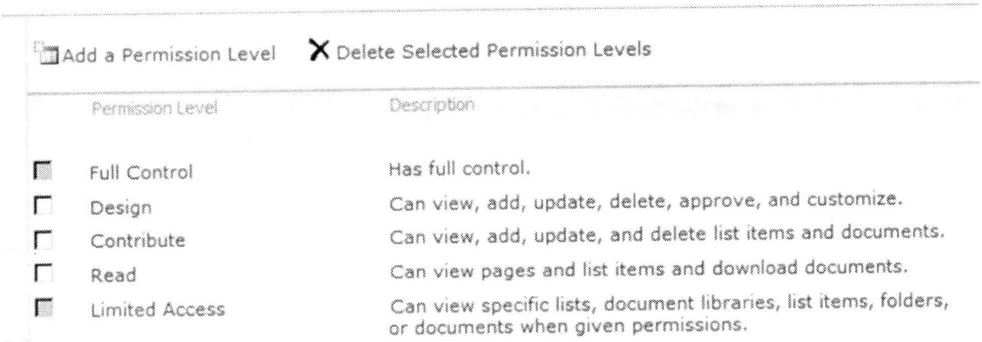

🗋 Add a Permission Level   ✗ Delete Selected Permission Levels

	Permission Level	Description
☐	Full Control	Has full control.
☐	Design	Can view, add, update, delete, approve, and customize.
☐	Contribute	Can view, add, update, and delete list items and documents.
☐	Read	Can view pages and list items and download documents.
☐	Limited Access	Can view specific lists, document libraries, list items, folders, or documents when given permissions.

Figure 12-26. *The various permission levels*

Click the full control link and it should show you the various permissions you can configure in any SharePoint permission level. Some of these permissions can be seen in Figure 12-27.

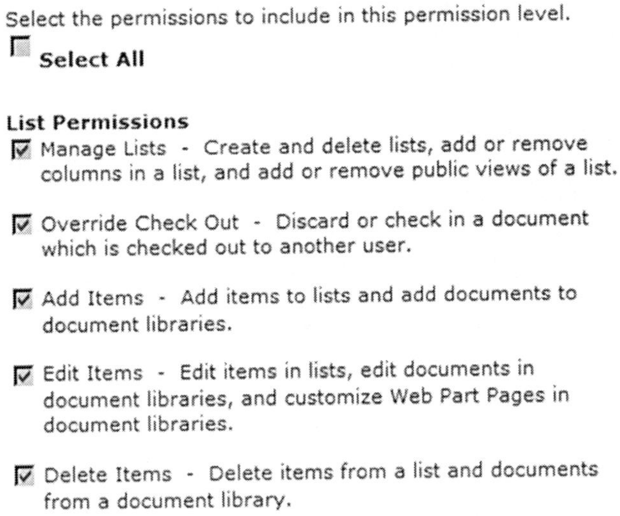

Select the permissions to include in this permission level.

☐ **Select All**

List Permissions

☑ Manage Lists - Create and delete lists, add or remove columns in a list, and add or remove public views of a list.

☑ Override Check Out - Discard or check in a document which is checked out to another user.

☑ Add Items - Add items to lists and add documents to document libraries.

☑ Edit Items - Edit items in lists, edit documents in document libraries, and customize Web Part Pages in document libraries.

☑ Delete Items - Delete items from a list and documents from a document library.

Figure 12-27. *Details of a permission level*

Specifically, in the object model, the permissions you see as check boxes are represented by an Enumerator called SPBasePermissions. SPRoleDefinition represents the levels such as "Full Control", "Contribute", while a Role Assignment contains a collection of Role Definitions.

Any object that inherits from SPPrincipal can be assigned a SPRoleAssignment. This becomes clearer when you observe all the objects in one single class diagram, as shown in Figure 12-28.

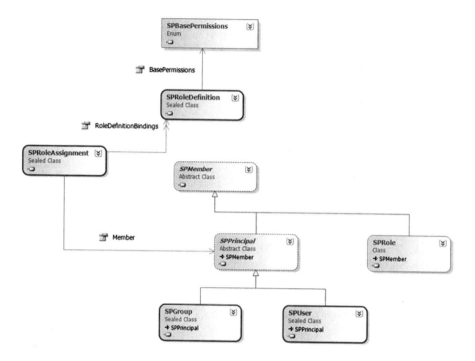

Figure 12-28. *Overall security-related object model in SharePoint 2010*

As you can see, the SPRole assignment object has a property on it called Member that points to an SPPrincipal. Therefore, an SPPrincipal such as an SPUser called "smalik", can have a role assignment that points you to two SPRoleDefinitions, "Full Control" and "Design", thereby giving you a union of SPBasePermissions between Full Control and Design. Please read the last sentence one more time because it is incredibly important to remember.

You can verify all the preceding by running the code shown in Listing 12-3 on your SharePoint site collection.

Listing 12-3. *Code to Browse the Security Setup of Your Site Collection*

```
private static void BrowseSecurity()
{
  using (SPSite site = new SPSite(siteUrl))
  {
    SPWeb web = site.OpenWeb();

    Console.WriteLine("\n\nUsers:");
    foreach (SPUser user in web.Users)
    {
      Console.WriteLine(user.Name);
    }
```

```
      Console.ReadLine();

      Console.WriteLine("\n\n All Users:");
      foreach (SPUser user in web.AllUsers)
      {
        Console.WriteLine(user.Name);
      }
      Console.ReadLine();

      Console.WriteLine("\n\n Site Users:");
      foreach (SPUser user in web.AllUsers)
      {
        Console.WriteLine(user.Name);
      }
      Console.ReadLine();

      Console.WriteLine("\n\n Roles:");
      foreach (SPRole role in web.Roles)
      {
        Console.WriteLine(role.Name);
      }
      Console.ReadLine();

      Console.WriteLine("\n\n Roles Definitions:");
      foreach (SPRoleDefinition roledef in web.RoleDefinitions)
      {
        Console.WriteLine(roledef.Name);
      }
      Console.ReadLine();

      Console.WriteLine("\n\n Roles Assignments:");
      foreach (SPRoleAssignment roleA in web.RoleAssignments)
      {
        Console.WriteLine("The following Role definition bindings exist for " +
roleA.Member.Name);
        foreach (SPRoleDefinition roledef in roleA.RoleDefinitionBindings)
        {
          Console.WriteLine(roledef.Name);
        }
      }
      Console.ReadLine();

      Console.WriteLine("\n\n Groups:");
      foreach (SPGroup group in web.Groups)
      {
        Console.WriteLine(group.Name);
      }
      Console.ReadLine();
    }
}
```

Elevating Security

Imagine that are you writing a simple WebPart which displays a disclaimer message to the end user. This disclaimer message has a little check box, allowing the user to acknowledge that he has read this disclaimer message. Checking this check box will update the list behind the scenes recording all the users that have accepted that disclaimer. Your WebPart is running under the same security credentials as the logged in user himself. Therefore, the same logged in user needs to have rights to edit the list in which you are recording the list of users that have accepted the disclaimer.

What this means is that after the user has accepted the disclaimer, he can go delete his list item from that list, which will clearly defeat the purpose of recording in the first place.

In situations like these, you need to be able to allow the user to update a list to which he usually would not have access to. This is commonly referred to as elevating the user's security rights. Elevation can be done in three different ways.

The first way to do elevation is to use Win32 API. This technique is shown in Listing 12-4.

Listing 12-4. *Impersonating Using Win32 API*

```
namespace NetworkAuth
{
  class Program
  {
    [DllImport("advapi32.dll", SetLastError = true)]
    public static extern bool LogonUser(
      string lpszUsername,
      string lpszDomain,
      string lpszPassword,
      int dwLogonType,
      int dwLogonProvider,
      out IntPtr phToken
      );
    public enum LogonType : int
    {
      LOGON32_LOGON_INTERACTIVE = 2,
      LOGON32_LOGON_NETWORK = 3,
      LOGON32_LOGON_BATCH = 4,
      LOGON32_LOGON_SERVICE = 5,
      LOGON32_LOGON_UNLOCK = 7,
      LOGON32_LOGON_NETWORK_CLEARTEXT = 8,
      LOGON32_LOGON_NEW_CREDENTIALS = 9
    }
    const int LOGON32_PROVIDER_DEFAULT = 0;
    static void Main(string[] args)

    {
      IntPtr hToken;
      string username;
      string password;
      Console.Write("Enter your username without domain (example smalik):");
      username = Console.ReadLine();
      Console.Write(
        "\nEnter your password (btw password will be shown as cleartext, so make sure no one
is looking):");
      password = Console.ReadLine();
```

```
    if (LogonUser(username,
       "domainAsString", password,
       (int)LogonType.LOGON32_LOGON_INTERACTIVE, LOGON32_PROVIDER_DEFAULT, out hToken))
    {
      Console.WriteLine("Success");
    }
    else
    {
      Console.WriteLine("Failure");
    }
    Console.Read();
  }
 }
}
```

This approach is useful when you're trying to impersonate with systems outside of SharePoint. Within SharePoint, however, there are a couple of other elegant methods.

The second approach to impersonate is to do so by using the SPSecurity.RunWithElevatedPrivelleges method. This approach will allow you to make changes to your objects using a fictional account called SharePoint\System. I say fictional because this account is not in your active directory; it is an account purely defined inside of SharePoint. This account has been given God rights within SharePoint, so it can do whatever it wishes. The problem this creates is that while God can edit a particular list item, if at a later date you wish to find out who exactly edited a particular list item, well, God edited it! So you lose any level of traceability.

This brings me to the third possible way of achieving elevation, or rather perhaps a more accurate term, impersonation. This is done by using a special constructor on the SPSite object which accepts an SPUserToken object. This can be seen in Listing 12-5.

Listing 12-5. *Impersonating to Another User*

```
private static void DemonstrateElevation()
{
  using (SPSite site = new SPSite(siteUrl))
  {
    SPWeb web = site.OpenWeb();
    Console.WriteLine(web.CurrentUser.Name);
  }

  Console.Read();

  using (SPSite site = new SPSite(siteUrl))
  {
    using (SPSite otherUserSite =
      new SPSite(siteUrl, site.RootWeb.AllUsers["WINSMARTS\\johndoe"].UserToken))
    {
      SPWeb web = otherUserSite.OpenWeb();
      Console.WriteLine(web.CurrentUser.Name);
    }
  }

  Console.Read();
}
```

As you can see from Listing 12-5, I'm first creating an SPSite object and I'm printing out the current user's name. In the second instance, I create an SPSite object by using a special constructor that accepts a SPUserToken for "johndoe". Running this application will produce output, as shown in Figure 12-29.

```
file:///C:/Code/SharePointSecurity/SharePointSecurity/bin/Debug/SharePointSecurity.EXE
WINSMARTS\administrator

John Doe
```

Figure 12-29. *Impersonation in effect*

As you can see, in the second instance, all code is now running as John Doe. Therefore, you now will be able to run code against your SharePoint installation under the permissions of John Doe. What is notable is that you were able to impersonate as both SharePoint\system and as John Doe without actually requiring any passwords. Therefore, these approaches are not allowed in sandbox solutions. Also, this reinforces my point that whenever you allow anyone to deploy code on the server as a farm solution you need to review that code very well for things such as impersonation.

Summary

This chapter covered the incredibly important topic of security. As I mentioned at the beginning of this chapter, security is something that you need to think of ground up. It is not something that you can think of later.

This also brings me to the end of this book. SharePoint 2010 is a big topic, so please view this book as only an introduction to SharePoint 2010. SharePoint itself is a huge product that integrates with numerous other huge products. There is no practical way that a single book could cover any one of these topics. Also, there is no practical way that one single individual can understand every portion of SharePoint.

As I learn more about SharePoint, I will speak about it, blog about it, and keep talking about it on my blog at http://blah.winsmarts.com.

Even though a book is a lot of work to write, finishing it and going through every bit of the product in the process of writing it is a very rewarding experience. Now that I can get back to regular paid work, I'd like to end by saying, that I love interacting with fellow geeks in real time. I hope you enjoyed this book and got some value out of it. If you're still reading by the end of this book, I am impressed so shoot me with an email with any comments or suggestions you have. I can be reached at www.winsmarts.com/contact.aspx.

Thank you for reading! :-)

Index

■T

■U

X

You Need the Companion eBook

Your purchase of this book entitles you to buy the companion PDF-version eBook for only $10. Take the weightless companion with you anywhere.

We believe this Apress title will prove so indispensable that you'll want to carry it with you everywhere, which is why we are offering the companion eBook (in PDF format) for $10 to customers who purchase this book now. Convenient and fully searchable, the PDF version of any content-rich, page-heavy Apress book makes a valuable addition to your programming library. You can easily find and copy code—or perform examples by quickly toggling between instructions and the application. Even simultaneously tackling a donut, diet soda, and complex code becomes simplified with hands-free eBooks!

Once you purchase your book, getting the $10 companion eBook is simple:

❶ Visit **www.apress.com/promo/tendollars/**.

❷ Complete a basic registration form to receive a randomly generated question about this title.

❸ Answer the question correctly in 60 seconds, and you will receive a promotional code to redeem for the $10.00 eBook.

THE EXPERT'S VOICE™

233 Spring Street, New York, NY 10013

Offer valid through 11/10.